THE
WHITE
HOUSE

BARN

VERMONT'S SMALLEST
COVERED BRIDGE.

Mrs. Appleyard and I

Mrs. Appleyard and I

Louise Andrews Kent

Houghton Mifflin Company, Boston

End paper decorations from sketches of
Appleyard Center by Beverly Hallock

FOR

Katharine

WHO TRIED HARD TO BRING ME UP
PROPERLY AND WHO WILL DOUBTLESS SAY:
"THAT CHILD NEVER SPOKE A WORD
OF TRUTH IN HER LIFE . . ."

☆

Contents

Foreword

I HAVE BEEN HOPING to see in the paper an advertisement reading like this:

> I am writing the biography of Susan Markham Appleyard and would appreciate the loan of pertinent papers — diaries, letters, etc., of which due care will be taken and material returned.
>
> Zabrinski Gabriele
> University of Upper Middlesex, Idaho

I would immediately send young Mr. Gabriele my diaries since 1932 and about twenty pounds of letters written not by Mrs. Appleyard but to her. You can find out a good deal from letters written to a person. Take the bills for instance. Does Mrs. Appleyard owe money for a mink coat or a black Jaguar car with a red lining? No, she does not, but she has recently bought two pads of paper and a bottle of ink. Does she have something sinister in mind such as writing a book? It seems all too probable.

Here is a bill, dated 1959 — so *that's* when she bought her new hat, the small purple velvet one. Then there are her income tax figures including a deductible item, "answering fan mail — $1.64." Some authors employ secretaries to answer their fan mail but Mrs. Appleyard, ever economical, does it herself.

So do I, and I have made some of my best friends that way.

What I would like Mr. Gabriele to do would be to get Mrs. Appleyard and me disentangled.

I never thought this confusion would arise and I don't really know just how it happened. Around 1940 I used to leap from my non-innerspring mattress in the cold gray dawn — about 9:15 — and by 10:00 I would have dashed to my desk. There I would find some illegible sheets of manuscript written in pencil, ink of many colors, crayon or other handy implement. It is not true, as my children have asserted, that I ever wrote on birch bark with a hot needle or scratched my thoughts on a clay tablet with a nail file. I always used paper.

Sometimes it took considerable ingenuity to find the manuscript. I would have to move Sibelius' Second Symphony, a bottle of turpentine, that jar of orange shellac, the chalk figure of George Washington which I was depriving of a coat of radiator bronze applied by some art lover half a century earlier, and such aids to literature as paint, glue and plastic wood.

I seem to remember oil of lavender too, for it was wartime and my early meetings with Mrs. Appleyard coincided with my career as a soap boiler. Soap was one of my contributions to the war effort. I knew I ought not let that bacon fat go to waste. The resulting compound, guaranteed to take everything off the hands including the two outer layers of skin, is well worth the sixty-seven cents a cake that it cost. I thought of giving away a cake with each of the first hundred copies of *Mrs. Appleyard's Year,* but my publisher said I had better keep the soap handy in case of a German invasion.

It happened that about this same time I decided to take up touch typing again. In those dim delightful days when I learned this art a typewriter had two banks of keys. On the upper one capital letters, numbers, asterisks and parentheses were plainly displayed.

I could shut my eyes and write rapidly about quick dogs and lazy foxes. I knew where the exclamation point was too.

In case anyone ever sees the typescript that deals with Mrs. Appleyard, it seems kind to conceal the name of the institution at which I learned to type. Manufacturers of typewriters, with typical American restlessness, have changed the machine a good deal since 1904. There is something called a shift key now and you never can tell where a percent sign may be lurking. Some typewriters make mistakes for you electrically, I hear. What won't they think of next?

Mr. Gabriele asked for pertinent material about Mrs. Appleyard. Among the Kent Papers I found several documents written by my children (impertinent, I'd call them) about the relationship between Mrs. Appleyard and Mrs. Kent. One states that:

> Mrs. A. is like Mrs. K. because she:
> Never has enough envelopes for her writing paper.
> Won't borrow or lend but will keep or give.
> Learns Greek every year.
> Does Christmas shopping so early that she often does not find
>   the presents till next spring.
> Gets homesick while traveling and lives on milk toast.
> Did not learn to tie her shoe laces properly till 1936.
> Treats books as friends and friends as books.
> Keeps dresses in Massachusetts and belts in Vermont.
> Has slips of conspicuous length.
> Is lethargic in winter; power plant of Appleyard Center in
>   summer.

Another says:

> Mrs. Appleyard, like Mrs. Kent, is the sort of woman whose children take her new bath sponges to wash their automobiles with. They listen to the resulting blue fire of oratory

with tolerant grins. (They don't mind ending sentences with prepositions; neither does she. In fact, Mrs. A.'s favorite sentence is a grandson's question: "What did you bring the book I didn't want to be read to out of up for?") Mrs. A. is better at whipping up a cheese soufflé than at playing hymns on the melodeon but will do either on request. She likes babies, kittens, double crostics, wind shadows in the grass, Renoir, Mozart, Queen Anne silver, Picasso, Berlioz, old chopping bowls, new cars, blue Delft chargers, old coats, old friends — and new ones, new books, new hats — and old ones. She does not like tripe.

I found also a paper that tries to tell how Mrs. Appleyard and Mrs. Kent are different. Mrs. Appleyard, this analyst avers, weighs more than Mrs. Kent, is taller, less careful about her appearance, less fussy about people sitting on her bed, more genial in greeting strangers, a better walker but a less restful driver, a better teacher and a determined non-handicrafter. She would rather do remedial reading than make plaster eagles by the lost wax process.

Probably these distinctions were valid when I first knew Mrs. Appleyard but time has worn them smooth. I have even stated in print — quite untruthfully — that it was Mrs. Appleyard who was blown out through the kitchen door while making plaster eagles. I am, in fact, the one who practiced this artistic exercise. I also invented this version of the lost wax process which is quite different from Benvenuto Cellini's, but it was not by this process that Mrs. Appleyard and I were welded into one. Something more subtle took place. I do hope Zabrinski Gabriele can find out what it was.

Mrs. Appleyard and I

Oral Tradition

BY RATHER AN ODD COINCIDENCE Mrs. Appleyard and I were born on the same day, May 25, 1886. I remember it perfectly and with a great deal of pleasure. It was the hottest May 25 in the history of the weather bureau. Apple blossoms and lilacs burst into bloom. Orioles whistled in the elms that arched over what was once an old Indian trail. It had become Walnut Street in Brookline, Massachusetts, one of the oldest streets in America. The orioles sounded both melancholy and cheerful as they wove their nests of string too short to tie, given to them by thoughtful citizens of the region. Boston is only just across the Muddy River; it had discarded Brookline for economical reasons when the inhabitants asked for a reading and writing master to teach their children, but this did not trouble the orioles or the scarlet tanager that flashed like a flame in and out of a young copper beech, or the big dapple-gray horses that clip-clopped past in the hot dust.

My father and my mother were discussing my name.

"I'd rather like to call her Lucinda, after Lou," my mother said. Lou was a favorite sister who had died not long before.

"Wouldn't it be better to call her Louise?" my father asked. "No one around Boston would be able to say Lucinda Andrews without putting an 'r' on the end of Lucinda. We could nickname her after Lou."

My father's being English explained this prejudice. He did not like such native expressions as "the idear of" or "I sawr him yesterday" either.

So I was officially called Louise, a name I have always disliked since it was used chiefly by schoolteachers when reproaching me for errors in long division. I was also called Lulu, which I thought even more hideous, or Lulie, which I rather liked. It's a nice name if you are around seven, I think, but it seems a little foolish when you are over eighty.

"Run up to Grandma's," my mother said to my sister Katharine, a responsible character almost five years old, "and tell them you have a little sister."

Katharine set off promptly up Irving Street to the corner where my grandfather's house still lifts its octagonal tower toward the clouds. I found the blueprints for it the other day. The architect had labeled them "Plans for James Wheeler Edgerly's Queen Anne Cottage."

The first story of this fourteen-room cottage was of red brick, brightened here and there with colored tiles set in geometrical patterns. Above the brick was wood painted dark green and carved to look gloomily Gothic. Stacks of tall red brick chimneys, designed to carry off smoke from marble fireplaces, worked fairly well when the wind was in the right direction. Luckily a wisteria vine was rapidly covering much of the house.

At the back door stood the ice wagon. A span of bay horses rested in the shade while the ice dripped onto the street. The iceman looked at the card in the kitchen window, then hooked his tongs around a fifty-pound chunk of ice well sprinkled with sawdust and carried it into the storeroom. The Edgerlys were modern; they had one of the first ice chests in the neighborhood. It was sturdily built of oak with shelves of slate. The top lifted up, uncovering a compartment that would hold a hundred pounds of ice.

The pan underneath had to be emptied every day. Usually the sawdusty water it contained was poured around the Salem grapevine in the backyard.

The family was still at breakfast when Katharine climbed the steps. Aunty was there sitting up very straight. Until her eighty-eighth year I cannot remember her ever leaning back in her chair. My grandmother, who had silvery waves of hair and small curls emerging from under a cap of lace and velvet, looked serenely beautiful. In the library was a marble bust of Clytie, which my grandfather had bought because he thought it looked like my grandmother. He was a gentle kind man with a friendly dancing twinkle in his dark eyes. He would have liked to be a sculptor but found the real estate business more practical.

Katharine was out of breath but she managed to make her great announcement: "I have a little sister — and her name is Aunty Lou!"

While my grandmother and aunt are getting out their parasols for their walk to Walnut Street, I will give a dash of genealogy. In Boston we like to get these matters cleared up early. Once — forty years or so later — I went into Boston to give a talk on old pottery and porcelain. At the end of it, I said I would be glad to answer any questions. No one asked anything about old china. Possibly I had already told more than the audience really cared to know. However one man did approach me. He asked in a slightly threatening tone: "Who was your *Mayflower* ancestor, Mrs. — ah — Kent?"

"Peregrine White — through the Josselyns," I said lightheartedly. I was rather pleased that I knew.

"Oh," he muttered, turning on his heel and shaking his head. "One of Edward White's lot!"

I have not yet learned just what Edward — I think that was his name — had done in defiance of tribal custom. Perhaps he read books. This is still a serious charge in parts of New England. Fortunately for me, writing them is just regarded as an amiable eccentricity. In fact people often say to me, "I'd like to write a book myself — if I just had the time." That's all you need, of course.

If I had time I might write a genealogy. I have a whole trunk full of papers but I don't intend even to glance at them. We had a talented genealogist in the Kent family, my husband's cousin Dorman Bridgman Eaton Kent. Dorman glanced at my papers and assured me that I could easily trace myself back to the Royal Lines — to John of Gaunt, time-honored Lancaster, and thence to Adam and Eve.

I was too lethargic to do it. It struck me almost at once that I had descended a long way, just like everyone else. I was more interested in some relatives more closely connected with me, David Wilder, for instance. David was a farmer in Leominster, Massachusetts. He was also the local lawyer, the local doctor, an elder of the church, at one time Treasurer of the Commonwealth and later historian of his town. He told in his *History of Leominster* how you could learn to be a doctor: You drove the doctor's chaise for him and he told you about his cases as you went along country roads in dust or mud or snow, sleet and hail. Learning to be a lawyer was easier. The student sat on a high stool and copied papers. One day a young man with innocent blue eyes, a head of fluffy yellow hair and pink cheeks like a plump baby's came to Leominster in a stagecoach and put up at the inn. Over the baked beans and brown bread he told the innkeeper that he intended to enter a lawyer's office. He asked, with just a touch of condescension, natural perhaps since he came from Boston, if there were any lawyers in town.

"Yes," said the innkeeper, "we have lawyers here."

"Smart ones?" asked the young man, settling his stock and smoothing his yellow hair.

"Smart? Yes — *and they eat goslings.*"

The young man took the next stage back to Boston.

David Wilder's interest in preachers dated from the time he was ten years old. There were several churches in town and he listened to sermons in them all, just as a broad-minded boy of today might try different TV channels. One of the most famous preachers he heard only once. David spoke well of the sermon but what interested him most was the baptism of Abijah Butler's youngest daughter, only a few weeks old. Sally was the name given to her.

"I thought," David wrote, " 'twas a pretty babe. I did not guess she was to be my wife."

Sally Butler grew up with clever fingers and a love of beauty. She learned to paint on velvet. I have one of her paintings — a big blue dish, succulently piled with peaches, pears, grapes and a huge pineapple.

When Sally Butler was to be married, in 1810, she longed for one of the porcelain tea sets that came from China in ships that sailed around the Horn. She earned the money by braiding straw. That was how straw bonnets or men's straw hats were made in those days. Girls picked up the straw in the field and when it was not too wet — and not too dry — braided it into long strips, which were later sewn into the fashionable shapes of the moment.

Sally's older brother Simeon promised her that he would drive her to Boston to buy the set. He told her that it would cost at least twelve dollars and a half. Sally braided so many yards of straw that at the end of only two summers she had the money. Simeon was a prosperous farmer and had his own chaise. When the harvest was in, he and Sally set out for the forty-mile drive to Boston.

A ship had come in from Canton earlier in the week. There were barrels of china in the warehouse. They had been opened and pieces of the sets had been set out on a shelf above the barrels. The shapes were the same but they were differently decorated. Some were done in what Bostonians called the Fitz Hugh pattern. Fitz

Hugh was a refined way of pronouncing Foochow, the Chinese name for the place where the tea sets had been decorated. This pattern came in blue or green or a rusty red. From Nanking and Canton came the blue willow pattern with the weeping willows and the bridge. From Canton, too, came the rose medallion with its mixture of rose and green and gold.

Sally Butler chose a simpler pattern. The pieces had dark blue borders with gold stars. On one side of each cup, on the teapot and on the helmet cream pitcher was a shield, with a mantling of dark blue and gold, lined with ermine. Gold tassels, touched with vermilion, hung down from the mantling. On the shield was a spray of gold flowers also lightly touched with red. There were a hundred and twelve pieces in the set and — as Simeon had said — the price was twelve-fifty.

The clerk in charge said, "If you order in advance you can have your own coat of arms or your monogram on the shield. It only takes two years. Of course there's a slight extra charge."

Sally wanted hers right away.

It was loaded into the back of the chaise and traveled safely to Leominster. It came back to Boston in 1850 when Sophronia Wilder was married to my grandfather and came to live there. It was moved often because my grandfather had a habit of building a house and living in it while he was building another. The houses became bigger as the family grew. One was a large mansard-roofed house on Kent Street in Brookline with gardens and green fields around it. They had eleven children so my grandmother had plenty to occupy her. She did not take much interest in old china. Sally Butler's tea set was broken bit by bit and thrown away. My Aunt Martha Wilder Edgerly — Aunty to family and friends — remembered seeing pieces of it in the ash barrels almost every week.

At last, when there were only four pieces left, she rescued them from the kitchen and put them into a cabinet my grandfather had designed. The cabinet is now in Vermont at Kents' Corner. The teapot, a small cream jug, the tea caddy and one cup of Sally Butler's tea set, with the pattern of draped shields and gold-starred blue borders, are still in it.

Sally's brother Simeon had a hobby — cabinet making. As his sisters married he made a chest of drawers for each of them. Since Sally was the youngest, hers was his masterpiece. When the sun comes into my bedroom in the morning, I see the swell front of beautifully grained cherry, the satinwood inlay, the oval brasses, and I think affectionately of Simeon.

David Wilder's father, also named David, and Sally's father Abijah Butler both fought in the Battle of Lexington and Concord. David evidently enjoyed writing about it in his history of Leominster. From him I learned that the surprise element of Paul Revere's ride had been somewhat exaggerated. According to David Wilder, the farmers for miles around Concord had known for weeks that the British would march out to Concord sooner or later to capture or destroy the powder and shot stored there. The question was when they would come and by what route. A system of alarm guns had been organized in many towns north of Boston. When they heard the guns, the farmers would know what to do.

It became certain that the troops would come soon when several British horsemen, disguised as civilians — except when their dark cloaks blew aside and showed their scarlet uniforms — rode out through Lexington. On the 18th of April, 1775, before Paul Revere saw those lanterns in the tower of the North Church, signal guns were fired on many village greens.

My great-great-grandfather Stephen Barrett of Concord and Carlisle also fought at Lexington and Concord and on the roads between. He was engaged to Lucy Kidder of Billerica and she had been busy for months making a present for him — a pocketbook of silk and linen. She began by gathering flax, retting it and spinning it into thread. She dyed it a green, which is still brilliant, and wove it into cloth for the lining. In the meantime her silkworms, carefully fed on mulberry leaves, made silk for the cover. She did not have many worms and it had taken a long time to collect enough silk for thread. She spun the raw silk and dyed it many colors — soft yellows deepening to orange, light tan and dark brown, pale and deep blues, several shades of green, and reds from crimson to rose and coral pink. She also wove canvas of coarse linen. On it she worked all her colors, shading one into another, in a geometrical pattern she called Turkish. She had just finished the pocketbook when the guns began to go off on the green.

When Stephen came to say good-bye, she gave him the pocketbook. He put two letters Lucy had written to him into it, put it into the breast pocket in the lining of his coat, shouldered his flintlock and trudged off to Lexington. He carried the wallet all through the war and brought it safely home. I keep it in Simeon Butler's cherry chest.

Stephen and Lucy were married soon after the war was over. Their daughter, Lucinda Barrett, married James Edgerly's father.

This is how I came so near being called Lucinda.

☆

"Did your father's family come over in the *Mayflower*," a genealogically-minded friend once asked me, "or in a later ship?"

"Later," I said. "A Cunarder."

"Oh!" said my friend, hastily sweeping such an embarrassing statement under the rug that Bostonians keep in the front hall in their minds.

☆

The Civil War had not been over long when my father came to Boston. Near where he lived in a boardinghouse on Charles Street, the Back Bay was being filled in. The place where Paul Revere had launched his boat to row to the Cambridge shore had already become land and now the Public Garden was being made. The dirt came from Needham and one of the first railroads in Massachusetts was built to haul the dirt for the Back Bay from Needham to Boston. Trains of flat cars ran all day and most of the night. Before dawn men began shoveling dirt into two-wheeled carts. Dusty horses dragged them. Dusty men drove them.

Charles Street had been newly paved with cobblestones. The noise of wheels and hooves went on all day and far into the dusty night. They filled in all the marshy land, much of it open water at high tide, from Boston Common to the Harvard Medical School, from the Charles River to Roxbury Neck. When the Edgerlys moved into one of the houses my grandfather built on Brookline Avenue, they lived on what had lately been a marsh. The children could still go fishing where the Beth Israel Hospital now stands.

When my father lived on Charles Street, there were still good places to fish in the Back Bay. Even at low tide you could wind through channels in a rowboat and fish in a salty lagoon near where the Chilton Club now stands. My father was not a fisherman but he enjoyed the small islands tufted with windblown trees and the smell of the salt marsh. The dust and the wheels rolling over the cobblestones at four in the morning made him homesick for England. He would lie in his dusty room thinking of green paths under the great trees of Epping Forest in Essex and of the rolling fields of nearby Suffolk.

Walter Edward Andrews was the youngest of the eleven children of Richard Bullock Andrews and Mary Miles Andrews. One of the sons was killed in an accident. The other children all grew up and married. Three of the brothers went to Australia and settled there. One spent much of his life in India. One sister married the governor of the Gold Coast and lived some years in Africa. Another sister came to America and settled in Maryland.

I always liked to hear about the big English family. They seemed a friendly group. Perhaps it was the letters that kept them so. They were written on thin paper and usually "crossed" — that is, written first from west to east, then turned and filled in from south to north. This writing between the lines grew smaller and smaller toward the end of the letter and thus packed much family news into a small space. Letters like these helped to bind Queen Victoria's empire together.

I used to hear the Andrews letters read aloud and I seemed to know the writers as well as if they had lived in Brookline. There was a dark brown photograph that hung over the mantelpiece. Two people were under an enormous old tree. The man was standing. He had a cocked hat and a long gun. His hunting dogs were beside him, looking up at him. He was Robert Andrews of the Auberies in Suffolk. His wife, Frances Carter Andrews, sat primly on an iron bench, which was almost covered by the wide skirt of her satin dress.

Gainsborough had painted the picture, my father said. He had never quite finished it. Mrs. Andrews was supposed to be holding in her lap a pheasant that her husband had just shot. It had never been painted, perhaps because such an exceedingly proper-looking lady would not dream of putting a freshly killed bird on her best new dress.

The photograph did not show the whole picture, just the two people. To their left there should have been a field where the wheat had been cut and bound into sheaves. Cornflowers and poppies grew among the stubble.

"There's a field full of sheep," my father used to say. "Their fleece shines the way it does only in England on a sunny day. The field is green — you've never seen green if you haven't been in England in June."

"What color is her dress?" I would ask although I knew the answer.

"It's the blue of a June sky between great towers of cloud. Or of a silky blue river when the wind stops blowing. You'll see some-day — you'll find I'm right."

"Do you think I'll get to the house and find the big tree and see the church spire across the fields? How shall I find it?"

"Ask for the Auberies. Anyone near Epping or Bulmer will tell you where it is. You'll see two stone leopards sitting on the gate-posts."

In 1939 I was driving a hired Daimler along a narrow English lane. The car came so near filling it that a man, who came along on a bicycle, jumped off and pushed his machine almost into the rose hedge. I asked if he could tell me the way to the Auberies.

"Gae till tha see twa cats on ta gyte," he said and then, realizing that I did not speak English, he said it again, slowly, patiently, po-litely.

I hope I have reported him correctly. At least I understood "cats," and a delicious prickle ran down my spine as I realized that they must be the leopards. And so they were, a sinister, smiling pair, perched on high stone posts with an iron gate only partly closed between them. We asked permission of a gardener to go into the grounds — the place had been out of the family for a gen-eration — found the old tree, touched its rough bark. It felt just as I always thought it would when I looked at the picture. There were even sheep in one of the green fields and the right clouds, the kind Constable and Gainsborough painted, hanging close to the church spire.

No wonder he was homesick, I thought. He had once told me that he had been for years.

"What cured you?" I had asked, and he had said, with his twin-kle, "Going back."

"You mean that, from England, America didn't look so bad."

"It looked rather well. And the family said I was Americanized. I shocked them by eating marmalade and toast with my bacon and eggs. They said I spoke American. I remembered suddenly that if I'd stayed in England I would still be sitting on a stool in a bank, copying letters."

☆

Leaving out a large number of honest or dishonest, hard-working or lazy ancestors, I now turn to the Villettes. They were French Huguenots who fled from France in 1685 when Louis XIV revoked the Edict of Nantes. This edict was a forerunner of the present ecumenical movement. It prescribed a certain amount of religious freedom for the Huguenots. They could, for instance, hold church services within five leagues of Paris. They were also allowed to trade, enter schools and inherit property. When the edict was revoked, memories of St. Bartholomew's Eve and of the Inquisition darkened Huguenot minds. Those who could escape from France did so in haste. One dark night the Marquis de la Villette, his wife and children rowed across the fierce waves and currents of the British channel in an open boat and at last came safely to London. One of my English cousins has the French Huguenot Bible they brought with them. My sister has a lace ruffle that belonged to the Marquise.

They soon became English. One of their grandsons was a clergyman of the Church of England. He was, in 1780, what was called the ordinary — that is, the chaplain — of Newgate Prison. One of his duties was to give prisoners about to be hanged their "neck verses," the cant phrase for what religious instruction and consolation he could give them before their execution. Men — and women too — were hanged for robbery, burglary, piracy, coining, forgery and theft as well as for murder and treason. John Villette knew all kinds of criminals. He wrote a four-volume work called *Annals of Newgate or Malefactors Register.* It began with Jack Sheppard and mentioned the most famous criminals of the fifty years that ended in 1776. The first three volumes were based on the records of earlier chaplains, the last on his own experience.

He hoped, he wrote, "to Expose the Deformity of Vice, the Infamy and Punishments naturally Attending those who Deviate from the Paths of Virtue and to Warn the Rising Generation against the Allurements and Dangers of Bad Company."

Besides being able to write good eighteenth-century English, Mr. Villette understood the private language of robbers and pickpockets and translated it for us. Rumbo was the nickname for Newgate. An alehouse was a boozing ken. There a flash cull might be found keeping company with some well-known prig or buzz — a thief in other words. A fence was already the term for a receiver of stolen goods. Pops were pistols, stampers were shoes. The chaplain would read the neck verses sooner or later to many patrons of the boozing ken. He would do so in a cell, lighted by a glimstick, the night before their execution on the nubbing cheat — the gallows.

Unfortunately the *Annals* end before what must have been the chaplain's most shocking experience in the criminal world of London — the Gordon riots in 1780. Today Lord George Gordon might be a popular member of the John Birch Society. He was one of those men who always recognized an enemy, no matter how well disguised. He was as irrational as the people who have called Eisenhower a Communist. Gordon's enemies were Roman Catholics. When George III's government introduced a bill to extend a small amount of toleration to Catholics, Gordon collected twenty thousand signatures on a petition asking for defeat of the act. The petition, an enormous roll of parchment, was carried, in what started as an orderly procession but soon became a mob, to the Houses of Parliament. Cries of "No Popery" sounded through the streets. The mob burned and plundered the houses and chapels of Catholics. There was looting and fire all through the city. Prisons were broken into and prisoners joined the mob. Even the walls of Newgate, one of the strongest prisons, burned one night. Many people died in the fires.

My father heard about that night from Betsey Villette, daughter of the chaplain. When my father was a small boy, she was a very old lady but still, he said, dark-haired and with very bright dark eyes, quick of motion and gesture, like a small brown bird. She remembered seeing the heads of traitors displayed on Temple Bar. Her father told her about the Gordon riots. She told my father. He told me.

The Villettes lived in a house near the prison. Part of the mob, which was piling barrel staves, odds and ends of furniture — anything that would burn — against the prison door, started to pile wood against the chaplain's door too. The dark street brightened as men ran down it carrying blazing torches. They shouted, "Burn Newgate, burn Newgate — set the prisoners free!"

They carried axes, mallets, iron bars, shavings, oil and turpentine from a paint shop. They had visited an alehouse and they stumbled and staggered as they laid their fire. Villette watched them from a window near the door with Betsey, not quite a year old, in his arms. He realized, as he stood there, that he should have taken his wife and children to their house in the country; that he should not be there waiting for men shouting "No Popery!" to burn the house of a Protestant clergyman.

A man came running through the smoke. He had a big pewter tankard in his hand. The mob stopped work and fell silent, watching eagerly as the tankard passed from hand to hand.

Villette picked up a silver spoon from the table and tapped the window glass. The baby in his arms jumped, crowed and held out her small hands to the men in the smoky light outside.

One of the torch bearers looked up and said approvingly, "A pretty babe!"

"Aye!" said another.

Then they turned and went on down the street, leaving the wood where they had piled it.

I am glad they did so and that the Villettes did not, like many innocent people, lose their lives in the Gordon riots. Otherwise I would not be sitting here, this morning of bright snow, writing about it. You have to have exactly the right combination of great-great-grandfathers, or you turn out to be someone else.

Memory

I AM two years old. I begin to remember things — nothing consecutive — only flashes of light against darkness. It is lilac time. A yellow swallow-tailed butterfly is on a purple lilac plume. We are in the country, far away from Brookline, ten miles probably, at Joe Lee's hotel near a river in Auburndale. Carriages drive up to the door and beautiful ladies are handed out of them.

As I look back, I realize that this was a task not to be entered upon lightly or unadvisedly. No woman in those innocent days had yet heard of calories, much less counted them. Since an eighteen-inch waist was considered large, they were laced into corsets as cozy as medieval suits of armor. They wore high-button boots in pastel shades — size three or smaller. Sometimes a fortunate man might catch a glimpse of a booted ankle as far as the fourth button.

Bustles, sweeping skirts, little jackets called Polonaises, bonnets with ostrich feathers, old family lace, mantles, veils, collars and bodices stiffened with whalebone, petticoats with layers of embroidered ruffles made women into bundles of upholstery. Within all this airy drapery was something that weighed a good deal.

Joe Lee was the first Negro I had even seen. I was sometimes afraid of strangers but not of this tall man with the deep soft voice. I remember his taking us to our rooms which looked across the

Charles River to wooded hills and a sunset of gold and pink. Then suddenly it was a dark night, and my father and mother were gone. Fear came on great wings out of the darkness and settled into my crib.

I began to whimper, to wail, to cry, to sob. I had quite a repertoire of lamentation when I really put my mind to it.

At last someone heard me. The door opened. Joe Lee's deep voice said, "Don't cry. I'll take you to your mother."

He carried me down a long dimly lighted passage where gas flames were blue and yellow butterflies, down through a hot dark kitchen that smelled of roasting and broiling and baking, through the pantry where stacks of white and gold dishes were being washed in great steaming tubs, through the dining room where the light shone on white damask and champagne glasses, across an empty hall and through tall folding doors into the big parlor.

It was crowded. Everyone was talking at once. Dozens of gas globes shone in the chandelier. Rainbows flashed from the dangling prisms that hung from its golden arms. The ladies all wore their best low-necked dresses — rose and violet and sky blue, lemon yellow and grass green and white. The fringes of hair over their foreheads had been newly frizzed with curling tongs. They had jewels almost as bright as the chandeliers. They carried jeweled fans of ivory and lace.

The men were in black with stiff white shirts, collars as sharp as letter openers and narrow white ties. My father's back was toward me but I knew him by the curly band of dark hair between his bald head and his collar and by the points of his beautiful whiskers. My mother was in the middle of the room right under the chandelier. Her black hair waved naturally so she did not have to frizz it. Her dress was a rose color like her cheeks and brocaded with a pattern of a deeper rose. She was taller than the women around her. They were all laughing at something she was saying.

Murmurs, insincere I'm afraid, about what a darling little creature I was — "image of her father, same dark eyes" — followed me
through the crowd. Translated they meant, "Goodness, what a
spoiled brat!"

"She got a little lonely, Mrs. Andrews, but I think she'll sleep all
right now she knows you're here," Joe Lee said.

My father carried me back. My mother went too and tucked me
up in my crib, covering me with a blanket she had embroidered
with forget-me-nots, tiny roses, pinks and pansies. This year, 1965,
it went to a christening in a Vermont church. The white wool has
turned a deep ivory and the colors of the flowers have faded a
little but every stitch is still perfect, as it was nearly eighty years
ago.

That summer my father rented a house in Beverly, Massachusetts. My brother Oliver was born there on the night of July 6,
1888, during a terrific thunderstorm. I remember the house only as
an enormous dark cavern lit by jagged flashes of lightning. My
father had a rather different memory of it.

The doctor sent him down to the kitchen for some hot water.
Doctors in fiction — and in fact — always demand hot water on
such occasions. I never heard of its being used. Perhaps it was a
formula for getting nervous husbands out of the way.

The kitchen was dimly lighted by one candle. The cook was
sitting, moaning with fright, by the polished iron stove.

There was a sharp snap and a smell of ozone. As thunder
crashed, lightning poured into the kitchen like a gold snake. It ran
around the water pipes, reached the stove, danced on it, leaped to
the cook's boots, melted all the rings that held the buttons into a
little pewter stream, knocked off the boots and went away from
there.

My father went over and picked up the boots. "Are you all
right?" he asked.

"Oh, yes sir," she said, got up, padded over to the table in her black cotton stockings and ladled herself out a plate of soup.

When my father left, with a pitcher of hot water, she was still eating the soup — with a two-tined fork.

Oliver immediately became my greatest joy in life. I would stand by the bassinet, newly done over with dotted Swiss muslin and pale blue silk, and admire his bald head and waving fists. He grew rapidly and soon had golden ringlets covering his head, brown eyes like my father's and a singularly sweet smile. Without his saying anything about it — he was a silent type — he let me know that we were friends.

We were so for more than forty years. I can't remember that we ever had a quarrel. Once, when I was about three, he did throw a small iron fire engine at me, but I'm sure that he did it for the pleasure of throwing rather than with any idea of hitting. Anyway it missed me by a good half inch.

That summer my father and mother, Katharine and Aunty all went to England. Oliver and I stayed with my grandmother and grandfather.

When I listened to my grandmother read their letters to my grandfather, I already had an interest in words. They gave me ideas even if I did not know just what the ideas were.

One letter told how my aunt and my mother were driving along in a basket phaeton, drawn by two fat black ponies with long tails, when my aunt pointed with her whip to a church across a green field.

"That," she said, "is the little Unitarian conventicle where Mr. Gaskell preaches."

I don't know if she knew she was talking to a Unitarian. I promptly added conventicle to my collection.

Oliver was sitting on a blanket on the floor with pillows around him so that he would not fall and bump his head.

"You are just a Unitarian conventicle," I said.

I meant no harm — I was only practicing — but he began to cry. My grandmother picked him up and took him on a tour of the pictures in the room. Oliver looked at them without much interest until they came to the copy of a painting by Morland of an eighteenth-century English village. There were dogs and horses in front of a tavern with a thatched roof, great old trees, red-faced men drinking ale from pewter flagons, pigs being driven to market. When Oliver saw the pigs, he bounced in my grandmother's arms and said, "Oink, oink!"

This was considered a highly intelligent remark. It was the only one he made until he was more than two years old. My father had the theory that Oliver was saving his energy until he really needed to say something.

Oliver made his first consecutive statement when he was not yet three. He sat up in his crib one morning when our mother came into his room, looked at her severely and announced, "There are earthworms in my bed. They run across my face at night."

In spite of her surprise at being thus addressed, our mother lifted him out and examined the crib. There were no earthworms in it but there was a small dead mouse. Probably its tail was the earthworm. Its brothers and sisters were soon caught in a round red trap and Oliver ceased to complain of his accommodations.

We had just moved into a house on Heath Hill. The Heaths had settled in Brookline when the road at the foot of the hill was little more than an Indian trail. Descendants of the original Heaths still lived in the old houses. The one my father rented was comparatively modern, built around 1840 perhaps. It had Gothic touches here and there, pleasant irregularities of arrangement, a big bay window, marble fireplaces. I remembered the one in the parlor as one of the most beautiful I had ever seen.

The present owner, a Heath descendant, showed it to me again recently and I had the pleasant experience of finding it as beautiful as I had thought in the texture of the white marble and in the carving of bunches of grapes and their leaves.

☆

In winter all ages coasted down the Atkinsons' hill into The Hollow. Our father built us a toboggan run with a splendid bump halfway down. I had a blue sled for Christmas and Oliver had a red one. At The Hollow the only heroic act of my life was performed.

It was Washington's Birthday, a brilliant day with crisp shining crust over sugary snow. Oliver with his red sled and I with my blue one were alone on the hill. As soon as Katy rang the bell for dinner, we would go in. She was making Washington pie for dessert. There was not a cloud in the sky.

The Hollow and the fields around it belonged to the Edward Atkinsons. Their cows grazed there when there was grass growing but, of course, in winter they were in the barn. They could not possibly gore us with their sharp horns or trample us to death. We were sure they would do both if they had a chance, for as Oliver often wisely said: "Akkison's cows is bulls."

We had just coasted down, our sleds going with special swiftness because of the glassy crust, when we heard the dinner bell. We hurried uphill toward the rail fence we must climb. We were almost at the top when the smiling hillside became a place of doom.

Through the still air from the Atkinsons' barn came a terrifying bellow.

Oliver panted: "The bulls is out!"

He slipped on the icy crust, hitting his head so hard that he dropped his sled rope. The sled flew downhill again. It was a red flame as it went. There was another bellow from the barnyard.

"My sled — the bulls will get my sled!" Oliver sobbed.

I said through chattering teeth, *"No, Oliver — I'll get it for you."*

I threw myself on the snow and rolled downhill, snatched the rope of the red sled and started up again. The hill seemed endlessly long. I fell three times and slid back but I never let go of the rope. The bulls still bellowed. I felt hot breath on my neck but I trudged on, with the sled scraping over the crust until, at last, I could say: "Oliver, here is your sled."

He stopped crying as if he had been turned off. For the first time I looked back. No bulls in sight. We thrust our sleds between the rails of the fence, climbed over it to safety, joy and Washington pie.

Three R's

I LEARNED TO READ before I went to school. When I opened my primer the first day and began to read, my teacher exclaimed in surprise, "Why, you can read five-letter words!"

"And six-letter ones," I said. "The cat jumped over two chairs."

The teacher was astounded at such virtuosity.

One thing led to another and when I was eight, I was reading Thackeray's *The Rose and the Ring*. When I finished it, I asked my mother if Thackeray had written anything else. She pointed out a shelf of books bound in leather and stamped with gold. I began at the left-hand end — *Vanity Fair*, the name of the book was — and went right through the lot. *Vanity Fair* and *Henry Esmond* were my favorites. For the next twenty years I read them both once a year.

In those days you were a partisan either of Dickens or of Thackeray. If you read one, you automatically did not read the other. My family regarded Dickens as sentimental and vulgar. Of course he is both — but then so is life.

I had to read Dickens clandestinely at other children's houses. I was like a drug addict, refusing to play games until I had had my dose. I was often dragged to the baseball field or croquet lawn, book in hand, reading until something had to be done about a ball.

Being nearsighted and being immersed in *Bleak House* or *Oliver Twist*, I did not develop into much of an athlete.

I have reread much of both Dickens and Thackeray lately and, at the risk of being disloyal to my tribe, I confess I prefer the open sentimentality of Dickens to Thackeray's sentimentality masked with cynicism. It is hard for me to think of books by either of them — or of *Middlemarch, Barchester Towers, Richard Feverel* or *The Heart of Midlothian* — as required reading. Imagine being required to read them or *Persuasion* or *Wuthering Heights!* I kept them, in turn, under my pillow and read them by candlelight until I was discovered and threatened with dire punishment, such as locking up the books.

I collected words the way some people collect shells or old pewter — not to use, just to enjoy having. I remember happily one day when Oliver and I went to dinner with the Copleys. The dessert was caramel custard. I thought it must have been accidentally scorched until Grandfather Copley tasted it and said: "Ah! Delightfully astringent!" Since I was the fortunate possessor of inner speech, I kept happily saying "delightfully astringent" over to myself. That's how I learned to like caramel custard.

I also learned certain things in school. My first school was Miss Pierce's. It later became the Park School, which now has several buildings and playing fields. In 1892 it was in a small mansard-roofed house on Walnut Street, next to the graveyard.

I had an annoying habit of declining to read books that stated facts about cats sitting on mats and of demanding something more interesting. I learned the whole multiplication table up to twelve times twelve the first week I was in school. I had thought naïvely that this would please Miss Pierce and that I would be allowed to sit quietly and read. Unfortunately the multiplication table was supposed to last the whole year and it was rather discreditable of me that I immediately learned that seven times eight was fifty-six and stuck to it no matter how suddenly I was asked.

Miss Pierce took a special interest in my handwriting. She wished from me a perfect copy of the following lines:

The alder by the river
Shakes out its golden curls;
The willow buds in silver
For little boys and girls;
The little birds fly over
And oh! How sweet they sing,
To tell the happy children
That once again 'tis spring . . .

There is more — much more — but I forbear.

I sometimes got almost six lines done without blot or error but sooner or later my rusty pen would catch in the paper. A blot would fall. I would start over.

Miss Pierce used to make a tour of the room during the writing hour. She would glance over my shoulder and say, "What, Louise! Is the alder *still* shaking out its golden curls?"

Yes, and it still is.

It is certainly strange that I turned out to be a writer.

Many years later after I had written several books and was a trustee of the Park School, Miss Pierce and I were on a committee to plan a dinner for graduates and former teachers. She told me that she was proud that she had taught me my three R's.

I said I was grateful for everything she had taught me — as indeed I was. I was not, however, thinking of reading, writing and arithmetic. What I knew of those subjects I had learned in spite of anyone's teaching.

Miss Pierce taught me something more valuable. Even writers, cowardly creatures, who would rather take notes on life than plunge wholeheartedly into it, need a little of this quality. I wish I had more but even a little is useful. It is learned only by practice.

It's called fortitude.

☆

My second year in school coincided with the panic of 1893. This was not a stock market crash like the 1929 disaster. It was a money panic; there was an actual shortage of coins. The longer the shortage lasted, the more people hid money under mattresses and the less money there was in banks. Pretty soon banks began closing their doors. Fortunately for our family the Brookline Savings Bank still stayed open.

Charles Storrow and Company, the firm in which my father was the junior partner, bought cotton in the South and sold it to mills in the North. My father used to go south and travel about, sampling cotton and ordering bales of the finest quality shipped to Boston. He always had some cotton in his coat pocket.

When small children needed entertaining, he would quietly take out a little cotton and pull it between his thumbs and forefingers until it was stapled; that is, until the long basic fibers were straightened out and parallel with each other. Then he would take a little silver ruler, two inches long perhaps, out of his waistcoat pocket and measure the staple. Good cotton thread could be spun if the staple were an inch long. Very fine cotton sometimes stapled an inch and a quarter, he would say.

At the height of the panic Charles Storrow and Company received notice that a shipment of cotton would soon arrive. The payment, due on delivery, was fifteen hundred dollars. No such sum was available. Their bank had closed. If they did not pay it, the firm could be declared bankrupt.

One night, after we had all gone to bed, our father came to our bedrooms — first Katharine's, then mine, then Oliver's — and explained to us about the cotton that must be paid for the next day. He asked us to lend him the money in our savings bank accounts. He had given most of it to us in the first place and he was the trustee so he could have drawn it out without telling us but, he said, if we were to be his creditors, he wanted us to understand about it.

That was how I learned about compound interest. He explained the whole transaction in a way that made us feel important, generous and businesslike, all at once. Naturally we agreed to lend him the money. He drew it out the next day. There was more than enough in the three accounts and the firm was saved.

The worst of the panic was over and banks opened their doors, but there was no money to send Oliver and me to private schools that year. We went to the public school at Marion Street; he in the first grade, I in the third. I was only briefly a pupil. During my second week I became an assistant teacher. Reading, spelling and mathematics were my subjects. My pupils were two little blond girls, one fat, one skinny, both frightened by words and numbers.

Miss Cartwright, the teacher, knew too much, I decided. She was too smart, too brisk. Ignorance and slowness annoyed her so deeply that her silvery curls stood on end and her velvety brown eyes flashed angry diamonds. Her weapon was the pointer. She grasped it so firmly as she tapped words or figures on the blackboard, that it seemed as if she might impale some hapless student upon its sharp point.

My sympathies are not confined to the victims. I feel sorry for the Miss Cartwrights of the world — male and female. If you are mathematically clever, it must be very annoying to spend your time with ignorant children.

As a teacher, I had the advantage of not knowing too much. Some of the best teaching, I've noticed, is done by someone who has just learned something and who is so excited about it that his one desire is to pass it on to someone younger and more innocent.

I tutored my pupils in the alphabet, three-letter words and addition as far as five and five. Both did well. I spoke softly. I used the pointer so gently that it sounded as if it had a poultice on the end. I praised the girls for their prowess. I was also rather pleased with my own.

Toward the end of the morning, Miss Cartwright came to inspect my work. I was too slow and dull and patient; she snatched the pointer from my hand. Her voice was high and shrill as she whanged the blackboard. Both little girls burst into tears.

"What's the matter — what have you been doing to them?" Miss Cartwright snapped.

"You frightened them," I said. "I can teach them if you leave us alone."

That reply, I have an idea, is why I was promoted so suddenly to the fourth grade.

The fourth grade was in the Lawrence School, an ugly building with dark brown woodwork, high studded rooms darkened by blackboards and by rows of dingy ink-stained desks. It smelled of chalk, gas and children, the Saturday night bath type, for the most part. I thought about Miss Pierce's, so full of starched elegance, of sunshine, of the smell of 4711 Cologne and Pear's Soap.

I clung to my mother's hand as the janitor, leaving his coal and ashes, showed us the door of Miss Rhodes's room and its coatroom. My mother helped me hang up my new plaid coat and my velvet bonnet with the ostrich feather curling over my left eye. She checked my boots to be sure that no button had missed its buttonhole. None had, for well had I plied the buttonhook. She smoothed my brown curls, made every morning over a curling stick while I screamed in agony. She straightened out my guimpe of muslin and Hamburg lace and my dress of soft red wool. She felt, I realized suddenly, as miserable as I did.

The moment could be postponed no longer. I must go in and face the fourth grade. There were more children in it than in Miss Pierce's whole school. They all stopped writing with their spluttering pens and looked at me, not with hostility, just with the professional interest with which a skulk of foxes might survey a stray lamb. Miss Rhodes, tall, thin, tense, energetic, showed me to an empty seat in the second row.

My mother was even taller than Miss Rhodes. She had on her new bonnet of white roses and bird of paradise plumes. She wore her best cape of dark blue, brocaded with the red of a bluebird's breast. Its folds fell from a high-collared yoke of rich blue velvet over which were sewn long triangles of Van Dyke lace. The cape was lined with the skins of many squirrels. There was nothing elaborate about it — just the sort of thing you ran up at home with the help of a seamstress.

My mother sat down, throwing the cape back against the chair, as Miss Rhodes cross-examined her about my qualifications. They seemed meager indeed. I did not write vertically. I was no geographer. I had not studied domestic science, nor had I used the right speller.

"Do they spell words some other way in the right speller?" I wondered miserably.

"Does she know The Poets?" Miss Rhodes inquired, making a sweeping gesture toward a row of pictures above the blackboard.

I looked up at them and decided that all poets were brown in color and had whiskers. My mother alleged that I had read *The Vision of Sir Launfal, Hiawatha,* "Snowbound" and "The Brook" by Tennyson.

"Then she knows The Poets," Miss Rhodes said. "Still, I think we should confer with the principal before placing her. Harold and Gwendolyn, I appoint you monitors in my absence."

Harold and Gwendolyn were almost as skinny and tense as Miss Rhodes herself. They paced the aisles, hungrily seeking breaches of discipline, noting those they found on the blackboard in their neat vertical handwriting. With my hands folded, I sat there, isolated from the human race. Robinson Crusoe was no lonelier on his island than I in the big brown room. Would I ever see my mother again or my father and Oliver?

Tears began to trickle down my cheeks. I sniffed in misery. The girl in front of me turned around. She was pale and freckled. Her straight sandy hair straggled out from under a round comb. She wore spectacles and braces on her teeth but, as she spoke, she looked as beautiful to me as Ellen Terry in *The Merchant of Venice.* She said, "Don't cry — your mother's coming back. *Don't you see she's left her cape?"*

And there it was, the hostage — velvet, lace, fur and all. I gazed at it happily through my tears. "Thank you," I said.

Gwendolyn came over to us. "Quiet!" she said sharply. "No talking in class — what's your name?"

I told her. She wrote our names on the board. My tears had dried and I could read: "Louise Andrews and Charlotte Wood — talking in class."

So I belonged to the class. And I had a friend, my first real friend.

We were friends as long as she lived.

4

Iron Bound

JOHN DONNE'S PHRASE "No man is an island" is often quoted. He is probably right, but to me people seem a little like islands or at least like small, rocky, prickly peninsulas, thrusting themselves out from the warm ground of our common humanity into mysterious and perilous seas forlorn. However, if I am any possible island in the wide world, then I am Iron Bound Island in Frenchman's Bay, four miles from Bar Harbor.

Iron Bound is sometimes considered one of the Porcupine Islands. Burnt, Bald, Sheep and Long Porcupine are the others. A few thousand years ago they must have been only the tops of rocky hills, pushing themselves above the fourteen foot tides that rush in and out of the bay. A long slow process brought seeds and soil and, at last, trees — pointed firs thrusting up like a porcupine's quills.

The rocks of all the islands and of the shores of the bay are not the same. There are many colors — brown, gray, pink, even yellow. Iron Bound differs in having purplish-brown cliffs with iron in them; hence its name.

It was once, my mother told me, two islands, each with high cliffs on the side facing Portugal, lying beside each other with a narrow, shallow channel between. Over the years this silted up and became the floor of a dark valley. When I walked there, ferns,

moss and Indian pipes, mushrooms and lady's slippers were growing under the evergreens. Yet, if you followed a steep twisting path
down into the valley and dug deep enough, you could find beach
pebbles, flattened and smoothly rounded by primeval tides.

On the east side of Iron Bound are some of the highest cliffs on
the coast of Maine. There are caves in them. You could scramble
down rocks and into the one at Great Head at low tide. If you
stayed too long, watching sea anemones change color as they
moved their pale fingers, catching jellyfish that melted into water
in your hands, prying periwinkles off the rocks, you might be
caught by the tide, might find yourself pulling your feet up over
humped rocks just ahead of curling green Atlantic waves.

Shag Ledge Cave was different. We could enter it only twice in
the summer at the highest tides of July and August; not even then
if there were storms. On the days of those high tides, we rowed all
the way around the island in the Black Boat.

It seemed like a very large boat to me. I suppose it may have
been twelve feet long. There was a broad seat in the square stern
and four seats — thwarts they were called by old salts like me —
for rowers. When I was very small, I sat with whatever grown-up
was in the stern and helped steer; that is, I pulled on a rudder rope
when I was told to. Later I was promoted to the bow oar. This is
like becoming an ensign, a proud moment. I never got beyond lieutenant, junior grade — second oar from the bow.

As we rowed in toward the cave, the ospreys would come screaming out of their nest to let us know they were on guard. They
would hover above us, drifting on the air currents. Once we saw
one plunge down close to our boat, catch a haddock and fly back
toward the nest.

There was a scream louder than the osprey's. A great bald eagle
swooped down out of a cloud. The sun flashed on his white head.
The noise of his wings cut through the still air like a saw buzzing

through a log. The osprey dropped his fish. The eagle swooped and caught it in his big yellow claws. The shadow of his wings darkened the sun as he flew over the boat and off to his nest near Seal Cove. We could hear seals barking as he screamed.

We shipped our oars and my mother steered the boat into the cave, letting the force of the tide carry us with it. It was very dark after the brightness of sun, sea and sky, but after a minute I could make out shelves of rock where barnacles, seaweed and anemones were sucking in the rising tide. My father showed me a rocky shelf far above my head — I could just see it in the darkness. He said that people thought that smugglers used to hide things there.

"Do you think my gold piece was ever there?"

He had found English sovereigns on the beach near the wharf and had hidden them in his bedroom so that Katharine and Oliver and I each found one.

"Who knows?" he said.

"But they couldn't get into the cave except at the spring tides," I said, for, being more than six, I was an expert in these matters.

"Not in a boat like this one, but they could in a canoe. They could carry canoes on their ship," he said. He knew about canoes on Frenchman's Bay.

The first time he came to Iron Bound, he crossed the bay in a birch-bark canoe paddled by a tall Indian. This was when my father had just come to Boston and before he had decided what business to go into. He had soon had enough of the noisy cobblestones and dust of Charles Street. He had met my aunts at a dance in Boston and had told them that he was going to Bar Harbor. They had said he must come over to Iron Bound and have dinner some day, so now, on a sunny morning with a calm sea, he was crossing the bay.

There were open fields on the island then. My grandfather's house was on a plateau high above the water. When they were a mile away, the Indian said, "See house." My father had turned his head and had seen James Wheeler Edgerly's summer cottage. It had been a New England farmhouse, built in the sensible pattern of continuous architecture. An ell containing kitchen, storerooms and woodshed connected it directly with the barn.

My father landed on the pebbly beach of Orrin's Cove and walked up the grass-grown road to the house, but found it looking empty and deserted. He was about to turn and go back to the canoe when, he said, the most beautiful creature he had ever seen came running around the end of the porch. She had wavy dark hair, cheeks like wild rose petals, big shining gray-green eyes.

She couldn't, he thought, be much over twelve years old. But I can wait, he said to himself. I can wait.

He waited seven years.

There was a wonderful dinner with everything grown on the island or in the sea around it: lobster soup, roast chicken, peas shelled almost as soon as they were picked, blueberry pie. They ate it around a big table in a room with a huge brick chimney and walls paneled diagonally with strips of pine. My father could see the bay, calm, pale blue at first; then — as the wind came in from the southeast — dark blue with whitecaps.

"Will it be rough on the bay?" he asked and was told that the wind, blowing against the tide as it went out, made those waves, called short chops — pronounced around the bay "shawt chawps."

They told him he had better start before the bay got rougher. He must come again, come often. Mary and her brother John showed him a shortcut to the cove where the Indian was sitting by the canoe. He nodded when my father asked if it was all right to go. They got into the canoe and shoved off.

When the children got back to the house, the family was all on the porch, watching anxiously. The Indian was not heading for Bar Harbor but for the eastern end of Long Porcupine.

"He's going back of Long Porc," John said, and my grandfather said, "He knows what he's doing. The sea won't be so rough there."

In a few moments the canoe, a mile away now, no bigger than a whitecap, disappeared behind the island. They watched for a long time, but the waves were running so high that they never saw the canoe come out from behind Long Porcupine and cross the open stormy stretch of sea between it and the next island. Even Mary's keen eyes did not see the white spot moving among the tossing wave crests.

At last my grandmother turned away, saying, "I'm afraid we shall never see that young man again."

It was, however, only his first visit.

As they left the lee of Long Porcupine, the Indian made my father understand that he must lie down and not move. All he could see was the grim-faced coppery figure against the sky, with its strong arms sending the canoe ahead. The waves seemed to run in all directions but the canoe rode them like a racehorse speeding over a foaming stream. Sometimes fine salt spray fell on my father's face but not once, he said, did the Indian let them slide into the trough of the waves, not once did a real wave break into the canoe.

The bay was almost calm behind Sheep and Burnt Porcupine and in Bar Harbor it was only a rough day with yachts tossing at their moorings. My father climbed the long slip at the wharf with nothing worse than saltwater stains on his new suit.

So that day he began his seven years of waiting. While he was waiting, he joined with a friend and founded the firm of Charles Storrow and Company, cotton merchants. He traveled a good deal, buying cotton and selling it, but of all the places he saw Iron Bound was his favorite.

☆

My grandmother had a habit of teaching people to read. She was a firm believer in education. Of course, not everyone agreed with her.

She started to teach Orrin Benjamin to read but Abijah Benjamin found out about it and forbade it.

"Larnin' makes rogues," he said.

Apparently the damage had already been done. Abijah's descendants fell, I'm afraid, rather naturally into roguishness. They did not, of course, like strangers on the island and they expressed this dislike in various ways.

My father liked to keep the old trails through the woods open. He would spend much of his vacation every summer chopping down young trees that were invading the paths and trimming off branches that pushed across them. He used to hire Orrin to help him.

One day with their axes, they were on the Seal Cove trail together. It curved through dark woods, past cliffs and bogs and fern-covered banks for half a mile before it came out at Seal Cove. My father heard seals barking, stopped to listen to them. Suddenly he became conscious that there was no sound of chopping behind him. A strange feeling in his spine made him swing around.

Orrin Benjamin was coming for him, ax raised, ready to strike him down.

My father said: "I wouldn't do that, Orrin."

Orrin lowered the ax, muttered that he was sorry, something come over him, he said.

My father continued to hire Orrin to help him keep the trails clear, but after that day, he told me, he always sent Orrin ahead — certainly a sensible precaution.

☆

We children used to pick blueberries and sell them to our grandmother for ten cents a quart. Later we ate them in pie, pudding or muffins. This was how we earned money to buy Christmas presents, an economic arrangement satisfactory to all parties. I often had more than four dollars at the end of the season. It was not all for blueberries. Some of it was for wild strawberries at fifteen cents a quart, raspberries at twelve and small mountain cranberries at ten. We also got pennies for learning passages from the Bible.

For learning the twelve tribes of Israel —

Reuben, Simeon, Levi, Judah,

Zebulon, Issachar, Dan, Gad,

Ashur, Napthali, Joseph, and Benjamin —

I received three cents, and well worth the money, considered.

Once I was picking raspberries in a tin quart measure. I had only a handful when Professor Jack appeared. He had just crossed the bay from Bar Harbor in Orrin Benjamin's skiff. I had been told that a botanist from the Bussey Institute was coming. I had been cherishing this information without knowing what it meant. Now I realized that a botanist was a tall man with small steel-rimmed spectacles, a big nose and a wide kind smile.

He asked if I would give him some raspberries.

"Take them all," I said, holding out the cup with at least two cents' worth in it.

He emptied them into his big hand and returned the empty cup. Only by some miracle it was far from empty. There were six vanilla caramels, four chocolate ones, two dimes, two nickels and four pennies.

I have had a special fondness for botanists ever since.

☆

During any summer day I had to attend to my reading, some of it clandestine. Among the luggage deposited on the wharf by the steamer *Ruth,* was the Book Trunk. Packing this for the summer was one of the excitements of the journey. It was a sturdy, flat, light-brown trunk, deeper than a steamer trunk but shorter. It held perhaps forty books. We were each allowed to choose some. *Little*

Lord Fauntleroy, Sara Crewe and *Herr Baby* went into it. There were also bird books and flower books, paperbound copies of Stevenson, Kipling and Frank Stockton, and novels by Mrs. Humphrey Ward and Sienkiewicz; for my family kept up with the latest thing, no matter how daring.

On hot pleasant afternoons, chairs were moved from the piazza into the deep shadow at the east end of the house. The ladies brought their embroidery and the gentlemen (I do not use these terms carelessly — they really were ladies and gentlemen) read aloud to them. Not being a lady, I was not invited to these readings. I was supposed to be having something falsely called a nice little nap.

My bedroom was almost a hundred feet from the reading party but by craft and guile, I would be present — at least till I was discovered. I waited until all sounds of clearing the dining table had ceased. I looked through a convenient knothole in the floor. If the white cloth had gone from the table and there was one of crimson damask in its place, I knew that the maids were in the kitchen drinking the good strong black tea they kept hot on the back of the stove. Now was the moment.

I stole downstairs, pausing at the turn to look down into the butler's pantry. Two large tables were heaped with dishes but no pans of hot water had been brought in yet. The coast was clear. I slipped rapidly out the back door and behind the water barrels, two big gray hogsheads and a smaller red barrel.

From behind the hogsheads I could hear my father's voice but not the words he was reading. I lay down on my stomach close to the edge of the porch. Woodbine and clumps of hollyhocks concealed me from the reading lawn. I inched along the grass till the words were easy to hear.

Ah! *Quo Vadis!* Lions killing Christians — good!

Not that I had any prejudice in favor of lions; I just liked something going on.

After a while my father handed over the book to another man, who read faster and less distinctly, dropping his voice in exciting places. I had to squirm nearer. I suppose I must have made a rustling sound. I was discovered, taken gently but firmly by the scruff of my neck and removed from literary circles. I felt honor bound not to listen again that afternoon. Naturally I did on other afternoons. I was usually caught but not always. In this way I heard pieces of *Quo Vadis, Marcella* by Mrs. Humphrey Ward and *The Master of Ballantrae* by Stevenson — all interesting works, I gathered.

I also tried everything in the parlor bookcase. These were mostly books bound in paper, brought on the train by guests and left behind as souvenirs of the voyage. I say "tried" not because I could not run my eyes over the page and find out, more or less, what was going on but because I was almost always discovered and told, "You may not read that book."

Always conscientious about any definite prohibition, I did not go on with that particular book. On the next rainy day I would choose another. Not all were snatched from my grasp. I was allowed to read Stockton and Henry James. I suppose it was thought that I would not understand James. I did not — I just read for the exercise — but *The Portrait of a Lady* became and has remained a great favorite of mine. So has *The Casting Away of Mrs. Lecks and Mrs. Aleshine.*

Once when we had rainy weather for almost a week, I was able to do plenty of reading. I heard my mother say to my grandmother, "That child really ought to be a librarian." Innocently supposing that librarians spent all their time reading, I made no protest.

I must have been a great trial to my mother, who was a natural athlete: tennis, shooting, swimming, riding — she excelled at whatever she undertook. She won the first golf match ever played by women in America, at The Country Club in Brookline, and received a cut glass inkstand with a silver top engraved with the record of her triumph. The Country Club (there is still only one in the eyes of its members) had one of the first golf courses on this side of the Atlantic. It is less well known that an earlier course existed on Iron Bound Island; that is where I played.

Because Iron Bound had more woods than fields, there were only seven holes on the course. The first tee was in back of the croquet ground. You could not see the putting green from it. You drove in its general direction, hoping your ball would not land in a large clump of exceptionally prickly rosebushes. The greens were mown by tethered sheep. Though they were well padded with wool, it was not supposed to be good for their nervous systems to hit them with golf balls. The duty of a caddy, after finding a ball in the rosebushes, was to go ahead and unhitch the sheep from the flag-staff that fitted into the cup on the green and withdraw to a safe distance. Still, sheep or caddy might be hit by an approach shot just the same.

The second hole ran up past the calendula bed and the petunia bed, good traps for balls but not prickly, and arrived at a green near the graveyard. This little square enclosure was surrounded by a gray post and rail fence with a frosting of moss and lichens. A white birch towered over the stones that marked the graves of early Benjamins and other pirates. In between the graves grew a tangle of blueberry bushes, bracken and enough blackberries to scratch the legs of unwary ball hunters; the graveyard was a magnet for balls.

The chief hazards of the third hole were clumps of huckleberry bushes. Sometimes a mother sheep and a lamb were tethered on the third green. At one time sheep ran wild on Iron Bound. It was not safe for children to walk in the woods. A wild ram might butt them down and gore them with his horns. The rams had been caught and killed for mutton long before my time but there was still a wild strain in the putting-green sheep. If they were protect-ing their lambs, they would always try to knock down caddies.

On the fourth hole the perils were Orrin Benjamin's cattle and the pigpen. Large red and white cows charged down fiercely on caddies. Enormous pink pigs grunted fiercely when balls were removed from their territory and made threatening rushes at intruders.

The fifth hole was the fourth in reverse. The green was near Orrin's duck pond, which was green too with slimy weeds, adhesive to bare legs. On the sixth hole, drivers often sliced into the spruces. Oliver and I might hunt in the woods for what seemed like hours before we found the ball. I suppose it is obvious that we were a rather specialized type of golfer, caddies in fact. That is why I remember the terrain so acutely.

For our services we received a cent a hole. All holes had their dangers. It was on the sixth green that Oliver was standing, holding the flag, when an especially wild mother sheep dove between his legs and carried him off into the woods. I can still see his look of annoyance as he rode backwards, trying to steer the sheep by the tail.

My mother always planned some project for the summer. Oliver and I met in the big bedroom of her apartment at the end of the house every morning at nine o'clock and worked for an hour. One summer we had collected flowers and ferns, pressed them and mounted them on heavy sheets of white paper. Another, we were writing essays on birds. A prize had been offered in our school for the best collection of bird essays: vast wealth — five dollars — loomed on the horizon for the lucky prizewinner.

First we had to report on what birds we had seen to our mother and identify them from pictures in various bird books. Then we made notes for our essays including descriptions of the bird and where we had seen it. Then we wrote the essay and, when my mother had approved the spelling and punctuation, we copied our remarks in our neat vertical handwriting on 5 x 7 sheets of fine writing paper.

What with caddying, painting, spying on birds through Aunty's opera glasses, picking berries and eating three hearty meals a day, we had little time to get into mischief. In fact, we were frequently so exhausted that we lay in hammocks slung between the piazza posts eating sponge cakes, hermits, dingbats, hard sugar ginger-bread, hard molasses gingerbread, apple turnovers or a few dough-nuts still warm from the kettle. Luckily for us no one had learned the ghoulish sport of counting calories.

Being a girl, I also had my stint of sewing to do every day. I hemmed sheets, put squares together for patchwork quilts, made needlebooks for Christmas presents and a silk cap to keep the drafts from my father's bald head. My pride that next winter when I saw him wear it in the evenings with his black velvet jacket is hard to exaggerate.

Since Oliver did not sew, some other project had to be thought of to keep him busy and to train his stubby fingers to some sort of skill. Fortunately we heard a rumor that if you collected a million stamps, you could get a Chinese baby girl. We had asked our mother while we were still in Brookline if we could keep the baby in case we won it. She said we could and we began work immedi-ately. I soaked the stamps and dried them. Oliver made them into packets of one hundred and tied them up with heavy linen thread. My mother would check the knots. If they were not square knots, holding the stamps in neat cubes, they had to be untied and done over.

We never collected more than about half a barrel full of these packets, perhaps a hundred thousand stamps, so we did not add a Chinese baby to the family, but Oliver became so good at making square knots that years later, when he was learning the cotton busi-ness by working in different departments of a cotton mill, he be-came a skilled loom fixer with no trouble at all.

Although we were short of our goal by about nine hundred thou-sand stamps, we did at least win the Bird Prize. It was given to us jointly. We did not squander the money, as we had planned to do, on penny candy. At our mother's suggestion we bought a handsome two-volume edition of *Nuttall's Ornithology*. I think we both realized that she, rather than we, had won the prize; not that she had ever suggested even a syllable to us, she was scrupulously fair, but simply that she kept us working regularly.

Someone asked me once if my mother had expected me to be a writer. I told her about something I had once heard my mother say. I was reading *Henry Esmond* for the second time in the room where the conversation took place. A courtesy aunt — we had several — said, foolishly, I thought, "Such a talented child, Mary! Are you going to encourage her to be a painter? Or a writer?"

My mother said gently, "Why, no, I'll discourage her from either as much as possible. Then if she has any talent it will be strong enough for her to use it."

She knew, of course, that I heard what she said. I thought it was a sensible reply. I did not, of course, know then that she had given me a tool as useful to a writer as square knots were to a loom fixer: the ability to sit down and do some work every morning whether you feel like it or not.

5

Fog

ON ONE OF THOSE TRIPS to Bar Harbor in the Black Boat we almost missed the ferry because of fog. Travelers no longer came by way of Bangor. The new steamer, swift, gleaming white, more like a yacht than an ordinary steamboat, carried passengers to several harbors.

When it was foggy, we could hear her whistle, a great clarinet sounding across the bay. No inlander quite understands fog. It is not simply a thing that makes vision difficult; other senses are affected too. Sounds sometimes seem muffled by fog, yet they may suddenly become louder than usual. The voice of a bell buoy, hardly heard on a sunny day, becomes a sound of doom — and of safety. A gull's scream is far off one minute, close in your ear the next. Fog smells salty, yet the scent of spruce and balsam may drift through it too, just before docks loom up ahead.

Wind laden with fog is wet against your cheek; whatever you touch is slippery under your fingers. You seem to taste it with each breath you draw and each breath comes harder, as you tug at your oar, than it does on a bright day. The wind, on the day when we so nearly missed the ferry, shifted suddenly into the east and fog came rolling in around us, the sun became first a bright golden cloud, then a drifting red cherry, then vanished. The water changed from

blue with white foam to dingy green with an occasional smear of
soapy gray bubbles. It looked like soup simmering in a great kettle
and we seemed to be in the kettle. Then, as our eyes grew used to
the darkness, we were in a small room with a tilting green floor and
walls of gray cloth. No matter how hard we pulled at our oars, the
walls were always close around us. My mother steered by a com-
pass so we knew we must be moving in the right direction. I could
hear a foghorn blowing on the Bar Harbor wharf and a steamer,
coming in from the southeast, a long way off, giving a choked
whistle.

Then all at once, the whistle was loud in my ears. There was a
dark shadow on the wall of our room. I heard a small bell ring
twice and the sound of water rushing hard beside me. I looked up.
The steamer that towered above us had reversed her engines just in
time not to hit us. I looked into a dark space with a jumble of
trunks, crates and barrels in it. A man stood close to the rail, not
far above the water. His cap was on the back of his head and his
mouth, under a bristly red moustache, seemed to be frozen open.
He reached out a long pole and fended off the Black Boat. The
bell tinkled again and the steamer went on her way into the fog.

☆

Oliver and I used to watch every summer for the arrival of the
White Fleet. In those peaceful times part of its duty was to visit
Bar Harbor. It was my impression that the work of its officers,
splendid in starched white uniforms, was to waltz with beautiful
young ladies in ports along the Atlantic seaboard. The fleet used to
come about the first of July and stay for a week or more. Oliver
and I went out to watch for it on Great Head one July morning in
1897.

When we got there, it was, as Orrin Benjamin would say, thick-a-
fog. The rocks on which we sat were damp. The air was so still

that I thought I could hear if anything moved on the bay. Nothing did except the rising tide gently filling the cave below us.

From a spruce tree close to us, a veery called to her mate. We sat so still that we saw him turn over moss and bunchberries, pause by a fringed orchis, listen a second with his head cocked toward the ground. He plunged his beak into the moss, came up with a wriggling worm and flew off to his nest.

"Audubon," I told Oliver learnedly, "drew a picture of the veery and he wrote, 'I drew this bird in Maine.' I think it was right here. It has the bunchberries and the moss and the fringed orchis in it."

"Did it have the rocks and the mountains and the sea and the fog?"

"No fog," I said and he said, "There won't be any soon. I feel a breeze on my starboard cheek."

I felt it too, coming gently from the northwest. The fog moved slowly out to sea. Soon it was only a high white wall at the mouth of the channel and the sun was shining on blue water. I consulted my Ingersoll dollar watch.

"We'll have to start back to dinner if the fleet doesn't come," I said.

"It's coming," said Oliver, "I hear the *Maine*'s whistle."

There she was, pushing through the fog wall. The whole White Fleet was there too. We knew them all from last summer, the *New York,* the *Brooklyn,* the *Massachusetts* and the *Maine*'s sister ship the *Texas.* Even J. Pierpont Morgan's swift black yacht did not thrust through the waves with the power of these shining white ships under their white smoke plumes. The sun showed us smoke-stacks of yellowish pink, dark portholes, great anchors, gun turrets, polished decks, flying flags, railings of shining brass.

Through the opera glass, we could see white-capped white and blue figures on the decks. We were not especially interested in the *Massachusetts,* although she was named for our native state. We had brought an American flag with us; it was to the *Maine* that we waved it. We were sure her crew had seen the flag and that they waved their caps to us. Perhaps they did.

The next day was the Fourth of July. We rowed across to visit the *Maine*. One of her lieutenants had invited us to come and see the ship. When we arrived at her gangway — I had my hand on it and was steadying the Black Boat so my mother could get on it — we were told that the lieutenant was across the harbor on the *Texas* and had left word for us to join him there.

Oliver and I were disappointed. It was the *Maine* we wanted to see. We'd see her another day, we were told, and anyway the *Texas* was just the same. We didn't really believe it. Still we enjoyed scrambling over the ship along shining decks, down companionways, past officers' cabins, each a miracle of compact order. We went into the galley, where the peel was being buzzed off potatoes by a handy machine, and into the forecastle which looked empty because all the hammocks were neatly coiled away. We were even shown a small room with walls of iron gratings where a sailor looked at us through the bars.

He couldn't, I thought, have done anything very bad. He looked the way our dog did when he was shut up in his kennel yard for chasing a wagon, ashamed but hopeful that we'd let him out.

I wished I could let the prisoner out.

On all five ships of the fleet, lanterns were being strung up for Fourth of July decorations. That night, as the sun went down and the stars came out, the lanterns began to shine too. The *Maine* and the *Texas,* on opposite sides of the harbor, were decorated in the same simple pattern of red, white and blue lights. The other ships were more elaborately trimmed. One of them — the *New York,* I think — had lights arranged in the shape of a crown. My father said it was a compliment to Queen Victoria in honor of her Diamond Jubilee.

Oliver and I did not entirely approve of this gesture. After all, why had we worked so hard setting off firecrackers? How about the Boston Tea Party and the lanterns in the North Church steeple and William Dawes riding through Brookline Village right past the very blacksmith's shop where our father had his horse shod? How about Bunker Hill? But we were not really too particular and by the time our father sent up the fire balloon, we shouted, "God save the Queen, George Washington and Thomas Jefferson!"

The fire balloon was like an enormous pear, vertically striped with bands of red, white and blue. It was taller than my father as he lighted it and lifted it into the air. The breeze from the west carried it toward the cliffs as it rose. It woke the eagles. They left their nest, were dark shadows against the fiery red, white and blue. Now it veered toward Shag Ledge. The ospreys woke too and added their hoarse voices to the din.

"I wish we could have gone on the *Maine,*" Oliver said that night. "They said the *Texas* was just like her but if the *Maine* had a prisoner it wouldn't be the same one, would it?"

"I bet they didn't have any prisoners," I said.

It was foggy again the day the White Fleet left. We were at Great Head watching but the ships were only dim shadows. We could not tell which one was the *Maine.*

We said to each other, "Well, we'll see her next year."

But — of course — we never saw her again.

6

Change

THE YEAR 1899 was one of change for our family. The lease of our house on Heath Hill had run out and our father had decided to buy a house. We would have liked him to build one but he said that fools built houses for wise men to live in. While he was considering which house to be wise about, we went to live at Mrs. Woods's boardinghouse on Walnut Street in Brookline.

I was charmed with the boardinghouse and its variety of people. They ranged in age from a little boy of five to an old, indeed ancient, lady almost as old as I am now, a Mrs. Cabot. Every boardinghouse has a star boarder, either a widower or a bachelor. Ours was a widower, Mr. Hovey. He was an editor, the first I ever knew. I decided they were wonderful. I was right, as usual.

There were shelves and shelves of books in Mr. Hovey's sitting room. He told me I could go in and read while he was out if I would always put the book back in its place. Something strange happened one day while I was sitting reading *The Decline and Fall of the Roman Empire*. Mary, a beautiful blue-eyed, black-haired Irish girl, had just taken away some faded roses and left the bowl with the June sun shining on it.

I am not sure just what made me look up. I still seem to hear a sound like the crumpling of a small piece of paper and smell some-

thing different from faded roses. I suddenly moved out of ancient
Rome and back into a room where the glass bowl of water, acting
like a burning glass, was sending a small cone of fire down on the
Boston *Transcript*. At first there was, on the front page, only a
small round hole with a black edge and a twist of smoke. Then,
before I could reach it, there was a ring of flame.

I tipped a little water over it. The flame sizzled out. I set the
bowl in a shady place. I put Gibbon back on the shelf and went out
to play with the boys. They were Oliver's friends, all slightly
younger than I. A thirteen-year-old girl is often stronger than a
younger boy. For a while I was a dominant figure in our gang. I
even knocked down some of those who challenged our group in
battle. The Cutler boys who lived farther up the street were considered dangerous. It was said that they would "do anything." Yet I
had once laid two of them low. Luckily they survived to become
some of Boston's most useful and distinguished citizens.

☆

One of these summers we went to Monument Beach on Buzzard's
Bay, near the beginning of Cape Cod, and the Purves family lived
across the salt marsh back of our cottage. The days were so wonderfully long that by evening we would have forgotten most of the
mischief we had been in. Danny Purves helped us get into a good
deal of it. It was with his aid and counsel that we caught fiddler
crabs and put them in the cook's bed. It was also his idea that,
while the cook had her afternoon nap, we should collect food from
the kitchen and store it in the old schooner rotting in the marsh, in
case we decided to go on a voyage to China. After several days we
had quite a good supply of pilot biscuits and fruit cake. Danny
called the cake "plum duff."

He came of a seafaring family. They were, he told us, the earliest settlers on the bay.

"Did they come in the *Mayflower?*" I asked.

Danny made a rude noise to show that the *Mayflower* was nothing to him.

"My family," he stated, "rowed here from Norway in a boat like a red dragon hundreds of years before the *Mayflower* was even built. There's this little old professor that comes to talk to my dad. He says this is Vineland and my dad's a real Viking."

Up to that time I had known no Vikings. As I look back on the Purves family, I do not wonder that the professor thought they belonged in Vineland. Harry Purves was an enormous man with red-gold hair and a moustache like a walrus. He towered over any man on the bay. He was immensely strong.

When the professor drove his chaise into a bog while he was hunting for runic inscriptions, six men tried to get it out. Harry Purves saw them struggling with it and strode out into the mud. He had on a bathing suit, dark blue with enormous white stripes. He was sunburned the color of a partly ripe bog cranberry. Great lumps of muscle rippled under his scorched skin as he pushed the six Lilliputians aside.

The horse had already struggled back to the sandy road.

"Maybe we'd oughta get an oxteam," suggested someone.

"Oxteam! — pah!" said Harry.

He lifted the chaise, professor and all, and set it back on the road.

"Drive on, Professor!" he said kindly.

By this time I had read about Vikings. I was sure Harry Purves was one. I could see him wearing a winged gold helmet, the Viking equivalent of a bathing suit, a polar bear's skin slung over his sunburned shoulders. Most of his seven children looked like Vikings, too, especially Danny. He was only a few months older than I but inches taller. He had a fine thatch of reddish-golden hair, a handsome straight nose, eyes as blue as Buzzard's Bay in a brisk wind. He looked sidewise out of them at me and told me of brave things he had done.

I adored him and believed every word he said.

He had shown his courage at many spots along the road and he remembered each act of heroism clearly. There was the place where the grass had rustled and he was sure there was a boa constrictor or maybe a poison adder coming at him.

"But I stood right there and just looked at where it was and it went away."

There was a thunderstorm so fierce that all his sisters cried and lighted whale-oil lamps.

"I bet you can't guess what I did."

I couldn't.

"I just stood by the sink and ate bread and molasses. I ate steady. The lightning never touched me," said Danny.

Danny glanced at the old boat and said, "Low tide. Loo-loo (that was what he called me in his spine-tingling voice) and Olly," he said generously, "it's time you had a little lunch. Cut into the house and snatch up whatever you can. I'll meet you at the boat."

We obeyed, of course. The cook and the waitress were taking their morning rest. We filled a basket with slabs of one-two-three-four cake, fairy gingerbread and blueberry muffins. These we split and buttered since we had learned that Danny did not like them plain.

We hopped along a tussocky path across the marsh and reached the old gray schooner. The tide had turned and water was beginning to gurgle up around it. Danny was in the stern moving the tiller and looking at the masts against the sky as if all sails were set. He had just frightened off a flock of herring gulls with one look, he told us. He was open-handed with the provisions, eating only about half of them and leaving the other half for Oliver and me.

When he had eaten, he made a suggestion to me that I will not quote; not because I cannot, I remember only too well — but this is Mrs. Appleyard's book as well as mine and she never writes anything that would bring a blush to the purest cheek. Of course it's a temptation; I like to think of one of Mrs. Appleyard's works with *Banned in Boston* prominently printed on the jacket. Still, I resist.

I merely state that when Danny paused for my reply, Oliver, five years old and half his size, knocked him into the marsh.

Thus ended our romance.

The next autumn I was engaged to Hamilton Copley. Hamilton was neither so handsome nor so heroic as Danny but he was rich — fifty cents a week allowance, fashionable, generous and well dressed. He had a fine talent for collecting and distributing food from the Copley kitchen. There was a certain currant cake that was pure ambrosia. He also stole his father's cigarettes and on one occasion, long to be remembered, a cigar. This was a kindness for which I shall always be grateful. With the Minot boys there were six of us who had a puff apiece.

"Take a good deep one," Hamilton said generously. "Miss Lowell smokes cigars and she's a poet. Perhaps you will be too."

Thus inspired I took an especially deep puff. Soon all six of us were lying on the autumn leaves in different attitudes of agony. Tobacco has never tempted me since. I am one who can see views of mountains, lakes and rivers without any desire to light a cigarette. Cantering horses, flags fluttering in a crisp breeze, a yacht crossing the finish line arouse no longing in me for a good cigar. Thanks to Hamilton, I am immune.

☆

What was called my education still went on from 8:30 to 1:30 five days a week.

In the eighth grade, for the first time I met a teacher who really cared about passing on knowledge. Miss Alice Bruce loved three things — Latin, French and children. I caught French and Latin from her as I might have caught the measles. I have never quite recovered.

At recess time we skipped rope and played hopscotch or prisoners' base on the asphalt surface of the schoolyard. Sometimes a hurdy-gurdy, bright with Venetian scenes, gilding and mother-of-pearl, came and played for us. On more than one occasion I denied myself a banana and gave the man some of my meager supply of pennies. He always swept off his hat with his left hand, bowed and smiled, showing very white teeth, kept on grinding out "The Carnival of Venice" with his right hand. The monkey on his shoulder in his little red flannel jacket bowed too.

Soon Banta would come along with his basket of penny candy — slabs of pink, blue or green rubbery sweetness or chocolate cigarettes. I was strictly forbidden to buy the candy; it was said to contain arsenic and I daresay it did. So did wallpaper and paint and a special tonic often prescribed for small children. We led dangerous lives. I was allowed to buy bananas. They cost two cents apiece.

My clothes were a problem that year. My mother had a friend whose two daughters were a little older than I. Their clothes came from Paris. When they outgrew them — and how fast those girls shot up and across! — the clothes were passed on to me. Hatred is a mild word for the emotion I felt toward those costumes.

I, who yearned to be suavely tailored like Katharine and her friends, who wanted a covert cloth jacket from England and a stiff straw boater to balance on my head, found myself dripping with ruffles of lace and silk. Furthermore these things had been bought for blue-eyed blondes who loved a dingy shade of greenish blue. Among other items was a matching ensemble — coat, hat, dress and button boots — all of this shade.

"There's probably arsenic in it," I thought mournfully as I balanced the hat above my King Charles Spaniel countenance. "Probably I'll go to an early grave — and just as well."

The hat was floppy. There were two layers of it — pleated silk above and lace below. The coat had bishop sleeves, adequate for a fairly large bishop. They dripped lace ruffles around the wrists.

The boots, I refused to wear. I alleged untruthfully that they hurt. Actually my quadruple A feet found plenty of room in them.

"Suppose it rains and I have to get off my bike and walk in the mud?" I asked with fiendish craftiness.

The boots with their turquoise buttons remained at home and so did the dress, which — my mother admitted — was more for Sundays.

Next to Latin my favorite subject was dancing. For years I went to Miss Carroll's dancing school. It was held in a building on Copley Square, convenient to reach either by train or by a horse-car that ran along Huntington Avenue.

I preferred the horse-car to the train. I liked the big bay horses in their thick winter coats, blowing steam in the icy air, tossing their heads and setting bells tinkling as the driver, in his big buffalo coat, cracked his whip.

The ballroom above S. S. Pierce's store on Copley Square was another world — one of warmth, elegance and beauty. Three great chandeliers with prisms of glass lighted the hall. The lights were different from any I had ever seen, not smoky candles dripping wax, nor lamps that reeked of whale oil or kerosene with wicks that might run too high and smoke a whole room, nor the yellow and blue flare of gas. These lights had a strange name — electric. You pressed a button far away from them. You could almost feel hot lightning run by strange magic along the wires. The lights in the chandeliers began to glow, first pink like a cloud at sunset, then slowly, a sunny yellow that made rainbows in the prisms.

Even if no one had asked me to dance I would have been happy just to see the lights go on and hear the music and watch Miss Carroll's slender feet move in elegant bronze boots on the shining parquet floor.

And I had turquoise boots at home, didn't I? They helped my morale a good deal though I wore black ankle ties.

I needed help for — let's face it — I was not often among the first chosen by the boys in their black broadcloth suits. I was not the last either because, though I lacked glamour, I was a good dancer.

I was sometimes chosen as an assistant to dance with some especially awkward boy. Some of the nicest men I ever knew, I met that way. They kept on dancing with me for years. Indeed it often seemed like years just in one afternoon. Some were fat and towered above me as they stepped on my feet. Others were so short that it was hard for them to place their hands under my left shoulder blade and support my steps with gentlemanly poise. They were more likely to sling skinny arms around my Roman-sashed waist and to leave poise and balance to me.

My Roman sash was my great pride and joy. It was woven of heavy silk in shades of ivory, turquoise and warm yellowish pink. Wide bands of these colors were outlined by narrow stripes of sea blue. I thought it must look like sunset over Venice.

I wore it with my favorite dress, which was white embroidered India mull as delicate as a floating cobweb. There was white China silk under it and then a petticoat with Swiss embroidery so there were three layers of fabric before the New England climate reached my flannel petticoat. This was the color of my mother's ivory-backed hairbrushes. Its warm silk and wool surface was simply decorated with feather stitching, French knots and buttonhole-stitched scallops — the kind of thing any child could do in odd moments. I doubt if it took me a week.

This was, of course, one of my best flannel petticoats. Those I wore on school days were of a more rugged substance and merely feather stitched. All my petticoats and my ruffled drawers buttoned onto the rows of bone buttons that encircled my Ferris waist. Some Ferris waists were stiffened with narrow strips of steel. Mine were made flexible with whalebone, brought — after incredible adventures of which I shuddered to think — from the Pacific. My stockings were made in England of lisle thread. I carried a Spanish fan. When I went home I put on a hat of French velvet and a coat of Scottish wool. The collar of the coat was chinchilla from South America and so was my muff. In fact, my costume was a lesson in geography. Now the whole thing would be made synthetically out of a few corn stalks — God bless America!

When the class was over, we would go down and wait in S. S. Pierce's until the bells of our horse-car were heard. My father often joined us there in the warm bright store. If Mother reported our behavior as nearly perfect, Father would buy us marzipan in shapes of fruit and vegetables. The only parsnip I ever liked was made of marzipan.

Queen Elizabeth I's head cook used to make her something splendid in marzipan — only they called it marchpane — every year for a New Year's present. It might be a castle or a ship or a great basket of fruit. Whatever it was, it tasted like Pierce's because both were made of almonds, sugar and egg whites. I'm glad that cook cannot read the label on a modern basket and see what our native ingenuity now uses for materials. I tasted some; I prefer parsnips. I can hardly say more — indeed I will not.

7

North and South

IN 1899 we went to North Hatley for the summer. A friend of my mother's had described it to her as The Earthly Paradise. The town was on Lake Massawippi in the Province of Quebec. The summer people were mostly from our southern states. They were charming, the scenery was beautiful — the lake lay among high hills with mountains beyond. There was a golf course, canoes, swimming, tennis, sailing, a good livery stable and the board was four dollars and a half a week.

This did not include lodging. You hired a cottage or took rooms in the Victoria Apartment House and went out for your meals. My father engaged six rooms, half the second floor at the Victoria, board for us at Mrs. Dave Jackson's and for his saddle horse at Bean's Livery Stable. The horse traveled comfortably in a special freight car from Boston. We went less luxuriously, changing trains at Wells River, New Hampshire, Newport, Vermont and Stanstead, Quebec. I seem to remember a good deal of switching of cars at White River Junction too. There was some headshaking in the boardinghouse over our recklessness in heading north for southern territory.

The dangers of our expedition had been exaggerated. I can never remember receiving anything but kindness in North Hatley.

The population, as I soon found out, was quite varied. There were generals and admirals who had fought on both sides in the war. They paced up and down the wide verandas of the Victoria discussing the Spanish-American War. I gathered that things would have gone better if they had all been in charge.

The porches that ran around the first and second stories of the Victoria were a meeting place for everyone on our side of the lake. Ladies referred to as Miz Colonel Smith, Miz General Jones or Miz Admiral Robinson — it took days for me to learn that Miz meant Mrs. — played whist there or crocheted fascinators or simply talked in bewitching accents.

No matter how hot the weather the older ladies always dressed in black. Even their feathered bonnets were black. In this uniform they supervised the comings and goings of their grandchildren who used considerable ingenuity in evading the glittering eyes of their relatives. Evasion was especially difficult on rainy days, for then the ancestors gathered around the fireplace in the lower hall near the foot of the big staircase. There was, they knew, no other way to get upstairs, so if they had not seen their granddaughters come down — nor any young man go up — they knew that the sexes were segregated.

This belief must be listed among the many things that people know that aren't so. Actually, as I well knew, there were plenty of beaux in their striped blazers on the upper veranda. A slender young maple tree grew close to the porch; climbing up and down it was no trouble at all. In fact it was so easy that it was considered more sporting to make an occasional trip over the stairs.

The chaperones, who would look up from their cards and make a mental note of all stairclimbers, would realize, when they saw one go up for the second time, that he had never come down, or — even stranger — one might be seen going down who had never gone up. It must have happened, they would think, carefully polishing their pince-nez, during some tense moment of the whist game. Perhaps they ought to crochet more — or read a book.

They probably consoled themselves by thinking that the boys had doubtless gone up to see those Boston girls. This meant my sister Katharine and her friend Dorothy Gookin. It was admitted by the chaperones that they were, for Yankees, well-mannered girls and handsome, if you liked that Gibson-Girl style, that starched, tailored look.

Two dashing young Southerners decided, as soon as they saw the Boston girls, to make an impression on them. Each took one of them out in his canoe and, as the moon rose, leaned forward, declared his passionate admiration, asked her to be his.

I don't know what a southern girl would have said in such circumstances. Katharine said she would ask her father. Dorothy said she would write to hers. Each inquired whether the young man wanted to be married right away; they said they did not approve of long engagements. There probably have never been two more frightened youths on Lake Massawippi. Both choked out sensible statements about perhaps they ought to know each other better and that maybe there wasn't all that hurry about asking their fathers. They had paddled slowly out into the lake. It was almost a race to see which would reach shore and safety first. The girls, who had been warned that these boys usually proposed the first time they took a girl out, went home and giggled most of the night over their success.

Hatley life, in my memory, centers on the canoe. No means of transportation — not even rowing the Black Boat on Frenchman's Bay — was ever such a combination of skill and poetry and danger. My father told us that we could paddle anywhere we liked so long as we obeyed the rules: *One:* Pass the test. *Two:* When boys take you out, no landings. *Three:* Start home when the ten o'clock train whistles. *Four:* Get home before the eleven forty-five arrives.

That first summer these rules applied to Katharine more than they did to me, but in later years I was able to use the same time-worn excuses: "The ten o'clock train was late, Papa . . . We started when we heard it but the breeze was against us . . ." etc., etc. The important thing in 1899 was to pass the test.

Oliver and I worked hard at it. We had to upset a canoe, first fairly close to the shore, later in deeper water, and with one arm across it, swim it to shore. Then, more difficult, two of us working together would turn the canoe right side up again, get most of the water out of it by rocking it from side to side, get back into it again without swamping it and splash out the rest of the water. We were taught to keep our paddles; that a paddle will help keep you afloat — this is true as I learned later — and that, if you can right the canoe, it is much easier to paddle it than it is to swim it to shore.

We loved upsetting canoes and getting into them again. We were soon given the freedom of the lake, a wonderful thing. One of my favorite places to explore was the marsh back of Bean's Livery Stable. It seemed a vast and mysterious labyrinth and did, I suppose, contain several acres.

One day I set out to find the cardinal flowers I had searched for so often. The marsh was rather like the maze at Hampton Court except that there you get lost while walking. Maneuvering a canoe in a passage in which it cannot possibly be turned presents special difficulties. I traveled between banks where, as I knelt in the middle of the canoe, marsh hay reached higher than my head. For a while the stream was so narrow that muddy banks crushed both sides of the canoe. Then the water widened into a small pool, thick with yellow pond lilies, edged with arrowweed and turtlehead. Around it stunted trees grew out of small islands. Water gurgled under my paddle. Bullfrogs croaked and splashed around me. Dragonflies whizzed past. A crow on top of a twisted cedar cawed disapprovingly at me. An old curved blackish log, lying among the tussocks, suddenly slithered into the water and oozed off about its snaky business.

Three streams led out of the pool. The middle one was the widest. I had tried it on my first visit. After many twists and turns I had found myself heading into a black muddy bank with horses neighing in the livery stable nearby. This time I took the right-hand stream, turned left, then right, had to back out, turned right farther on. Here the stream ran under an arch of cedars whose branches brushed against my hair. The green tunnel was dark but at the end of it I saw lily pads. When I came out into this pool it was into the blaze of the unbelievable color — scarlet, crimson, vermilion — no word is quite right — of cardinal flowers.

There were blackbirds in the hay beyond them. They rose, showing their gilt-edged red shoulder flashes, and sailed over the marsh, leaving me alone with the flaming cardinals. Their stalks thrust high above the water and showed again deep down in the watery mirror below. There were hundreds of stalks, thousands of flowers. I edged the canoe up so close to them that I could reach out and touch one of the flowers. It looked like velvet but it felt more like satin.

One blossom had fallen into the water. I picked it up and took it back to my mother to show that I had found the secret pool. She was delighted and she planned to go herself and find it the next day but something happened to prevent her going and she never saw the cardinals in bloom.

☆

The years run together in my mind. I am not sure of the dates, only of the mixture as before: the lake and the hills, driving with my father to see the sunset, dancing and laughter, old friends and new ones.

Oliver's great friend was Gardner Aspinwall, who had his own sailboat. With Oliver as crew, he explored the whole lake. They were in that happy phase, so soon outgrown, where girls are regarded as a nuisance. Many had tried to go for a sail in the *Kittiwake* but in vain. I had been on her but I was not classed as a girl — more as a sort of stewardess. I had helped put on the *Kittiwake*'s latest coat of white paint. Some of that golden spar varnish had been applied by me too. Such handiness made me tolerated.

Not so a girl from Georgia with a voice as thickly sweet as the best maple syrup. She came along, all ruffles, ribbons and lace, to Joe Goodwin's wharf just as Gardner and Oliver were getting into a canoe to paddle out to where the *Kittiwake* lay at her mooring.

"Oh, Mr. Aspinwall," said the girl, "don't you know I told you I'd be here this morning. And that's your lovely '*Kittiwink*' out there! Isn't it the cutest thing? I just never saw anything so cute. Now, you'll take little old me for just the teensie weensie bit of a ride on her, won't you?"

"No," said Gardner.

"Why, Mr. Aspinwall, I just know you don't mean that. He doesn't mean it, does he, Mr. Andrews?"

"Yes," said Oliver.

"Now Mr. Aspinwall, you're just joking. You wouldn't leave me behind, I know. Now you just tell me what you're really going to do this lovely morning with that cute little old '*Kittiwink*.'"

"Going to take the darn boat out and sink her," Gardner said morosely.

Then he and Oliver shoved off, leaving me to listen to some uncomplimentary remarks about darn Yankees. What she said was not, I realize, entirely undeserved.

"They're just stupid little boys," I told her. "Everything will be different next year."

This was true. Everything was different at Hatley every year — yet always the same. Plenty of girls went on the *Kittiwake* the

next summer though not the one Gardner always called little old
Miss Fluffy Ruffles.

Harford Powel was a poet who used to take me to dances, but
not until he had asked Harriet Jaques and Elizabeth Read and they
had said they were going with someone else. I was pleased to be as
high as third on his list. On the night of the Gypsy Dance at the
hotel up the lake, I wore an accordion-pleated skirt that swirled
around my ankles, many strings of beads, ribbons of bright colors
twisted around my waist and into my long black braids. Just before
I left, I met Mrs. Summerfield Bond. I had on my covert cloth coat
over my costume. She was wearing a sort of brigand's cloak she
had bought in Italy. It was long and heavy with an extra cape over
the shoulders.

She said: "That coat spoils the effect. Change with me — the
cloak will be the finishing touch."

I realized she was right and I slung the cloak over my shoulders.
I was delighted with the dashing effect it gave my costume.

"Is it really all right to take it?" I asked.

She said that of course it was. It wasn't as if it were a wet evening. She knew she could trust me to bring it back safely. I promised I would.

Harford Powel and Paul Powell arrived in the Powells' big
white canoe just ahead of the steamer.

They were Gypsies to the extent of charcoal moustaches, red ban-
dannas around their heads and brass curtain rings strung over their
ears. Both seemed depressed by these decorations. Gypsy dancing
made them morose too. Neither had any impulse to snatch a tam-
bourine and salute me by thumping and jingling it. In fact, neither
of them asked me to dance at all. They sat on either side of me and
glowered at their friends who were leaping through waltzes, polkas
and mazurkas.

"This party," Harford stated accurately, "is a gloom. We'll stay for supper and then take you home. I hope it won't be Gypsy stew."

From that danger at least we were safe. We finished our ice cream and chocolate cake, thanked our hosts and got into the canoe. I was careful not to let Mrs. Bond's cloak touch the water. She had said it took two days to dry if it was even out in a heavy mist. It was not misty that night but there were heavy black clouds now over the moon.

The inlet on which the hotel stood was sheltered from the rest of the lake by two long wooded points of land. It was not until we were almost at the tip of the southern point that we realized that a strong wind was blowing down the lake. By the time we knew it, we were among fiercely foaming waves and it was too late to turn back. Both boys were strong paddlers, used to canoes since they could walk.

"We'll just run with the waves," Harford in the stern yelled to Paul, who never turned his head but said, "All right," and kept paddling.

The clouds were so black above us that his white shirt was only a faint patch of light in the darkness. The waves, which boiled by with a sizzling splash, looked whiter.

We were still not far from land. We knew that if we could turn across the waves, we would reach the shore in a few moments. We could not turn; the wind carried us fast, as if we'd had sails set, toward the middle of the lake. We were at least half a mile from shore when the wind shifted, howled suddenly from another direction. When sailing, I had seen these sudden veerings of the wind, but never a change so swiftly fierce as this. Waves broke into the canoe.

I heard Harford say, "Swim for it, Lulie. She's sinking. Grab her when she comes up."

She sank. I was in the water trying to swim but tangled in the black cloak. Its weight increased as I went down. I came up again, still could not move my arms, sank again, struggling to push the cloak aside. It was completely soaked, heavier than ever, as I went down for the third time.

I almost gave up then but I heard my own voice say: "Bring the cape back — you promised."

I made one more try, got an arm out. Behind me I heard the boys calling, "Where's Lulie? I can't find her . . . I can't find her!"

I was being dragged down again but I reached out blindly. By good luck I caught a paddle that was being blown past me. It kept me afloat till the canoe followed it. The sky had lightened a little and I saw its long white shape, upside-down, coming fast just beyond me. I swam three strokes, thrust my left arm over the canoe, drew enough breath to call to the boys, still hunting for me: "Harford. Paul. Here. On the canoe!"

Then they were there, Harford at the stern, Paul at the bow, swimming the canoe along, trying to turn her across the waves and get to shore. It was no use. At last they gave in. We could go only where wind and waves carried us, on a long diagonal down the lake.

We knew the steamer would leave Glen Villa at midnight. We must have been in the water more than an hour when she passed us, with her lights shining, the Gypsy Canadian band playing "Alouette." We called "Help!" twice but no one heard us, so we joined in the singing. It was probably a good thing that no one heard that either; it would be hard to say which of us was the worst singer.

I was more interested anyway in trying to follow the rhythm of the canoe. I had struggled out of the wet cloak and had managed to pile it up just ahead of me. Down the center of the canoe ran a sort of keel, a long narrow strip of wood. I kept my left arm over the canoe, holding on by the far side and swimming with my right hand. This would have been easy in calm water but, at irregular intervals, the waves dashed the canoe against my side. For years a bulge on that side showed where three of my ribs were broken that evening. Fortunately a drunken driver ran into my car recently and the ribs on my right side were broken against the steering wheel so now I am well-balanced.

We were lucky in being able to land at the only place on the west side of the lake where there were lights still burning — Commodore Stebbins's cottage. The family was still up, playing bridge, when we knocked on the door. They gave us dry clothes, fed us soup and sandwiches. The boys walked home with me; it was only a mile. They took turns carrying a tarpaulin containing Mrs. Bond's cloak. I hung it up on a hanger on the porch — where it dripped dry without injury — and went to bed. It was two o'clock.

Katharine woke for a minute, said, "Are you safe home?"

"Yes," I said, "safe home."

I still wear a heavy gold snake ring that Katharine and my father bought me in Montreal to show me they were glad I wasn't drowned. So am I, every time I look at it.

I hated to leave Hatley. As the wheels clicked along, I said over the names of people I liked: Bond, Bergland, Powell, Aspinwall, Thomas, Armstrong, Brown, Cary, Cochrane, Stebbins, Catlin, Daves. They ranged all the way from small babies to the chaperones in their black silk dresses. I liked to think of Commodore Stebbins at the tiller of his sailboat, of Paul Powell in his father's big white canoe, the steadiest on the lake, of Mrs. Catlin in her rowboat.

Mrs. Catlin lived down the river. Every night, before supper, she put on an elegant silk dress that fitted her like the paper on the wall, some said. Others declared that she looked as if she had been melted and poured into it. These admiring clichés of the period were not lightly awarded. Mrs. Catlin was plump but not flabby, far from it. Her black foulard silk with the white dots encompassed her firmly. Her button boots shone like satin. On her head, firmly anchored between her front and her chignon, both of her own hair but detachable, was a bonnet sparkling with jet. She wore white gloves.

This was her rowing costume.

Every evening she rowed up the river along the lake shore for some distance and then back again, about two miles altogether, for the exercise.

I think Mrs. Catlin had no children. She spoke much of her nieces who were charming girls, she said, especially one called Wallis Warfield. She hoped Wallis would come to Hatley someday and that I would meet her. I never did. I heard later that she was married three times, once to a man called Simpson, and that she became one of the world's best-dressed women. I wish Mrs. Catlin could have known this.

I wonder if her niece ever went rowing in white gloves.

8

A Good Name

MY FATHER didn't find a suitable house to buy right away so we spent two winters at the boardinghouse. I think my mother enjoyed not keeping house. As in everything else she did, she kept house with skill and apparently without trouble. Still, as even I knew by that time, it is not by accident that brass and silver glisten, that three-minute eggs are cooked three minutes, that shirtwaists are starched and damask tablecloths shine. She taught these skills — and many others — to a succession of good-natured Irish girls who stayed till they had learned their trade and then moved on to higher wages in more fashionable families.

By that time they could cook and serve company dinners — nothing fancy, just homemade consommé, scalloped oysters, roast grouse with bread sauce and apple fritters, ice cream and macaroons, Camembert cheese and toasted crackers. The ice cream came from Vogel's and so did the macaroons. They were baked several times a day. Any that survived long enough to become at all dry went into their special macaroon ice cream. Our favorite form of ice cream was a big melon mold with macaroon inside and orange sherbet outside.

Oliver and I missed those parties after we left Heath Hill. We always used to inspect the dining room just before the guests came.

The place cards I had painted would be resting on the cloth of silvery damask. Green and ivory Wedgwood plates would have green glasses and lovely crystal-clear glasses beside them. There were white candles in the old branched candlesticks. Each candle had a bobeche of gold-edged glass below it and a shade like an inverted water lily above.

My mother had made the shades and she had embroidered the sideboard cover. William Morris had made the design. That morning she had taught Latin, history and mathematics to pay for Katharine's tuition in the school to which she went. In the afternoon she may have given a lesson in duplicate whist—the latest thing in card playing. She had mended a tear in my new dress so it was almost imperceptible. She had studied what she was going to teach tomorrow. As my father used to say, she could teach anything if she had a book and half an hour's start. She certainly had a love of learning, the ability to find out quickly and kindly what you knew and the force to sweep you on from there. Several of her grandchildren have inherited this gift.

On the nights of dinner parties, we sat at the head of the stairs, following the dinner by our ears and noses. We heard the slide between the kitchen and the dining room open and shut as things were passed through; heard china and silver being stacked in the china closet; breathed in the flavor of roasted meat.

We heard our mother telling a story—not the words, the rhythm—and the laughter, soprano, alto, tenor and bass, that followed it. There would be music after supper, we knew. The ladies would naturally have slipped a sheet or two of music into their muffs—"just in case." And of course, Miss Vane, our English visitor who had dropped in for a weekend, which had already lasted five months, would sing. Some of the men had brought their instruments. Perhaps there would be a quartet or even the Trout quintet—our favorite. We stole farther downstairs so we could catch a ravishing glimpse of the company as they went into the parlor — the men's tailcoats and white shirtfronts, the ladies' bare arms and necks. Oliver and I edged our way into the dining room and looked through the crack between the folding doors. We could see the piano and Miss Vane in her crimson velvet leaning in the curve of it, ready to burst into Schumann or Mendelssohn. Her repertoire, range and volume were such that the other ladies never took those sheets of music out of their muffs.

We were not fond of Miss Vane. She thought — and had said that very morning at breakfast in her clear soprano — that American children were badly brought up. Why did we not have a governess? she asked my mother.

My mother said that, of course, everyone makes mistakes in bringing up children. If you make the mistakes yourself, at least you have some idea what they are. She didn't think it was sensible to pay someone to neglect children; you could neglect them yourself. She was called to the telephone at this point. Oliver and I, left to ourselves, started to show what American children could do.

We both reached for the maple syrup jug — a red and blue Crown Derby jug with a silver lid. Oliver got it and started around the table, whirling it as he went. I followed him, a lap behind. He ran so fast that, though he waved the jug up and around and upside down, no syrup ran out of it.

As we passed the screen with the English hunting scenes for the third time, we heard my mother ring off the telephone. We resumed our seats. When my mother came back, Oliver had annointed his flapjacks liberally with maple syrup and was politely passing the jug to Miss Vane. It was unharmed by its morning exercise. I still use it.

Miss Vane had turned a fine English peony color. She glared at us through her pince-nez and opened her mouth as if to speak. We looked straight at her with eyes of threatening innocence. We were right; she did not dare say anything. After all, where else would she get free board and lodging — such as it was?

☆

There were new people in the boardinghouse that fall. So many came and went that Tyler Safford and I got out a newspaper with a society column to record what went on. The handwritten paper proclaimed on its masthead that it would circulate at "3 cents a read." Inflation got to work as the years went on. A generation later it cost five cents to read the *Kents' Corner Grazette.* However, Tyler and I were well pleased with our earnings. We regularly took in twenty-four cents, sometimes more. Luckily we had a solid backlog of subscribers.

☆

Mr. Hovey once said to me, "You know, you might be a writer someday."

"Did you read my poem?" I asked.

"Well, yes," he said. "But what I had in mind was your column of advice to young girls. Now, as one editor to another, this will go no further — do you write both sides?"

I replied honestly that I did. It was, I said, because no one had asked me anything yet.

"Standard practice," Mr. Hovey said approvingly. "I like the interview with Hidasaburo Yoki too."

Mr. Yoki had come to Boston to study. It was a convention of the day to say that any Japanese who came to this country was "the son of the J. P. Morgan of Japan." Mr. Yoki was no exception. It seems to have been a large family and, if Hidasaburo was typical of it, a pleasant and gentle one. In my interview, I had asked him about his work. He was studying at the Museum of Fine Arts where there were, he said, some of the most beautiful Japanese

"scleens" in the world. The interview went on for some time before I realized he was talking about screens. He spoke lovingly of
every cherry blossom, every deer, hawk, fish, duck or sparrow. He
evidently was a great animal lover.

Gerald was with me. He stood between us, panting — as he
often did — and wagging his silky tail. I believe it should correctly, in an Irish terrier, have been of a bristly texture but I loved
Gerald for his charm and wit, not for his pedigree.

"Do you like dogs?" I asked Mr. Yoki.

He put out his hand timidly, touched Gerald's curly head, smiled
suddenly, turned off the smile and said, weighing each word: "I-
rike–dogs, not–so–much."

In the presence of other people's dogs, I often think of Mr. Yoki.

☆

One of the things my mother found time to do with us, now that
she no longer kept house, was plenty of bicycle riding. We all had
bicycles. On Saturdays and Sundays, sometimes on weekday evenings, our whole family would ride around Jamaica Pond together.
Hundreds of other families did the same thing. I remember one
evening, a warm one for September, almost like summer, when
there was a traffic jam of bicycles at the point where the Fenway
reaches the pond. Machines with glowworm lights on their handlebars zoomed in from three directions. There was a strong smell
of kerosene from the lamps as the cyclists came together in a good-
natured tangle of handlebars and pedals. There were so many that
all the riders had to get off and "push their wheels" (this expression was the slang of the moment — our parents frowned upon it)
along the crowded road.

This was the best chance I ever had to see all kinds of bicycles
and the costumes in which to ride them. There were still a few old-
fashioned ones with wheels higher than my head. Their riders bal-

anced perilously in the smoky, dusty air, looking rather like monkeys. Oliver said that they really were monkeys; that they slept in
trees and dropped down on their wheels early in the morning.
There were dashing riders in the crowd, girls riding men's bicycles.
They dressed in skin-tight suits of corduroy, bright green or scarlet
jackets and knickers. Their hair was as golden as earnest attention
to the peroxide bottle could make it. They would swoop down
small hills with their arms folded, their visored caps on the backs of
their exquisite heads. When they pedaled uphill, muscles bulged
amazingly through their white silk stockings. My own safety bicycle, shining though it was, my neat divided skirt of Oxford gray,
my brown hair in a pigtail, looped and tied with a bow of black
ribbon at the nape of my neck, even my Gibson shirtwaist, seemed
pretty drab by contrast.

Many tandems were without glamour. They were ridden by ancient married couples, thirty years old or more. The man would be
in a tweed suit with baggy knickerbockers and his wife, of course,
would be modest in a divided skirt. However, separate bicycles
were the usual thing for married couples. For many years President
Eliot of Harvard and his wife rode from Cambridge to Brookline
every Sunday to have dinner with some relatives. Such a trip might
be an adventure. Not all horses were accustomed to bicycles.
Sometimes an apparently sedate horse might shy, rear and bolt
with a great whanging of iron wheels on cobblestones. People
might well be killed in great numbers on our highways if this sort
of thing kept up, pessimists said.

Luckily the horses in the Jamaica Pond traffic jam that night
were in a relaxed mood. A victoria with two ladies in it passed us
with a young coachman in bottle green with silver buttons, sitting
high on the box. The carriage lamps shone clear through polished
glass framed in black and silver. The coachman waited while cyclists dismounted and stood aside, then drove gently along,

touching his whip to his hat to greet my mother as he passed.

He was one of her Boys' Club boys, I saw, and he was driving the best carriage from his father's livery stable. Sometimes, on stormy days, he drove us to school in a hack. My mother had started the club because the sons of coachmen and choremen, who lived in a little settlement not far from us, often dropped out of school early. She thought that some of them at least might stay in school if they had a place to go in the evening where they could find books to read and get some help with their studies. One of our neighbors lent an old barn. The boys worked to fix it up. There was a room for reading and study, another for hobbies. Stamp collecting was one of them, I remember.

The boy who was driving the carriage that night told me, many years later, that my mother had encouraged him to stay in school and study and had introduced him to the generous neighbor who helped him through M.I.T. I wish she could have known that he grew up to be one of the town's ablest and most useful citizens.

At last the bicycle traffic jam untangled itself. Jamaica Pond was wreathed by a long stream of moving lights. The tandem girls sailed downhill, arms folded, visored caps rakishly askew on their bright hair. Oliver and I helped push Mr. Robert Minot uphill on his tricycle. He had often taken us to ride on it when we lived on Heath Hill. It was built like a dogcart with a backward-facing seat for passengers — or pushers. We would sit on that while he pedaled on the level or coasted downhill. When the grade was against him, we would leap off into mud or dust and push so he would not have to dismount and wheel the machine.

We went back to our bicycles. My father and Katharine in her new brick-dust-colored suit had gone on ahead. My mother was waiting for us downhill below the big rock.

"I'm glad you helped him," she said. "They were always such kind neighbors."

We joined the river of smoky lights and moving wheels and started around the pond. Music went with us. There was whistling and singing. We passed a group thrumming guitars. A boy rode toward us playing "A Hot Time in the Old Town Tonight" on a concertina. Impossible to do — but he was doing it. We stopped and applauded him. My mother laughed and clapped as loud as we did.

That night stays in my memory as a mist of gaiety and happiness and light and music.

When I said good-night to my mother, I said, "This was my happiest day." She said, "It *was* fun, but you'll have many just as happy, I'm sure. Happier perhaps. Shall I say you something to put you to sleep?"

"*Horatius,* please," I said, for that was the longest.

Usually I was asleep by the time the bridge crashed into the Tiber, but that night I was still awake to hear her say:

> *In the dark nights of winter*
> *When the cold north winds blow*
> *And the loud howling of the wolves* . . .

So I heard it all except the last few lines and — even now — I can still hear them in her voice.

I remember her voice again when the ladies on the porch were talking of their investments. One had thought of telephone stock but her trustee had advised against it. He said the distances in this country were too great for it ever to be profitable so he advised something safe, like the New Haven Railroad. Another lady, one well trimmed with jet, said she was not sure about trustees; they embezzled sometimes. She had not decided whether to leave her property directly to her children or in trust for her grandchildren.

"What do you plan to do, Mary?" she asked my mother who

smiled and said, "Oh, I haven't anything to leave the children. Except, I hope, a good name."

It was only three months later that she left it to us.

☆

My mother had never, so far as I could remember, had a day's illness. She caught something called, that year, the Asian influenza. Staying in bed, as she did for a day or two, was so tiresome that she got up and went out too soon. She died of pneumonia three days later. She was forty years old.

Our family had endless kindness poured out on it. I am still grateful for my share of it but there is no use pretending that it made up for what I had lost. My mother once showed me the motto around a sundial: *non nullas horas nisi serenas* and asked me if I could tell her what they meant.

I had learned this in school and said so: "I count only the sunny hours."

"Yes," she had said. "Try to learn to do it, too. We all ought to carry our own sundials."

This was not an easy lesson for me to learn. Perhaps I have never really learned it but I do know — almost seventy years later — that when you find a friend, you both make an unspoken compact. You say silently to each other, "One will go — the other will grieve, and yet still keep our happiness."

If friendship were a matter of bookkeeping — so much joy in one column, so much sorrow in the other — everything would cancel out and you would, it seems, be left with nothing. Yet there must be another factor in the equation, for somehow the joy outweighs the sorrow.

People are mortal; while memory lasts, relationships are not.

☆

In January of 1900, I went to live with my grandmother and aunt in their house on Irving Street. I had a warm comfortable room for studying on the second floor and an unheated bedroom at the top of the octagonal tower.

On warm spring evenings my tower was a lighthouse. My friends would whistle in the street below and I would hang dangerously out the window talking to them. Bert Windham used to try to get me to come down and meet him but, knowing that he meant me no good, I did not go. I had lost interest in gangs of boys. I had real friends, girls of my own age.

Beth Farley and Leila Tuckerman had decided they liked me. The result was a triple friendship that brought me happiness when I needed it most. Beth was a natural comic. She could always make us laugh. She had bright pink cheeks, even brighter hazel eyes, curly brown hair touched with gold. She was like an affectionate puppy. Leila and I felt she lacked seriousness toward her studies. We worked hard on her education.

Beth and I also tried to reform Leila, that golden-haired creature with a nose and mouth beautiful enough for a Greek statue, who would turn wild-rose pink and laugh till she cried over our witty remarks.

I always thought that she and Beth chose me for a friend because I looked so melancholy. For the first two years of our friendship I was, of course, dressed all in black. Our whole family, according to the custom of the time, wore black for two years. During the last part of the second year Katharine bought me a black shirtwaist with small white dots on it. An older friend, seeing me in it, told me quite seriously that she did not like to see me look as if I were forgetting my mother so I put it aside and went back to wearing plain black.

It was in our senior year that we all became inhabitants of Miss Eaton's laboratory at Miss Haskell's school. With three other girls

we were all being prepared for the Harvard-Radcliffe examinations.
It had long been the custom for girls to take these, not necessarily
because they were going to college. My mother took them so early
that — since Radcliffe did not yet exist — they were called the
Harvard Examinations. She got all A's but, of course, she was not
allowed to enter Harvard. When Miss Eaton was beating physics
into the heads of some extremely unscientific young ladies, it was
still considered peculiar for girls to go to college.

One of our group of six may have had some scientific ability but
the other five certainly did not. Miss Eaton, however, was not one
to be defeated by even the shoddiest human material. She was a
short plump woman who had apparently been designed by a geo-
metrist in a humorous mood. From her round flat feet to the bun of
gray hair on top of her round head, she could be expressed in a
series of circles. Her black skirt was one circle, her black shirtwaist
another. This was accented by three pairs of circular eyeglasses,
hooked onto it here and there. She often had to try all three hooks
before she found the right pair, mounted them on her round nose,
in front of her round eyes, looked us over with good-natured con-
tempt and, through her small round mouth, trumpeted forth her
scorn of our ignorance.

On one occasion, slapping our papers sharply against a homemade device for finding out about specific gravity, she said, "Nevertheless, you are *all* going to have perfect notebooks, you are *all*
going to take the Radcliffe examinations and you are *all* going to
get A's."

Five miracles happened: we all did get A's!

9

Edge Hill Road

IN 1902 my father, at last, found a house big, solidly built, ugly and inconvenient enough for our family. It was at 44 Edge Hill Road within half a mile of the streetcar line, near his partner Charles Storrow's house, not far from my grandmother's. It was built in the American Queen Anne style of deep red brick with dark green trim. Its entrance was a brick arch suitable to a medium-sized jail. Inside everything was of the best materials: oak floors, chestnut banisters and stair rails and doors. The general effect was a dull depressing brown.

Katharine and I, in an attempt to cheer things up, chose a wallpaper for the front hall with crimson poppies the size of footballs surrounded by twisting leaves like giant spinach. Perhaps family pride makes me claim that it was the ugliest wallpaper I ever saw though I must admit that I have since seen some specimens in my house at Kents' Corner that were strong competitors for this distinction. I will say for the poppies that they took your eye off the woodwork.

The pleasantest room in the house was the library with bookcases nine feet high and a big bay window with a cushioned window seat. The photograph of the family Gainsborough hung over the mantelpiece. On cool evenings an open fire always burned in the fireplace and the glow of a German student lamp vied with blue gas flames in glass globes to light the dark room.

Sliding doors opened into the drawing room and displayed a Persian rug, a grand piano and other furniture I had not seen since Heath Hill days. There were two furnaces in the house besides fireplaces but the drawing room preserved its native chill. This did not prevent various young gentlemen from courting Katharine in it. They used to stay while she read favorite passages from the works of George Meredith aloud to them. They were a sturdy breed.

The supply of staunch visitors even increased after the Storrows gave a dance for Katharine. There was dancing all over the big house. Even the billiard room, usually as cold as our drawing room, was heated. Katharine kept me supplied with partners. I waltzed and two-stepped as many miles as anyone with older men, some of them over twenty. Stephen Fitzgerald, tall, a wonderful dancer, handsome as a drawing by Du Maurier, brought me strawberry ice cream and talked to me about Latin. He thought I would enjoy Terence even more than Cicero.

Terence and I never met. My days as a Latin scholar were almost over. In spite of my record on the Radcliffe examinations — I had even, terrified by Miss Eaton, done well in algebra and geometry — I did not go to Radcliffe. Leila was going but I did not mention to anyone that my idea of happiness was to go with her. If I had even murmured my wish, my grandmother and aunt would have sent me, I feel sure, but I knew they had another plan. Since it seemed to make them happy, I followed it — to a certain extent.

Simmons College was about to move into its new building on the Fenway. Fortunately — or so it appeared to my aunt and grandmother — that meant a School of Library Science within walking distance, two miles, from our house. They remembered that my mother, seeing me with my nose in a book as usual, had once remarked, "That child ought to be a librarian!"

This they interpreted as her wish for me. It did not occur to anyone that the last thing a librarian has time for is to sit curled up on a comfortable sofa all day, reading *The Wings of the Dove.* Well, at least they had not thought of sending me to the School of Household Economics so there was no danger of my getting mixed up with a lot of cookbooks, for my view of that science was also unrealistic.

Of course, there was always the hope that Simmons might not accept me. This proved a vain imagining. They snatched me up as uncritically as a kitten will a yellow butterfly. While I was being escorted to the Library School, my aunt stayed in the office. I rather suspect her of having, in an underhanded way, mentioned my marks on the Radcliffe examinations including that A in physics. The secretary told me when I came back that she was sure I would enjoy the course in physics required in the Freshman year.

While I was trying to think of an answer both polite and truthful to such a remark, she handed me a pen and I signed where she told me to. I was caught in the trap — and have never regretted it.

To save carfare I walked back and forth between Simmons and the library and then my two miles home every day. This routine may account for at least part of my distaste for walking. My allowance — two dollars a week — was generous since carfare was only five cents. The rest of the money was supposed to be for my lunch. By going without lunch and by walking through various types of New England weather, I was able to buy books. My whole greenbound set of Kipling was acquired in this way. I patronized the works of Arnold Bennett and H. G. Wells too.

Ann Veronica came out about this time, a daring book, in fact shocking. To show my father how sophisticated I was, I suggested he should read it. He read several chapters and returned it to me.

"Didn't you like it?" I asked, and he replied, "The love affairs of the common housefly have never been of great interest to me."

I have realized since that they are not very interesting to me either. Still, at that earlier time, they did have a little more sparkle than a bibliography of the textile business.

☆

My father rode on weekdays as soon as he came home from town. Either Katharine or I would meet him at the stable where he kept his horses and ride with him for an hour. We had both taken lessons at Classen's Riding School back of the firehouse. There was a ring strewn with tan bark and roofed in, dressing rooms, a bank of seats from which parents could watch their children as they bounced around the ring under the Classens' direction.

They were both Germans. Mr. Classen was a Prussian type, very military, with pointed moustaches thrusting their spikes out of a face of reddish brown leather. I never remember seeing him without a whip. Mrs. Classen was an enormous woman dressed in a habit of bright green velveteen. She had golden hair that often shook itself down over her fat shoulders. She could canter around the ring on her white horse and pin up her tresses — I think that's the correct term — as calmly as the Lorelei combed her hair on that fatal rock.

Looking at Mrs. Classen, whose face was like a pink spongebag, I used to wonder whether the Lorelei, the Valkyrie and Rhine maidens in general were as seductive as reported. She was, I believe, something better — a conscientious, hard-working wife who would give riding lessons all day, be sure that no horse was lame, that all were well groomed and smile as she punched your ticket that showed how many lessons you'd had.

Lessons lasted half an hour, but it took another half to change into my riding habit and back into my ordinary clothes again. The riding habit was of black broadcloth. My hat was a well-stiffened black derby. My father had taught me how to tie the white ascot stock that upholstered my neck. I had — and still have — a riding crop with a head of horn, a silver band with my initials on it and a leather loop at the end of the Malacca cane.

My father did not approve of whips with lashes like Mr. Classen's. Classen needed it in the ring, he said, but what a rider needed was a way of signaling to his horse, not a weapon. Mr. Classen certainly loved to crack his whip. He would stand in the center of the ring with it under his arm, look us over wearily and give his regular speech. I had studied enough German so that I understood most of his English.

The gist of it was that, since no woman could ever ride cross-saddle properly, it had been necessary to invent the sidesaddle. Because the legs of the rider were on the left, she would lose her balance and fall unless she kept her shoulders at right angles to her horse's neck. The left shoulder must be brought forward and around; the right shoulder around and back. Do not hold on by the "hhrreins" (excuse me — reins). Balance, always balance. Rise from the knee, not the stirrup, at the trot. At the canter, throw back the weight. Balance, always balance!

The horses would then be led to the mounting block. When the groom brought mine, I would take the reins in my gloved left hand, put my left foot in the stirrup, swing my right knee over the pommel, tip my hat slightly over my left eye, be sure my hair was tightly nailed in place and ride on.

When I telephoned to say I would come for a lesson and that I would like to ride Joe, Mr. Classen would say: "Sure, Choe, at three o'clock."

Everyone wanted Joe. He was a little dark brown horse, not much bigger than a pony, with an easy gait and a disposition to match. Often something of quite a different size, shape and color would meet me at the block.

I would say: "But Mr. Classen said I could have Joe," and the groom, giving a cross Prussian stare, would assert: "Dis is Choe; it's yust you don'd know him in his vinter coad."

Winter or summer coat, Joe never panted like a freight engine with a heavy load. Still I had to ride whatever they brought me, for Mr. Classen would be cracking his whip and shouting at me to mount and ride.

"Left shoulder hhrround, Miss Andhhrews! Hhhright shoulder back. Hhrise from ze knee, Miss Andhhrews, not from the stihrrup. Left shoulderr vorward and hhround!"

Crack would go the whip; it felt as if it stung me under the right shoulder blade. I can still feel it, especially when the barometer is falling. Probably a touch of arthritis of the spine, a doctor once told me when I mentioned it.

Nonsense! I know Classenitis when I feel it; I still bear its honorable scars.

At last I graduated from Classen's. My father bought a sturdy amiable little black cob called Polly for Katharine and me to ride. Evelyn Heston also had a horse; that is, she said it was hers. She was one of the most beautiful girls I have ever seen, and could always make me almost believe what she said even when I knew better. This one black horse of hers also drew the hearse for Mr. Mooney's livery stable, which was conveniently near the Hestons' house. When Evelyn rode out with the admirer of the moment, she always rode one of the blacks — Duke or Prince — unless there was a funeral. In that case she would tell her escort that she was not feeling well.

On my rides along the Fenway bridle path, I often met Evelyn riding with different men. As autumn came, I noticed, the man was often Ambrose Copley. One October afternoon he asked her to ride with him. As she accepted, she told me, she felt that this was a special occasion. She turned out to be right. Ambrose had said he would come at one. It was Saturday. Days were growing short: they must start early and catch the sunshine, he said. Evelyn said she would be ready.

So she was, in spite of difficulties. When she asked for "her" horse, Black Prince, Mr. Mooney said: "You'll have to take the chestnut, Miss Evvie — Prince has to draw the hearse for old Mrs. Barton. The funeral's at three."

Evelyn said she almost had to cry to get Mr. Mooney to let her take Prince. (The pretence that he was hers was discarded for the moment.) She had to promise she would have him back at ten minutes past two. She borrowed Mr. Mooney's little boy's dollar watch and tucked it into her pocket so she would be sure to be on time.

"It doesn't leave us much margin, Miss Evvie," said Mr. Mooney anxiously, "to unsaddle and groom him, put him in harness, drive to the Bartons', near though it is and — and so forth — be at the church, though it's almost next door, at quarter to three. It's cutting things close, Miss Evvie."

"Don't worry a bit, Mr. Mooney," Evelyn said, "and thank you — this is a special day for me and Prince."

The day was special in various ways. On a quiet road leading off the Fenway and twisting uphill, a road where gold leaves were drifting down that blue and gold October afternoon, Ambrose Copley told Evelyn that he loved her and asked her to be his wife.

She accepted him at once. She would have preferred to be less brisk but she had glanced at her watch. Ambrose was a slow and lengthy speaker. It was almost one-thirty; time to start back. She turned Prince's head toward home. Ambrose protested but Evelyn said she had promised to be home at two. This was especially important now as Ambrose must ask her father's consent.

Ambrose did not take kindly to this schedule. He wanted to linger in the sunshine now that she had made him so happy. He wanted to ride slowly downhill with his arm around Evvie's waist.

"Someone might see us," Evelyn said primly. "I wouldn't like people to think I'm fast."

She did hold Prince back until they reached the Fenway. Prince knew as well as she did that he ought to go home to his next engagement. He tugged hard on the bit. Ambrose did not notice but talked of how they would live in a house west of Boston; he knew just the one, old colonial, fine stables. They would hunt with a famous club. Was Prince a good jumper?

"Only fair," said Evelyn, who had once jumped a beam resting on two bricks in Mr. Mooney's stable yard.

"I'll buy you one that will make you fly in the sky," Ambrose said.

They now crossed the Fenway to the bridle path. Prince started cantering for home and none too soon. The watch said two o'clock.

"I'll race you," she said to Ambrose. "If you win, I'll give you — something."

"Did he know what you meant?" I asked.

"Of course — I kissed my crop to him."

I was amazed at such daring.

They dashed on, treading yellow leaves into the soft black dirt, Prince always a little ahead. When they left the bridle path and were going uphill on the hard road, Prince fell back. Or did Evelyn pull him back? Anyway Ambrose won — by a yard at least.

A groom was at Mr. Mooney's gate. He snatched Prince's bridle and led him away quickly. Prince had foamed during the race. He was, Evelyn said, as much white as black. Ambrose led his horse and they walked on toward the Hestons' arguing about whether he had really won and when he would receive his reward.

"After you have talked with Papa," Evelyn told him.

He was talking to Mr. Heston in the back parlor when, from a front window, she saw the hearse come careening down the street — Prince still white with foam — and go racketing along to Mr. Barton's. Mr. Mooney was using his whip.

They made it to the church — we heard afterwards — by two forty-eight. It seems probable that Mr. Mooney holds the record for this particular racing event.

10

Best Friends

I HAVE SAID so little about our dogs that one might think there had been none in my life. Yet they were an important feature of it. The first of them was John Bull. When my father and mother became engaged, he asked her whether she would like a solitaire diamond in her engagement ring or other stones too. She replied that she didn't want a ring — just a Boston bull terrier. She got John Bull and later a sapphire and diamond ring.

J.B. — as he was sometimes called by people who were on informal terms with him — was about twice as big as any Boston terrier I have seen lately. He was a handsome tortoiseshell brindle with a neat white shirt front, large intelligent eyes, ears which he raised when something interested him. He had natural dignity, poise, authority. When I was less than three years old, in a moment of frivolity and audacity, I kicked J.B., then ran away laughing across a sunny, sandy beach. He followed me, looked me straight in the eye, took the offending foot — the left one — between his jaws and pressed his sharp teeth together. He did it so gently that he could not possibly have broken the skin. Yet he made sure that I felt it.

When he was quite certain that I would never kick a dog again — I never have — he released my foot, licked my hand to show that all was forgiven and lay down again in the sunshine. He was already an old dog when I remember him. He died when I was five. My first knowledge of illness and death came to me then. He was buried in my grandmother's garden, the place marked by a slab of white marble bearing the words "J.B., a faithful friend."

For many years we continued to have Boston terriers. Molly, Boxer and Jasper were well-mannered dogs. Kenty was a terror. He once kept Katharine and me on top of a fence all one Valentine's Day morning. He jumped up and threatened to bite our feet every time we moved. Finally the postman chased him off and we were able to get into the house for lunch.

The Gypsies stole our dogs quite often. Sometimes the police got them back for us. When they stole Kenty, I think no one tried very hard to get him back. The idea seemed to be that it served both the Gypsies and Kenty about right. Mr. Mottram, from whom several of our dogs were bought, gave it as his opinion that another dog might suit us better.

I went with my father to help choose one.

Mr. Mottram looked at me with professional interest. "Ah," he said. "Small ear — like the father. Large eye — like the mother. Color of hair — brown, like the father."

I was much flattered at being considered practically a Boston terrier.

My father bought Victor that day. He was a gentle, charming little dog, the color of a partly ripe horse chestnut. He was with us at Heath Hill and was still living with the family when my mother died.

☆

Before I went to live with my grandmother, my father talked with Katharine, Oliver and me about where we should go to church. Up to this time he had rented a pew in the First Parish Church —

Unitarian — for the family and one in St. Paul's Church — Episcopal — for himself. He used to go to the Unitarian church with
us sometimes. Occasionally one of us, usually Katharine, went to
St. Paul's with him.

He told us now that he thought we all ought to go to church
together. He wanted us to be happy about it so he would leave it to
us to decide which church it should be. We mustn't be in a hurry,
he said, but think it over carefully and then vote on it.

Oliver and I exchanged a glance. It said all we had to say on the
subject without our speaking a word. We knew that for the first
time in our lives we were in a position of power over Katharine;
that she would like to be an Episcopalian and that with our two
votes we could make her a Unitarian. She tried a little propaganda
for the Episcopal church on us separately and got from both the
same answer. We said we would think it over.

While we were considering the matter, the family received calls
of sympathy from the ministers of the two churches. Dr. Lyon was
the Unitarian minister. He represented the New England tradition
that allowed no town to be incorporated without a settled minister.
This insured there being a gentleman and a scholar in every New
England town. By 1900 there were many churches in Brookline,
but Dr. Lyon was respected by the whole town as still typical of the
old relationship between town and church. He was an intellectual
man, an inspiring and eloquent preacher. He had baptized me and
I still remember a feeling of both kindness and spiritual power in
the touch of his hands. I feel sure that he felt genuine sympathy for
our family but it was difficult for him to express it — as indeed it
was for anyone who knew us. The call, I felt sure, was even more
painful for him than it was for us.

Dr. Storrs from St. Paul's came a few days later. He was a big
hearty red-faced man, more than six feet tall. I thought he was like
a sporting parson in some book of Trollope's.

He was as embarrassed by the call as Dr. Lyon had been and he was much more awkward. Oliver and I felt sorry for him as he sat on a chair too small for him, with crossed knees, waggling one of his enormous highly polished boots in the air. We were fascinated by the boots. So was Victor.

He approached quietly and began licking the shining surface of the boot on the floor.

Dr. Storrs looked down and said: "D - - - the little brute — he's lickin' the blackin' off my boot!"

Oliver and I glanced at each other and nodded slightly.

We became Episcopalians.

☆

Victor disappeared not long after this good act. We supposed he was stolen but though it was Gypsy season — they were camping as usual near Hammond's Pond — he was not in the camp nor in any of the pet shops the police checked. He would have been easy to identify because of his chestnut color and his long, slightly kinked tail. Boston terriers were supposed to have short screw tails. It was the custom at that time to cut off long tails, but my father considered it cruel to dock the tails of either dogs or horses. He said they enjoyed their tails and should be allowed to keep them.

After a time Katharine had a new Boston terrier, Baloo —a beautiful tortoiseshell brindle with white markings, gentle, friendly, musical. He would sing with me in happy melancholy while I played the piano.

That summer we met the Melbourne sisters. There were five of them, all athletes, splendid swimmers, dancers, golfers, riders. We heard that in winter the youngest one waltzed on skates better than most girls did in slippers. The oldest sister, Miss Jane, played golf with my father and he often took her driving to see the sunset.

Of course, I did not really want a stepmother; I liked things as they were. However, if I had to have one, I would choose Miss Jane. Katharine, I found, had reached the same conclusion. We decided to behave beautifully. Later in the summer, my father said to Miss

Jane, in our hearing, that he hoped she would come to Boston and stay with us at the time her sister, Rose, came on for the skating competition. We both urged her to come and she accepted.

We knew the visit would be no ordinary one when my father told us he was going to get rid of the old grand piano and get a new upright. It could stand in the library against the sliding doors. The drawing room was too cold and the old grand was no longer tunable, he said. The change took place a week before Miss Jane arrived. We had invited her to stay a week; we were quite sure it would be longer.

We planned delicious menus. The first night we had lobster soup, filet of beef with mushrooms and rice croquettes. Of course the ice cream and the macaroons came from Vogel's. After dinner my father asked Miss Jane to play. Baloo was downstairs in the kitchen having his supper when she sat down at the piano.

"Why, this seems like a perfectly new piano!" she said.

"We haven't had it very long," I said accurately.

She played delightfully — Chopin, Schubert, Brahms. All was calm, all was bright. The fire burned on the hearth. Its light flickered on the backs of books. The double German student lamp glowed softly.

She had stopped playing when Baloo came in. Baloo was so musical that to him each note was an exquisite pain and he could not suffer in silence. My father should have remembered this when he asked Miss Jane to sing.

"Won't you sing 'Greensleeves'?" he asked. "I'll play for you."

Miss Jane stood up. He sat down and began to play. All went well for several bars but when Miss Jane's fine mezzo-soprano proclaimed: "Greensleeves was all our joy," Baloo joined in.

"OO-oo-oo-OO-oo-oo-OO!" he sang with his head on one side.

We were all so used to Baloo's obbligati that we did not notice him much at first, not in fact until Miss Jane stopped in the middle of one of his high notes and asked, "Does he always do that?"

"Do what?" asked my father. "Oh — sing, you mean. Why, I believe he does occasionally. Katharine, keep the dog quiet."

Katharine did her best. She slapped him, she choked him, she held his jaws together but sounds of happy pain still escaped from them. He was evidently exactly attuned to Miss Jane. At last Katharine took him down to the kitchen and left him there. Unfortunately his voice came up through the pipes of the hot air furnace almost as loud as if he had been in the library. After a few more duets with him, Miss Jane announced that she was tired. She went to her room and the Andrewses all took up their reading in pleasant silence.

The next night we went to see the figure skating so there was no home concert. Miss Rose did beautifully but she did not win the prize. Miss Jane was disappointed. She felt that the Boston girl who won was not especially graceful. She said she supposed it was natural for the prize to go to home talent.

We had more music the next night. It was Sunday and we all, including Baloo, joined in the hymns. When Miss Jane started to play one of my father's favorites, one of Mendelssohn's "Songs without Words," Baloo did his best to supply the words. Or did he sound more like an infatuated oboe? It's hard to say, for the piece was never finished.

Halfway through, Miss Jane got up, shut the piano with ladylike quietness — it would have been less frightening if she had banged it — and said: "I shall play no more in this house."

Nor did she.

Monday morning Mr. Mooney's hack transferred her to the hotel where Rose and the other skaters were staying. We read in the paper that Rose had won the waltzing competition and we were glad.

I, for one, could not help being glad too that Baloo had won the singing competition.

One Thing Led to Another

IN MY SECOND YEAR at Miss Haskell's I met one of the best teachers I have ever known. He was a plump ironical young man with thick spectacles. Pierre la Rose was his name. He taught English at Harvard and he also came twice a week to Miss Haskell's to dissect the themes we had written for him. It was from him I learned that criticism is not necessarily a bad word; that it may mean interpretation and illumination; that a writer is fortunate indeed who has an intelligent reader who takes the trouble to listen to what the writer is trying to say — and makes him be sure he has said it.

Every now and then Mr. la Rose would read over a phrase he liked, as if he were tasting something pleasant, and say, "Not bad — not bad at all." This sometimes happened to me. I would feel myself turn pink with happiness. The blood would beat hard in my ears above my stiffly starched collar. Once he laughed out loud over something I had written.

Afterwards he said to me: "Keep working, writers have to work, you know. Digging ditches is much easier."

I nodded solemnly — as if I really knew — and took the paper from his neat plump hand. It was marked A–. He had explained early in the year that he saved A's for Chaucer, Shakespeare, Keats and a few other teacher's pets. Henry James was one of them. Certain stories of Rudyard Kipling's received praise from him too, though he did not have my uncritical reverence for every word Kipling ever wrote.

When school was over that June, Leila, Beth and I went to visit Lucy Holbrook in Brattleboro, Vermont. Kipling, after a quarrel with his brother-in-law Beatty Baleister, had left his house — "Naulakha" — suddenly. Lucy's father had bought it, just as Kipling had left it, furniture and all. I was already excited about the house before I had ever seen it, even more so when I caught my first sight of it.

It was a long, low shingled house, weathered silver-gray by Vermont wind, rain and sun. Though it had been designed like a bungalow in India, it looked as if it had grown out of the green fields and dark trees. It faced June sunsets and waves of blue hills that turned deep purple when the sun had gone. I ate supper that night sitting in a chair Kipling may have used, eating with a fork he may have touched, watching — as he must have done — the sky change from flame and purple and clear turquoise to a faint golden glow with great elms dark against it.

After supper Lucy showed me a small room at the end of the house where Kipling used to work. His writing table, a plain oblong of pine with one drawer, stood where it always had and just as he had left it. The blotter had, in reverse, words his pen had written. In the drawer was paper he would have written on if he had stayed. There were pens, stubs of his pencils, erasers. His ink bottle, still partly full, stood on the blotter.

I doubt if any author now exists who would arouse the blend of reverence and excitement I felt for these relics. Quite literally, I trembled at the sight of the blotter. I was in a sort of trance for the rest of the evening.

Small wonder that I could not sleep that night. I could hear the soft wind ripple the June grass and make the birches whisper. An owl sleepily asked, "Who are *you?* Why are *you?*" I could not answer. A deep-voiced clock thrummed the hours. I heard it strike three. After that I must have slept for a while. It was beginning to be light when I woke with a story clear in my mind. I lay there watching it happen, listening to it happen, feeling the force of gestures, gasping over the danger, the mystery.

Then, before it faded, I stumbled out of bed. I had brought a pad of yellow paper with me.

"Always have plenty of paper," Pierre la Rose had advised me. "You can't tell when you'll need it."

I needed it now — all ten sheets of it.

I took it down to Rudyard Kipling's desk. I sat down in his chair. I looked for a moment, as he must have looked sometimes, at ferns and at cobwebs with dew on them, at the last stars fading and the sky just brightening. Then I picked up one of his pencils. My hand moved over the paper as if I were writing something I knew by heart. This story had everything — love, suspense, dual personality, self-sacrifice, mystery and sudden death.

When I reached the bottom of page ten, it was over. Sun and wind were drying the grass and rustling the silk of June maple leaves. The clock struck six. I put Mr. Kipling's pencil back in the drawer. I went to bed and slept till Leila and Beth dragged me out of it.

"You look as if you'd seen a ghost," Beth said.

I said I'd had a queer dream about writing a story at Mr. Kipling's desk. Then I noticed the pile of yellow paper on my bureau.

"I guess I really did write something," I said.

I folded the papers and stuffed them into my bag, thinking that I must read the story over some day. I never had time that summer. It was fall and I was at Simmons before I read it again.

By great good fortune I was in Helene Buhlert's section in English composition. She was not much older than I. She had only just graduated from Wellesley. Helene was an example of the fact that you can't tell about the contents of a package by the envelope. Who would think that this pretty girl with flaxen gilt hair and brown velvet eyes was a fanatic about the writing of English? Oliver Cromwell was enthusiastic about his day's work. So were Dante Gabriel Rossetti, Thoreau and Robespierre. None brought more zeal to his task than did Helene to hers.

When she demanded a ten-page narrative, I remembered the story I had written at "Naulakha." I copied out the yellow sheets in my best library hand, changing not even a comma, and handed in the narrative upon the appointed day.

When the class met again, Miss Buhlert (of course, I never called her Helene until years later) announced that something strange had happened.

"Someone," she said, "has written a *good* story. I am going to read it to you."

It was certainly a strange story — everyone agreed on that. At the end of the class Miss Buhlert asked me to stay a minute. She handed me back my papers saying with a sort of fierceness: "That story is publishable. Type it, double space. Send it somewhere right away. Enclose return postage."

Naturally I sent it to *The Black Cat* since this was the most daring magazine I knew. In less than a week — mail traveled briskly before automation — I had a letter from the editor, Mr. Umbstaetter, asking me to come in as soon as possible and discuss it with him. I asked permission to be excused from my classes that morning. Miss Wiggin, the librarian, was almost as excited about the letter as I was.

"I don't blame you a bit for wanting to go right away," she said with a kindly twinkle. "Good luck — fame and fortune!"

I caught the next streetcar and was soon walking along High Street in Boston. It was a narrow street of dingy buildings. The *Black Cat* office was in one of the dingiest. I climbed steep stairs, dimly lighted by unshaded gas flames, and came into a small untidy dark room. Black cats from old covers of the magazine leered at me from the walls and looked up at me from the clutter of papers on Mr. Umbstaetter's desk. He was sitting in it, a big man whose white shirt was without a collar. He wore a green eyeshade and he had not shaved recently.

He did not look much like an editor to me — I had supposed they were slender, intense, with wavy hair pushed back from noble brows and with floppy black bow ties — but I handed him his letter anyway. He took off his spectacles, held the letter a long way from him, looked dubiously from it to me.

"You're telling me you wrote that story 'His Alter Ego'?" he asked.

I realized that I might not look like an old experienced writer. I blushed and nodded speechlessly.

"Hm," he said. "Guess it's here on the desk somewhere."

He scrabbled among the papers and came up with it. Then he began to make noises like a possible purchaser. It was not, he said, a good story. It would take a lot of editing. (He licked a large inky thumb as he turned over my immaculate double-spaced pages.) It was a good length, he admitted grudgingly.

"But how did you know how a man moves when someone plunges a dagger into his back? Hm?"

He seemed to think I must have killed someone that way.

I stammered out guiltily that it was just an idea.

He said quickly that of course that's what the whole thing was, just an idea. He'd have to do a lot of work on it. Still he'd consider buying the idea . . .

"Would you take twenty-five dollars for it?" he asked fiercely, like an eagle pouncing on an osprey to make it drop its fish.

Twenty-five dollars! An incredible amount — just for an idea!

The osprey dropped its fish. The eagle caught it deftly.

I left the *Black Cat* with twenty-five dollars in my purse.

The last I saw of Mr. Umbstaetter, he was sitting at his desk reading Rudyard Kipling's latest story. I felt quite sure that Kipling had written it; I just held the pencil.

I never read a copy of *The Black Cat* again so I don't know whether "His Alter Ego" was ever printed. Perhaps the idea was too difficult for Mr. Umbstaetter to edit.

Although I wrote no more stories, people thought of me as a writer. I'd received money for words on paper, hadn't I? The idea still lingered around me when Beth Farley's brother became publisher of the Boston *Herald* and of the *Traveler,* as the evening edition was called. I heard that they wanted a column that would be of interest to women for the *Traveler,* not a society column but something about local affairs. Frank Buxton, editor of the *Traveler,* liked my idea of a group of people sitting around chatting about practically anything. He published the column under the title of "Theresa's Tea Table" and over the signature of "Theresa Tempest."

I am not sure if any women ever read it but I did have several male readers — among them Philip Hale, my favorite dramatic, literary and music critic. Also one of the editors of *The Youth's Companion,* a Mr. Ira Rich Kent, read it faithfully. In fact he encouraged me to strike for more pay. He thought four dollars a week for six columns was not enough. Spurred on by his interest I asked for more and received several advances, finally reaching the dizzy height of ten dollars a week. When, after a year and a half, I asked for twelve, I was fired.

That was in 1911. I was delighted. I still remember how relaxed I felt when I could go out and dig dandelions instead of digging for ideas at my desk. On May 23, 1912, Mr. Buxton called me on the telephone. I was rather busy that afternoon.

"Couldn't you take a message?" I said to the maid who had answered the call.

"He said it was important."

"Oh well, I'll go, but wait and help me with my dress, please."

Mr. Buxton asked me to come back and write the column. It seems unlikely but I think he mentioned fifteen dollars a week, starting the next day.

I said, "Mr. Buxton, do you ever read the society column in the *Herald?*"

"Not if I can help it," he said.

"Well, take a look today," I suggested. "You'll see why I can't accept just now — but thank you. Perhaps later. But aren't you coming this afternoon? Didn't you get the invitation? I addressed it myself."

"Invitation? What to?"

"Why, to my wedding," I said.

The gasp that greeted this information is still a great pleasure to me.

12

Miss Andrews at Home

SOMETIME before I went to college, Katharine became engaged to a fascinating young Englishman with several names, one of them hyphenated. He had real violet eyes and a Cupid's-bow mouth. His forehead could only be called a brow. Golden brown hair swept off and over it. He had a wing collar, an ascot tie and a handkerchief up his sleeve. He proposed to Katharine the second time he met her, thus interesting her to some extent. He continued to ask her to marry him every time they met. After a few months she accepted him. The ring he gave her had a ruby in it about the size of a postage stamp and there was a wide border of diamonds around the ruby. Having presented this, he went back to England. Letters asking her to visit his family arrived by every ship.

At last she went to England and on her return was strangely happy to be back in America, I thought, for one who had always felt so English, whose heart must be there.

It turned out that life in a suburb of London was somehow not just what she had pictured. Women were less free in England than in America, she said. Going to church and keeping house were supposed to be all the interests they needed. They had relatives but no friends. No one dropped in casually as people did in Brookline. Her future mother- and sister-in-law seemed perfectly happy mending holes in men's socks, of which there was an incredible supply. There were six men in the family but too many holes, she considered, even for six.

The men played golf on Sundays while the women went to church. The golf course surrounded the church, a great convenience; the men could clank their bags of clubs down on the church porch, dodge in, receive communion and then go back to the links.

Men went shopping and bought new clothes but women used what they had, chiefly tea gowns. You could also put new ribbons on them or a bit of old family lace. As she reflected on this life Katharine became more and more American. After a while she sent the ruby ring back to England, heaved a sigh of relief and was disengaged.

Aunty felt she ought to meet someone new. She gave several evening bridge parties in Katharine's honor. A Mr. Kent, an editor, was often among the guests. Having met an editor, Mr. Umbstaetter, I felt I knew the type without seeing him.

In the fall of 1905, I did not go back to Simmons. I had to attend to the serious business of being a débutante. Katharine felt it would be foolish to try to study at the same time.

"You would never be able to go to the Sewing Circle luncheons on Wednesdays," she pointed out. "And you'll be up too late dancing to get to those nine o'clock classes."

My grandmother, my aunt and Simmons all saw how difficult it would be for me to combine these disciplines. I was given a year's leave of absence from Simmons and was soon launched into a whirl of parties. Having clothes made to wear to dances and teas was an occupation in itself. My tailored suits — the black velvet, the violet tweed, the black broadcloth — were made by Bergstein, whose shop was near Classen's Riding School. The velvet suit and the violet one were rather daring; the skirts barely covered my ankles. The broadcloth was more conventional. It almost touched the ground in front and had a small train behind just long enough to make boarding a trolley car a minor triumph of manipulation. The whole skirt was edged underneath with S. H. and M. skirt binding, a clever device that kept the broadcloth out of mud and slush. The binding looked like a three-yard velveteen snake. Before you put on the skirt, you had to brush the dried mud from your last excursion off the binding.

Some of my evening and afternoon dresses were made at my grandmother's, where I would stand patiently while Ellen Murphy stuck pins into me and while her assistants stitched the bones of whales into linings to support me during my working hours. Ellen always referred to "my work" which was, of course, "to meet a man."

Ellen would stand a short distance from me and, making sweeping motions with enormous shears, she would cut wildly into satin and tulle and velvet. I felt like a trembling lay figure as I stood there with her fierce little green eyes on me and the shears clicking around me. When the cutting was over, the pinning began. This was even more uncomfortable. Pins pricked the lay figure's skin. It turned out she was human after all. Ellen objected to any wincing.

"Save your dancing for the ballroom floor!" she would say crossly.

At last she would be pleased. The smile of the satisfied creator would run over her freckled face as she stood off and surveyed her handiwork.

"We'll get him with this one, Miss Lula," she would announce confidently.

When she started work on a new dress, she would always begin by asking: "Well, did we get him, Miss Lula? Did we get him with the pink?" Then, as I shook my head in shame, she would add grimly: "Well, we'll knock him over with this one, I can tell you!"

A dressmaker whose shop was on Copley Square in Boston made

me a beautiful ball dress of rose and ivory brocade. Mr. Storrow's daughter had brought the material — the joy of my life — from Paris. It seemed wise to entrust it to someone less impetuous than Ellen. This was peaceful dressmaking, involving merely six trips to town and back. Miss Zinn, the designer, was so gentle that I never felt I was going to be tattooed with pins or wounded with scissors. She took measurements and told them in French to her assistant. The metric system bewildered me but the dress fitted perfectly.

If — as the winter wore on — I said of a dance, "I think I'll wear my brocade," the seal of approval was set on the entertainment.

My friend Margaret Whitney had a different standard.

"Do you think," she would ask, "that so-and-so's party will be worth snarling my hair for?"

She had lovely brown-gold hair with a natural wave, much enhanced if her pompadour was brushed the wrong way inside.

Something special was wanted for my coming-out tea. Aunty had been told by a friend of a real genius among dressmakers, one with the French touch, who lived only two miles away. As Ellen had all she could do at the moment on a violet satin — with which she was bound we would get him this time — it was decided to try Madame Henriette for my white dress. Aunty and I drove over in one of Mr. Mooney's hacks the first time to a small house, very neat that day and smelling of a delicious pot-au-feu. Madame was fiercely fashionable. She had little sketches of dresses straight from Paris to one of which she and Aunty decided to make me conform.

It would evidently be expensive to bring me and the dress together in perfect harmony but there was an economy feature, as Madame pointed out. There would be two blouses, one with a very low neck for evening, the other with a high collar for afternoon affairs. The same skirt would be worn with either. It was practically two dresses for the price of one.

She got the idea from Worth, Madame said modestly.

Considering all she planned to do to change my appearance, the price seemed moderate. There were yards of taffeta for the lining, yards of ivory grosgrain for the dress, yards and yards of creamy lace to drape over it and — literally — hundreds of yards of ribbon to be quilled into flower shapes and sewn all over the lace. There was also a large box of rhinestones, called "diamants" by Madame except when she forgot and said "dimonds." These were going to be the centers of flowers and be scattered everywhere over the lace.

Madame herself would supply "the findings" — whalebone, skirt binding, hooks and eyes, spools of silk.

I thought it was silly to sew rhinestones all over the beautiful lace but naturally no one asked my opinion so it remained unspoken.

My tea was to be on the twenty-third of November. Madame began work early in October so there was plenty of time to make the dress. At first Aunty went with me to the fittings but when she was quite sure that the skirt and both blouses would fit me perfectly, she said I must learn to be responsible for my own clothes, so I went alone.

The house, I noticed, became less neat as the days went on and Madame's accent became less French and more midwestern. She did less and less work between fittings. The house smelled of rancid bacon and of Madame's tonic. She had to take the tonic for her nerves. Quilling up all that ribbon made her nerves tingle something fierce, she stated often. She kept the tonic near her and drank it out of the unlabeled brown bottle from time to time. It had a heavy sweetish smell, strange and unattractive. I was glad to get out in the fresh air and walk the two miles home.

Madame promised the dress would be ready on the sixteenth but I had to report to Aunty that neither of the blouses was ready and that there was still lots of ribbon to be quilled for the skirt.

"But the tea's only a week off!" Aunty exclaimed.

"Madame's nerves are troubling her," I said. "She had to take a lot of tonic while she was hanging my skirt."

"Tonic?"

"For her nerves. They tingle. She drinks it out of a bottle."

"We'll soon see about that!" said Aunty grimly.

We got into one of Mr. Mooney's cabs and drove to Madame's. The light was on in the fitting room. Through the window I could see Madame. She was asleep in her chair with lace and silk heaped around her. "Diamants" flashed. The bottle of tonic was on the table among loops of ribbon.

"I think you'd better stay in the carriage," Aunty said.

I felt sorry for Madame, dragged out of paradise into a world of pins and needles by a jangling bell. In a short time Aunty came out and I helped her carry an enormous box containing all the materials for the dress.

"Don't worry, darling — Miss Bowes and I will finish it," Aunty said kindly, and added, "You know you are almost grown up now, old enough to understand about that unfortunate woman. She drinks. That tonic of hers is rum. Let this be a lesson to you."

As rum has never been a temptation to me, this may have been a fortunate experience. It did not seem so at the time. Aunty, Miss Bowes, my grandmother and even I quilled ribbon and sewed on rhinestones, yet it soon became obvious that if we finished the skirt, neither of the blouses would be ready on time. Aunty decided that I should wear the blouse of a white dress from last year with a few ribbons and rhinestones scattered on it here and there.

Luckily, when the great day came, there were dozens of bouquets of flowers. From them, Katharine chose a haystack of pink carnations, a sheaf of red roses, a bunch of a thousand violets and a spray of lilies of the valley. She pinned the lilies on my shoulder, the violets at my seventeen-inch waist (into which dimension she herself had laced me) and gave me the other flowers to hold. When I looped my arms around them, they covered most of my blouse. I was just able, at suitable intervals, to disengage my right hand for precarious handshakes.

Katharine and I received our guests in front of the drawing room fireplace. It was a beautiful day. Hundreds of people came: old friends of the family, Katharine's young married friends, our neighbors on High Street Hill, débutantes in their best dresses with trains that swept the floor and hats like cartwheels, Harvard freshmen in their neat dark blue suits. There were admirers of Katharine's, so sophisticated that they seemed to be wearing two waistcoats — dark ones that matched their coats and white linen demivests under them that cut across their splendid neckties.

I recognized almost everyone and beamed upon them across the room while they were still in the line. Late in the afternoon someone I did not know came through the door. He was a tall distinguished-looking man in a cutaway coat, a well-tied ascot and one of those double waistcoats. Pince-nez edged with tortoiseshell rested on his fine aquiline nose.

Katharine nodded to him and he bowed politely.

"Who's that?" I asked.

"Why, it's that Mr. Kent, that editor who comes to Aunty's bridge parties."

Ah! How pinkly fat-faced and stupid those freshmen looked in their double-breasted blue suits! Here was a man of the world, a writer, an editor. How different from Mr. Umbstaetter he appeared as he worked his way along the line! How lucky Katharine was that Aunty had found him for her!

A number of years later my friend Carol Holcombe's husband consulted me about coming-out parties. Carol planned to give one for one of their daughters. Arthur, head of the Department of Government at Harvard, a statistically minded man, thought such occasions foolish. He was asking everyone for figures bearing on this matter.

"As I understand it," he said, "such parties are given with the idea of a girl's meeting her future husband. Now, Lulie, can you possibly believe that girls meet their husbands that way? Think carefully, be honest, please. This is important. Do you really think so?"

"Yes," I said.

"Why?"

"Because I did," I said.

"An isolated instance, statistically unimportant," he said.

It wasn't to me. I never thought of statistics as Mr. Ira Rich Kent looked down kindly at me. For the first time that afternoon I forgot that my blouse did not match my skirt. I even laid down my burden of roses and carnations. He stayed beside me while several people came past. He asked me if I played bridge. For the first time in my life I was sorry I did not.

After a while, he asked where my aunt was. I said she was in the dining room, seeing that different débutantes took their turns at pouring tea and chocolate or serving ice cream.

I wished I were in the dining room. It sounded like fun from across the hall.

Mr. Kent came back before long. He asked if I were going to the Harvard-Yale game the next day. I had to confess my shame.

"No," I said honestly, "no one's asked me."

"Would you like to go with me? I asked your aunt if I might take you and she said yes — unless you were going with someone else."

(Loyal Aunty would not, of course, admit the blot on my scutcheon.)

I said it would be wonderful, that I'd love it more than anything. He said that he'd go along and see about tickets; that he'd call me in the morning.

It was not until years later that I heard how he got the tickets. He went to all the speculators. There were no tickets left — none, not even on the Yale side.

"Not at any price?" he asked and was told, "All gone, mister. Money's no help."

Full of gloom he went to have dinner at the St. Botolph Club. There he met a friend who looked downcast too.

"Are you all right, Alfred?" Rich asked.

"Oh, I'm all right but Rhoda was going to the game with me and her aunt was going to chaperone us but they're both down with the flu — and here I am with three tickets — had to get them from a speculator — and I'm broke."

"How would you like me to take two of them off your hands? At whatever you paid, of course," Rich asked generously.

"They're on the Yale side," Alfred said.

"Since I am a Tufts man that will not embarrass me," Rich told him.

"How did that happen?" asked Alfred, startled by such unconventionality.

"My family are Universalists and they did not want me to get mixed up with a lot of pagans — Unitarians, Episcopalians even. So they sent me to Tufts. This afternoon I've almost wished I were a Harvard man."

"Perhaps they'll get licked," Alfred, an M.I.T. graduate said, brightening up, slightly.

In spite of this Tufts affiliation, Rich brought me a corsage of crimson chrysanthemums. I wore it with my black velvet suit and a crimson hat. I was rather surprised to find myself with people yelling "Boola! Boola!" around me. By an odd coincidence Rich knew the man sitting next to him — a rather depressed-looking character — and introduced him to me. He seemed neutral about the game, shouting for both sides drearily. Rich was for Harvard in a restrained way. I shrieked in their favor until I realized that perhaps

I was being impolite to beautiful girls wearing bunches of violets. I am not sure who won the game. I remember only a pleasant feeling that I had.

We walked back all the way from the stadium to Brookline in the soft November sunshine. Rich told me years afterwards that he decided that afternoon that he would like to marry me — because I laughed at his jokes. He had a Vermont deadpan way of delivering them that concealed from most people the fact that they actually were jokes. I found out that afternoon that his conversation was on more than one level; that I liked to listen for the sound of the quiet stream of humor and irony running underneath it.

The following Tuesday he began his courtship with a nourishing attention, five pounds of marrons glacés. He also made his party call. The parlor maid — we had one that year to cope with just such emergencies — carried in two calling cards on a small silver tray to Katharine and me in the library. We received him there in front of the fire. Katharine, who took housekeeping seriously, had given the following instructions to the cook: "Be sure to have something delicious for tea every afternoon." Her commands had been obeyed and pretty soon it was brought in.

This kind of thing went on for almost seven years. Rich always left two cards. They would be dumped into the big card tray, a convenient sized charger about right for carrying a boar's head, and would be gradually covered by others. After a few years Katharine and I went over the big tray and threw most of the cards away. Those engraved Mr. Ira Rich Kent, however, we put in a clean envelope. We returned them to him the next time he called. Perhaps this sign of thrift should have been attractive to a Vermonter yet, in this representative of the state, extravagance seemed more typical than economy.

When he sent violets, the bunches were the size of wheels — for a rather small bicycle, it's true — but wheels anyway. He often just

happened to have tickets for the latest plays, just about as coinci-
dentally as he happened to have those Yale game tickets. I was so
busy that year that it was often Katharine who went with him.
Aunty, of course, regarded him as Katharine's property. She let me
understand that anything he did for me was simply kindness to
Katharine. I was sorry because I liked him better than anyone I had
ever met. Still it was only natural. After all, Katharine was something special.

One day he showed enough interest in practical affairs to ask me
if girls' clothes were very expensive.

"I don't know what you mean by expensive," I said. "My best
hat cost forty-five dollars and I've worn it twice."

"Is that the big black one with the two white flowers?" he asked
without great enthusiasm.

"Yes — gardenias," I said and the conversation lapsed.

Later he told me that this accurate report put off his proposal for
two years.

The fact that my aunt put clothes on me as if she were playing
with a doll and that I was no more interested in them than a doll
would be did not occur to him.

By this time it was almost May and I was getting ready to pack
the more summery part of my wardrobe for a visit to Baltimore. I
did not see Mr. Kent — as, of course, I called him for the first seven
years of our acquaintance — until the next fall.

It was in Baltimore that I first learned to know and like beaten
biscuit, hominy grits, kippered herrings, soft shell crabs and Kossuth cakes. Kossuth was a Hungarian patriot in the Revolution of
1848. Later he was an exile and visited this country. The enthusiasm for his career could not have been expressed more agreeably
than it was when Baltimore named those cakes for him. They were
domes three inches across, rising with airy lightness from circular
cases of crinkled paper. They were filled with whipped cream and

frosted with chocolate. These were the original models, I was told, but there was a more recent type, filled with strawberry ice cream, covered with strawberry frosting or with pistachio ice cream and frosting to match.

When you went to a little afternoon card party in Baltimore, you would be refreshed, after your labors, with crab salad, exquisite sandwiches, some of them rolled up and tied with ribbon, Kossuth cakes and iced tea. With these rewards in mind, even I joined in the new game of auction bridge.

I had a letter about this time from Mr. Ira Rich Kent, written from Kents' Corner in Calais, Vermont. It was, he said, only a crossroads hamlet. One of the houses was solid planks under the clapboards. His great-grandfather Remember Kent came there in an oxteam over a blazed trail in 1797 and built the house. About a mile away lived descendants of his great-great-grandfather Abdiel Bliss. In their stable lived a direct descendant of the horse Major Bliss had ridden in the Revolution.

I had known residents of ancestral houses but never a horse who lived in an ancestral stable. I was much impressed.

13

"It'll Be the Last"

BY DECEMBER OF 1910 Ellen Murphy had grown pessimistic about my chances of getting my man. In fact, she had ceased to say "your man" — as if she were sure there was one with my initials tattooed on him — and had substituted the indefinite "a man." I understood: she decided I could not be particular. However, when I said I was going to Baltimore again for a visit, she cheered up. She felt I might have a chance in fresh fields and she began work on a creation of pink satin and tulle diamanté.

She said, when she showed me the picture, in which sparkling tulle billowed over satin and where wings of tulle sprouted from the model's shoulders, "In this, Miss Lula, you'll be the angel of victory. You'll get a man yet."

I was not wearing my pink dress, though, when it occurred to me that she might be right. I had on a shirtwaist with the sleeves rolled up, the skirt of my old gray suit and a checked apron of blue and white. I was busy trimming the front hall for a New Year's dance in honor of Elizabeth Read and Lydia Bond. Lydia was a débutante in Baltimore that year. She and Elizabeth had come up to Boston to go to some parties and were staying with me. My dance would take place next evening; the night after that we were all taking the Federal Express to Baltimore.

At the moment the girls were upstairs snarling their hair. I had sent them away so that when they came down to tea, my decorations would burst on them in their full magnificence.

I had almost finished. I had looped long ropes of laurel around the drawing room doors and windows, over the seven doors of the front hall and I had twisted laurel around the banisters. After it was in place, I had fastened fruit—real oranges, apples, lemons and bunches of grapes, red, deep blue or pale green, to the laurel. I felt that if Della Robbia lived in Brookline, this was the way he would trim his front hall.

I perched on a stepladder just wiring the last orange into place when the doorbell rang. The maid opened the door. I turned to see who it was. The stepladder skidded. I fell off it, rolled down six steps and landed at the feet of Mr. Ira Rich Kent.

As he helped me up, he said: "How is it possible to fall so gracefully?"

I looked at him through my hair, which had come down in several directions, and thought: "Why I believe he's in love with me!"

It seemed the most reasonable explanation.

Ellen did not get the pink dress finished in time for the dance so I wore my yellow dress, one that used to have quilled ribbon around the bottom of the skirt and the train. Most of the ribbon had disappeared suddenly at a dance. A short man, a wonderful dancer, was swinging a tall blond girl around doing the Boston. Mr. Kent, six or seven inches taller than I, was piloting me. A loop of quilled ribbon detached itself from my dress. The tall girl caught her foot in it. Another loop twined around her partner's foot.

The "Blue Danube" played on. We danced on, all four tied together. More and more ribbon entangled us. Someone noticed our situation and began to laugh. Pretty soon all the other dancers were standing in a ring, watching our maneuvers. After a while the blonde could move no longer. She and her partner sat down on the floor. Mine and I kept our feet. Victory! Someone brought a pair of scissors. We were cut apart; my dress was unquilled. Well, I never like quilled ribbon anyway.

At my dance the decorations were much admired. There was a five-piece orchestra and a beautiful supper, planned by Katharine. The "Blue Danube" was played for the last dance. I danced it with Mr. Kent. He said he always thought of me when he heard it. I felt that if I had only had my new pink dress on — oh, well! Ellen finished it the next morning in time for me to pack it into the trunk I took to Baltimore.

I wore it to the first ball we went to. Early in the evening someone stepped on the sparkling tulle billows of my train. Diamonds crunched under his patent leathers and the tulle came off in waves. Enough of it was left so that others trod upon it. Soon it was so ragged that I tore most of it off, leaving a short ruffle around my waist. My angel sleeves still streamed down over the pink satin but no man was conquered by this costume. Obviously Ellen would have to think of something else.

Her next creation was American beauty satin with gold lace and black chiffon veiling its surface here and there. When Ellen stood off from it at the last fitting she looked from it to me in a threatening way and uttered her ultimatum.

"And if you don't get him this time, Miss Lula, it'll be the last I'll make for you — it'll be the last, I say."

Before many months were over I might have reported success but I did not tell anyone, not even Ellen. I had a beautifully written letter, signed Ira Rich Kent, asking me to marry him. I was much pleased and I wrote to tell him so. I said I would never marry anyone else but that I did not think I would make a good wife. Somehow — yes, that is what I said — marriage did not appeal to me.

My opinion of marriage had been formed by listening to my young married friends. They spoke much of the sanitation and nutrition of their infants, all said to be miracles of wit and beauty. Having looked over a number of them, I had decided that the miracle was that their mothers were obviously sincere in this opinion. To me, babies seemed as unattractive as half-fledged robins. No wonder, I thought, that their mothers turned them over to nursemaids and spent as much time as possible on the golf course or around the bridge table. If I married, would I be driven to playing golf and to telling about that grand slam in hearts? A grim prospect.

Inconsistently I was puzzled that Mr. Kent — as I still called him — did not mention marriage again. He seemed to have forgotten the whole thing. He left two calling cards as usual. He still sent candy and flowers to both Katharine and me. Still it was to me that he sent the *Encyclopaedia Britannica,* Eleventh Edition, twenty-six volumes and the Index.

Katharine was shocked when it arrived and said, "You can't possibly accept it."

I replied that she had always said that it was proper to accept candy, flowers and books. These were certainly books, weren't they?

"I shall consult Papa," she said.

I had to tell Mr. Kent that I could not accept such a valuable present. He took this statement calmly. He said he would write my father a letter. When it came, my father read it to me.

It said that "in the devious courses of an editorial life" he had acquired the Encyclopaedia. (I wondered if a non-editor might acquire one in a similar way — by purchase, for instance.)

He went on to say that, since his bookshelves were crowded, he would be glad to have permission to store it temporarily in our basement. My father gave permission.

As I packed up my American beauty dress and started to Baltimore again to be maid of honor at Elizabeth Read's wedding to Francis Cadwalader, I felt pleasantly secure in knowing that I had the Encyclopaedia on hand.

On the day of the wedding a letter came from Mr. Kent saying he would be thinking of me walking up the aisle. He said he missed me. I telegraphed Katharine saying I would go straight home.

It was a little after seven in the morning as I turned into Edge Hill Road and passed the William Sedgwicks' house. Mrs. Sedgwick, stately in her dressing gown of purple brocade, had her head out her bedroom window. She was taking long breaths of the crisp golden morning air.

"Why, what are you doing here?" she called down. "Katharine said you were going to stop in New York."

"Oh, I decided to come home," I said.

"There's a man in it!" she said and slammed down the window.

"There is — there is," I thought, "and he's going to ask me again."

Perhaps at Thanksgiving, I thought, but it was soon December and he had not said anything. I vowed that something would happen before Christmas. It did — on Christmas Eve.

The sun was just setting as Mr. Kent and I started for a walk around Jamaica Pond. I wore what I regarded as my most seductive costume — a black velvet hat with a bush of ostrich plumes trailing over the high brim, my amethyst suit with a blouse of linen and lace, heavy black silk stockings clocked with white and black leather pumps. My gold lorgnette dangled from a wide black ribbon. I glanced through it occasionally at swans, at elms against the pink sunset, at small boys — nature lovers presumably — throwing pebbles at the swans. They raised their wings from the pink water, thrust out their long necks and hissed at the boys.

Mr. Kent wore a suit of gray tweed and a derby hat. His gold watch chain and his Phi Beta Kappa key gleamed against his waistcoat. He carried a Malacca cane, topped with gold and ivory.

When the boys grew tired of annoying the swans, they turned their attention to us. One of them picked up a small stick and swaggered along with it. The other raised an imaginary lorgnette to his eyes.

"I say, Algernon," he asked his friend, "do you really think it's cold enough to carry a cane?"

Then they rolled over on a grassy bank, laughing at their wit. We laughed too. The sunset was fading as they finally ran off. Lights began to show along the road and in houses and in the still water of the pond. We walked along in a silence that would have been happy for me except for a nagging voice in my brain.

It said: "You swore you'd say something before Christmas . . . before Christmas . . . only — suppose he's changed his mind . . . changed his mind . . ."

It was almost dark when we reached the bench, the one across from the entrance to the Sargent Place.

I said, "I've got pebbles in my shoes. I'll sit down a minute, if you don't mind, and get them out."

When I had dumped them out, I said, "I'm wondering if you'd still like to marry me."

I was lucky — he hadn't changed his mind after all.

Of course we were not engaged yet. Rich, I told him, would have to ask my father's consent. He turned pale at the thought.

"All I have in the bank is an overdraft," he said.

I told him that I was not marrying him for his money. He gave up trying to escape that way and went into the library where my father was. Dinner was announced as he came out into the hall from the interview. He nodded speechlessly. I was engaged.

I liked what my father said when he and I were alone after dinner for a few minutes. I know that he had tried several times to make up his mind to become an American citizen. He loved this country; his work and his life were here. Yet every time some basic loyalty held him back and he remained a citizen of Great Britain.

When I asked, "Is it really all right — about Rich and me?" He said, "Of course, darling. He's a good American and I can't say more — for anyone."

I think that when Winston Churchill died, I heard people say at least fifty times on radio, TV and to me, face to face, "Of course, his mother was an American."

About the fiftieth time I heard this cliché, I said, "So was mine — and wasn't yours too?"

The speaker said disapprovingly — she seemed to think I was frivolous — "But his father was English."

"And so was mine," I said.

I was not being frivolous. I was expressing my belief that you can make many things by computer — but not people; not yet anyway, thank goodness.

Nothing I ever heard was less mechanical, more American, more British too, than the moment in the funeral service for Churchill when the choir burst into "The Battle Hymn of the Republic." As I heard "Mine eyes have seen the glory," I thought not only of Julia Ward Howe, still beautiful at ninety years old, but of Churchill as American as he was English. Across the voices of the choir, I heard his voice saying, "We will fight them on the beaches . . ." and felt again his contagious courage.

On Christmas Eve of 1911, wars were far behind us; peace was normal. It never occurred to me, as we went to Beacon Hill to hear the carol singing, that we were living in a vanishing world. The Hill was an island of candlelight and music. No one was allowed there except on foot. Groups of singers — Dr. Richard Cabot was leading one of them — moved against a background of illuminated windows and shining Christmas trees. One was all white stars and white lights and icicles.

While I was looking at it, Rich asked, "Would you like to live on the Hill?"

"Yes, oh yes!" I said.

"Of course it isn't always just like this," he said, honestly.

Yet after all these years that is how I think of it.

We went home, as we came, by trolley.

Katharine and the suitor of the moment — I can't remember which one — were at the back of the car. Rich and I were at the front. When we got home and she and I were alone, she rebuked me.

"You ought not to look at Mr. Kent the way you do — unless you intend to marry him, of course."

"But I do," I said. "Sometime in May, we thought."

She was delighted and began to make plans for the wedding. I did not tell her that I had proposed to him; in fact, I did not tell anyone.

☆

Years later Rich brought to Houghton Mifflin one of their most successful authors, Lloyd Douglas, who wrote *Magnificent Obsession* and *The Robe*. He always said Rich was the best editor in the world. I was inclined to agree with him and Lloyd became a great friend of our family. He always gave me copies of his books before publication. I was reading *Disputed Passage* when I came upon an oddly familiar episode. A young couple had been kept apart for years, but the book ended happily. They walked around a pond. She got gravel in her shoes and made it an excuse to sit down on a bench. After she fixed the shoes, she proposed. She was accepted.

I went running up two flights of stairs to the study where my — at the moment — unfavorite editor was at work.

"Rich Kent," I said, "did you tell Lloyd Douglas about my proposing to you on that park bench?"

"No," said Rich.

"Well, will you please tell me how he happened to write about it — even the pebbles in my shoes?"

"He didn't write it," said Rich. "I did. He agreed with me that it was just what the book needed."

I said: "I always heard an author would get blood out of his mother's arm and use it if he ran short of ink. But really! I believe editors are worse." Then I added, "I say, Algernon, do you think it's cold enough to carry a cane? Come on — let's leave this den of iniquity and walk over and sit on our bench for a while."

14

Wedding Day

I CANNOT SAY that I spent much time reading my encyclopaedia. Between December and May I worked conscientiously at buying my trousseau. My father had recently repaid me with compound interest the money he had borrowed from me in the panic of 1893. Now he doubled it so that I was able to indulge in enticing extravagances — petticoats with layers of embroidered ruffles from Switzerland, damask tablecloths and linen sheets from Ireland, napkins of Italian cutwork, an English suitcase, porcelain from China.

Mr. Storrow took me to Shreve's to choose my silver. He was pleased when I rejected what the salesman said was the latest thing. I chose the same heavy plain pattern that my mother and grandmother had used. Another person who took a great interest in this wedding project was my Aunt Eleanor Clarke from Philadelphia. She was not really our aunt but Katharine and I had always called her so. She and our mother had been girls at school together. After our mother's death, Aunt Eleanor was endlessly kind to us. A wedding gave her a special chance to express her generosity.

A whole dinner service of blue and white Minton china arrived suddenly. Silk slips and nightgowns, silver dishes, a pin of diamonds and pearls appeared. She wrote that Rich and I must visit her at her country place outside Philadelphia on our honeymoon. There was a tennis court, she said, and a golf course nearby. She had heard that Rich was always winning golf and tennis trophies.

This was true but I was trying not to brood on it. A little tennis I could stand. I had a good system for mixed doubles. I simply kept out of my partner's way and let him do all the work. When it was my turn to serve, I did so with a gentle accuracy that often proved trying to our opponents. Many of my serves were returned with too much force and the ball went outside. This evened up the score for the serves I returned into the net. I thought we might have a happy marriage in spite of tennis — but golf! Would I find myself on a golf course?

After a while I nerved myself to speak about it.

"What," I asked Rich, "is your opinion of women on golf courses?"

"That woman's place is in the home," he replied.

"Oh Rich!" I said. "You are the most wonderful man in the world!" — an understatement if I ever made one.

Naturally Aunty and Ellen Murphy were not idle during this period. Ellen worked mostly on underclothes, threading blue ribbons into slips and petticoats and pink ones into nightgowns. It was shocking to her that most of my dresses were ready made. She felt so badly that she was allowed to make me a dress to wear to receptions. It was the color of a flamingo flying by fast. It had a train and a sort of waistcoat of gold lace. I cannot say that I ever wore it to a reception nor did I, as Ellen said I would, find it handy to slip into for dinner at home. However I cherished it as a souvenir of Ellen's interest and a sort of triumphant announcement that at last, with her help, I had got him.

Aunty had decided that the wedding dress must be made by someone terribly fashionable "in town" so Mrs. McDiamond was decorating heavy white satin with lace from my mother's and grandmother's wedding dresses.

These were happy days. Rich came to tea or dinner or both almost every day. Henry Edgeworth Frick, an expert in shipbuilding, was often there too. He owned an automobile — a Maxwell. It was a new model, so new that a horn had come with it at no extra charge. It also had a device for keeping the headlights going a good deal of the time. When it came snorting up Edge Hill Road, it was no secret that its owner was calling at our house. Before long he and Katharine were engaged; secretly, because with typical generosity, Katharine did not wish to take any of the shine off my wedding so she would not announce her engagement till June.

I chose May 23 as my wedding day. I told Rich that if he came home and found me sobbing because he had forgotten our wedding anniversary, at least he would remember my birthday on May 25. This precaution proved unnecessary. He remembered both dates rather better than I did.

Perhaps the matchbox helped him. It was my wedding present to him. I had it made for him. It was of gold and just right to hold the wax vestas he liked, also just right to go in one of his waistcoat pockets and balance his watch in the other one. His initials and the date — May 23, 1912 — were engraved on it. McAuliffe and Hadley made it. I ordered from them also for my father a gold snake ring, like the one he gave me to show he was glad I was not drowned in Lake Massawippi.

When I went to get the box and the ring, Mr. McAuliffe showed Katharine and me a new brooch that had just been made with a blue moonstone, as blue as a star sapphire, surrounded by small diamonds and pearls. We both thought it was the most beautiful thing we had ever seen. It did not occur to me that I was any more likely to wear it than I was the Kohinoor. Rich had an excellent jeweler of his own. A few days after we were engaged, a box had

arrived for me by special messenger with a note from Rich, saying
he hoped I might like one of the rings in the box. If I did not, the
maker would design whatever I liked. In the box were a solitaire, a
ring with five diamonds, a sapphire surrounded by diamonds, a
larger sapphire with two diamonds — and an emerald, bordered
first with small diamonds, then with a border of small square cut
emeralds.

I did not even try on the others. This was my ring; we
recognized each other at once. I have always worn it except when it
was being repaired. If you garden, cook, clean ovens, make miniature furniture, paint ceilings white and paint pump houses red and
make plaster ornaments by the lost wax process, a ring gets a good
deal of wear. In fact mine needs to be rebuilt again only I don't feel
I can spare it just now.

Presents began to come every day. Tired horses dragged away
trash carts to which I contributed tissue paper, chewed up paper,
excelsior and boxes of wood and cardboard, but more boxes kept
coming. The present I liked best was not wrapped at all. It filled
the back of a small delivery wagon.

Every now and then my father had said of our drawing room, "I
wish we had a convex mirror over the chimney piece. A room
needs an eye of light, you know. I saw a girandole once but I
couldn't afford it . . ."

The horse dragging the delivery wagon walked so slowly that I
realized, as I passed the cart, that my father had found his eye of
light. There it was with the gilt balls around it, its shining eagle
and laurel leaves and branching candlesticks. It would hang in
rooms I had never seen and gather up pictures of them just as it was
now reflecting lilacs and apple blossoms and blue sky on Edge Hill
Road. I wondered if I could take proper care of it. It occurred to
me for the first time that I would have to learn to be a housekeeper.

It did not, of course, enter my mind that, in 1959, the mirror would be moved to Kents' Corner in a case specially made for it; that the movers would drop the case and feel so guilty that they would take it and the resulting hash of gilded plaster back to Boston. It would have been easier to repair the girandole if I had had the pieces. I took only about a week to make them out of plaster of Paris and Elmer's Glue-All and put them in place and gild them. Marriage is certainly a very remarkable institution.

The same day the girandole arrived at Edge Hill Road, I had to sign for a small box from McAuliffe and Hadley's. I couldn't understand when I opened it, how Rich could possibly have read my mind. The explanation was simple. I had told Rich about having McAuliffe's make the gold snake ring for my father. Rich had gone into the shop and asked Mr. McAuliffe if he thought there was anything I would especially like.

"Well," said Mr. McAuliffe. "She did seem to appreciate my blue moonstone."

So there it was shining up at me.

Elizabeth Cadwalader was with me when I opened it.

I said, "Oh no!"

"Don't you like it?" she asked.

"Better than anything — but so does Katharine. I hate to show it to her."

"I'll break the news to her," Elizabeth said.

She went into the next room as soon as she heard Katharine go into it.

"Rich sent Lulie something so pretty," I heard Elizabeth announce.

"Some sort of little pin, I suppose."

"Not very small. Perhaps you can guess what it's like."

"Oh," Katharine said. "I suppose it has a few small diamonds and pearls and perhaps a sapphire or an emerald."

"Diamonds and pearls, but not a sapphire or an emerald, rather an unusual stone."

There was a pause and then Katharine said: "Not — not a blue moonstone? Well!" and then, after another pause, "Well, if he'd asked me, that's just what I'd have told him."

She would have too.

Aunt Eleanor gave a luncheon on my wedding day for all the girls I would have liked to have for bridesmaids. There were about a dozen of us altogether at the Hotel Touraine. Since a good many of the guests were from out of town, I took them on an excursion that ought to be — but isn't, I'm afraid — traditional for brides of greater Boston. Dressed in our best spring silks and our biggest hats, we went to the Public Garden and rode on the swan boats.

I heartily endorse this preliminary to a happy marriage.

After we had been paddled around the pond among shining willows and beds of hideous Victorian plants shading enormous pansies, it was time to walk across to the Touraine. We must have looked like a swarm of butterflies. Luncheon was early so I could have plenty of time to dress for the wedding. I would have if it had not been for Mr. Buxton's call, inviting me to a career as a newspaper woman. It took a few minutes to make him understand that I would not change my cocoon of satin and lace and orange blossoms for all the ink of India.

I was just in time to get into Mr. Mooney's brougham with my father and drive at a brisk trot to St. Paul's Church in Brookline. Bells were ringing as we drove up to the door. Outside it was standing Mrs. McDiamond, the maker of my dress. She had come for an important part of the ceremony — to turn the train of my dress when I changed from the side aisle to the middle aisle. The ushers were already lined up and Leila was there looking lovely in pale green with a hat the size of a haystack.

I thought of Beth who had died some years before and of how I wished she were there too. She would have been delighted that Leila was on time. For a moment I felt that she was standing beside Leila and that we were all laughing together. Then Oliver, who was one of the ushers, came to help me out of the brougham. He was wearing his new cutaway coat and gray striped trousers. The moonstone pin Rich had given him shone among the folds of his silver-gray ascot. I straightened his white carnation for him and he carried my train until he could put it down on the red carpet.

While Mrs. McDiamond was arranging it, I said to Oliver, "Is Rich there?"

"Don't worry," he said. "He's not going to leave you in the lurch."

As soon as I came in I saw that he was there but it seemed a long time before we met. First the church choir — small boy sopranos and altos, tall tenors and thick-chested basses — all came up the side aisle singing "Onward Christian Soldiers." It took several verses before they had crossed to the main aisle, had marched down it and were safely settled in the chancel.

The church was full of people, many of them singing. After the hymn came a moment of silence, then the first notes of "Lohengrin." The ushers paced ahead slowly. Leila proceeded with Wagnerian dignity. Of course her hat helped her.

I was inclined to go too fast.

"Don't hurry," advised Mrs. McDiamond, as she turned my train.

She had help. Ellen Murphy slipped out of her seat and gave the final necessary twist. All seemed going smoothly.

My father had given me his left arm because — as he often told me — "A gentleman keeps his sword arm free." I had accepted this adage uncritically. His not having a sword did not worry me. Neither did it occur to me that, after he had given me away, he would have to walk around my train to get into the family pew on our left. He was not at all troubled by his position either.

When the time came to leave me, he simply leaped over the train, murmuring as he did so: "Lucky I was bred in the deep ditch country, darling!"

This touch of life in the hunting fields was the high point of the wedding. Not long ago a friend who was there told me that her favorite moment in my wedding was when Mr. Andrews gaily jumped over that white river of satin and orange blossoms.

If I had known how much the choir was going to sing, I think I would not have said "yes" so glibly when the rector, Mr. Perry, asked if I would like the full choral service.

It was a long time before Rich finally agreed to take me as his wedded wife. He had plenty of time to change his mind. However he stuck to it. At last Mendelssohn sounded. Soon Mr. Mooney was driving us away.

Small boys on bicycles swooped around us yelling, "Why don't you kiss her, Mister? Now's your chance!"

Sensible advice, which was, I'm glad to say, accepted by the bridegroom.

The wedding reception is a pleasant blur. There are photographs to show it took place. There is one that a friend christened "Well, I've got him!" It never occurred to me to send a copy to Ellen Murphy, though she certainly deserved one.

I remember music at the reception — Viennese waltzes punctuated by the popping of champagne corks — and I suppose there must have been food but Rich and I did not have any. When we went away, we got into Mr. Mooney's brougham. It was trimmed with white ribbon and old shoes. This decoration did not trouble us because we had a secret. Mr. Mooney's first automobile, an enormous black limousine with everything a car should have, including a glass vase for flowers, was waiting for us on a road west of the hill so we had a way of escape.

Just as I was settled in the brougham and was brushing off the confetti, Katharine put Baloo, with an enormous bow of white ribbon on his collar, into my lap. Someone blew a bugle. Baloo sang loudly. The horse went fast and our pursuers were soon left behind. However, seeing Baloo with us, they were bright enough to guess that we were not going far in the brougham. As we got into the limousine, leaving Baloo sobbing behind us, Oliver and his friends came rushing down the western slope of the hill. We got away before they reached us. We had left the horse and buggy age.

We were soon on our way to Portland, Maine. From there we were going to Boothbay Harbor and after that we would sail to Monhegan Island where some friends of Rich's had lent us a house. Our seats on the train were at the end of one of the Pullmans. Rich sat in the one next to the door and politely turned around so that he faced me. He looked very distinguished in his new suit of English tweed, fine black and white check barred with blue. He had a dark blue tie and a white carnation in his buttonhole.

In a few minutes, when I leaned forward to tell him how Mr. Buxton had called me that morning, I saw that he was almost asleep. I suppose I must have disturbed his nap because he opened his eyes, smiled kindly upon me, said, "I hate women with thick ankles," and went to sleep again.

Did he mean my ankles? I looked down at them anxiously. My skirt was daringly short, fully six inches from the ground, and I could see them well. But were they thick or thin? I couldn't tell.

"So this is married life?" I thought with a certain lack of enthusiasm.

I was wrong.

Rich woke up quite soon. The lady with the thick ankles was halfway down on the other side of the car, he told me. All was well on the way to Monhegan.

15

Here and There

OUR VOYAGE TO MONHEGAN was by sailboat. It was as peaceful as a swan boat. The gentle steady wind seemed to follow us all the way. Our cottage, covered with silvery shingles, was close to the water with a view that reminded me of Iron Bound. I did not see it again till the day we left.

Fog shut the island in that night and insulated us from the continent. Usually fog means quiet seas but this fog covered a storm so fierce that for days no boat entered or left the harbor. We used to walk to the ocean side of the island and watch the Atlantic break on the tall cliffs. We could hear the crash and roar of the waves and breathe their salt spray long before we could see them. Even the worst storm I had ever seen on Frenchman's Bay did not equal this one. The fog gave me the feeling that the island, with its cathedral woods and screaming eagles, its ring of white foam, its ferns and wet rocks, had left the ocean floor and was quietly drifting wherever the storm took it. At any moment it seemed as if it might be dashed against the mainland and smashed to pieces.

Fortunately such fancies did not interfere with my appetite. We took our meals at the boardinghouse next door. Our hostess, Miss Fenwick, apologized to us every day because no boat had come in so there was no "shore meat"; all she could give us was lobster. Every day we assured her that her plain boiled lobster with melted butter, freshly baked hot rolls and asparagus picked from her garden were things we could manage to endure.

Miss Fenwick also made the best chocolate cake I have ever tasted. It never, alas, occurred to me to ask for the rule. Mrs. Appleyard would have been more efficient but — perhaps fortunately — she was not on our honeymoon. She might have tried to improve the syrup Miss Fenwick served with pancakes at breakfast time. Rich, I noticed, corrected me patiently when I called it maple syrup, as Miss Fenwick did. Rich thought she made it herself out of dark brown sugar and maple extract. Not having yet visited Kents' Corner, I did not realize what a damaging statement this was. It would not have been tactful to mention it to Miss Fenwick.

She had told me several stories unfavorable to off-islanders. The stories usually ended by the invaders of the island being given a boat and advised to row back to the continent. I am glad that we were sufficiently congenial with the islanders so that we were encouraged to stay and eat lobster till the storm was over.

When we got back to Brookline, there was still confetti in the privet hedge. The day after we arrived, Katharine and Ed Frick announced their engagement.

"What's struck your family anyway?" Mrs. Sedgwick called out the window to me.

I replied sententiously: "The first olive in the bottle is the most difficult to extract."

I seem to have recognized a trend. Rosamond Capen, daughter of Aunty's best friend, announced her engagement to Oliver soon afterwards. The two ladies had been busy with wedding plans for some time. They had planned to marry Oliver to Rosie and Katharine to Rich, who had been living with the Capens. There was a slight inaccuracy so far as Rich was concerned, but on the whole their average was pretty good. After several other matches had been arranged successfully, Aunty turned her attention to her friend, a widow. Soon Mrs. Capen became Mrs. Sumner Robinson. Mr. Robinson, when I first saw him, had a beard but he soon shaved it off. I am not sure whether Aunty had advised him to remove it as one of the conditions of her blessing the wedding, but anyway he did and the marriage was a happy one. Aunty herself became engaged about this time but perhaps the engagement was only part of the general epidemic.

It was, she told me, a ridiculous idea. She broke it off before it was announced to anyone but the family.

Rich and I spent the rest of our honeymoon in Baltimore, Philadelphia and New York. We were in time for strawberry Kossuth cakes in Baltimore and soft shell crabs and creamed terrapin with boiled turtle's eggs the size of robin's eggs arranged around it. I don't know how it was cooked. (Yes, Mrs. Appleyard, no doubt you can guess, but this was not going to be a cookbook — remember?) We also had terrapin at Aunt Eleanor's country house outside Philadelphia. The house was white and longer than the biggest battleship that ever came into Bar Harbor. The door was always opened by a butler in a dress suit and a footman in green and gold. I have seen similar teams at other doors now and then — blue and silver is becoming to handsome young footmen too — but I never was quite sure whether the footman was needed because the butler could not manage the card tray alone or because it might be necessary to knock down a gangster or a child selling cookies. I'm afraid the time for me to learn has passed.

Rich got plenty of tennis and golf at Aunt Eleanor's and I was able to catch up on my reading. I was not reading anything special, just whatever there was around. Since my marriage I had fallen rather below my standard of a book and a half a day. Lately someone accused me of always reading three. That was only in the hospital while I was not writing a book. Nothing interferes with one's reading like writing, though arithmetic can be distracting too.

In New York we went to theaters and to a supper club where we ate chicken simmered in the French manner. I think it was Diamond Jim Brady who bumped into me and almost knocked me over. Anyway it was someone whose diamond shirt stud would have been quite abrasive if it had hit my nose instead of my shoulder.

We found, when we got back to Brookline, that my father had made arrangements to sell the Edge Hill Road house. He was going to live in Milton with Ed and Katharine. She was already energetically cleaning out closets. She had noticed in me a tendency, common in Boston, to wear my clothes long after the statute of limitations had expired, so she began her work by giving my long-cherished evening dresses to the Salvation Army. I have often wondered who got my pink and ivory brocade.

Rich and I were happily married until one afternoon in the middle of August when he came home and made the following statement: "After tea," he said, "I am going to teach you to balance your checkbook."

"I have no checkbook," I said.

He showed me one. It was neatly bound in dark blue and had three checks to a page.

"This is yours," he announced. "You must learn to use it." I said, "Yes, but not *today* when I'm so *happy!*"

"If you were having a terrible day and were unhappy, you wouldn't want to either," he pointed out, for he had evidently been sneakily observing certain traits in my character.

"I thought men balanced checkbooks," I said. "If I wanted to, I wouldn't be married — I would be a banker."

"You see," Rich said patiently and preposterously, "you are going to manage the family finances. I opened a joint account for us today. I deposited my salary in it. Just sign this card with your usual signature . . . Thank you . . . Here's the deposit slip; just enter the amount there . . ."

The extraordinary thing is that, after more than half a century, this account still balances. Why do I make such a fuss about it? After all probably few more than fourteen thousand checks have been written by me in this period. My oldest granddaughter would dispose of them correctly and electronically in a morning. Why am I boasting of this trivial feat?

Well, for one thing, I have made, in my time as an accountant, about forty-five different kinds of mistakes. Every time I balance my books there are at least forty-five things I can think of to do to each check to make the balance come out wrong. These ingenious mistakes range all the way from simple errors in subtraction to subtleties such as making out the stub for one amount and the check for another. You probably think you have made some interesting errors yourself but I feel sure I can duplicate them.

Of course, the bank, especially since it became electronic, makes mistakes of its own. The week it triumphantly announced its complete computerism to me, it made an error of $978.50 in my account. When I make a mistake, it is more likely to involve ten cents but computers spurn such trifles. I must admit I took a certain amount of simple pleasure in pointing out this error to them.

My view of the banking business is no doubt conditioned by another early experience. Claude Gibbons, one of my favorite dancing partners, knowing that I was a Simmons graduate, thought of me as the right person to carry out an idea he had. He worked for a large Boston bank. It occurred to him that the bank could increase business by encouraging women to open separate accounts. He thought — and how right he was — that if women had their own accounts instead of being doled out an occasional two dollar bill, money would circulate rapidly.

Only, he wondered, would women ever learn to balance checkbooks? Perhaps, he thought, if there were a pleasant room in the bank with mirrors where makeup could be repaired (quite a number of Boston women now owned powder puffs) and where hats could be set at the right angle, women would do more shopping and cash more checks. He thought a sensible, well-poised woman who understood accounts should always be on hand to help. One women's department would be organized at the main office first. He was sure the idea would spread to other offices, even to other banks.

"You are just the person to start it, Lulie," he said.

What queer things people think about people!

I listened spellbound while he told me how I would straighten out checkbooks and suggest sound investments. He said I might rise to be a vice-president someday.

He added, "Now do me a favor and say yes."

"Claude," I said, "I am going to do you a favor: No."

That is why this particular bank is still in thriving condition. I had learned enough about libraries at Simmons to leave them without my skill. I had also learned enough about accounts to know that no bank where I practiced them would survive long. However Claude's idea was a good one. The next Boston débutante he asked to fill the position did so well that she became a vice-president of the bank and later head of all women's banking organizations in the country.

By August of 1912, I was already in what was then known as an interesting condition. It was obvious that I was no use either in cleaning out the Edge Hill Road house or in settling the apartment at 66 Chestnut Street in Boston. It was decided that I had better accept an invitation from Lydia Bond and her mother to visit them in North Hatley. Rich would join me there later and take me to Kents' Corner.

I felt better as soon as I got to Hatley and I made myself useful in several ways. One of them was shingling a roof. I found I could do it even when I felt quite dizzy. I was interested to learn that you start at the bottom and go up. Left to myself I should have begun at the top.

Perhaps, I thought as I pounded in nails, hitting my fingers only occasionally, my health is not so delicate as I have always supposed. Probably I am just a hypochondriac.

Looking back over my eighty years of health — most of it bad — this seems the most likely explanation. I remind myself of an old lady whom a favorite neighbor, Nora Gallagher, told me about.

This aged Vermonter lived through many afflictions and died at the age of ninety-six. Her affairs were in good order, for she had always been preparing for the event. Even her tombstone was ready except for the final date. Cut into the Vermont granite was her message to posterity. It said: "I told them all the time I didn't feel good."

I feel sure she had told them.

Mrs. Bond and Lydia were so kind to me that I wished I had a chance to do something special for them in return. One morning when I went out into the sunshine I met Mrs. Bond with tears on her face. She wiped them away hastily, said she was being foolish and managed a smile.

It was just, she said, that she had lost the diamond out of her engagement ring. She was hunting everywhere she had been that morning for the stone but she had just given up. I had some idea how she must feel. Her husband had died some years before. She had told me once that every time she looked at the ring she felt that he was still near her.

With my astigmatic nearsightedness, finding things was hardly my special skill. Yet this loss struck me so keenly that I heard myself saying: "I'm going to find it for you. Tell me where you've been, what you've been doing."

"I've been everywhere — emptying trash, in the garden pulling up weeds, down at the dock dumping water out of canoes."

"Go and lie down," I said. "I'll find it."

Again I heard myself say this in a firm voice not really mine. It was as if someone else were speaking. I walked quickly down to the strip of pebbly, sandy beach near the dock. I did not examine it or the canoes but stood looking down into the clear water. There were a few motorboats on the lake now. One of them zoomed past the cove stirring up the still water into greenish-white waves.

As the first wave reached the shore, I saw something flash among the pebbles near the end of the dock. I walked out into the water — it came to my knees — plunged my hand down where I had seen the flash, came up with a clutch of small stones.

One of them was the diamond.

This is so obviously impossible that I can scarcely believe that I'm not making the whole thing up. I'm not though.

I ran to the house with it. Within a few minutes Mrs. Bond and I were on the front steps crying. I have seldom been happier.

16

Vermont

THE DAY after my psychic diamond dredging, Rich came to take me to Vermont. We traveled, first by a few railroads, then in a buckboard drawn by two horses, to the Lake Mansfield Trout Club near Stowe. The road to it was so muddy that the horses bogged down and we traveled the last quarter of a mile on foot.

Rich's father had been one of the founders of the club. One of the first things I saw there was his portrait. He had a look of kindness and humor that made me feel at home. The clubhouse, a shingled building with wide shady porches, was close to the lake, which had been made by damming up a small clear stream. In what had once been a mountain valley, trout now flourished.

It was the duty of the guests to catch enough trout for dinner every day. Members might give fish away or take them home, in which case they paid for them by the pound. Otherwise trout were cooked at the club about as soon as they came out of the water. While the men were out fishing, the women picked blueberries for pies or puddings or muffins. They husked corn from the garden and peeled early apples for pandowdy.

My appetite came back. It was no hardship to eat perfectly cooked trout twice a day. I was surprised that many of the guests, especially the men, preferred roast beef or pork to the fish. However everyone ate pancakes and maple syrup for breakfast. I quickly saw what Rich meant about the Monhegan brand of syrup. The remarkable thing was how happy our honeymoon had been in spite of that substance.

I began to have a special feeling about Vermont, not only because of its beauty — the lake with the high wooded hills around it, the torrent of bird song at dawn, the cool freshness of the mountain air — but because somehow it seemed familiar. I wondered why until I heard a conversation between Rich and Mr. Soutter from Massachusetts. He was not a member of the club. Someone had invited him to dinner.

He had come up to Vermont for a wedding in Burlington, Mr. Soutter told Rich.

"Was that the Allison wedding?" Rich asked.

"Yes, do you know them?"

"The bride is a cousin of mine — on my father's side," Rich said.

"I suppose the groom's your cousin too," Mr. Soutter said.

"Not really," said Rich. "He's my great-uncle's wife's nephew." Mr. Soutter said disgustedly, "Vermont isn't a state — it's a club!"

Yes, I thought, it's a club and I belong to it.

That very afternoon, while helping husk corn on the porch, I had heard a clubbish conversation that delighted me.

Mrs. Evans said to Mrs. Breck, "Laura, I've been having trouble with my waxwings. How have things been with you?"

"I have been having problems with mine too," said Mrs. Breck.

She did not have time to give details because a new arrival, who had been looking at the lake, turned and said, "Oh, I have trouble with my waxwings too!"

Mrs. Evans smiled kindly upon the speaker and said, "I wonder if you would identify yourself for us."

The newcomer said, "I live in Lower Cabot. I am Mrs. Ezra Childe. My maiden name was Albee. My mother was a Fox."

"Oh," said Mrs. Evans, "I somehow thought we were related. Through the Albees. May I introduce Mrs. Breck from Breck's Hollow and Mrs. Kent, LeRoy Kent's daughter-in-law? Now do tell us about your cedar waxwings."

Now that everyone was identified, we listened to Mrs. Childe's waxwing problems. I had already learned something: people should not be expected to listen to your problems unless they know who you are. Not in Vermont anyway.

The waxwings' problems had to do with string, which they need for domestic purposes. Mrs. Childe and the other ladies had all given their climbing plants string to climb on. It seems that a waxwing will tweak string away from a morning glory or a clematis and weave it into its nest. The solution is to lay out short lengths of string in convenient places, convenient to the waxwings, of course. This is what Vermonters can do with the box marked "STRING — too short to tie."

Years later, I was sitting on the porch at Kents' Corner rolling up a ball of short pieces of string. Suddenly there was a flutter of wings; a piece of string was tweaked out of my hand and carried to the big maple across the road. I spent the rest of the morning cutting the best and softest pieces into suitable lengths. To the masked and crested bandits with their well-groomed plumage, their feathers tipped with red sealing wax and their yellow-bordered tails, I identified myself.

"I am Mrs. Kent of Kents' Corner," I said.

They politely accepted my string. I have never had to give them any since. Waxwings still nest in the maple. I suppose they economically use the same nest. When I see them flying in and out of the trees I happily assume that they are descendants of the pair to whom I gave the string twenty years ago. I had already seen their courtship that morning. The lady waxwing sat on a dead branch of a tree, smoothing her feathers. As she sat there, she gave an occasional whispered squeak, like the hinge of a very small door that needs oiling. After a while the male bird arrived with a wild cherry in his beak. Through my field glass I could see it shine like a ruby. He gave it to the lady, who accepted it graciously. As they flew across the road into the green depths of the maple, I was sure they were engaged.

The day we started from Lake Mansfield to Kents' Corner, low-hanging clouds, out of which rain poured unceasingly, shut out the hills. We traveled by buckboard, trolley car, railroad and automobile as far as the Pavillion Hotel in Montpelier. A large carryall with two horses was waiting to take us and our luggage to Calais. Rich had engaged the carryall, rather than a motor car, because he thought a carriage was less likely to get bogged down than an automobile.

He told the driver to go up North Street because it was the shortest way and we could see the view, in case the clouds lifted.

"Ay-ah?" said the driver.

His tone did not imply that cloud lifting was likely that day.

Rich described the view to me as we drove along through the cold rain. He told me the names of every peak in the Worcester Range and showed me where Camel's Hump rose high in the distance above one end of the range. His descriptions were so good that at moments I thought I could see them, but all I saw were thick clouds that came to the edge of the road on both sides. We might as well have been back on Monhegan.

Rich told me where maples would soon be like hills of fire and where apple trees were covered with striped pink and yellow apples.

I kept saying, "It must be beautiful!" and he kept adding miserably, "If these clouds would only lift."

Once it seemed as if they were lightening and Rich said so to the driver, who said, "Ay-ah?" and the heaviest rain yet fell on us. It was mixed with a little hail, which drummed on the roof of the carryall and made the horses whinny. We drove into the darkness under a big maple and waited until it turned to rain. I had not supposed I would ever be delighted to see rain.

Rich told me we were in "The Horn of the Moon." I did not question this statement. Anything seemed possible that day. Later I learned that it was the name for a place where one of the main roads traveled in a crescent shape. After the hail stopped we followed a piece of it and Rich told me that the view had changed now; that to our right — if the clouds would only lift — we could see the whole range of the Orange Mountains. I said they must be beautiful. Not long after that he told me we were almost halfway home.

I said, through chattering teeth, "That's nice!" and swallowed a sound part sneeze, part sob and part hiccough. That meant only another hour unless, of course, we got stuck in a mud hole. We almost did, near something Rich said was Bliss Pond. Luckily the driver snapped his whip at the right moment and the horses heaved the carriage forward to a gravelly bit of road. Of the pond I saw only a strip of water about a foot wide and several lily pads. We passed one of the old brick houses built by the Bliss family. I saw its shadow through the fog. Dimly too, I saw the doors of the Old West Church but I had to take its spire, with the golden arrow of the weather vane, on faith.

Over a hollow in the road, tall elms arched up into the clouds and dropped dark branches over us. A brown stream of water gushed under the bridge.

Our driver uttered his first and only sentence. "Guess I'll go round by Maple Corner going back in case this bridge goes out," he said.

I half expected Rich to say "Ay-ah?" but he only remarked politely that the plan seemed a sensible one.

We climbed slowly up a long hill and began to go down the other side of it.

"The best view of Kents' Corner is right from here," Rich said.

I believed him and in a few minutes I saw that it really existed. There drifted out of the mist barns painted like railway stations — ocher and maroon, a big brick house, a little white farmhouse. Below the brick house was a white one with lights shining into the windows. This was his mother's, Rich said, and there were several other houses hidden away in the fog.

We drove right into the grassy yard of the "White House," cutting deep ruts into the lawn. This struck me as too bad. It still does when a large truck drives in and plows up my lawn on a wet day. However it's traditional, so Ralph Weeks and I heal the wounds as best we can with hay chaff and chunks of sod and wood ashes so the lawn still looks green.

We have had to do away with the mounting block because it could not be used with automobiles. In 1912 I was glad to dismount to it from the carryall. Rich then led me through the double front door with its panels of engraved glass into the front hall and left me there while he went back for our baggage. The hall was just as dark and chilly then as it still is on a cold, wet day — like this one, for instance. All the doors into the hall were shut. It was papered in two cold shades of gray. Under my feet was a mustard and maroon-colored carpet. The black walnut hat rack had a gray golf cape hanging on it. I felt like wrapping myself in it but Rich came in with the bags so I just tried not to shiver as he put his hat down on the white marble slab of the hat rack.

I tried to think of something nice to say about the house. I tried to smile.

I only sneezed.

On the other side of the dining room door was warmth and the smell of wood smoke, kerosene lamps and frying doughnuts. Rich's mother had been too much occupied in getting them just right to hear us come. She was a handsome woman with bright dark eyes, silvery curly hair and pink cheeks. She was the only woman I ever knew who looked stately in an apron. I was a little taller than she but I always felt shorter. I had not seen her since our wedding.

She allowed me to kiss one cheek and Rich the other.

"You are cold," she said to me disapprovingly, removed a well-browned doughnut from the kettle, turned some slices of fat salt pork over in the pan. She had a cook but naturally did not let her do anything important like fixing salt pork with sour cream gravy. This, I learned uneasily, was one of her son's favorite dishes.

The cook, shadowy in black, was slicing beets in a timid way.

"Not so thin, Elvira," said Mrs. Kent. "This is Mrs. Rich Kent, she's a writer. Don't let the dried applesauce burn."

Elvira looked more frightened than ever but she cheered up when Rich shook hands with her and asked after her six children.

"You're looking peeked," Mrs. Kent said to me. "You'd better go and lie down."

Evidently she guessed that I would fall down if I didn't lie down. Had she also guessed my secret? I learned later that she knew it as soon as she looked at me but had kindly ignored it.

I stretched myself out, but not very far, on a short black walnut sofa in the back parlor. Its black horsehair covering was both prickly and slippery. There was more of this substance on chairs and other sofas. I was resting in the ugliest room I had ever seen, except perhaps the front parlor.

The favorite color scheme in 1870 when Blanche Hollister Kent was a bride seems to have been maroon and mustard. No expense was spared by LeRoy Abdiel Kent to make his wife happy. Mustard and maroon chenille portieres hung between the two rooms and harmonized with carpets, window curtains and window shades. Maroon, lightened with copper, gave the wallpaper a sullen glow. White marble chilled the tops of tables. An enormous black air-tight stove was cheerful in its hideous way. Red light came through a mica panel in the door. Its black pipe made right-angled turns and vanished through a grating in the ceiling. Near it hung a lamp with a mustard-colored shade and dark ruby pendants.

The front parlor was much like the back one except for a large pool table among the horsehair-covered furniture. It was covered with bright green baize. This addition to the color scheme made me feel dizzier than ever.

When it was time to get ready for supper, Rich escorted me up to two rooms above the parlors. They were warmed by pipes from the stoves below and decorated in the maroon and mustard scheme. The bureau, besides slabs of marble and walnut, had a mirror that, like the head of the bed, reached the ceiling. I saw myself in it. I looked even worse than I had expected. A greenish mustard, harmonizing well with the decorations, was my general color. I learned later that this gruesome tint was partly supplied by the mirror. Even in rugged health you can still look pretty green in it.

"Well," I thought, "at least I'll look all right with the billiard table."

I heard the clicking of balls. When I got downstairs I found Rich and his mother shooting a little pool. I wished they would go on indefinitely so supper could be postponed. I felt that salt pork, no matter how well disguised with sour cream, would not agree with me. At this meal Mrs. Kent followed the practice she continued during my whole visit. She cooked her masterpieces, set them before us and kindly seemed not to notice that I ate only small scraps, a little potato, an occasional Montpelier cracker. Hospitality had always been a tradition of the "White House" — so called to distinguish it from the "Brick House" north of it. As I look back, I think Mrs. Kent's merciful respect for my secret was about the finest example of hospitality I ever encountered.

After supper Rich went up to see his cousin Herbert Kent at the Brick House to find out if a visit from us would be acceptable.

"What did he say about bringing Lulie?" Mrs. Kent asked when Rich came back.

Accurately Rich replied: "He said, 'If she doesn't mind folks that have hair on their teeth, bring her up.' "

"He means you're city folks," Mrs. Kent translated. "Never mind — you can't help it."

Thus encouraged, I went out shivering into the fog.

The Brick House, now the Kent Museum, was decorated much like the White House and almost as cold in the front hall but cheerful in Helen's bedroom where a fire was burning in the open fireplace. There was a baby — Howard — only a few days old in a cradle. Three older children — Edwin, Josephine and Laura were admiring him. He was asleep and looked as if life at Kents' Corner agreed with him.

I thought he was an especially nice baby and said so. My opinion was accepted as valuable though I was not exactly an expert. This was the first five-day-old baby I had ever seen. I hoped mine would be like him. It did not occur to me that some babies are girls.

The fog and rain lasted all the week of our visit. I never really saw Kents' Corner. Rich described the rolling hills around the house and the view down the valley and made me feel a certain pastoral beauty behind the cold curtain of mist. One day we walked through mud below and rain above to the store at Maple Corner. It had all the traits of the country store of the day: counters of dark wood whittled here and there with initials, cans of kerosene with potatoes for stoppers, a cracker barrel, hams hanging from the rafters, smoke from a cast-iron stove.

Well surrounded by cuspidors was a table at which faithful patrons chewed tobacco and played poker while they waited for the mail. A small muddy automobile known as "The Stage" brought the mail. Automation had not been invented so a letter posted in Boston Monday morning arrived in our own mailbox, outside the gate of our house on Monday afternoon. Now I go to the post office to collect my letters. The time for a letter to make the journey from Boston to Calais varies from day to day, but I feel pretty sure of getting a letter posted Friday morning by the following Tuesday.

"It will take two weeks to process your driving license," my granddaughter was told lately. "The machines are stuffed and they're tired."

Well, we are an inventive people — we'll probably work out a good system for mail from the moon.

I did a little exploring of my own. The third floor of the White House seemed like another planet. The innocent furniture of the pre-horsehair era had been carried up there for the hired girls to use. I found old Windsor chairs, beds of curly maple, tables of pine and cherry, bureaus painted with roses and forget-me-nots. A seventeenth-century banister-back chair stood at an eighteenth-century dressing table. Braided and hooked rugs covered the wide boards of floors spattered to look like tortoise shell.

A cloak such as Washington wore crossing the Delaware hung in one of the closets. It came down to the Hollisters from one of their Carroll ancestors, a member of the family of Charles Carroll of Carrolton, Rich told me. There were tall beaver hats and chromolithographs and linen towels, woven and spun from home grown flax, and patchwork quilts. All the interesting things were not on the third floor. One day, in the back parlor, my eye caught the flash of silver on the melodeon. Skirting the billiard table and dodging past a horsehair rocker bent on tripping me up, I picked up two silver oblongs. The name Ira Kent was engraved on one, in what is called bright-cut, and Polly C. Kent on the other. They were the coffin plates of Rich's grandfather and grandmother. Interesting certainly — in a depressing way.

I had already seen the cemetery. Vermonters love cemeteries. LeRoy Kent's gravestone was an immense plain block of granite.

He had died only the year before and it was set in place during one of the days of our visit. His wife's name and the date of her birth were cut on it below his.

"Do wives always have their names on their husband's stones?" I asked Mrs. Kent.

"If they're not looking for a second husband," she replied. "It's restful for bachelors and widowers if they know you're not in the market," she added. "They can talk to you without worrying about a breach of promise suit."

It was still foggy when we left Kents' Corner. I never saw any of the views. (I was right in trusting Rich. They were all as beautiful as he said, I found out five years later.) We went by automobile to Montpelier and spent the night at the Pavillion Hotel. Lafayette stayed there once. I got the impression that it had not changed much since his time.

Dorman and Agnes Kent had asked us to dinner at their house on Kent Street. The steep hillside on which it stood was so high and the fog was so thick that we could hardly see that we were looking down on the lights of Montpelier. We had been asked for six-thirty and we were there by six-twenty-nine. When Rich touched the bell, the door flew open.

Agnes was standing there fair-haired, serenely beautiful. I had been told she was lame so I was not surprised to see her on crutches. Two small boys, immaculate in white jackets and knickerbockers, stood in front of her. Richard, the younger one, had his hands in his pockets.

Bennett, who had opened the door, said: "How do you do, Cousin Rich? How do you do, Cousin Louise? We are glad to see you."

Before we could acknowledge this nicely learned greeting, Richard made his gesture of welcome. It was spontaneous, unrehearsed and, I rather think, unique.

He held up his hands. In each was a large beautiful brown Vermont egg. He clashed them together like cymbals. I have never seen egg yolk so suddenly or widely distributed. Both jackets were white and gold. Not only were the eggs broken — so was the ice. I can pretty well guarantee that this method will do away with any formality between new relatives.

While the boys were changing into their second-best suits and Rich was scrubbing the vestibule, Dorman showed me his antiques.

"What do you think of this highboy?" he would ask.

When I said, "Why it's one of the most beautiful I've ever seen!" he would add, "Ought to be, had to give twenty-five dollars for it."

I think he had four, each acquired at about the same price.

The house seemed perfect to me. There was something beautiful wherever I looked. The dinner was as distinguished as the furniture — a perfectly cooked roast of beef, vegetables just out of the garden, a wonderful deep-dish apple pie. Agnes, moving around on crutches, had cooked it all herself.

"Do you always get everything just right?" I asked.

"She does," said Dorman. "I hope you're a good cook," he added.

"Well, I'm not quite sure," I admitted. "I've never even boiled a kettle of water yet."

Bennett spoke up.

"If Cousin Louise can't cook, what is Cousin Rich going to have for dinner?" he asked.

Dorman said he supposed the neighbors would send in a covered dish now and then.

I liked to think of the residents of Chestnut Street, Mt. Vernon Street and Louisburg Square leaving baked beans or fishballs at my door.

"I doubt if I'll get anything as good as this," I said.

Conversation, as it often did when a few Kents were gathered together, turned to the Kent family — especially to old Remember

Kent who had come to Kents' Corner over a blazed trail in 1797. He had the Kent highboy with him on a sledge drawn by oxen.

Dorman told me so many things that evening about Remember Kent and his eight children, seven of them sons, that I began to feel that I knew them well.

"You know," I said, "Rich never told me what remarkable people the Kents were."

"Because they weren't," Dorman promptly replied. "The Kents didn't amount to much. Remember Kent was moderate. (A damaging adjective: Vermont for lazy.) He'd never have had a farm if Abdiel Bliss hadn't cleared one for his daughter Rachel who was Remember's wife. Abdiel had seven daughters and he cleared a farm for each of them. No, there's just one talent the Kents all had."

"What's that?" I asked.

Dorman looked kindly at Agnes and me.

"They always knew how to choose good wives," he said.

"Do you suppose I can learn to be one?"

"Oh, I wouldn't wonder," Dorman said.

I decided to try.

17

Chestnut Street

KATHARINE HAD FINISHED clearing out the Edge Hill Road house while we were in Vermont. She was really extraordinary. She hurled furniture around the landscape as easily as if she were blowing soap bubbles. My things landed in Chestnut Street, hers in Milton. Some went into my grandmother's attic to be kept for Oliver and Rosie. The Salvation Army got the rest. No mistakes were made; nothing was broken.

In August, before I went to Vermont, Katharine had paused in these activities long enough for her wedding. She slipped briskly into the family wedding dress one afternoon and adjusted the veil just right. She gave our father instructions about walking on her left up the aisle — none of this nonsense about keeping his sword arm free and vaulting over her train. I was disappointed; I'd hoped to see him repeat that famous leap. Almost before I realized they were married, she and Ed had hopped into the Maxwell and were puffing off down the street. Without Katharine the house seemed like a dark cavern, a cavern strangely scattered with rose-petal confetti and crumbs of wedding cake. We didn't, I saw, really live there anymore.

We came back from Vermont to 66 Chestnut Street. Katharine and Rich had the apartment in good order except that no one had put the *Encyclopaedia Britannica* on the bookshelves. The living room of the apartment was the drawing room of the old house. It had beautiful woodwork in the style of Samuel McIntire. The convex mirror hung over the fireplace and acted as an eye of light. One of the things it reflected was The Surprise. Rich had told me in May that he had bought me a birthday present for a surprise; it would be delivered when we moved into the apartment.

It was across the room from the mirror so it was distorted into strange curves but —

"How did you know just what I wanted?" I asked with my arms around Rich's neck.

"I didn't think there was room enough for a grand," he said. "I hope an upright will do."

Would it do?

I was already sitting down at my Mason and Hamlin piano, playing the easiest part of the "Beautiful Blue Danube." When I stopped, we took a few turns around the room.

"We'll have to get someone in to play for us while we dance," I said. "Oh, Rich, you're the best dancer! Did I remember to tell you? That's why I proposed to you."

"I always wondered."

The piano seemed to be just the tonic I needed. Rich went to *The Youth's Companion.* He walked across the Public Garden to the office on Berkeley Street. I spent the morning unpacking books. The dining room was full of bookshelves. It was a big room downstairs in the basement but only halfway below the slope of Chestnut Street. You could see people almost as far up as their waists as they walked up or down the brick sidewalk. When I met fashionable ladies buying lobsters or filet mignon in the Charles Street shops, I used to recognize them by their shoes, spats and skirts.

One of my Brookline friends lived at a distinguished address —

Greenough Street, Within. I dated my letters Chestnut Street, Beneath.

Just to get from the coal stove in the kitchen to the dining table, Leila Page's wedding present to us, if you were carrying — say — a dish of scrambled eggs, was an adventure. The coal stove was near the back door. It heated the kitchen cosily. Next to it was something I had never seen before — a gas stove. Because of danger of explosion and asphyxiation, we did not use it much. Next you passed the soapstone sink and entered a pantry with flour and sugar bins.

From now on, you left any indication that the sun ever shone. What light there was came from yellow and blue gas flames. They guided you through the shadows of the wood cellar, coal cellar, vegetable cellar and preserve closet. They let you see the doors to two bedrooms, each with a fireplace and a wood-burning stove. These were modern improvements. The open fireplaces had been bricked up around the pipes of the stoves. The old mantelpieces, not quite so elaborate as the one in the drawing room, had been left in their places.

Still carrying the eggs — remember? — you passed tool, broom, clothes and china closets. The passage now made a sharp turn, which took you into the dining room pantry. It was lighted to some extent by gas globes. There was a sink with copper showing through tin and shelves for china. The blue Canton was already on the shelves. So were the Minton soup tureen, the gold-trimmed champagne glasses and other daily necessities.

You had now reached the dining room-library. Our red Persian rug glowed on the bare floor. A fire was burning in the fireplace. Pictures were stacked against the wall. The room smelled of linseed oil — I had started giving the dining table a heat-proof finish with oil and pumice when we were still at Edge Hill Road. It was beginning to get a good surface. It was set for lunch with china, linen, silver and glass.

The scrambled eggs were still warm after their trip.

Had I — who had never boiled water — already learned to scramble eggs? Had I been taking clandestine cooking lessons all the time?

Nothing so sensible; the eggs had been cooked by Minnie Wiggs.

It was, in fact, Minnie who had made the trip from the alley to Chestnut Street. I had become familiar with the route only by escorting her to the kitchen and showing her the bedrooms on the way.

Minnie spoke well of the subterranean bedroom and accompanying lavatory. She said it was more convenient than in her last place, where the bedroom was on the fourth floor and the lavatory in the cellar. She also said it was handy having the set tubs in the kitchen and so near the back yard where she'd hang out the laundry. And did I like my eggs beaten with the eggbeater or just with the fork?

Not to show my ignorance, I spoke as much like a gourmet as I could at short notice.

"Not slippery," I said. "Rather firm with the whites showing just a little."

"'Tis with the fork then," said Minnie and I agreed.

She had heated the plate so hot and had sped so swiftly through the passages that the eggs and the beautifully browned English muffins were the best thing I had eaten for days.

Minnie beamed upon me when I told her so.

She said: "I don't know much. I was just a kitchen maid with an awful cross cook. They don't want you to learn anything but I guess I could learn — only you'll have to teach me, ma'am."

This — though I did not know it — was the moment Mrs. Appleyard entered my life.

I heard myself saying kindly: "I'll be glad to tell you anything I know, Minnie."

To myself I vowed: "And I'll learn something to tell you. Right now."

I then used my fingerbowl, for we had gracious living in Chestnut Street, Beneath, said I would rest a little and then speak to Minnie about dinner before I went marketing. I handed her a copy of Miss Farmer's *Boston Cooking School Cook Book*. Fortunately I'd had two copies for wedding presents. I studied the drawing room copy while I rested. When I had finished my rest, and my work, I knew how to broil lamb chops with mushrooms, to bake potatoes, cook green beans and make corn muffins. I confided my freshly acquired knowledge to Minnie.

When she hung her jaw open, looking bewildered, I looked up the proper places in her copy of the cookbook, put in slips of paper and suggested she should study them while I went marketing. She must come and see me if there was anything she didn't understand, I said. When I got back, I'd be in the dining room, unpacking my books.

All went well. The market delivered the food in plenty of time. Minnie understood Miss Farmer perfectly. Our first dinner at Chestnut Street was an instance of a theory I've had ever since. If you can read and have a good cookbook and want to cook, you can cook.

Rich approved of the dinner. It began with cream of lobster soup, made by my grandmother's rule, written in her clear, strong black manuscript hand, and ended with apple turnovers and Vermont cheese. The turnovers were homemade — at my grandmother's. She had spoken of Rich's welfare and she had looked a little worried as she handed them to me. She need not have been troubled. With Mrs. Appleyard and Miss Farmer on the inspirational end of the job, Minnie continued to turn out some of the best meals ever served under any roof of ours. She was well worth the four dollars a week we paid her. She was delighted when I raised it to five.

"And that cook told me I didn't know nothing!" Minnie exclaimed. "But she wouldn't tell me nothing — she didn't want me learning her secrets. Secrets! I was noticing what she did all the time. Only I can't cook if I'm frightened. Now you never frighten me, ma'am. Would you like I should try a cheese soufflé for lunch? That cook made it out of The Book and I've studied it good, it might turn out all right."

Of course it was all right.

I was learning too. Fortunately about this time I read an article in the *Ladies' Home Journal* by Arnold Bennett. He said that in marriage no matter how much people love each other they always try to change each other. This is impossible — but you can change yourself. A wife, for instance, may not be able to change her husband but she can find out what she does that annoys him most and stop doing it; thus something is accomplished.

What, I wondered, do I do that irritates Rich the most? Could it perhaps be the Andrews' habit of using chairs as tables? As I glanced around the drawing room, I noticed interesting collections of objects on every chair. The piano bench was crowded too. I seemed to remember a certain politely patient look on his face when he came home and looked for a place to sit down. He was extremely neat himself. Each of his suits was on its own special hanger and had its own pair of braces attached to the trousers so the suit was always ready to put on. He wore a different suit every day. Every night he took all the things out of his pockets and laid them in the same pattern on top of his high chest of drawers. He was never late because he had mislaid something.

It did seem just barely possible that wifely untidiness might be annoying to such a husband.

"I will be neat," I vowed, "if it kills me."

It pretty nearly did.

I began work on the drawing room chairs. I removed little garments I was embroidering from three Queen Anne chairs and a pile of magazines from a Chippendale. I took paper and string I was saving off the piano bench and my hat and coat off the Martha Washington armchair. The room ceased to have that lived-in look; I had even taken the socks I planned to mend someday and the hammer and screwdriver off the piano. Now that the room was so bleak, it was obvious that I'd better dust it. Though my back was beginning to ache as if I'd been beaten, I began work.

Dust was a problem. Charles Street and Chestnut Street were not paved except for cobblestones sunk deep in mud or dust according to the weather. You could scrape mud off your boots on the handy iron foot scrapers on the front steps of the houses but, of course, it soon became dust again and was swept along the streets by the wild wind. Coal was burned all over the hill so chimneys were coated with furry soot, which was also impartially distributed by the breezes.

Minnie and I battled with these substances but our hearts were not in that type of work. At the moment we were experimenting with potted pigeons. With such a project in view, Minnie and I had been taking a rather languid interest in dust. I had removed the larger concretions of carbon from the windowsills but neither of us knew that dust can fall on a vertical surface and cling there cozily. On the afternoon when I had decided to use chairs merely as chairs, I also discovered the geophysical fact of vertical dust. Looking around the drawing room with my usually restful myopia, I became aware of something odd about the pier glass. It seemed to have words written on it.

I inspected it closely and read in Katharine's energetic script the following message: DUST! K.M.F. October 14, 1912.

This remark had been engraved by using the forefinger to clear away a thick coating of dust. As it was now the twenty-first of October, I reasoned that the remark had been there a week. Even I could figure that out. I remembered now that Katharine had called on me that afternoon and, Minnie had said, had waited awhile in case I came in.

I decided to clean the mirror. It was not much trouble to remove the inscription, which was in easy reach, but the pier glass thrust its gilded top right up to the ten foot ceiling. Determined to make myself over to please Rich, I wrapped a cloth around the hearth brush and dusted as far as I could reach. There was still a cloudy area at the top. Placing a Queen Anne chair in a strategic position, I climbed on it and went to work with sweeping strokes. The chair slipped out from under me. I hit my head only a glancing blow on the marble shelf under the mirror — just enough to knock me out briefly.

When I came to, I decided my neck was not broken. I was able to get up and make the room beautifully neat before Rich came home. How lucky that my pompadour concealed the bruise! I staggered down the twisting stairs to the basement, returned the hammer and screwdriver to their places, sampled the pigeons — they were delicious — and took piles of papers, books and sewing off the dining room chairs.

I have almost never used a chair for a table since.

Now if I had also learned not to use chairs as stepladders perhaps that bean pot would not have fallen on my head in 1959.

Oh well!

My friends all agreed that it was a wonder I hadn't lost the baby. It was the custom in those days for experienced matrons to tell expectant mothers awful stories about childbirth. By November I had little hope of surviving the experience. Several times a day, to emphasize the brevity of life, an undertaker's vehicles passed the window where I sat sewing. They came along West Cedar Street, turned down Chestnut and went on to Charles.

One of them was just an ordinary cart, only very black with a black horse. Another was a black box on wheels with doors at the

back. There was also a black hearse with nodding plumes and —
this made me cry over the small silk and wool nightgowns I was
making — once in a while a white one. These were drawn by
horses but, a modern note, there was a large, motor-driven hearse.
It carried either a black casket or a white one. I grew so used to the
sound the hearses made that I knew they were coming long before I
saw them.

I never told Rich about them. It would be hard enough for him,
I figured, when it happened. We might as well be happy while we
could.

Members of the St. Botolph Club had given us a present I am
still enjoying, a pair of bronze and gold bowls copied from some
early Greek ones. With them had come some handwritten verses
containing good advice to brides. A refrain after each verse told the
bride always, no matter what the circumstances to "Greet the old
man with a smile."

I had them framed and kept them on the bedroom mantelpiece
and read them often by the gaslight that burned there all day. By
the time Rich came home I would manage a smile. I deserved a
good mark for this, perhaps a B-, because the bedroom was almost
as depressing as the living room. It had no hearses parading by but
it was as dark as a crypt. Its only window was a narrow slit which
opened on a dark passage well furnished with ash barrels and leading to the alley. Through this passage on sunny days from eleven
to quarter past, enough sun penetrated the bedroom so you could
turn off the gas and still see.

By an odd coincidence the real estate agent had shown us the
apartment on a sunny morning at eleven o'clock. It was only after I
moved in that I realized why he had hurried us from the front hall
into the bedroom and had so carefully closed the door after we had
seen it without gaslight.

Such sunlight as penetrated glowed upon two of my few non-antiques. I had yearned to have something modern and with my savings I had bought twin brass beds with box springs and hair mattresses. They were a perfect investment of my lifetime earnings as a writer; that is, almost perfect. Jordan Marsh, a benevolent but sometimes absent-minded institution, had sent fraternal rather than identical twins. The posts of one bed were cylindrical and of the other square. In order to fit into the bedroom, they had to overlap the fireplace with its chimney piece of black marble. The effect was of a dark cavern barred by gold posts of two shapes. I think it's safe to say that you never saw anything just like it.

I was in correspondence with Jordan's for over a year before the identical twins were united. Their letters contained polite suggestions that I should pay for the beds, mine said briefly: "I will pay for this merchandise as soon as I receive what I ordered; twin beds with square posts."

I realized late in 1913 that I was foolish to have said "square" so often. When the twins became identical they had round posts. By that time I realized that Jordan's must know best what I needed.

"She doesn't," no doubt they reasoned, "want her little ones — she said she had twins, didn't she? — falling against those beds and whanging their heads on square posts. So abrasive. Round ones will be safer."

They were right. Until I reverted to curly maple and sold the brass beds to a junk dealer in Hardwick, Vermont, they injured no one. Long may they shine!

18

New Friend

MY MELANCHOLY ceased suddenly. Again the *Ladies' Home Journal* came to my rescue. This time the article was about happiness. It mentioned William James's observation: that you do not merely smile because you are happy; you are also happy because you smile. The writer added that to have a happy marriage you must begin with happiness; that happiness was as contagious as the common cold and much pleasanter. He advised all brides to take — and therefore give — happiness in massive doses.

I decided to be happy. It was a conversion. I suppose I had enough Puritan background to have accepted too easily the idea that there was something virtuous about a melancholy face; that a good wife ought to look as if she had a slight toothache. From then on, I decided, like the sundial, I would count only the sunny hours. Of course, I had set myself an impossible task but I decided it would do no harm to try. At least I stopped listening for plumed hearses.

Walking, I had been brought up to believe, was a cure for everything. I took to walking across the Common and doing my shopping in Faneuil Hall Market. This was supposed to be economical. On Charles Street eggs cost twenty-five cents a dozen. I could buy two dozen in Faneuil Hall for thirty cents.

One day having made this substantial economy, I had reached the violet-tinted windows of Beacon Street on my way home. I tripped over a protruding brick in the pavement and fell upon the eggs. Thinking myself alone, I said, "Damnation." Then, seeing polished black boots near me, I changed it to "Oh, dear."

The owner of the boots gallantly raised me and my dripping boxes. He looked as if he had been carved out of the same wood as the Sacred Cod and by the same artist. However, he was human.

He almost smiled as he said, "Better have an omelet!" lifted his derby hat and walked off to the Somerset Club, where some of the best omelets are still made.

Minnie took his advice. She added a few mushrooms she happened to have on hand and a few *fines herbes*. It was an excellent omelet.

As I crossed the Common on these forays, I used to think of pirates hanging from the Old Elm, Quakers being chased out of town and witches in various uncomfortable situations. I also remembered a less dramatic episode that took place near the Frog Pond before I was born.

Mrs. Wyndon, mother of a friend of mine, had not been born in Boston. She and her husband decided when they were first married that they would like to be Bostonians. They bought a house on Mt. Vernon Street. They soon found that being a Bostonian is not something that happens overnight. Though they often saw the same people, no one spoke to them. After some months, however, somebody's second cousin once removed mentioned Mrs. Wyndon to a friend on Louisburg Square and Mrs. Wyndon was invited to an afternoon tea.

Now, she thought, I'll meet my neighbors.

The hostess spoke kindly to her but did not introduce her to anyone else. She felt lonelier than ever in her best dress with the bustle and her bonnet trimmed with rosebuds. Still there was a bright moment at the tea table. The lady who poured the tea was friendly. They agreed that there was no tea like Lapsang Souchong and that the tiny cream puffs filled with lobster were delicious. Mrs. Wyndon had a second one and also a Delmonico wafer like a doily of bronze lace. She went home feeling happier than she had for weeks.

It had been slow, she thought, but now that she knew someone, things could never be quite so bad.

The very next morning, crossing the Common she met the lady of the tea table. They exchanged bows and smiles.

In the next mail came the following note:

> Dear Mrs. Wyndon:
>   I feel I should explain to you that when I met you on the Common this morning I mistook you for someone else. Thinking we had been introduced, I bowed and smiled. Had I recognized you, I would, of course, have bowed — but I would not have smiled.
>   Yours sincerely . . .

Except for Mrs. Wyndon's name, which I have changed, this is a true story. I am glad to report that she got to know people.

Mrs. Wyndon did not — though this seems strange — automatically like everyone she met. There was Araminta Smoot for instance. Unmarried, with plenty of money, Araminta had time to collect the gossip of the hill, embellish it with her own variations and pass it on loudly to anyone who would listen.

One day when she was walking up Chestnut Street, Mrs. Wyndon saw Araminta starting down the hill. Feeling she could not bear a dose of the Smoot mixture that day, Mrs. Wyndon hastily turned up the steps of the nearest house and took sanctuary in the vestibule.

It happened that the owner of the house, a complete stranger, was at the front door waiting for her carriage. Seeing the shadow of someone dark against a side light of the doorway, she opened the door.

All that Mrs. Wyndon could think of was the truth and she said it: "Araminta Smoot is coming down the hill."

The owner of the house said: "I understand perfectly. Come right in!"

Thus Mrs. Wyndon was not only saved from danger but she made a new friend. She was driven home to Mt. Vernon Street in the brougham just as soon as Araminta had gone safely past.

Out of morbid curiosity I would have liked to see Araminta, but she was only a memory when I lived on the hill. She had long since taken her talents to California where she found new scope for exercising them. Beacon Hill and Boston Common became as peaceful as they were when only the Indians lived there.

In December I turned my attention to our Christmas Eve open house. Minnie and I stopped potting pigeons and poaching collops of venison in vinegar and currant jelly. When I say "we," of course I mean it editorially. I understand that in joint authorship there is one writer who supplies the ideas and another who "holds the pen." Having, so far as writing is concerned, always been the pen-holder, I realize that ideas are the important thing. Getting them on paper can be done by anyone who has the time.

With Minnie I provided the really necessary thing — the inspiration. She just held the spoon or the rolling pin. I helped her by tasting things and suggesting another pinch of nutmeg. I praised her for never touching pastry except with a cold spatula and a pancake turner. I told her that hers was almost as good as my grandmother's. I spoke well of her meringues too.

It began to snow early on Christmas Eve. The punch was ready. Rich had edited it with traditional gusto. Fires burned in the drawing room and in the dining room, new candles were ready to be lighted in all our wedding present candlesticks, including those of the girandole eye-of-light. There were big bowls of holly. Gold shone on glass and china, on silver I had polished with my own hands. Sandwiches were as thin as the Declaration of Independence. Meringues were so light they almost floated off the plates. Fruitcake counteracted this levity in a solid way.

Rich and I went out early and walked around the hill. The snow gave an extra dimension of beauty to shining windows.

"It's even more beautiful than last year," Rich said.

"Yes," I agreed, "but it's lucky there wasn't any snow on that park bench. We might not even be engaged."

"Oh, you'd have given in pretty soon," he said.

I had just begun a retort to this conceited and truthful statement when I slipped on an icy spot. Rich caught me before I fell and said, "Perhaps we'd better fight it out at home."

We were soon looking down into Chestnut Street, Beneath.

"I bet someone nice lives here. Let's go in and see if they'll give us some of that punch," I said and we went down into the candlelight.

There followed one of those bleak moments when you wonder if anyone will come to the party. All the feet went on past our door and up the hill where voices were singing "Oh little town of Bethlehem." When the singers moved over to Mt. Vernon Street, we began to have our share of visitors. The punch was appreciated. Minnie's coffee-chocolate with whipped cream hit a number of the right spots for on this happy evening no one had heard of calories or cholesterol.

Someone said: "I wish I knew how to make these little lemon tarts."

Someone replied: "I'll give you the rule."

This voice sounded familiar. In fact, it bore a certain resemblance to my own. I did not realize until years later that it was really Mrs. Appleyard's.

This was the only Beacon Hill Christmas I ever spent inside, looking out. There are advantages, I know, to being a guest — no Chelsea coffee cups to wash, no punch spilled on the table, no fragments of meringues and fruitcake and lemon tarts trodden into the rug.

Still, when Minnie said the next day, "Well, it isn't much they're after leaving us!" I detected more triumph than regret in her voice. It was the true hostess-note sounding. I said, "It wouldn't have been much of a party without you, Minnie" — as indeed it would not.

We had decided already that our next Christmas would be in Brookline. I liked Chestnut Street, Beneath but not as a place to bring up a baby. The dust, the soot, the endless rumbling of carts on the Charles Street cobblestones, the icy pavements in winter, the mud of spring, the humid heat of summer did not add up to a suitable environment for our first child — that unique and sacred creature. By January we had signed a lease for 25 Waverly Street, a house flooded with sunshine and facing a green park. The task of subletting the apartment we gave to the same man who had shown it to us.

He came several times, always, I noticed, at eleven o'clock on sunny mornings. How brightly that ray of sunlight shone on the almost twin brass beds! Before long another happy couple had fallen in love with the place. They could hardly wait for us to pack up the Encyclopaedia and the china and leave the shelves to them. To oblige them we moved out on the 28th of February, 1913.

Our new house resembled the apartment in having woodwork that might have been designed by Samuel McIntire. It was really a double house built to look like one eighteenth-century mansion. Our front door and pillared porch looked as if they belonged to the whole house. Actually they led into about two thirds of it. At one side there was another front door for the other tenants.

They were a friendly couple with a parrot and two small Yorkshire terriers, to whom the parrot spoke sarcastically. They had all been there before we came. They stayed during the ten years we lived there and were such good tenants that when we sold the house we described them as our greatest asset — as they were indeed.

Another splendid feature, new and strange to me, was that the house was lighted by electricity. The bulbs, which glowed pink when they were first turned on, were supplied free by the power company. When the man came to read the meter, he brought us new lamps for old. We had no other electrical devices. Minnie, who always turned the lights on timidly, fearing electrocution, swept the floor with a broom until I had an attack of modernity and bought her a carpet sweeper.

Rich stoked the coal furnace and set out barrels of ashes for the ashmen who came, wearing dusty dark-blue coats, in dusty pale-blue carts drawn by ash-colored horses. Clothes were washed by hand or sent to the Sunshine Laundry, known to its clients as the best laundry in the world. The iceman came often, bringing in twenty-five, fifty or a hundred pounds of ice according to which way Minnie placed the ice-card in the china closet window.

I had invested some of our wedding present money in aquatint engravings from Audubon's elephant folio. I could not afford the large birds — the wild turkey or the birds of prey — but luckily it was the smaller birds I liked — warblers, the chipping sparrow, the yellow-throated vireo. These cost about four dollars apiece. In a moment of extravagance I paid ten dollars for the forktailed fly-catcher and the blue jays. By the time I had hung them against the wall of silvery-gray grass cloth, it was time to have the baby.

I plan to be reticent about this fascinating experience. I have noticed that when two or three women are gathered together, each enjoys telling about the birth of each of her children. Each politely waits her turn even when the first speaker has six children. I have noticed also that no one really listens to the others. Token listening is done by each, but only as a sort of down payment on her turn to speak.

Moreover, on each of the three occasions I had a baby, I was assured by the doctor, a fine competent man, that my whole pregnancy and its conclusion had been normal and easy so why should I mention it? Of course, I realized he must know all about it but I did wish he'd try it himself — just once.

The only person who seemed at all upset by Elizabeth Kent's arrival was Minnie. Just as the doctor announced in a disappointed tone, "It's a girl," Minnie fainted in the front hall. Rich heard her shriek — the only shriek uttered that day as I was having this easy time — and caught her as she fell. He called for the doctor who, seeing that all was normal upstairs, went down and revived her.

While he was busy, the nurse brought Elizabeth in, all neatly dressed, to entertain me. I began to laugh as soon as I saw her. She looked like a determined poet with her head bald on top but with a long fringe of silky black fur that hung down over the collar of her nightgown. Her eyes wandered around the room as if she were sizing up the accommodations. On the whole she looked pleased. I felt that we might enjoy each other's society; in fact, I swiftly acquired a taste for hers and have never lost it.

Minnie finally revived and went back to washing the breakfast dishes. The doctor said Elizabeth was a fine specimen and went away — to collect others, I suppose. Rich came up to see us. I told him she was the most comical thing I had ever seen. By this time she was in her bassinet in the next room. The nurse introduced him to her.

"*I* think she's very pretty," Rich told me in a slightly reproachful tone.

He then went off to help edit *The Youth's Companion* and I went to sleep. I never had a sleep I enjoyed more.

I understand that it is now modern to have babies at home rather than in hospitals. I heartily recommend it. Rich could drop in any time and sit down comfortably on the foot of my bed, holding the baby. The neighbors brought in delicious things to eat and flowers from their gardens. Elizabeth's birthday was April 28. Forsythia, early tulips and daffodils came to welcome her. Life was a sort of perpetual party.

The only shadow was cast by Minnie. It seems she did not like babies. Not like babies? Not like Elizabeth, one of the most remarkable ever born? It hardly seemed possible, yet such was the case.

"I'll stay till you're settled, ma'am," Minnie said. "But you know, ma'am, it's a cook I want to be. They tell me I can get maybe eight or nine a week with all I know now. And soon have a kitchen maid under me, peeling carrots and such. And thank you, ma'am, for all you taught me."

So farewell, Minnie! Good-bye, lobster soup and cream puffs filled with caviar. Au revoir, lemon soufflé and guinea fowl with bread sauce. So long, mixed grill with mushrooms and bacon and chicken livers and welcome — with moderate rapture — celery in flourpaste sauce and strawberry jello. Welcome, solid, chilly mashed potato and overdone chops. Welcome, in fact, standard Boston cooking, including chunks of haddock dipped in corn meal and fried almost enough. And welcome, thrice welcome, Mary O'Brien who thinks Elizabeth is the cutest thing she ever saw.

19

Wishing Stone

IN NO TIME AT ALL it seemed as if we had always lived on Waverly Street. Every sunny morning Mary O'Brien pushed the big English carriage containing our treasure onto the side porch. From the dining room windows we could see just what Elizabeth was doing. Sometimes she was asleep. Sometimes she was waving her fists. She was soon skillful at kicking off unwanted blankets and looking at her toes. Each day was marked by new accomplishments. Early in June she began to try to catch one hand with the other; she soon succeeded. She was less than two months old when she turned over and around, appearing with triumphant chuckles with her head toward the foot of the carriage. It was generally agreed that she was very remarkable.

By a strange coincidence all the mothers I knew in the neighborhood had extraordinarily bright children — something about the air, perhaps. Grace and Ted Defriez lived halfway up the street. Their daughter Polly was about two years old. She already spoke clearly and wittily. Leila Page was staying with her family, the Tuckermans, in the big double house near the corner of Cypress Street. Her daughter Cary had been born a few weeks before Elizabeth. Cary was beautiful as well as bright, a blue-eyed, fair-haired baby with Leila's lovely pink cheeks.

Across the park lived Burton Powers, the son of our family doctor. At two years old, he had blond curls and an intelligent and kindly, though slightly skeptical way of surveying the world from the stroller in which his mother pushed him around the park. I decided early that he was going to be something special. However it was some years before I invited him to be my lawyer.

I was determined to be a good mother. I soon made my first failure in this line of work. After a few weeks of Elizabeth's life, I could no longer nurse her. An impressive specialist came and put her on a formula. I asked him about pasteurized milk, but he frowned upon it. Freshness was important, he said, and heat destroyed it. I bought milk fresh and raw from a special farm at a special price. I sterilized everything — except the milk — and fed Elizabeth the resulting mixture, fresh and full of interesting bacteria. She soon became extremely ill with colitis. The doctor came often, shook his head and prescribed frequent doses of castor oil. This treatment is so medieval that I feel as if I must be making up the whole thing — but I'm not.

When cold weather came, the expensive germs I had been buying became less powerful, I suppose, because things went fairly well through the winter. By April the cycle began again. At birth Elizabeth had weighed eight pounds. On her first birthday she weighed ten. She looked like an Indian famine sufferer. All the other year-old babies I knew were beginning to walk. She had barely strength to crawl. It was common in those days for children not to survive their second summer. I remember the frightening intonation with which older women used the phrase.

Two things helped her survive it. One was her natural toughness. Life, on any terms, interested her. Though she could not walk, she could already talk. Her conversation was fascinating — to her mother anyway. However she needed more than her native vitality. It was Grace Defriez who made the suggestion that helped the most.

Grace went to Nahant in the summer. She and her friend Lily
Fay decided that I should go too. They said there was a remarkable
young doctor there who had helped children through their second
summers. The clean sea air would be good for the baby. Rich
would like going back and forth between Boston and Nahant on
the boat; all the men did. Lily found a cottage on Valley Road that
would be big enough for us and — since it was on the unfashion-
able side of Cold Roast Boston — not expensive. We went there in
June of 1914.

The second day we were there, Dr. McKissock came to see Elizabeth. She was fed only on the diet the specialist had given her —
the best fresh raw milk and white bread.

"Poison," said Dr. McKissock. "Pure poison! We'll soon have
her out of that. She'll get Vitalait and whole wheat bread and vegetables."

He had taken her in his arms and was walking up and down
talking to her. She was crowing and laughing and grabbing his
hair while he told me about Vitalait.

"It's a culture of good bacteria," he said, "grown in pasteurized
milk. It's really yoghurt. The stuff that makes Bulgarians live to be
a hundred years old. I'll go and get you a culture right now and
show you how to make it. I'll order yours for you. It will come
three times a week. That will make plenty for Elizabeth and some
left over for you. Now you start with pasteurized milk —"

I asked him if it was true that pasteurizing spoiled the freshness
of milk. He said it did but that we'd make up for it by giving
her orange juice and a varied diet just as soon as the colitis was
cured.

The change was extraordinary. It began to show after only a few
days. All I had up to that time was the framework for a child.
Flesh began to grow on it. Her muscles strengthened. She began
to pull herself up in her pen and take steps holding onto the side.
The first time I saw her do it, I sat there crying tears of complete

happiness. I had not let myself know how dark the cloud was until I saw it lighten.

Mary O'Brien loved to wheel Elizabeth out in her basket-work stroller. She would admire the flowers in the gardens they passed.

She would say, "Pretty flower!" chuckle and hold her hand out, squinching up her eyes and taking long breaths as if she were inhaling delicious fragrance. The owners of the gardens would put flowers into her hand. She and Mary often returned from their walk with a well selected bouquet.

☆

As the July days of 1914 went by, war seemed to hang over France and England. Not over America, of course. We were safe with the Atlantic Ocean between us.

The last few days of peace were far from peaceful on Valley Road. Our neighbors next door bought a phonograph, the kind with an enormous trumpet shaped like a morning glory, and a collection of records. Out of patriotism, I suppose, they played nothing foreign — no arias by Caruso, no songs of Schubert's. The noise was all genuinely American — "Yankee Doodle," "Tar Ra Ra Boom De Re," "The Stars and Stripes Forever," "Alexander's Ragtime Band." The records were changed with commendable agility. There was scarcely a moment of silence.

Yet one August afternoon the music ceased briefly.

A man came running along Valley Road with a bunch of newspapers in his hand. He ran across our lawn to the house next door, leaped over the railing upsetting the phonograph. As it ground to a screaming stop, he shouted, "War! War!"

For a moment I felt that the world as I knew it had come to an end. Just at that moment an extra big wave dashed up the beach across the road. As it receded, so did my instant of truth. After all, I thought, the ocean is still there.

When we got back to Brookline, we all had something especially wicked in the line of a malady called the Spanish influenza. Just before Elizabeth had it she had seemed ready to take her first steps alone but I realized the fever had made her too weak for walking. At last she was well again. I took her out one morning into the September sunshine, leaving her sitting on the front steps while I went to get her stroller. When I came back she was gone. She was not walking up the street, she was running. I had to run to catch her. She has — as we say disapprovingly in Vermont — "liked to go" ever since. I share this frivolous taste, especially in her company.

Autumn saw a change in our family. Mary O'Brien married and went to live in Baltimore. We shopped together for her wedding present. She chose a Sheffield tea set, one of the last to come out of England at that time. I wish I could find one like it now.

Fanny Campbell from Nova Scotia was Mary's successor. She cooked better — when she felt like it — than Mary did. She dusted with more energy — if she dusted at all. I do not mean to imply anything derogatory to Nova Scotia when I say that Fanny came from there. She was unusual in Brookline and no doubt in Nova Scotia too. Her home life seemed complicated. She had told me she was a widow so I was surprised when she introduced a sandy-haired, freckled, young man to me as her husband. He was going to spend the weekend, she said.

"But I thought you were a widow," I said.

"A grass widow," Fanny said impatiently. "Charlie is just off his ship. We've made it up."

Charlie's ship made short voyages. He spent several weekends with us. The food was always excellent while he was there. During the week we had a good deal of lukewarm minced lamb with scorched beets but nothing was too good for Charlie. We were allowed to share ham mousse with mustard sauce and well broiled steaks with him. Marketing was easy. Rhodes Brothers, three blocks away, delivered orders four times daily. If Fanny forgot a yeast cake or thought Charlie would like a few chops for supper, she just told the driver and he delivered whatever she needed on his next trip.

Fanny had two brothers who also made our house their home when they visited Boston. Neither looked at all like her. She was a spare, erect, quick-moving woman with sharp blue eyes, a sharp nose that would have looked well on the figurehead of a ship, a sharp chin and salmon-colored skin. Her hair hung in tawny wisps. She had several white teeth and some gold ones over which she snapped her mouth tightly shut when she finished speaking. She spoke a great deal, giving me good advice.

She loved Elizabeth. She said Elizabeth was the image of a baby she had lost. She also spoke well of Rich, alleging that he was a lovely gentleman, but she was not pleased when his mother dropped in to breakfast one November morning.

"Mark my words, there'll be trouble — she's planning to spend the winter," Fanny said darkly.

"No. It's just for a few days," I said.

I was wrong. Mrs. Kent did spend the winter.

Fanny, however, did not.

For a while after Mrs. Kent's arrival, neither Charlie nor either of Fanny's brothers visited us. When they began to come again, just before Christmas, Mrs. Kent took a strange view of this happy family. She did not think Fanny was married to Charlie and she thought the brothers were not related to Fanny at all. She had acquired this opinion while teaching Fanny to make sour cream johnnycake. She spoke as if this dish, a special favorite of Rich's, acted as a sort of talisman, conferring clairvoyance upon the eaters.

Rich — perhaps because he had just eaten two pieces of johnnycake with plenty of maple syrup — said that he too was uneasy about Fanny's visitors. He and his mother both thought that I had better tell Fanny to go. Neither was at all nervous — as I said I was — about breaking the news to her but they made it clear that she who hires, fires.

Luckily Fanny herself increased my meager supply of courage.

Our set of blue Minton china was supposed to be used only for company. As I had explained to Fanny when she came, we used the blue Canton for everyday since, if any were broken, I could easily replace it at Hatch's where my mother and grandmother had always bought theirs. In the kitchen pantry there was also plenty of English willow pattern but neither this nor the Canton was good enough for Fanny's company. She always served them on the Minton.

My natural cowardice made it impossible for me to speak harshly about this to Fanny. I did just mention it a few times. Fanny broke something everytime I did so. She was still serving Charlie delicious meals on blue Minton between Christmas and New Year's. I had told Rich and his mother that I couldn't possibly turn Fanny out into the snow during the holiday season. They agreed to this postponement.

"But after New Year's," they said.

It was January 3. Bert, one of Fanny's brothers, was leaving after his New Year's visit. I came into the kitchen to make yoghurt and found the sink piled high with Minton. The big soup tureen was there, also soup plates, dinner plates and the extra-large coffee cups. There were frying pans and saucepans in the sink too.

Fanny was beating up eggs for a sponge cake.

I said, "Fanny, I'm afraid that you've forgotten that I asked you not to use the Minton in the kitchen."

Fanny replied, "Yeah, so you did — and this eggbeater ain't no good."

She threw it and the bowl across the kitchen. They landed in the sink, breaking every piece of china in it.

As the sound of the crash died away, I heard my own voice saying, "I'm sorry, Fanny, I'll have to give you a week's notice."

"That's what you think, kid," announced Fanny, taking off her apron. "You can wash these (obscene) dishes in your own (obscene) sink. Bert! Bert — wait! I'm going with you. Come up and help me with my bags."

Within half an hour she had departed, wearing a dress, coat and hat I had given her. They looked, I thought, as I shoveled the Minton into the trash can, much better on her than they did on me. I felt strangely lighthearted. I had fired Fanny and there couldn't be more than a hundred dollars' worth of Minton in the sink. I would soon save that just by not buying steak for Fanny's family. I'd order the china from Plummer's in New York. It cost only fifty dollars but that did not include the tureen. For that, Plummer said, I would have to wait till after the war.

I'm still waiting.

In the meantime I acquired a new maid, some lemon queen cakes and a dozen clover leaf rolls from the Woman's Exchange. Theresa Fallon was the maid's name. She was neat, cross, careful with china and a poor cook. You can't, I realized, expect perfection for six dollars a week — nor for sixty either, I understand, from my friends who are lucky enough to have their green beans scorched for them, instead of doing it themselves.

"And Theresa," I pointed out to Rich who had mentioned that he preferred uncarbonized beans, "is undoubtedly respectable. I'm sure she'll never make this house into what your mother called it."

"True," said Rich, "and besides we'll never have to eat antigonish salad again."

This dish — a concoction of gelatine, fruit, marshmallows and whipped cream — had been a favorite of Bert's. Fanny had often made it for him. Rich used a derogatory term for it — feminine food, he called it.

Luckily I did not have to think much about Fanny anymore. I had a new interest. Some months earlier I had been up to Walnut Street and visited the Wishing Stone. I had found the small square of ruby-colored stone in the wall of pudding stone. According to ritual, I had licked my thumb, pressed it against the wishing stone, shut my eyes, breathed deeply and wished hard for my son, Hollister.

He arrived on March 1, 1916 after another normal, easy birth. The doctor got there almost two minutes before the baby did. According to the nurse's directions, I was giving myself ether when the anesthetist arrived.

He said, "I found the door open and Doc's hat on the floor and his coat on the stairs so I thought it was all right to come up."

He did not give me any ether but I was glad to pay his bill. I had realized by the tone in which the doctor had exclaimed, "Well! We've got a boy for you!" that expense must not be spared.

He's been well worth it.

20

Montessori Mother

ALONG WITH MY SON, I had acquired two beautiful quilts. After the first day I was calling him Sam. Rich had given me a choice of names for him: either Samuel Dwight Hollister Kent or Hollister Kent. The first seemed ponderous for such a small item — he weighed only six pounds and soon not much over four — so I decided on Hollister. That seemed formal so he became Sam. As a result people have often thought we had two sons. Samuel and Hollister both used to get invitations to débutante parties.

Rich had given his mother and me a book telling how to make the quilts.

I said as soon as I saw it: "Oh, I'd like to do that!" and Mrs. Kent imprudently told me, "I'll quilt all you patch."

In no time at all we were busy on Rosebud for Elizabeth and Rose of LeMoyne for me. We both worked on them every day and when Mrs. Kent left for Vermont in April, she took them with her. They came back beautifully quilted in an amazingly short time.

I had seen the quilting room on the third floor of the White House. It was really two bedrooms. LeRoy Kent had had most of the wall between them removed so his wife could set up her quilting frame and have plenty of room to walk around it. I still have the patterns she used. I had planned to learn how to quilt but I had been discouraged by hearing that you had to prick the forefinger of your left hand at every stitch to be sure the needle had gone through all the layers of material. Old quilts often have small blood stains on them, Mrs. Kent said, and the maker's left forefinger is rough and often raw. I gave up the idea and started crocheting a necktie for Rich. Heroically, he wore it several times.

Since I had learned about pasteurized milk, we were able to spend the summer of 1915 in Brookline. Dr. Richard Smith, Boston's best pediatrician (this is not just my opinion and don't try to pick a fight with me about it) put Sam on a sensible formula and things went well. Rich had a box, really a small porch, built outside a window of his upstairs study. It held Sam's basket nicely and took in the morning sun through its screened top and sides. An awning could be lowered to keep out rain. As Sam grew bigger we substituted a mattress that covered the bottom of the box for the basket. It gave him plenty of room to roll around. All day — and often at night too — he lived in fresh air. I used to attribute his easy disposition to The Box and I have read long scientific articles that proved I was right. I am inclined to think now that it was as natural as his curly hair. Fortunately it did not disappear when the hair did.

By midsummer Elizabeth had developed enough mobility so that she ran away for the first time. I chased her around the block, catching up with her near the Public Library. She was already starting to read. Perhaps the library was a natural goal for a literate two-and-a-quarter-year-old. I was so glad to see her that I forgot to reproach her. We had a policeman on our block. She regarded him as her personal property and spoke accurately of him as "my fat policeman." He used to bring her home when he noticed that she had run away again.

One evening when the robins kept her awake, she crept down the back stairs and got safely through the kitchen. Theresa, an excellent waitress, was passing the overcooked peas, soggy potatoes and well-toughened veal chops. Some small sound aroused my maternal instinct. I caught the runaway just as she was squeezing through a gap in the picket fence. I carried her screaming back to bed.

Perhaps it was Theresa's cooking that made Rich say, "That child ought to be spanked."

"Go ahead," I told him.

He said that spanking was not his business. Apparently he considered it like balancing checkbooks — suitable for women — so I went upstairs and began spanking her. At first I was rather incompetent and disliked the exercise but as I warmed to my work, I found I was rather enjoying it.

I stopped in mid-air, thinking that cruelty, like anything else, improves with practice. I doubt if this makes her better, I thought — I just know it makes me worse.

I discarded spanking as a sport. I had just read a book about Montessori and that morning I had bought the Montessori teaching material. Either a challenging intellectual life or the spanking made Elizabeth stop running away. The Montessori equipment was certainly ingenious. To help a child learn to dress himself there were frames with two pieces of cloth on each. On one piece of the cloth were buttons and on the other were buttonholes. The buttons varied in size on the different frames. Elizabeth did the big ones at the first try and was soon doing small ones as fast as I could.

Another frame had a row of hooks and eyes. There was also one with eyelets and shoestrings. You never told a Montessori child to use any of the apparatus. You used it yourself quietly in his presence. If he showed no interest, you put it away. Someday he would get interested and start work.

Buttons and shoelaces were more plentiful on children's clothes than they are now. Elizabeth not only buttoned things quickly but she tied her shoelaces correctly. I suppose she must have seen Rich do it. Neither of them taught me. When I was almost fifty years old, I was still tying the bows of my shoelaces so that they ran parallel to my feet rather than at right angles to them. My friend Margaret Wight's son, Delano, noticed this peculiarity and patiently taught me to tie a proper bow knot. He did not, however, teach me to join two pieces of string with a square knot. I had to wait for a second world war and training as an air raid warden to learn that.

Elizabeth did not know she was learning to write by the Montessori method. She thought she was playing with cases of wooden cylinders. There were three cases each containing ten cylinders. In one case the cylinders varied in diameter, in the second in height, in the third in both. You never told a child what to do with them. You picked up a cylinder, ran your fingers around it and around various holes until you found the right one. Then you dropped it in. The free flowing motion was the first step in writing. You never mentioned the connection to the child.

Elizabeth learned to match cylinders and holes faster than I could. She would dump out all thirty cylinders on the dining room table, at which she sat in her mahogany high chair, and put them back in place with uncanny swiftness. Another part of the writing process was an alphabet of sandpaper script letters of heavy cardboard. These we matched in the same way we did the cylinders — by running our fingers over them.

In their own time, Montessori said, the child will explode into writing.

Elizabeth did not hurry, possibly because she had been clandestinely learning to read. Her method was to make me read Stevenson's *A Child's Garden of Verse* to her until she knew it by heart. After that she would sit down, look at the book and recite the verses. Next she began on the activities of two children called Peter and Polly. She was soon reading anything she got her hands on.

My chief problem was to get her not to read. This was a losing battle, especially at night. In the daytime I could at least take her out to the park where she played tag or ran in circles with other children or turned handsprings in the white clover. At night she quickly learned that, if she turned her light on, I would discover it. She adopted other methods of illumination — a flashlight under the bed clothes, the large arc light across the street, moonlight. About a generation too late I decided that reading addicts had better have a good reading lamp beside their beds and use it.

I had a night out every week and I used it for work at the Boston Simmons Club of which I had become president. The Society for the Preservation of New England Antiquities had recently moved into the Harrison Gray Otis house. This handsome eighteenth-century mansion had been used as a lodging house. The beautiful rooms had been divided up into cubicles for immigrants. Now it was being done over under the direction of William Summer Appleton. A suite of rooms on the third floor had been cleaned up and these were leased by the Simmons Club.

As I had to spend most evenings with the children, I took my war work home with me and turned it in once a week. What I did during the winter of 1915–1916, was to pick oakum.

Before the days of antibiotics, pads full of oakum were considered good for large open wounds. I began work by picking fragments of tarred rope to pieces and then to smaller pieces and then to soft tarry fluff. This work I had often read about. It was usually done not by average Simmons graduates but by convicts. My output, I believe, compared favorably with that of the less deft criminals. Picking oakum is really suited to hands more rugged than mine, and then I don't imagine many convicts are distracted from their work by being Montessori mothers.

The oakum was as hard as old pemmican or dried maple chips. Yet with determination and a strong nail file, it was possible to pry it into small chunks and then to pull it back into the original rope fibers. Certain hard bits of tar had to be discarded and after a while

I would have a mass of fibers with no uncomfortable angular pieces. I would then enclose the oakum in cheesecloth to make a pad perhaps six by eight inches in size. These pads were distributed at first by Dr. Harvey Cushing's organization. There were enough tarry-smelling, brown-fingered oakum pickers around Boston so that a good many pads were turned out.

The summer of 1917 we went to Peterborough, New Hampshire. Rich drove us there in our first car, a second-hand Dodge touring car. He came for his vacation and also for most weekends, making daring drives sixty miles long. We lived in a converted barn, which looked out over fields and woods to Monadnock's classic profile. We had ten acres of land but the barn was within a few feet of the road.

Our favorite neighbors were the Batchelders, who lived across the brook at the bottom of the hill in a beautiful old house under great arching elms. The house was full of eighteenth- and early nineteenth-century furniture, china and glass. Mr. Batchelder was a naturalist. His finely pressed and mounted specimens of plants reminded me of the comparatively clumsy work I did as a child at Iron Bound. The Batchelders' warm hospitality reminded me of Iron Bound too. The island, the life there, my years in my tower room were all especially clear in my mind that summer. My grandmother had died not long before in her ninety-second year.

She entertained her club, known as the Elderblow because you had to be a grandmother or great-aunt to belong, a few days before her death. She helped to arrange the tea table with the sixty Minton cups she kept for such occasions. Most of the refreshments came from the Woman's Exchange, but she still enjoyed baking things herself so there were small tarts of her puff paste and fluted oblongs of spiced hard sugar gingerbread.

She wore her cap of rose-point lace with its black velvet bow and her heaviest black silk dress, trimmed with jet and white lace. Her hair still waved and curled. Her handshake was warm and strong.

The resemblance my grandfather had seen when he bought the bust of Clytie was still there, I noticed, as I saw the bust at the end of the library. She was not especially tired when the party was over. Sunday she walked across the street to church. Monday, when I came to see her, I told her about a young man, grandson of a friend of hers. He had shown me a picture of an extraordinary suspension bridge on which he was working. He said I might drive around New York someday using it. It would be finished before long.

My grandmother said: "I've just thought of something strange. That bridge had reality before it was ever built. It existed before it existed. The idea is as real as the bridge itself or there would be no bridge there."

Many years later one of my children, looking at the George Washington Bridge, asked, "What keeps the bridge up?"

I thought of my grandmother.

"The idea," I said.

When I came to see her the next day, she was in bed, propped up against her pillows. The doctor had been to see her and he had sent a nurse who had just come.

My grandmother was speaking to Aunty about some pies. There were, she said, two mince pies and an apple pie she had made yesterday in the cold room. One of the mince pies could be served for dessert for the family. The other she wanted to send to her friend Miss Jones. Dr. Sabine liked her apple pie so she would like to send that one to him.

"For these hands," she said, looking down at them and folding them, "will make no more pies."

I delivered the pies. When I came back, she had gone.

Of the many letters written about her, Mrs. Sabine's, I thought, best expressed my grandmother's personality.

"I shall always miss," she wrote, "the serene presence across the way."

So, I knew, would I.

21

Thunder

THAT SUMMER OF 1917 there was, of course, a great deal of talk about war. Oddly, it seemed closer in Peterborough than it had in Brookline. There was talk of German spies and of strange lights among the hills; signals to and from submarines, outside Portsmouth, was a popular explanation of them. I had the uninteresting idea that they were automobile headlights showing before they actually mounted the hills on the up and down roads.

Some of my neighbors regarded the very large number of thunderstorms that summer as German work. The man who sold us milk seemed to feel that the Germans produced the storms in order to upset his cows. When I asked him how they managed it, he replied: "You don't suppose the Kaiser would give away the secret, do you?" and then added, "What are you, anyway, pro-German?"

I told him I was not; that I was half English and that one of my English cousins had been killed fighting in France. I'm not at all sure he believed me.

It is perhaps not strange that I found the Batchelders' conversation more congenial. Its content was wonderfully varied. It might start with the peculiarities of fringed gentians and travel, by paths as mysterious as submarine signal lights, to the time British soldiers moved into the Boston house of one of Mr. Batchelder's ancestors at the time of the Revolution. The piece of furniture most cherished by the Batchelders had belonged to this great-grandfather whose name was Foster. It was a secretary desk made in Chippendale's workshop; its dark mahogany was carved with such effortless skill that it seemed as if it must have grown into that shape in some tropical forest. The heavy brasses might have been made by a jeweler. It also had something I had not seen before and have never seen on another piece of furniture. The feet of this secretary, instead of being like the feet of lions, were shaggy bears' paws, strong enough to support the biggest of grizzlies.

Mr. Foster had only a short time in his house before the British officers took it over. He spent part of it in pulling one of the drawers out of the highboy and, with a sharp piece of chalk, writing his name on the underside of it. When the British left Boston rather hurriedly and Mr. Foster came back to his house, the highboy was gone. It had been moved, as I remember it, to the customs house, and the new officials — good Americans — did not wish to part with it.

"How do we know it's yours?" one of them asked.

Mr. Foster signed his name on a piece of paper and handed it to the officer saying, "If you pull out that drawer and turn it over, you'll find my signature on the bottom of it."

It must have taken a sturdy yoke of oxen to carry it back to his house.

I once borrowed the highboy but it was not heavy to carry. With no trouble at all I transported it to the banks of the Connecticut River and put it into a book I was writing called *The Terrace*. Writers have lots of fun.

Mrs. Batchelder used to come to tea with me in my red barn. The architect who made it into a house had been very clever. A big fieldstone chimney, which carried off smoke from two fireplaces and the kitchen stove, was in the center of the barn. Balconies built along two sides contained bedrooms on the second and third floors.

There was a cozy dining room under one of the balconies. The living room ran all the way up to the barn roof. It looked out on Monadnock. You could see the weather being made there and know it would come across country to you later.

I enjoyed the high airy living room in the daytime. In the evenings, as I sat there alone, I sometimes wished it were not quite so picturesque with its exposed beams, its roof that disappeared into the darkness above the single hanging electric light, the odd noises in the shadowy corners. It was soon after I turned on the light that the rats would come back from their day's work, eating grain in unconverted barns. Though there was no grain in my barn, they were still loyal to the old homestead. They always followed the same course — through the dining room, up the wall by a post to a beam eight feet above the living room floor, along the beam on the south side to the east balcony, up a post to the third floor to spend the night in the storeroom.

Every night I too followed the same course. I kept my riding crop beside me. As soon as I heard the first claw scratches, I would jump up, crop in hand, and chase each rat — there were only two, old bachelors, I think — along the beam. Sometimes I succeeded in touching one with the loop of my crop but I never turned one back. They were much too smart for me. I think they rather enjoyed the sport.

I told Mr. Batchelder about them. The rats I knew in Brookline were gray. These were black. Were they a different kind I asked?

Indeed yes, he said. They were descendants of old Anglo-Saxon rats that had come over on the *Mayflower* and other sailing ships from England. At first these old aristocrats stayed along the seacoast but later, as parvenu, plebeian gray rats came in from European ports, the black rats retreated to the country.

I was pleased, of course, to realize that I was entertaining only the elite among rats; at least, I was pleased until I was asked to a luncheon party so fashionable that I decided to wear my best hat. I had put this treasure carefully away in its own big hatbox in the third floor closet. My riding boots were there too and also the white linen and lace dress I planned to wear.

The hat was bright red, wide brimmed with a domed crown covered with shining red cherries and green leaves. That is, it was when I put it away. In the meantime the box had been gnawed through by the descendants of *Mayflower* passengers. The outside of the cherries must have been delicious, not a trace remained. On each stalk was only a wisp of the cotton with which the cherries had been stuffed. The riding boots had been gnawed too, but I had not meant to wear them. Unfortunately the lace dress had not escaped attention. Certain threads that held the broad bands of lace together had proved nourishing. I went to the party in my blue and white foulard silk and a blue sailor hat.

The tennis racket that I kept beside my chair in the evenings was for the bats. They came out soon after the rats had been chased up to their third-floor cafeteria. At first the bats — I don't know whether they were Anglo-Saxon or not — would fly in the darkness near the roof of the barn, but as the shadows deepened, they would swoop closer and closer to the light. I would be ready for them with my tennis racket. I rather prided myself on my record. I quite often hit one to the ground and one evening I got both. I wore gloves for this sport so I could pick them up and put them outdoors. Of course, they were always back the next night. Just how they got in I don't know, but as once, at Kents' Corner, I saw a bat flatten itself to just the right thickness and go into my bedroom between the closed door and the threshold, I assume they had little trouble.

At the luncheon someone said, "I hear you live in a converted barn."

"Yes," I said, "converted — but not enough."

That summer was the only time I ever read the complete works of Jane Austen with gloves on. At first I used to take them off when I turned the pages but by September I was quite deft at doing it in gloves. It makes a sound unpleasant but not disagreeable when compared to the squeak of bats and the slithering of rats along rough-hewn beams. I always read Jane Austen during wars. Her complete lack of interest in Napoleon's activities has a soothingly insulating effect.

I needed relaxing reading that summer because of the thunderstorms as well as because war seemed coming nearer. Theresa was afraid of thunderstorms. She began to moan and mutter and scorch beets and carrots as soon as lightning began to play around Monadnock.

The only way I could control Theresa's hysterics was by telling her that if she promised not to shriek at every thunderclap, I would let her hold Sam and would myself cut the green beans we were canning. This system worked well. Sam loved the thunder. At every crash he crowed joyfully and bounced in Theresa's lap. The louder it roared, the higher he bounced.

By evening, when Rich arrived, I had had all the lightning I cared for. In fact I was just as frightened as Theresa only less truthful. Having awarded Sam to her I not only had to can beans, I also had to serve them for supper with roast chicken and bread sauce.

Rich praised me. He said he never knew I could cook.

"Neither did I," I admitted.

"How did you manage it?"

"Why," I said, "I just did the things I used to tell Minnie to do."

"Don't you ever tell Theresa?" he asked.

"Yes, but she knows better — better than to bother, that is."

Rich asked thoughtfully, "How would you like a job on the *Companion*, testing receipts? The food editor is retiring. I'll recommend you if you like."

"What will you say — that if I can cook it, anyone can?"

Rich thought this over and edited it.

"I will say that if my wife, with her somewhat limited experience, can follow the *Companion*'s prescriptions for sound American cooking, the subscribers should have no difficulty in producing interesting meals."

☆

When I came back from Peterborough in 1917, I joined Herbert Hoover's Food Conservation Administration. I carried on my duties in one of the coldest houses I have ever lived in. It was often twenty below zero, which feels as cold in Brookline as forty below does in Vermont. Coal was scarce. Once we were down to a few shovelsful when the cart arrived with half a ton. We had ordered five.

We had some firewood, old chestnut trees that had died on our land in South Brookline near Lost Pond. I used to build a fire in the living room, set trivets around it, hastily carry food in through the frosty dining room and keep it lukewarm near the fire. We ate it sitting as close to the fire as we could get.

The kitchen was physically comfortable because of its stoves — one coal, one gas — but no room containing Theresa could be described as comfortable. It was bad enough to have to test receipts for *The Youth's Companion* in her company.

A good many of those submitted at this time involved whale meat. Whale meat — the adviser would say — is like steak. The proper place for such steaks, I soon decided, is in *Moby Dick;* read about it, don't eat it. If you like steak flavored with fish, just cook mackerel along with your steak or marinate it in cod liver oil. It would then be like whale meat only not so tough.

Luckily there was a good Pennsylvania cook who sent in a rule for scrapple about this time. To escape from the sperm oil prob-

lems and deal with a pig's head was a real pleasure. Theresa
scowled less for several days as she cooked scrapple for breakfast.

There was no real rationing under Mr. Hoover's food program.
Saving food for our soldiers and for our allies was voluntary. On
the whole, the Hoover plan worked about as well as the strict rationing system of World War II. In both wars selfish people
hoarded food. In the second war, ration books were stolen and
foodsellers were bribed to forget about coupons. The same kind of
people went without things. The same kind had all they wanted.

Wheat flour was the scarcest thing in the first war. If you bought
five pounds of it you had to take rye flour, corn meal or barley flour
with it. Some of the worst bread I have ever eaten was baked in my
kitchen out of these ingredients. As one of Mr. Hoover's food ad-
ministrators, I was supposed to go and show my clients how to
make something delicious out of them. I did make fairly edible
things of rye flour and corn meal but I never learned to cope successfully with barley. Yes, I know you can make barley gruel but
you have to be an invalid to be meek enough to eat much of it.
There's always barley cream but it implies cream. We Hooverites
denied ourselves cream so it could be churned into butter and sent
to England.

It was depressing to get letters from our English friends telling
what they thought of the butter. Any extra space they filled with
remarks about American bacon. It was as if a bride, writing thank-
you notes, should tell what she really thinks of the wedding
presents.

Our table never saw bacon. The small amount of butter we had
was used for the children — and of course by Theresa. She made it
clear from the first that she was in no mood to help the British.

My territory, as outlined by the Food Administration, ran around
Emerson Park, included part of Davis Avenue, Waverly Street,
Thayer Street and a block on Washington Street. I visited about

forty families. Most of the women read the leaflets conscientiously and did their best to follow them. I felt foolish when experienced housekeepers twice my age asked my advice about cooking whale meat.

I used to say, "I haven't had much luck broiling it. Mostly I make it into a stew with onions and carrots and spice."

"My husband doesn't care for stew," the ladies often stated.

My husband did not care for whale meat stew either but I did not like to admit it. There was something about that Moby Dick flavor that pinches of allspice and cayenne and hints of garlic did not extinguish. Simmering it all day with gourmet flavoring made it just possible to chew and swallow it — if you thought hard about the war effort.

I had trouble with one lady who always gave her husband two thick pork chops for breakfast. Mr. Hoover's suggestion of some nice scrambled eggs and barley muffins merely aroused a scornful "Ha! Ha!"

I suggested scrapple and gave a blow by blow description of how to make it.

She listened politely but, as I paused for breath, she said, "Mrs. Kent, I guess I haven't made things clear: my husband is a man who appreciates his stomach."

Food became more and more of a problem as the spring of 1918 came along. I worked harder than ever with my clients. My stomach ached so sharply that I slept very little. When I dozed off after one of the children had called me, I would wake again suddenly, thinking I heard furniture being dragged around in the attic or boards creaking under stealthy footsteps. It sounded as if Bert might be visiting us, but one thing I could say for Theresa — she had no relatives.

I went on testing receipts for the *Companion*. For this purpose I had been able to buy a large bag of white flour. I had asked Theresa more than once to keep it in a metal container I had bought for that purpose, but she preferred to leave it out on a chair near the stove.

On Thursday, her day out, I remembered that I had seen the bag on the chair that morning. It was still there. As I picked it up, something jumped out of it, slapping my bare arm with a cold gray whip. It was an enormous rat, not black like the Peterborough aristocrats but the color of tarnished pewter. It crossed the kitchen swiftly and vanished into the dark closet under the stairs.

I followed it, found a hole in the plaster, heard it scrabbling to the third floor. When I reached there more slowly — I had to use the stairs instead of posts and beams — I found out what had been keeping me awake at night.

The box with my wedding dress in it had been dragged to a dark cozy corner near the furnace pipe. Sharp teeth had bitten through the heavy cardboard. The mother rat, seeking a comfortable spot for her lying in, had not bothered to undo the string and paper. I did so and found that every bit of tissue paper in the box had been chewed into confetti. Strangely enough not a thread of the rose-point lace had been touched. Orange blossoms, satin and the English lace veil were intact too. The dress was stained but a trip to the cleaners made it all right.

I was not pleased to realize that I was hostess to a whole family of rats. I am afraid there was annoyance in my voice the next morning when I told Theresa that the flour was ruined because she had left the bag out on the chair.

"So it's my fault the house is full of rats is it?" Theresa inquired. "It's me that's brought them from New Hampshire, I suppose, so we'd have them winter and summer. Well, Mrs. Kent, I give you a week's notice."

Had I heard correctly? Was it possible I was free? Was that an oriole singing as it flashed through young elm leaves? Was that forsythia coming out?

Joy!

"You'll want to be looking for another place," I said, "and you'll need a vacation. I'll give you a week's wages, starting now."

I tried not to beam with delight as I said this.

Theresa looked slightly taken aback.

"You mean I've got to get out this minute?" she asked.

"After lunch," I said generously, "so you'll have time to pack."

Her mouth was still half open as I left the kitchen, saying that I was going to the Woman's Exchange and would be back soon. I put Sam in his box. Elizabeth and I danced down the street. At least she danced and I had no trouble keeping up with her. I felt better than I had for months.

The Woman's Exchange had many treasures — antique china and glass, lemon queen cakes, Parker House rolls, jams and jellies. This morning it also had Margaret O'Malley. She was sitting in the employment office part of the shop, not far from a magnificently frosted bride's cake.

Joyfully I told Miss Fogg, who ran the Exchange, that I needed a new maid.

She said, "Margaret O'Malley has just come in. Perhaps you would like to talk to her."

Margaret looked her full seventeen years. Her round cheeks were bright Irish roses and her eyes a sparkling gray green. Her black hair waved cheerfully in several directions. We smiled at each other and I asked about her experience. She didn't have much, she said. I asked if she could bake good bread.

"Maybe — if I had the right flour," she said. "I'd do my best."

"Do you have a reference?" I asked.

I could hardly wait to take her home with me but I felt I should be professional.

"I don't know," she said. "They're mad with me because I'm leaving."

"Oh well! Would you like to come and live with us?" I asked and gave her a brief sketch of the family.

When I finished it, Margaret said, "I seem to like you all right. Sure I'll come."

She came the next morning and stayed seventeen years.

It seemed too soon when I went to her wedding and sat in the front pew. Like the mothers of most brides I felt a little tearful.

The house — I remembered — was always cheerful after she came. The children loved her at once. She used to tell stories about leprechauns while they and their friends gathered around her in the park. I got the impression that I might see a leprechaun pop out from under the forsythias any time.

She addressed Sam as her little goldmine. He returned the compliment by calling her Goldie, still our name for her whenever we meet. She now spends her spirited goodness and charm over her own family. She and her husband have five children and many grandchildren but they take a friendly interest in my grandchildren too.

Her earliest contribution to life on Waverly Street was the way she threw herself into the Battle of the Rats. We were not the only ones who had them. Armies of them — sent by the Kaiser on submarines, some thought — had invaded Boston and were moving west until they found comfortable homes, Brookline seemed ideal to many. My Food Administration clients and I discussed them. I received many suggestions about entertaining them.

Different kinds of traps, poisoned crackers, buckets of water thickly sprinkled with oatmeal and barley were all recommended.

One by one they succumbed. The last one died honorably in the wall, making us the maximum of trouble and expense. The expert who dug him out said he was the biggest rat he had ever seen.

22

Armistice

IN THE LATE SPRING of 1918, Rich went to the officers training camp at Plattsburgh. We had planned to stay at home that summer so that I could carry on my Red Cross and Food Administration work and so he could wind up his affairs at *The Youth's Companion* before going into the service. When he came home late in June with a fine record and a sharpshooter's medal he took one look at me and said: "I'm going to take what's left of you to Vermont for the summer."

I had to admit I had been coughing and running a temperature while he was gone but I felt I was indispensable to the war effort. He sneakily got Dr. Powers to drop in and see me. Between them they persuaded me that I would help my country most if I rested for a while and ate country food.

It is easy to make the trip now in about five hours. In 1918 it took two days.

The second day we crossed the Connecticut at White River and drove along a Vermont gravel road. Rich had often told me of the superiority of Vermont turkeys, cheese, butter, maple syrup, politicians, venison, Latin teachers and Guernsey cows to those in any other state. Still I was not prepared for his first remark as our wheels touched Vermont soil.

"You see," he said seriously, "this Vermont gravel is a little finer than the New Hampshire gravel."

By five o'clock I saw Kents' Corner for the first time. There was no fog to hide the view of it Rich had said was the best. The fields were the greenest we had seen all the way. The tall lady elm thrust itself out of the greenest one of all, beyond a foaming brook. Back of it the hillside was a patchwork quilt of various grains and grasses. I recognized a blue-green square of oats, a darker one of corn, waving silvery-green squares of tall timothy. There were others besides that I did not know. The cubes and triangles of the Kent houses were arranged in an agreeable pattern.

We drove past the Brick House and I saw that in the sunlight its bricks were light pink, dusty rose, terra cotta or almost purple rather than ordinary brick red. For the first time I saw that the shutters on the White House had faded to a green like the patina on an ancient bronze horse mixed with the blue of a wave just before it breaks. We drove in over the lawn of well-mown grass and white clover past the sprangly old apple trees hung with little green globes and stopped at the mounting block. I knew suddenly that I had come home.

The next day Rich asked me if I would like to ride over to North Calais to the old Ainsworth mansion and look at some antiques there. It was a big brick house, rather like the one at Kents' Corner. It has burned since but it was then in good condition with the date — 1823 — painted clearly above the front door. Most of the front wall, with its empty windows and the door, is still standing. It is the only genuine ruin in our part of the country and the only one I've ever seen that is dated.

When I saw it that first day, it was empty except for the things for sale, which were piled up in the old bell room. I asked the price of six country Hitchcock chairs. The owner said in a truculently plaintive tone that she guessed she ought to get twenty cents apiece.

Rich told me afterwards that she expected me to beat her down but — extravagantly and branding myself forever as "city folks" — I agreed with her. We took the chairs back to Kents' Corner. Rich opened the door of the carriage house and set them down between a carryall and a one-horse chaise. He set one chair on the workbench, gave me a box of broken glass and some sandpaper and left me to scrape off the six coats of paint that had been put on it in the last seventy-five years. I was cured by the time I had scraped the first rung.

The children spent the afternoon dancing on the mounting block and rolling down the grassy bank near it. Goldie was in the kitchen helping Grandma Kent cook supper. Cedar waxwings flew in and out of the apple trees. An indigo bunting flashed its lapis lazuli wings among the black raspberry bushes near the springhouse. A light breeze moved leaves and grasses just enough so that what had seemed like silence became a giant singing whisper. The sound of broken glass moving across the chair seat became a tone of the symphony. So did the thud of horses' feet in the dust and a bumblebee buzzing into a hollyhock. The whine of the saw and the noise of rushing water came from one of Vermont's oldest saw-mills. I heard water trickling into the springhouse too.

I could smell clover and drying grass. In the field below the house, John Graham, tenant of Rich's farm, was tossing hay into cocks, each one a work of art. I took a rest from my scraping and complimented him on them. I asked him if the children could ride to the barn on the hay sometime. He said he wouldn't wonder. I inquired after the health of the Morgan stallion. Not too bad, John said. I pointed to a pale blue mountain peak that melted into blue sky above rolling green fields with white houses and two round red barns.

"That hill?" said John, "don't know it's got a name."

I found out later that it was about three thousand feet high and called Spruce Mountain.

I went back to my scraping and John returned to his hay cocks. As long as he lived I enjoyed his understatements and he took pleasure in my ignorance. He set traps for me and would remind me years later how I had fallen into them. His favorite happened when I told him I would like to have the back lawn leveled for a croquet ground.

He asked if it would trouble me if it sloped a quarter of an inch in sixty feet. I thought it over carefully and said I guessed it would be all right. John would slap his knee and laugh loudly everytime he quoted this conversation.

When I was called to supper that evening, I had a strange feeling. I was hungry. Something smelled delicious. I could hardly bear to wait while I ladled out water from the rainwater barrel in the woodshed and washed my hands with homemade soap.

Supper turned out to be a dish of new potatoes and peas from the garden, a sort of chowder with tiny dice of salt pork in it.

"What is the substance the vegetables are cooked in?" I asked.

It was deep ivory in color and tasted like my idea of nectar or ambrosia — or both.

"In Vermont we call it cream," Rich said.

"No wonder I didn't recognize it," I said.

I had no desire at all to churn it into butter and send it to England.

Rich went back to Boston the next day. I stayed all summer. I finished the six chairs. I stopped coughing. I gained five pounds. I picked berries. I carried pails of water from the spring. It is surprising how clean you can keep with a few pails of water if you have to carry them yourself. As at Iron Bound, we washed in rainwater and drank springwater. To entertain the children, I used to fill my red-rimmed white pail half full and whirl it around my head without spilling a drop.

When Rich got back to Boston, he learned that the army would not accept him. He was above draft age and they considered his work on the *Companion* important to the war effort. He had to stay at home and attend to it and forget about being a sharp-shooter. He was already in a militia unit known as the Motor Corps. That was the right place for him, the army told him.

He came to see us on several weekends. On one of them John Graham gave a corn roast in his honor. He built a fire across the brook, near the cornfield so the young roasting ears could be picked and brought at once to the fire. Grandma Kent had brought a plate and a sharp knife. She cut her corn off the cob and ate it with a fork.

"I am not going to risk my false teeth gnawing corn off any cob," she stated firmly.

This was the first time I realized that her handsome teeth were not original with her but were carefully fashioned of hand-carved ivory. I congratulated her on their artistic verisimilitude.

"Yes," she said. "I told that dentist those teeth are going to fit my mouth and not any china cup of water by my bed or there'll be one dentist missing from Boston, Mass."

This remark seemed to have terrified the man into work beyond the power of ordinary tooth designers. The other ladies present all agreed that their teeth caused them trouble of various sorts. Details were given. I was kindly asked if mine were comfortable.

"Why, yes," I said.

I did not like to say more but she wanted statistics.

"How many are your own?" she asked.

"All of them — such as they are."

"How many have you had pulled?"

"Well — not any."

"You mean you have thirty-two? Dear, dear!" she said com-miseratingly.

The others all clucked with kind but threatening sympathy over this statement. "Your time will come," seemed to be the general verdict. No doubt they were right and I know a new set would be decorative. How splendidly they shine on TV, those undersized tombstones of white marble! With my well-seasoned vanity, I fully intend to put the original thirty-two to the test when the corn is ripe. It is already tasseled out; it won't be long now.

I have never enjoyed corn more than I did at that first corn roast. Sam husked it, sitting on an overturned sap bucket, first in the last sunset glow, next in firelight. Then a great coppery moon came up above the sugar place. For a moment I saw the lady elm, with its vase-shaped top and the trailing garlands of branches around its trunk, dark against the glow.

I said to John Graham: "That elm is the most beautiful tree I've ever seen."

John said, "I hate an elm."

"Oh, why? Why?" — as Henry James would say — I beauti-fully wailed.

"Toughest tree there is to cut," John replied.

"You — you won't cut this one will you?"

"Guess that would be quite a bit of work," he said.

This was one of the naïve conversations John used to enjoy re-calling.

"Remember when you almost cried when you thought I'd cut down that old lady elm?" he would ask laughing and slapping his knee. "Guess it will last your time."

The elm and I are rather battered but still here.

The hillside has corn planted on it this year and the elm towers above the tasseled stalks. Machines instead of oxen or horses will bring the corn to the silo. In 1918 it was horses. I told John I wished it were oxen. He had no use for picturesquely putting clocks back but he found a small yoke, used in training calves. He said he would yoke up two Holstein calves; that Sam and Elizabeth could drive them and Rich could take a picture of them.

This was a lively occasion. Luckily the picture was taken before the calves decided to run away. I suppose a Spanish bull in a ring may travel as fast as those calves but I doubt it. Harry Graham, John's oldest son, was some distance up the road. He managed to catch them as they went by. The picture, a peaceful pastoral scene, we used as a Christmas card.

Rich came up from Boston several times by train during the summer but he did not take the two-day drive until Labor Day when he came to take us home. He stayed long enough for us to drive over to Lake Mansfield one day and bring back trout the next. We drove back from Montpelier up North Street so that I saw the view Rich had tried to show me when the horses dragged us up through rain and fog in 1913. It was — and still is — even more beautiful than he could possibly have told me. We could not stay to see the full change of the foliage but I saw it at what is still one of my favorite stages — when around a pond, bluer than the sky, swamp maples are scarlet and crimson and deep plum color, almost purple; when sugar maples hang out their first flags of gold tipped with rose color; when there are enough red leaves on the mountains so they look violet rather than blue.

Mown fields are at their greenest. Cattle are turned out of their own close-cropped golden pastures into the green ones. They make new patterns of tan and ivory and black and white against green. Elms, green last night, shine suddenly pale gilt through the morning mist. A mountain ash is covered with purple finches pecking at clusters of vermilion berries.

Some of the New Hampshire hills, as we drove home, were more brilliant than our Vermont ones — Rich had to admit this, yet seemed to think it a little blatant and overdone — but Massachusetts preserved its respectable dingy greens. Still I was glad to see it. Our own house looked pleasant in the green shade of the big elm.

While Rich and Goldie were unpacking the car, the children ran around the house patting things.

Sam kept saying: "What a pretty table! What a nice chair! (It was a battered Chippendale my aunt had discarded.) See the fireplace!"

Elizabeth said: "Look in the mirror, Sam. It's a convex mirror. See how funny we look. And see the bird pictures. I know that one — it's a — a forked-tailed fly swat."

By this title Audubon's fork-tailed flycatcher is still remembered in our family.

One Indian summer afternoon I heard bells begin to ring. They rang from churches, schools and the firehouse. Someone raced past me yelling, "Armistice!"

I ran, pushing Sam in his stroller with Elizabeth racing beside me, toward Paine's in the village. As we reached Washington Street, we heard sirens. We stopped at the firehouse. Our favorite firemen were seated on their new motor-driven engines, tooting horns and sounding sirens. One of our friends was pulling the rope of the big bell.

"War's over, Mrs. Kent!" he yelled.

Every face we saw, in the firehouse or on the street, was broadly smiling. Even some of my food conservation clients greeted me genially.

"No more whale meat!" one cried.

Could it be true? There were no papers yet at Paine's to tell about an armistice. Mr. Paine said that someone from one of the Boston papers had telephoned him the news; that even then the bells had been ringing. He didn't see how the news had spread so fast.

It was still spreading. Now sirens were sounding from the other firehouse, the one at the foot of High Street. Factory whistles began to join in. The streets were full of people — men laughing and slapping each other on the back, women laughing and crying. Flags were being hung out. I bought one for each of the children. They waved them as we walked home.

When we got there, the noise was calming down. The tooting from the firehouse had stopped.

"Well, I suppose they couldn't keep it up forever," I said to Goldie.

Yet I had a feeling that, if the war were really over, the sounds of joy would keep on into the night. When Rich came home, walking from the new *Youth's Companion* office, as he did in fine weather, he said that at the *Companion* they thought it was only a rumor. He had called several newspaper editors for confirmation. None had heard anything official.

Little by little the noise grew less. Bells stopped. Whistles faded into the general noise of the city. Automobile horns blew only because drivers were annoyed with each other or with jaywalking pedestrians or with apoplectic policemen who fostered traffic jams by their casual gestures. Soon everything was disappointingly normal.

Yet the disappointment left hope behind. Even a false armistice seemed to foreshadow a real one.

People said, "There's always a false dawn before the real one, you know."

I could not quite believe that a lie told often enough and loud enough becomes the truth.

Yet as I dished out the whale meat stew that evening I said to Rich, "I think it may be the last."

☆

The first week in November Rich left early one morning to drive to Vermont. He planned to drive through to Hardwick, where his mother's winter house was, in one day. He said he heard the roads had been improved. If he could average twenty-five miles an hour, he thought he could make it. He planned to make another one-day trip home on November 11.

While he was gone, the news came that the Allies really were discussing an armistice with the Germans; that if it were signed, the war would be over at eleven o'clock on the morning of November 11 — about six o'clock in Boston.

I woke myself up at a little after five that morning and lay there in the darkness listening. It was a windless morning. I could not even hear the sound of dry leaves rustling. Once the silence was broken by a horse's feet and the clink of milk bottles. Wheels grated off along Waverly Street and everything was quiet again.

It was a little before six and still dark when I heard it, far to the east, hardly more than a whisper, the sound of a whistle. Another joined it from some other distant factory, another and another — piccolos, flutes, clarinets, oboes, bassoons, louder and louder, nearer and nearer. Then the bells began, first in distant church towers, then in our own. The whole great symphony swept over us, traveled beyond us to the west.

It went on all day. Motor horns tooted, drums beat, sirens howled. People used whatever noisemakers they had: sleigh bells, castanets, bugles, cymbals, tambourines, dinner bells, penny whistles. I took the children to Paine's and bought a bright new flag to hang from the porch. There was no doubt about it this time. The war that would end war forever — and leave a world ruled by wisdom and kindness — was over.

That afternoon there was a regular monthly meeting of the Simmons College trustees. I had recently been elected to the board. I took my duties so seriously that except for President Lefavour and the secretary, I was the only trustee present. I enjoyed the idea that all the dignified Bostonians on the board were running around the Common among squirrels, sailors and pigeons, setting off firecrackers and singing "Yankee Doodle." Or perhaps they would be rendering "Old Hundred" on the hand bells used on the Hill on Christmas Eve. Since there was no quorum for our meeting, I decided to visit the Common and see for myself.

It was a soft Indian summer afternoon. As I walked toward the center of the city, the noise grew louder. To my disappointment proper Bostonians were scarce on the Common. The Navy had taken it over. Every sailor seemed to have two pretty girls, one on each arm, each twirling a clackety wooden noisemaker with her outside hand. Sometimes they joined other trios and went swinging and swaying across the grass in long lines. Small boys swooped along on bicycles pinging their bells. Two walked sedately carrying alarm clocks, which they wound up often.

Bells rang in the towers of Park Street Church and King's Chapel and St. Paul's. I went into St. Paul's, knelt there in incoherent thankfulness for a few moments, then sat there for perhaps half an hour. Music sounded softly from the organ. The church was dimly lighted by candles. You heard bells all the time but, when the heavy doors were shut, the minor noises were only a blur of sound.

The church was almost always full. The congregation changed constantly. My seat was at the back so I saw people, some with noisemakers or penny whistles in their hands, pass in front of me, drop to their knees for a moment, then sit there briefly listening to the music. They soon went out again. Every time the door opened, a great wave of sound rushed into the church. Noisemakers clacked. Firecrackers banged. Bugles blew. Voices sang and shouted . . . "Over There" . . . "Tipperary" . . . "It's a Long Long Trail" . . . Then, with the shutting of the door, would come comparative silence and peace.

I left it at last and walked through the noise up Park Street. My father had invited me to have dinner with him that evening at the Union Club. He, Katharine and friends of hers were already at the club. Katharine had been living near Philadelphia for some time. Her husband had gone first to a small shipyard, which was much behind its schedule of construction. Ed had reorganized it so that it actually began to produce ships. The Hog Island yard, the largest in the country, was also behind schedule. Because of his success at the small yard, Ed was put in charge of construction at Hog Island. Before long, ships began to be launched there too. I had been down myself to see one launched by Albert, King of the Belgians. He and I arrived at the gate at the same time. He was in a big black touring car with the top down. I was on foot. He was the only king I ever saw close enough to observe that he had not shaved that morning. He had many golden bristles pushing through skin the color of a ripe peach.

He waved me politely ahead, but I was polite too. I let the big Packard go first, walked through the gate after it. I was in my place in time to see the champagne bottle break and foam over the bow of a ship as she slid down the way.

It was unusual for a ship to be launched by a man. King Albert's defiance of Germany had won him lasting popularity and respect, and he was forgiven for not being a woman. The moment of the launching was always one of suspense. There was always a chance that the ship would get going too fast and that the bottle would miss it.

King Albert came to Boston too. Rich, as a member of the Motor Corps, was on traffic duty at the corner of Arlington Street and Commonwealth Avenue early one mild December morning as the King's car came from the North Station. The streets were empty except for his car. Rich and he exchanged salutes. Rich also welcomed Marshal Joffre and later Marshal Foch at the same street corner.

Sam and I went to see Marshal Foch receive an honorary degree from Harvard in Sanders Theater one winter afternoon. Rich had to be on traffic duty so he sent Sam in his place. Sam wore his best overcoat with the brass buttons and a sailor's cap of scarlet. He was not yet three years old and small for his age, but when he saw Foch he whispered to me: "I like that general — he's a very small general, isn't he?"

The Marshal's charm was not all in his neat, precise appearance and small size. Part of it lay in his voice, which was large enough for a much bigger man. In its easy rhythm, its range of tones and perfect clarity, it reminded me of another French voice — Sarah Bernhardt's.

Sam was delighted with it too.

He whispered to me, "Mother — he's *talking!* He's talking *French!*"

I think we both felt we understood every word.

23

The Police Strike

KATHARINE and her two children, Olivia and Barbara, and my children and I spent the summer of 1919 at Pocasset on Buzzard's Bay.

Trains still ran conveniently to Cape Cod from Boston, so Rich came to see us on weekends. Ed could come less often. One week when we knew he was coming we decided to greet him with a clambake. Our next door neighbors were the Westons and Mr. Weston was a great expert on clambakes. He drove with me in my first car, a Model T Ford, almost a year old, to what he said was the best place for getting clams. I ordered both clams and lobsters and said I would pick them up Friday. The owner of the shop took the order but he warned me that by Friday the local clam and lobster men might be out on strike.

"You can always drive over to Plymouth and pick up some," he said.

When Friday came there was not a clam anywhere around Buzzard's Bay or on the Cape. By nine o'clock I was on my way to Plymouth. There were no clams there either, or in Duxbury.

"Better go to Boston," the fishmen said.

I was determined that the clambake should go on. The pit was dug, the stones were ready, the children had collected bushels of seaweed. I telephoned Rich to say I was coming and turned the nose of my Model T toward Boston. I stopped in Quincy, Milton and Mattapan to inquire for clams. There were none anywhere.

More for consolation than with any hope of clams, I went to Rhodes Brothers and told my story to my favorite salesman, Mr. Hutchins. He raised his bushy black eyebrows almost to his bushy white hair and led me to the fish counter.

As I go into supermarkets now and see a few tired slabs of frozen swordfish wrapped in plastic, I often think of that counter. They took fish seriously at Rhodes Brothers. Displaying it was an art.

The square counter was made of white Vermont marble. Its sloping top was covered with crushed ice. Every morning on this surface the head fishman made a new design. That day the silvery-gray of haddock and flounder, the black and silver stripes of mackerel were emphasized by the scarlet of boiled lobsters. In the center an enormous pink crab clasped a lemon in its claws. Around the edge of the design was a border of shrimp and — my eyes could scarcely believe it — clams. They had come from north of Boston where the fishermen were not on strike. There would be plenty of fresh ones, Mr. Hutchins told me, by seven in the morning.

I telephoned the good news to Katharine and spent the night at Waverly Street. By seven the next morning Rich and I were in the Model T outside Rhodes Brothers. A bushel basket of clams and a dozen snapping lobsters, packed in seaweed, were put into the back of the car. We covered them with many newspapers and a tarpaulin. We put the top of the car up to shade them.

I drove fast, often at twenty-five miles an hour, and our marine treasures arrived at the seacoast in plenty of time to go into the bake. Mr. Weston was just starting to pack in seaweed over the hot stones in the bottom of the pit. In went chickens, potatoes, lobsters, clams and corn with seaweed in between and on top.

The bake was covered with a tarpaulin. All we had to do while supper was cooking was to take turns cranking the freezer full of peach ice cream and breathe in the fragrance of sea air outside and of Parker House rolls and brownies and sponge cake in the kitchen, for Goldie had not been idle. Ah!

The bake was perfect, opened just when chicken legs were smokily tender, when every lobster claw was scarlet, every clam just opening, every potato mealy, every kernel of corn full of cream. No child on this happy occasion had to try to swallow a clam if he could not. He could eat chicken legs and hot rolls with butter and beach plum jam, drink lemonade and — after dancing on the sand — be ready for ice cream and brownies.

Our guests said there had never been such a bake. Luckily there was enough left over for a chowder next day. (No, Mrs. Appleyard — don't tell how to make it. Let them figure it out for themselves.)

Our clambake was the last one of the season. Soon afterwards Katharine moved into the Larkin house in Portsmouth, a beautiful eighteenth-century brick house on Middle Street.

Our family went back to Brookline in time for two interesting events: Elizabeth's first day at the Park School and the Boston Police Strike. Soon after we got home the police left their posts and rioting began in Boston. Governor Coolidge finally yielded to the police commissioner and made his famous speech about striking against the public interest, which later won him the presidency. The Militia was called out to protect property. The Motor Corps was put on traffic duty all over the city. Rich lived in barracks. His first traffic post was in Haymarket Square.

Five roads came together there. Traffic lights had not yet been invented and much of the traffic was horse drawn. Wagons with spans of big Percherons jammed into the square. Whips were cracked by drivers of wagons loaded with barrels, sacks of potatoes, bales of hay. Smaller wagons were sandwiched in between them.

Automobiles of all kinds — elegant limousines from the North Shore, Model T's with brass bands around the radiator — crowded in honking their horns. Bicycles slipped under horses' noses. Pedestrians, with that admirable independence handed down to Bostonians by their colonial ancestors, jaywalked as jauntily as if they were hurrying to throw tea into Boston Harbor.

Rich did so well in unsnarling the traffic jams of the square that he was promoted to a post near the North Station, where he dealt with all the elements of the Haymarket traffic plus trolley cars and taxis racing passengers to the station.

He had to keep doing his work at the *Companion* but he found time to stop in and tell us the news. Once it was that he had been put on evening traffic duty so he would have more time for his editorial work. The night squad of the Motor Corps soon decided that they would have a better chance of survival if drivers of cars could see them. As camouflage, their khaki uniforms and broad-brimmed hats were well designed. Even under arc lights their figures melted into shadowy, dusty streets.

Someone suggested wearing bands of broad white tape crossed on their chests and backs. This device, invented by the Motor Corps, has been used by policemen ever since in various forms. A sort of luminous atomic red is fashionable at present. The Motor Corps also worked out an organized and intelligible system of signals to drivers. Up to that time each individual policeman had sent traffic ahead or stopped it in his own casual way. Under drill, signals became clear and easy to follow.

There was a threat that Boston firemen might strike too, to support the police. This meant that even a small fire might grow into a conflagration that would consume the city. Boston's police and fire commissioners met with the commissioners of Brookline, Cambridge and other neighboring towns and got permission for the Motor Corps to be trained to drive fire engines.

Rich was sent out to Cambridge and learned to drive the biggest and newest fire truck the city had. Knowing the verve and zip with which he drove a Dodge touring car, I thought it would be dangerous indeed if the Boston firemen struck. Fortunately they heard about it too. They may also have heard that no striking policeman would ever go on duty again. Anyway the firemen gave up the idea of striking. Officially Rich was relieved by the decision but I think he had a lingering yearning to drive that monster of scarlet and go to a fire. Just once.

Elizabeth loved her first day at the Park School. As mothers do on such occasions, I felt strange after I left her. I supposed that sending her on her first step into the world was what made me ache all over, especially low down on my right side. I had often felt the same during my oakum picking and whale meat days but the pain always stopped after a time. This attack was just as bad the next morning. I tried to pick up a hair brush I'd dropped. Finding I couldn't, I sent for the doctor.

He glanced briefly at me and sent for an ambulance.

"I'll dress," I said. "You'll go as you are," he said. "Don't move."

Luckily I had on my new Jaeger camel's hair dressing gown, a warm and comfortable garment though not precisely seductive.

In a few minutes I was carried out on a stretcher into the autumn sunshine. They got me to the Massachusetts General Hospital and got my appendix out before it burst. I made an excellent recovery. Rich was allowed to sleep at home instead of in barracks so he could add keeping an eye on the children to his editorial and police work.

He drove Elizabeth to school in the mornings. Aunty came and took Sam to play in the park while Goldie did housework and tested recipes for the *Companion*. Mrs. Riley, the laundress, lent a hand with the meals when Goldie was out. A taxi driver, an old friend, brought Elizabeth home every day in a Red cab.

So, as I told one of my visitors, everything was going smoothly.

"Yes," said she, perhaps not with the acme of tact, "somehow one's place is always filled."

"Well," I said, "at least it's taking five of them to do it."

I must have been some use, I thought. Apparently, from what I heard, the entire lower school at Park was kept busy by Elizabeth too. She seemed to have shaken things up a good deal. The first day she came to school she could read. I admitted this to Mrs. Harris who said "Really!" in a disapproving way. By way of apology I had added that she could not write so Mrs. Harris looked less disapproving. The second day, while I was taking my ambulance ride, Signora Montessori's prophecy was fulfilled. The time had come for the Montessori child to explode into writing; so she did.

She took a piece of paper. She said she thought she had better write to her mother who was in the hospital. She wrote, in a fine Italian-American hand:

> Dear Mamma:
>   I am sorry you are sick. I miss you. I hope you will be well soon. I like school very much.
>
> Your loving daughter,
Elizabeth Kent

Rich brought it to me and the news that they had promoted her to the third grade.

"The teachers," he said, "seem to think she's abnormal. Mrs. Harris was pretty stern. She implied you'd taught the child to write on the sly."

"Mrs. Harris looked so disapproving when I told her Elizabeth could read that I didn't dare say she might explode into writing. It was Montessori's fault not mine," I said.

"Fortunately the school is still standing seems to be the general idea. By the way you don't need to be formal and call her Elizabeth. She has a new name," he said. "The big boys in the third grade treat her like a toy. They poke her with pencils to see if she'll speak. They seem to think she's a sort of talking doll. They call her Kenty."

I tried not to fall into this habit but I have succumbed to it in company with philosophers, publishers, college presidents and other dignitaries. She has remained Kenty ever since.

Regardless of visiting hours at the hospital, Rich was allowed to stop in to see me when he came off traffic duty. Naturally I would have liked to see him neatly dressed in a Brooks Brothers suit and his English Burberry coat but it was fun to be visited by him and his fellow policemen in uniform, armed to the teeth.

"You look so fierce — I hope you don't frighten pedestrians to death," I said to Rich one afternoon.

He had received another promotion to the corner of Park and Tremont Streets, where jaywalkers have always been especially active. He thought that perhaps the supply of ladies from Beacon Hill promoted jaywalking.

"They act as if they were driving old colonial cows around the city," he said. "I have to speak to them about it."

"What do you say?"

"Oh, not always the same thing. For instance, today there was a dear old lady from Beacon Hill in a bonnet and a sealskin cape. She couldn't make up her mind to cross when I had the traffic stopped. As soon as I waved it on she'd plunge into it under horses' feet and the radiators of cars and then jump back to the curb again. She did it three times. When she started to do it the fourth time, I stopped traffic, left my post, walked over, saluted her and said: 'Madame, I must request you, as a favor, to step back on the sidewalk, remain there until you receive my signal and thus cease impeding the flow of the traffic.' She stepped back."

"Without your pointing your revolver at her?" I asked.

"Yes."

"And she didn't faint?"

Rich said no and I laughed until my scar began to ache. He

laughed too. A nurse came in to reproach us, but seeing a policeman, she relented.

I have always regretted that the police strike stopped before I
could get down and do a little jaywalking at Park and Tremont to
keep Rich in practice. However perhaps he didn't need it. My
friends who saw him on duty reported that he was one of the best
traffic officers in the city. I always accepted this understatement politely.

Years later, but before there was an overpass where Routes 1 and
9 intersect near Muddy River, where Boston becomes Brookline,
there would be immensely complex traffic jams, especially on Saturday afternoons. I would hear motor horns braying and tooting
for what seemed like hours. The house where we lived then on
Hawthorn Road was about half a mile away.

One Saturday Rich left his trolley car near the intersection to
walk the half mile home just at the time the traffic was jammed.
Listening to them I noticed that they seemed especially loud but
that they did not go on so long as usual.

"I suppose a policeman has come," I thought.

The policeman was dressed in a new brown Burberry and wide-
brimmed hat of French felt. He carried the briefcase from Mark
Cross I had given him for Christmas. It was flexible pigskin made
in a pattern he liked. He kept it well polished with saddle soap.
He was also carrying a tennis racket.

Thus equipped he had walked into the center of the traffic jam,
established his authority and untangled the mass of cars. He had
each stream moving smoothly when the regular policeman came on
duty.

"What did you do with your briefcase and your tennis racket —
use them for signaling?" I asked.

"Kept them between my feet."

"Perhaps the police force would give you a job," I said.

Luckily for me, he remained an editor.

24

The Twenties

I HAVE READ so many dashing accounts of the twenties that I feel pretty humdrum to remember them as a period of quiet happiness. For me, their chief feature was that Posy was born on May 16, 1922. It was a beautiful morning with orioles singing in the big elm tree outside the bedroom window. As usual the doctors announced that with me everything had been easy. The only difficulties were theirs. They talked a good deal about their skill in dealing with them in terms that sent me to sleep.

When I woke up, I did not hear the baby crying.

"Is she all right?" I asked the nurse, who said, "Perfectly. Sound asleep. She's a very good sensible little baby."

"You mean you can tell already?"

"Certainly. Babies are all different. Some of them are furious at being born. Now she's a philosophical type. She's accepted the world and has decided to adjust herself to life."

I was much impressed by this wise attitude of my daughter's and have been ever since.

Posy's eyes were brown from the first, not the usual blue that will turn some other color later. My grandmother had told me that it was not true — as I had been taught by one of my friends — that all babies' eyes are blue at first. Most of them are, my grandmother said, but her son John's were always brown and so, she said, were mine.

There was a little difficulty about the baby's name. I had thought she was going to be a boy and I had been calling her Nicholas Wilder after a sixteenth-century ancestor of my grandmother's. Since this name did not seem to fit the circumstances, Rich and I decided to call her Martha Wilder after Aunty, who had once told me that the only thing ever named for her was a goldfish. I thought I could show my appreciation of Aunty's kindness to me by naming the baby for her. The nurse was already calling the baby Pinky Posy. That seemed a little informal for a philosopher so Rich telephoned Aunty from his study next door to my room.

"The baby is safely here," I heard him say, "and we'd like to name her Martha Wilder Kent for you."

I could not hear what Aunty said — only that she was talking longer than seemed necessary to accept the compliment graciously.

I heard Rich say, "If you'll just hold the line a minute I'll tell her."

He came in with the look a recent father has when he isn't sure if his wife will have hysterics over what he's going to say.

"She says she won't have it," he reported. "She says she's always hated the name Martha and she won't have that beautiful little creature called that. I don't see how she knows how beautiful she is — I didn't tell her. She wants to know what you'll call her."

"Nothing," I said calmly. "Say she can name the baby herself and let us know what she decides."

In about ten minutes the telephone rang again.

Rich came in and said, "Aunty says the baby's name is Rosamond Mary."

"Tell her I think it's a perfect name," I said.

So everyone was happy and we kept right on calling her Posy. She now teaches philosophy and she has almost succeeded in teaching me to use the term "philosophical" correctly. Nothing annoys a philosopher more than the assumption that he is a person who accepts the rough spots in life cheerfully when what he is really interested in are subtleties of logic and negation and fallacy. I have also tried to train myself to know who is being talked about under the name of Rosamond — a fine dignified name. I assumed for some years that it meant Rose of the World. It was a surprise when I looked it up, found that it was derived from the German words *Ross* and *Mund* and that it means Horse Protection. Kenty and Sam called her that for some time but dropped back to Posy, which is, after all, less cumbersome.

Posy had an unusual effect on our house. Small though she was, she made it shrink. There was no bedroom for her on the second floor. She shared Kenty's and they had a beautiful time. Kenty used to steal Posy out of her crib and take her into bed.

"She warms me up," was Kenty's excuse for this maneuver.

Under this arrangement we had no guest room. Before Posy came, we could move around in various ways to leave a room free. The result was not exactly comfortable. Guests associated with more stuffed animals and building blocks than they really needed. Their clothes had to hang beside hand-smocked-by-me dresses and English sailor suits from Rowe of Gosport. I would clear out the top drawer of the bureau and line it with fresh paper. The fascinating contents — dolls, automobiles, old valentines, handkerchiefs and flashlights for reading in bed — I jammed into a box and set the box on the closet floor.

In spite of the hospitality involved in these efforts, guests still had to live chiefly out of their suitcases. Things were even more congested after Posy came.

"We need a larger house," Rich said after his mother had camped with us for several weeks. "One with a real guest room."

We found one with eight bedrooms at 17 Hawthorn Road. It

was a nineteenth-century copy of an eighteenth-century Salem house. It faced another not quite identical twin across a small terrace. The houses stood high above the road. A sloping green lawn, always rolled and coasted on by the children of the neighborhood, and a semicircular path led up to a broad flight of steps. Iron lamp posts with glass globes, an attractive target for the juvenile delinquents of the period, topped the stone wall above the steps. This was really an extension of the high foundation walls of the houses. An ugly but practical feature, they supplied excellent cellars but made the houses look very different from the Salem ones from which they had been copied.

Laurels, rhododendrons and other shrubs planted along the cellar walls covered them, though not enough. A great wineglass elm soared up on either side of the steps. They let sunshine into the front rooms in winter but shaded them pleasantly on hot summer mornings. Their branches seemed to be reaching out to touch each other over the front steps. I always hoped I'd see them do it. I did so in the thirty-sixth year I lived there.

Orioles made nests in the elms all those years and still do so, I hear. Syringas still flower around the lamp globes. When I go there, I see shrubs and trees I planted — forsythias, viburnums, cedars, lilacs, flowering crabs, hawthorns. There were no hawthorns on Hawthorn Road until I planted mine.

The houses were painted gray. Their Greek cornices and columns were white. There were three full stories in both houses with hip-roofed attics above the third. Chimneys for four fireplaces thrust themselves out of the high roofs. Forty-five sticks in my mind as the number of windows I paid for having washed.

The houses had been built by the George Pages, friends of Aunty's. They always rented one and lived in the other. They spent a good deal of time abroad and used to move into whichever house was empty when they came back. The houses had been built with a view to accomplishing woman suffrage. Mrs. Page was a leader in the struggle for votes for women. Her houses were designed with big sliding doors between living and dining rooms so that suffrage meetings could be held there. Ladies who wished to free themselves from being enslaved by their husbands would sit on folding chairs or on the curved window seats along the bay windows and listen to men telling about how oppressed they were. Afterwards they would have a delicious fattening luncheon.

Now that I know so many girls who teach, keep books, nurse and work in shops to help make doctors, lawyers and merchants out of their husbands, I sometimes wonder if those ladies were really so enslaved as they thought. Perhaps the whole thing was just a male plot.

Aunty came to live with us. Soon after my grandmother died, she had moved to Walnut Street where, as usual, she had planted a flower garden. In seasons when flowers were scarce, children liked to walk precariously on the fence or swing, heads down, on her gate and on that of Miss Susan Storey next door.

Miss Storey, gentle and kind, used to worry about these exercises. One day she said to Aunty: "Martha, there were three more dear little children swinging on the gates today. I asked them for their names and addresses, telling them I would have to report such dangerous pastimes to their parents. I have written the letters — they have the most unusual names and live on streets I never heard of; how Brookline is growing — and I think this may save their lives. I hope, Martha, that you think I did right."

"Frankly, Susan," Aunty replied, "I do not. It seems to me desirable that as many dear little children as possible should swing upside down on our gates in the hope that some of them at least may break their dear little necks."

Luckily there were no gates at Hawthorn Road.

There was practically everything else and it was moved there, a car full at a time, some from Aunty's house, some from mine. The hardest way to move, in my opinion, is to a house a mile or less away where you do most of it yourself. Rich brought a final car full of this and that several days before the professionals took over and then asked what he could do to help me most.

I said: "Hang the girandole over the living room fireplace and then take Kenty and Sam to Vermont."

He did and the rest was easy. I drew plans for each room in the house, marked on them just where each piece of furniture should go, labeled and numbered the pieces. At the end of the day everything was in its own place: Rich's shirts in the proper drawers, his suits on hangers in his closet. The attic was nicely furnished with Victorian chairs, boxes of bonnets, domed trunks containing ancient dresses of brocaded silk, small plaster casts showing the Elgin marbles. These all came from Aunty's attic. Mine contributed a canary's cage, roller skates, Montessori learning materials and a goldfish bowl. I carried them up myself. When I had moved all my miscellany to appropriate spots in the house, I went for Aunty. She was telling the movers what she thought of people who dropped large paintings of waterfalls.

"It will have to go into the attic now," she told them.

The men, who knew by now that to reach the attic from Hawthorn Road you have to climb about seventy-five feet into the air, looked gloomily at the picture frame. It showed only too clearly that it was made of gilded plaster. They drove off with their load while I filled the car with things too precious for their hands such as a Wedgwood copy of the Portland Vase, a Chelsea teapot and the portrait of my grandfather by Henry Alexander.

I had wadded sheets and blankets around them and was ready to start when Aunty said, "Oh, darling! I forgot John Bull's tombstone!"

When she moved to Walnut Street, I had brought the oblong of white marble for her from my grandmother's garden, where it had

been for more than thirty years. Now I picked it up from among
the chrysanthemums and put it into the car. It seemed heavier than
I had expected. By the time I unpacked it at Hawthorn Road it
weighed even more. I ran my fingers affectionately over the raised
letters — "J. B. a faithful friend" — thought of the satin smoothness of his brindled coat and put it down temporarily among the
prickly rugosa roses.

"I'll carry it up tomorrow," I said, "and put it in the ivy under
the laurels. Somehow I feel a little tired."

"Really?" Aunty said. "That's strange — well I suppose the
piano was a little heavy."

Actually, as she well knew, it had taken four men, all with interesting vocabularies, to carry the piano from street level to its appointed place in the living room. They had a little stool with
wheels on which they pushed it. When they came down, the fattest
one grabbed it and threw himself on it to coast down the walk.
Steering was difficult. He landed in the rugosas. I remember some
of his remarks but they would only be of use to some more modern
author than I.

I did little more that day than hang my grandfather's portrait
and the one of Grotius, possibly by Van Dyke. Everything was now
in place. Even the silver was in the drawers of the Queen Anne
lowboy. When I went to sleep that night, it was as if I'd never lived
anywhere else.

One of the first things I did in the morning was to stroll down to
get John Bull's tombstone.

It was gone.

I hunted all through the rugosas. I found the mark it had made
in the soft dirt behind the stump of an old willow but no other sign
of it.

Disgusted at my carelessness and laziness, I went up and told
Aunty.

"I'm so sorry — I can't think how it happened," I said miserably.

Aunty took the calamity calmly and with a sensible explanation. "Don't feel badly," she said. "It seems quite simple to me. Obviously someone came along who happened to need a tombstone for a faithful friend whose initials were J. B. So he took it. Probably it's all for the best."

Well, at least I did not have to carry it up to the laurel bush.

☆

Our first winter at Hawthorn Road was an anxious one. Sam started running a slight temperature in the afternoons and had to spend most of the time in bed. Neither Aunty nor Rich nor I said the word tuberculosis aloud but we all thought of it. There had been a great deal of it in both our families and it was still a menace of which we were always conscious.

Part of the problem was to keep Sam in bed yet not make an invalid of him. Kenty brought his lessons home every day and he and I worked on them in the mornings. He also worked on his stamp collection. I don't really recommend this as a bedtime occupation — stamps have a great tendency to get lost in the bed clothes — but it made the long days pass by. During his hours of fever, I used to read aloud to him. I became practically a talking book.

My friend Margaret Whitney brought him a set of pencils of different sizes ranging from minute to enormous and a splendid supply of paper so that he could always draw pictures. It was she, too, one raw March day just after his eighth birthday, when I was feeling especially discouraged, who said as she went out the front door: "Lulie, I think he's made the turn — I notice his ears have turned just slightly pink since I was here last week."

It was true: he began to have a normal color instead of looking either waxen white or flushed. His temperature curve became normal too. When his chest was X-rayed in May it showed small healed scars on his lungs.

One of the best features of the house was the big sunny playroom on the third floor. The children were allowed to keep it in whatever disorder seemed best to them. Their bedrooms had to be neat but the playroom could have a half-built fortress on one side, railroad tracks on the other and pretty nearly anything in between.

Aunty's bedroom was next door to the playroom. She had been given her choice of bedrooms and had chosen one almost in the top of the elm tree. Until she was eighty-nine years old, she used to whip up and down the stairs almost as quickly as the children did. As they grew up and went away to college, I would suggest a second floor room to her but she always said she'd rather stay in her treetops. Rich had his study on the third floor too, and the guest room, to acquire which we had made the move, was there.

I also spent a good deal of time up there. Kenty's occulist had suggested that it would be a good idea to interest her in something besides reading. It occurred to me that doing over the dollhouse might be a project that would take more varied eye movements than just following lines on a printed page. It was about the time that Queen Mary's dollhouse was being written about. We had a book with pictures of it and I found that I could buy goblets and tumblers and pitchers made by the same people who made them for Queen Mary. We began collecting them.

The dollhouse itself was a sturdy four-roomed structure built for Katharine about 1887. It needed painting and papering. Its old furniture had gone, so on weekends we used to shop for more. We also scraped off old paper and paint. Many skills were needed and we both developed them. One was to hang tea-chest paper on the walls of a room too small to get into. The two upper rooms were done that way. I thought the dining room walls might be covered with some substance less difficult to handle.

"What would you like for the dining room?" I asked my daughter who replied, "I think a landscape paper showing the landing of Columbus would be nice."

It was less fussy to handle than the tea-chest paper but as I had to paint it first, it was not much less trouble. It is still in excellent condition more than forty years later and many of the furnishings — such as a rusty iron sink in the kitchen, a small kerosene heater and the telephone — have become antiques just by standing there.

Exactly what the effect on Kenty's eyes was, I can't remember, but we both acquired a sense of scale, which has come in handy in my work on my miniature rooms. She has often found small toys and pieces of pottery for me and the scale has always been just right so that they have fitted the place for which they were meant. To see the small thing in the large and the large thing in the small is one of the great pleasures of miniature work.

I remember forty years later the pang of delight with which I realized that I could make a girandole to hang against the Columbus wallpaper out of a curtain ring, the convex lens of a flashlight bulb and a few cultured pearls from a broken string. When I wanted to make one for a miniature room a few years ago I suddenly woke up to the fact that times have changed. I still had some pearls — in Boston even the pearls are cultured — but flashlights were no longer convex. They had flattened out without my noticing it.

Like Aladdin I offered my friends new lights for old. At last Louise Pierce found one but not until I had worked out another solution. I woke up at two o'clock in the morning thinking: "The left-hand lens in my spectacles used to be quite curved before my eyes improved. I bet there's an old one in that Chinese cabinet on my bureau."

Sure enough it was there, ready for just such an emergency. I did not work on it that night but I slept peacefully, and in the morning

I knew just how to do it. I lined the lens with chef's foil to give it a reflecting surface. I used the same mixture I made when I repaired the big girandole — plaster and Elmer's Glue-All. I made the eagle and the wreath of laurel leaves of it too. I sank the pearls lightly into a ring of the mixture. I gilded the whole thing with a brush no bigger than a feather of a hummingbird's wing. I hung the mirror over the marble-topped table in my Victorian alcove, giving it just what it needed — an eye of light.

No one has more fun than I do.

25

Roofs and Shingles

WE ACQUIRED the White House in 1924. Grandma Kent decided that it was too big and troublesome to take care of. Rich and she had owned it jointly since his father's death. Now he bought her share and when we arrived, we found that she had bought two smaller houses a little way down the hill — the house now owned by the Lewis Manlys and the Remember Kent house, which had been out of the family for a generation.

It is the oldest of the Kents' Corner houses. It was built in 1797 and then stood at the crossroads. When Ira Kent, Rich's grandfather, built his new farmhouse in 1810, the old house was moved to its present site. It was solidly built of heavy sawed planks. Clapboards now cover them so that it looks like an ordinary frame house. Just try to change the electric wiring and you will have a surprise.

Grandma Kent planned to rent one of the houses and live in the other. It was hard to decide which she liked best so she lived in both.

"The brook's running so loud today — I won't sleep in Remember's house tonight," she would announce. "It keeps me awake." Or, "It's going to be hot tonight — guess I'll move back across the road. The brook cools things off."

Neither house was ever locked. One afternoon some out of state visitors invited her to go for a drive. She accepted gaily and got into the car.

"Mrs. Kent," said her host, "you didn't lock your door."

She got out of the car, went back into the house. After a slight interval, she came out with the key, locked the door and again got into the seat beside the driver.

With the kindly patience city folks show to elderly rustics, he said: "But Mrs. Kent, you left the key in the lock."

"Yes," she said. "It may be dark when we get back. It will be much easier not to have to fumble around fitting that key into the lock."

The last time I had seen these friends, the Wellmans from Iowa, was in the living room of the White House one hot thundering afternoon. Mrs. Kent gave a ladies' party for Mrs. Wellman while Rich and Mr. Wellman went fishing. The living room was familiar to Mrs. Wellman with its maroon and mustard plush curtains, the horsehair rocker and the pool table. She must often have dusted the melodeon and the parlor organ and swept the carpet and cleaned the hanging lamps with their red and amber glass pendants.

She had, she told me, been one of Blanche Kent's hired girls.

This was an honorable position, rather like going to an exclusive finishing school. The girls — there were usually two of them — lived there and had Sunday afternoons off.

"It was dreadful," Mrs. Wellman confided to me. "I was homesick only two miles from home. I used to cry myself to sleep. The things Blanche would say to me when I broke a dish! Once when I was carrying some garbage out to the pigs, I spilled a little grease on the woodshed floor. I had to scrub that whole splintery floor on my hands and knees while Blanche Kent stood over me and said what she thought. I hope to tell you I never spilled anything again."

Graduates of the White House School of Home Economics married well. They were not only trained as experienced housekeepers — there was culture too. They were encouraged to read aloud while sewing was going on. In the evenings they got the flavor of foreign lands by looking at the big collection of stereopticon pictures. They sang and played the organ or the melodeon. They painted milking stools. Their wages — two dollars a week — were deposited for them in LeRoy Kent's bank. They also had a little spending money. A girl would have over two hundred dollars saved at the end of two years.

They went to lectures, to neighborhood suppers and dances. Inspired by *Godey's Ladies' Book,* they made themselves dresses of complicated outline. They pieced quilts and quilted them. They were, in fact, fashionable heiresses.

On that hot August afternoon, I remember, Kenty sat under the billiard table and listened to the ladies talk about old times. Rich had brought in ice from the icehouse and washed the sawdust off it before he left. It clicked pleasantly in the best lemonade glasses. The sour cream cookies were delicious — if you like them. I didn't. It was a distinguished occasion and Mrs. Kent (Blanche, to her former hired girl) had on her new black and white checked gingham dress. It was unusual for her to buy a new dress right out of the shop. Usually she had them made over or just wore them as they were. She was a firm believer in the theory that if you keep a dress seven years it will be in fashion again. I myself have never found that system very dependable. On the whole I think it's more practical just to keep on wearing a suit till the elbows wear out. This happens earlier with me than it would with most people because of my habit of writing. People who just walk or drive cars seldom need elbow patches.

Mrs. Wellman had been looking Grandma Kent over carefully. She said: "Your dress suits you real well, Blanche. You know I bought one ready made of that same material and when my laundress was pressing it, if she didn't scorch a piece right in the middle of the front breadth! Do you happen to have any of the material left, Blanche? It wouldn't take only a narrow strip."

"I'll go and look," Grandma Kent said. "Lulie, pour some more lemonade. This is the hottest day for two years, I wouldn't wonder."

I poured more lemonade for Mrs. Wellman and her friends, wondering as I did so just how Mrs. Kent would supply a new front breadth for Mrs. Wellman's dress. I knew very well there was no extra material.

However Grandma soon appeared with a large piece of it. She was no longer wearing the dress.

"Excuse my slip, girls," she said genially. "That dress was really too hot. Come on, Emma," she said to Mrs. Wellman, "let's shoot a little pool. You used to be pretty good." She took the tray off the table and set it on the melodeon. "Oh, here's your material, Emma. I'll just leave it on the sofa."

"Thanks, Blanche," Mrs. Wellman said and chalked her cue.

Thunder crashed above the click of the balls. Sam joined Kenty under the table. Mrs. Wellman jumped every time she heard thunder.

"It puts me off my stroke," she complained.

Nothing put Grandma Kent off her stroke as she moved about in her embroidered china silk slip. After she had won the match, she said: "Thunder's cooled things off now. Guess I can stand a dress."

She went and put on one of her newer ones, barely five years old. After the guests had gone I said, "Grandma, you cut the front right out of your new dress, didn't you? Why did you do it?"

"You don't think I was going to have Emma Wellman go back to Iowa and tell the Vermonters there that Blanche Kent had failed so much she wouldn't even trouble to find a piece of gingham to help out one of her girls, do you?" she asked.

My father was fond of saying that fools build houses for wise men to live in. With this principle in mind, I suppose it was sensible to buy the White House rather than to build another sixteen-room cottage. My chief occupation since 1924 has been to keep it standing up. As I write this, Ralph Weeks and assistant are in the cellar jacking it up. There are strange creaks and it feels like traveling in a large unsteady canoe. If it were not jacked up regularly the whole thing — including the Kent highboy and Rich's collection of glass paperweights — would have fallen into the cellar long since.

I had, I suppose, been misled by the solidity of our houses at Waverly Street and Hawthorne Road into thinking that buildings automatically stood where they were placed. I am now in a position to tell anyone who will listen to me that it makes a difference what a house is built on. Our Brookline houses were built on rock. Both went through sharp earthquake shocks without anything worse than a few pictures hanging crooked.

The foundations of the White House had to be completely rebuilt the year we bought it and twice since. The reason for this was tersely expressed by the first Vermont mason I knew.

When I spoke, I'm afraid in a slightly peevish tone, about this project, he said, "Well, if folks will build their houses in a side hill swamp . . ." and continued to push a large rock back toward the North Pole.

The walls of the house and of the buildings around it — the barn, the carriage house and the corn barn — all tend to move south. This is because of the way the Vermont winters act on the wet clay soil around us. Winters when snow comes late are especially bad for foundations. Along the north sides of buildings, the water in the clay freezes and expands, pushing walls slightly south. In 1924 the north foundation wall of the house had moved so far south that the house was just barely resting on it. Stones from the wall lay on the cellar floor.

A winter of deep snow helps insulate the foundations but temperatures of 40° below zero — not uncommon here — penetrate even through the snow. One year, not long after we rebuilt the foundations, there was a period of 60° below zero temperatures. They threw this house around so violently that our newly plastered walls cracked. I began to wish we had built an igloo for our summer cottage.

About that time I read a book. This activity is one looked on with suspicion by practical Vermonters. They would not have objected to my reading poetry or stories about the Wild West. They even view the writing of books with a certain tolerance. It comes under the heading of "women's work," which also includes washing windows, hanging wallpaper and scrubbing floors — a nice hobby really. Women are supposed to bait mousetraps too, though a man, properly wheedled after a favorite menu — say baked ham basted with maple syrup and rhubarb pie — sometimes will remove the mouse when caught.

The books on the censored list are those on practical subjects.

"He gets his ideas from books," is a damaging thing to say about a man.

Of course, a woman who gets her ideas from books and then imposes them on men is even more dangerous. It was a book called *Practical Hints for Building* that made me think I could have a picket fence. When I told Rich, he groaned deeply.

"In this soil and climate," he said, "it won't stand up two years. It might get through one winter but two will heave it about so it will be flat on the ground."

"But Rich," I said, "it says right here in my book —"

The fence has now stood up through forty winters.

Rich, being an editor, had a certain respect for books. He allowed me to do what the book said. The holes for the posts were dug very deep and were much larger across than the posts, which were creosoted to a point slightly above the level of the ground. At the bottom of the holes good-sized flat stones were placed. Smaller stones were wedged in around the posts. Large pebbles, then pebbly gravel, then sandy gravel were poured in all the holes. When this mixture settled, more gravel was added until there was enough so that it sloped slightly away from the posts. The gravel supplied drainage and also cushioned the posts against the pressure from frozen, expanding clay.

The same principle was used the next time we rebuilt the foundations. A deep trench, dug along the north side of the house, was filled with pebbles and gravel. The house still edges slightly southward but not nearly so fast as it used to. Next year I hope Ralph can fix a few doors so they shut easily. It's pleasant to be able to look forward to such useful activities.

Even while the masons were putting the house back on its foundations, I began my attack on the maroon and mustard color scheme. Papers were torn off walls, carpets off floors. Horsehair furniture was carried to the third floor. Eighteenth-century pieces, banished fifty years earlier, were brought downstairs. We began that summer a project on which I still work sometimes — painting birds and flowers seen by the family on the walls of the front parlor. We all worked on it. Even Posy was big enough to scrape old wallpaper off the lower part of the walls and to notice birds.

I began painting on the inner wall of the room as soon as it was papered with a heavy, slightly off-white paper. I drew a tree with twisting branching arms. It was similar to the tree on one of my old Indian print bedspreads. What I planned was a New England Tree of Life with birds perching on it and flying around it, with flowers growing below it and on its branches.

For more than a week the tree was completely bare. Then one morning Posy came in, her eyes shining with excitement, saying: "I've seen a blue jay — put him on the wall!"

The next thing was to find a suitable picture to copy, for I was no painter of birds on the wing. We looked through all our bird books and framed prints. She chose a blue jay she liked. I enlarged it to what the book gave as a blue jay's measurements (it came out rather more than life size) and began work. I stood on one of my twenty-cent, wooden-bottomed Hitchcock chairs, now decorated to look like old, and placed my tray of poster colors on a newspaper on the melodeon. I drew the outline lightly in pencil, climbed up and down to change brushes and colors. It takes black, white and several shades of blue to paint a blue jay. One thing I'll say for mural painting: unlike most of my occupations it is not sedentary.

For a while the blue jay was the only thing on the tree but after a time Kenty and Sam began to bring in flowers and ferns and to paint them just above the wainscot. Even Rich, who had the basic distaste for nature of a city lover brought up in the country, found a closed gentian and brought it home for me to paint.

Someone once suggested to me that I must feel sympathetic toward Michelangelo and the uncomfortable way he had to work on ceilings. I replied that from my point of view he had things easy. I would have loved to paint lying on my back. What I found hard was climbing up and down to wash my brush or to measure and enlarge a rosebreasted grosbeak's tail feather or a cedar waxwing's crest and to stand off from my work and wish it looked better.

I still add things to the tree occasionally but my technique is different from the one I used in 1924. I paint quietly, sitting at a table in the Winter Kitchen while I am baking a sponge cake or an apple pandowdy. When the bird is finished, I cut it out and paste it on the wall. I choose a place where the paper cracked when the house was heaved around by frost. There are often new cracks where a screech owl or a luna moth or a pileated woodpecker comes in handy to heal the winter's wounds.

On the other walls of the room are larger birds — a flight of ducks, a blue heron. Last spring there was one balanced on a cake of ice, fishing goldfish out of my pond and eating them as hors d'oeuvres. I thought of adding portraits of my favorite fish — Scarlet O'Hara, Bianca d'Oro, Silver Rose and Fin Feather, senior to the heron picture but I haven't got around to it yet. Perhaps next summer — if I'm not writing a book . . .

Someone asked Kenty what the effect of this educational project was on her. She replied: "When anyone asks me what some bird is, I say, 'Ask my mother, she knows.' "

"Too bad it wasn't a success — all that work!" the interlocutor commented.

I said I thought a project might be considered successful if even the mother learned something.

In spite of skeptics, we kept working on walls. In the back parlor we did maps. Kenty put all the roads, streams and ponds on a map of Calais. She also did a star map of the August sky. Sam helped me on other maps — of Vermont, of the United States, of the world. To make me feel at home there is a map of Frenchman's Bay showing Iron Bound and Sorrento and Mount Desert.

It took me most of one summer to do the map of the world. During the 60° below zero nights of the next winter, the house was tossed around so much that in the spring I found the map cracked from New York to California and points west. It was such an annoyance to me every time I looked at it that several years later, I decided to do something about it.

I consulted Ken Smith about building bookcases and a mantelpiece around an old Franklin Stove. He made the plans and Harold Townsend did the work, using wide old pine boards for cupboard doors and mounting the stove on brick tiles baked in Abdiel Kent's brickyard a century earlier. For the space above the mantelpiece, I used a piece of Sheetrock. Before the cracked map was hidden, I had made a tracing of it and had transferred it to the Sheetrock.

The family all helped me. By the end of a week we had inked in the outlines, redrawn the small pictures of Drake's ship and Lindbergh's plane, of a covered wagon crossing Kansas and of Columbus reaching the Indies. We had lettered names and painted lakes.

When I look at it, I am always dimly conscious of the original with its disfiguring crack, lurking miserably three feet behind the Sheetrock, and of paintings of the *Flying Cloud* and of the *Constitution* now covered by bookshelves.

The map of North America, which took me most of one summer and part of another to do, is still in good condition. Visitors who look at it are often heard to say: "Yes, there's my old home town — only it's about half an inch out of place."

Sometimes they estimate the error in miles. On the whole I think that, when you drive around the continent, you'd better take a Texaco map.

Our family projects were not all carried on in summer. The affairs of the Kent Casting Company kept us busy in Brookline for three winters. We organized it because the Park School stated that Hollister Kent had little grasp of financial matters. It occurred to me that the management of fifty cents a week hardly gave a mathematician a wide view of investments.

Sam had some molds for making lead soldiers. We found two shops, one in Boston and Paine's in Brookline, where they said they would display the soldiers if they were painted and sewn in boxes. They sold all we could make. Sam did the casting and the bookkeeping. The structure of the company was complicated enough for Dupont's. We sold shares to members of the family, we issued bonds, we borrowed on notes, we paid interest, we kept records of materials. I still have the company books which show, in Sam's writing, such facts as how many pounds of mixed lead and antimony we had on hand, amounts paid for paint and brushes, and our sales figures. We got a dollar a box from individuals but with the shops, as I heard Sam tell a friend, we were on a forty and sixty basis.

"What's forty and sixty?"

"We get sixty percent of every dollar's worth of sales and the store gets forty percent," Sam said wisely.

I was so pleased that my hand trembled and the stripe I was painting on a soldier's trousers had to be wiped off and done over again.

When we got a rush order, the whole family used to gather in the playroom and paint figures. They were not all soldiers. My enthusiasm for war not being great, I tried to think of peace-provoking toys. We increased our capital and bought molds for a farm with many animals, others for figures for a Christmas crèche. Arthur Perry, a Quaker, suggested our making our military band over into a Harvard band. He gave us one of our best orders. Sam cast the figures as usual. While they were still warm, he cut off the tops of the helmets, thus changing them into caps. We painted their jackets crimson and gave them white trousers. We also did some Yale bands with blue jackets. Few were sold — after all, we were not in New Haven. We had to take them back and paint the jackets red.

Sometimes we were so busy that even Rich had a brush thrust into his hand and was given some simple task, such as boots. We were on an assembly line basis, each doing the part assigned. I painted faces, Sam did horses, Kenty bugles and trumpets. Posy did palm trees and sheep for the crèche. Aunty made one of the most important contributions — she sewed the figures into boxes. We used scarlet stocking boxes, given to us by a local store when they were empty. We disguised them slightly with the Kent Casting Co. hand-lettered label.

When Sam went to Milton Academy, we wound up the affairs of the company. We retired the stock, the only one on my investment list that paid ten percent right through the stock market crash of 1929 and the worst of the depression. The bonds and notes were paid off. We still owned almost three hundred dollars' worth of molds and we had two hundred dollars in cash. With it we bought a canoe, which traveled many miles, paddled or sailed, on Curtiss Pond in Calais. Sam and I both had slight cases of lead poisoning but the school had ceased to comment unfavorably on his arithmetic. On the whole the project was a success.

I do not mean to sound frivolous when I say that I rather enjoyed the depression. This was not because I could buy two pounds of the best butter for fifty-two cents or because I could wear my old suits indefinitely and feel virtuous. I suppose I felt a sort of triumph in somehow surviving it and in being useful to my family.

It was not uncommon in those days for women to announce to each other: "Of course, we lost everything in the crash." I heard this statement so often that I came to assume that Rich and I had too.

Then one day someone, feeling perhaps that I was left out of the conversation, said, "I suppose you lost everything too?"

I shocked the group by saying, "Nothing I cared about."

"Really!" some one commented and went back to statistics about Electric Bond and Share. "Didn't you have any?" she asked me sternly.

"Just a little," I said.

This was true. I had just sold what was supposed to be fifteen thousand dollars' worth. I got six hundred dollars and paid a school bill for one of the children. I felt I was lucky to get cash for those pieces of paper, lucky that we were all well, that Rich had his job at Houghton Mifflin, that we had a roof over our heads.

This was an understatement: we had more roofs than we could conveniently keep shingled. Suddenly I became responsible for some more. One morning at Kents' Corner, Sam got up as usual at half past six and carried the well-sterilized white milk to the barn. This was in 1928 and there was no pasteurized milk at the Maple Corner Store. I had designed a pasteurizer and had it made by the local tinsmith. Sam would milk a beautiful Guernsey cow, kept by John Graham especially for our use, into the white pail. When Sam brought the milk down, I would pasteurize it. While I was doing so, he would get ice from the icehouse, wash the sawdust off it, smash it up and mix it with rock salt. We would set the container of pasteurized milk into a pail of the freezing mixture to chill it rapidly. After that it would be kept in the refrigerator. This milk was for drinking. The evening's milking was poured raw into special pans and used for cooking or for making cheese. The cream skimmed off it was like deep ivory velvet.

On this particular July morning, it was chilly. As I put on my five-year-old Jaeger dressing gown — it hung cozily around my ankles — to wear during pasteurizing, I heard Sam running across the porch. He usually went across the lawn to the kitchen door.

This time he burst through the front door, saying, "Mother, come quick! Hurry! The Girards are knocking down the Brick House chimneys. Go and stop them!"

"It's their house," I said, "they've a perfect right to." But I ran up the road in my dressing gown just the same.

Several of the Girard boys were on the roof with their father. The air was full of whirling bricks, which thumped down on the grass.

I yelled up to Mr. Girard, "How much apiece for the bricks?"

At the mention of money, activity ceased for a moment.

"How many did you want?" asked Mr. Girard.

"All of them," I said.

"Cent a piece uncleaned — two cents cleaned," he said.

"Cleaned," I said.

"Where'll I put them? Want to buy the house? It's for sale."

"Could they go in the cellar?" I asked. "No — I'm afraid I can't buy it."

Mr. Girard agreed politely to taking care of the bricks until I needed them. He was, he said, improving the house. It needed a new roof. Without the chimneys he could put a sheet of tin right over the whole thing and make it neat. He liked things neat, he said.

I said I did too. I was gradually becoming enough of a Vermonter so that I understood that neat was a term of high praise. I went back to my pasteurizing and Mr. Girard went back to his improvements.

That autumn Atwater and Mabel Kent came to stay with us in Brookline.

"What do you find to do in Calais? Isn't it rather quiet?" Atwater asked.

"Quiet!" I said and told about my morning trip to the Brick House.

Mabel was fascinated.

"Oh, At!" she said. "Buy it and put the chimneys back!"

"All right," said Atwater, "I will."

It was bought in my name and he told me to keep it, but Rich would not let me accept it. He alleged that we had plenty of roofs to keep shingled. Atwater said I could use it as a guesthouse and he would keep the roof shingled — unless I preferred it covered with tin. We used it as a guesthouse for the next fifteen years.

26

Walls

GRANDMA KENT took a progressive attitude toward the changes we made at the White House.

She summed the situation up this way: "And when my friends — as of course they do — try to get me groaning about things here, I say, 'Nonsense! Don't talk that way — I like everything they've done. I like to see something going on.' "

I heard one of our neighbors say of another: "She knows but she don't realize."

This could never be said of Blanche Kent. She realized not only the present but the past and handed it on to me.

"That's a beautiful pine tree," I said one day as we drove past Bliss Pond. "It looks almost primeval."

"It was only a foot high in 1795 — not very old," Grandma Kent stated and told me its story.

In 1795 two brothers settled near the pond. They cut down trees, sawed them at Abdiel Bliss's sawmill and built themselves a small plank cabin as a temporary shelter.

"We'll have a real house someday," James, the older brother, said to Peter, the younger. "We'll build it right there — where we can look out over across the pond to the mountains."

"Then I'd better pull up that little pine," said Peter. "It'll be right in the view."

"Don't do that," said James but Peter had already done it.

"I'll plant it back," James said. "When we build our good house, it'll be big enough so's we can make panels for our front door," and he pushed the tree back into the ground.

"I don't want it in my view," said Peter and yanked it up.

"Listen, Peter," James said, shoving the tree back into the hole again and tramping in the dirt around it, "that tree's got to make boards for our front door. If you pull it up again, I guess I'll have to thrash you."

So Peter pulled it up again and James had to thrash him.

"This time," James said, "you'll plant it yourself and you'll stay right here on your knees till you promise to leave it grow."

So Peter promised. The brothers never got around to building their good house so the tree is still there. It would make twenty-inch boards for someone's front door now but luckily no one has had the energy to cut it down.

Some of the people who lived near the tree in 1843 were Millerites. They knew exactly the date when the world was going to end. They were so sure they were right that they deeded their property to their skeptical neighbors, gave away their cattle, dishes, silk dresses and cameo pins. When the last night came, they gathered in the Old West Church, dressed only in clean sheets, waiting for midnight when the earth would vanish and they would mount to heaven.

Somehow, when midnight came, nothing happened. They were still there when their candles burned out and they saw dawn touch the cool blue paint of the balconies and the sounding board and the blue edges of the box pews of deep golden pine.

Some of the people who had received deeds to Millerite property were merciful enough to tear up the deeds and let the unhappy saints go back to their farms. Others said, "Well, guess you meant it, didn't you? Deed's legal — seem's though."

Ethan Drew was one of the formerly prosperous farmers whose

property was kept by the man to whom he had deeded it. Out of "charity" his family were given back some of their clothes. They were allowed to live in the cabin near the pine tree so they had walls and a roof. Someone gave them a wild young heifer, a rooster and two hens. Perhaps if Ethan worked hard and had good luck he would have a farm again some day. In the meantime to get a little — a very little — cash, his daughter Lydia went to work for the Patons, prosperous neighbors half a mile along the road. She lived there but she had Sunday afternoons off.

Without those afternoons, she told Grandma Kent, she couldn't have stood it. Each week seemed endless. The Patons quarreled, said bitter things to each other in harsh jangling voices. They had a natural gift for cruelty and kept it in condition by conscientious practice. They united in criticizing Lydia and sneering at Millerites.

"Well, is the world going to end tonight?" they would ask every morning and cackle over their wit.

Lydia once brought Mrs. Paton a bunch of wild flowers but she was told to throw it out. Flowers, Mrs. Paton said, were for outdoors, not for making a house untidy.

"I want things neat," she would say.

She contrived to make this simple statement frightening. Lydia trembled as she scrubbed the kitchen floor and polished the six silver teaspoons that had belonged to Mrs. Paton's mother, for she came of a rich family. Lydia also scrubbed pewter plates with sand and vinegar. She made soap. Every day she turned the big cheeses she had made. She washed sheets (jokes about them were part of Mr. Paton's sense of humor) and made — as even he admitted — excellent baked beans. ("Wouldn't get any like these in heaven," he'd say.) For a while she sang while she worked, but Mrs. Paton did not approve of singing.

On Sundays, after she had washed the dinner dishes, Lydia would walk home to the cabin. There she would be sure of peace and love

and gentleness for an hour or two. She would have left things
ready for the Patons' supper, all spread out on the table under the
raspberry-colored netting that kept the flies away. The Patons
would have eaten but there would still be dishes to wash. She had
to be back by six.

It was hard to start back. As she reached the turn of the road
past the big pine, she looked straight toward the Patons' white
house. It rose out of the greenest, best mown lawn anywhere. Its
white columns shone with fresh paint. So did the white picket
fence around the garden. All the flowers in the garden were white
— white mallows, white hollyhocks, petunias, phlox. It was
neat.

"And when I'd come along to the turn and see the walls of the
house shining so white, with those white columns and that white
fence and all the white flowers," Lydia told Grandma Kent, "I used
to say to myself: 'I wonder if hell has a marble front.' "

The stories about the various houses we passed gave an extra
dimension to the countryside. I felt as if I knew the people who
had lived in them and those whose names were cut on slabs of
granite in the old cemeteries.

In the East Calais cemetery Philip Sidney Bennett is buried. He
was a peddler of small wares at a time when women could seldom
visit stores. He used to come to Blanche Hollister's house on Hollister Hill when she was a small girl. He was deaf so there was no
use trying to interrupt him when he had started his spiel. Like most
heavy men, he usually sat down in a fragile chair.

He would place his pack at his feet and, tipping back in his chair,
begin: "Now ladies, what'll you have? What'll you have today?
Why what have I got, what have I got? Ribbons — pink, blue,
yellow, red; hairpins and combs of tortoiseshell to go in your hair
— my, such pretty combs for pretty hair! Lace for those lovely
petticoats, ladies, and needles to sew it on with, pins and pincush-

ions, pens and pen wipers; buttons — seventeen kinds of buttons, including copper ones with an embossed portrait of Sir Walter Raleigh, the same as put down his cloak over a mud puddle for Queen Elizabeth to walk on; thread — linen, cotton, black, white; tape measures, whalebone, collars and cuffs; screws and screwdrivers, gimlets, curtain rings; nails and hammers for pounding them. Flower seeds for your gardens, ladies — marigolds and nasturtiums of which the seeds are pungent in pickles. A doll for a girl, a top for a boy — whatever it is you most enjoy!"

How could all these things be in the pack? Blanche Hollister used to wonder, but they were all there and more besides.

Sidney Bennett would always go through his whole spiel before he would open the pack. Blanche and her brothers and sisters would be dancing with impatience but you could never stop him. One day he tipped so far back that the chair collapsed under him.

He never stopped speaking but lay with the pieces of it around him on the new braided rug saying, "Pens and pen wipers. Seventeen kinds of buttons . . ."

He designed his tombstone himself and had it made before he died. On the big block of granite, in large letters, it says BENNETT; below in smaller ones, *P.S. The old nuisance.*

"Everyone," he said, "will know who that is."

And indeed people still do.

It was a long drive with a horse and buggy or a sleigh from Kents' Corner to Hollister Hill, ten miles at least, but LeRoy Kent used to drive across the hills to take Blanche to dances.

Her mother had said to her before she had ever been anywhere: "Now, Blanche, I won't have you going out with anyone excepting only Roy Kent from Kents' Corner."

The alliance between the two kingdoms was arranged and a new wallpaper was put on the front hall of the Hollister house for the wedding in 1870. Blanche Kent had an oval bonnet box covered with the original hand-blocked paper. It was French with a couple in eighteenth-century costumes sitting under a great old tree, blue sky, green grass, gushing fountains. I found it among her things after she died in 1938. Rich told me that the paper had come from Hollister Hill.

Some years later I took the box with me and went to the old house. I explained through the screen door to the owner that I was interested in the paper; that if Strahan reproduced it she could have enough to repaper her hall. Strahan had already reproduced the original wallpaper in the hall of the Brick House.

"I thought," I said, turning the box around so she could see the figures and the tree and the fountain, "there might be some of it in an old trunk in the attic."

"Unh — *unh.*"

"Or perhaps someone used what was left over to paper a closet."

"Unh — unh."

"Sometimes," I said miserably, "there's a piece lining a bureau drawer."

"Unh — unh!" At which remark I thanked her — for what I'm not sure — and was turning away in disappointment when she pushed open the screen door, almost knocking me off the granite door step, as she said, "But I know where there *is* plenty."

"Where — oh where?" I said.

"Why right under the new paper, of course. If you call it new. It came loose last winter. You can see the other under it. Tear off all you want. I'm going to have it papered anyway. No — I don't like that old stuff. I want something modern, neat."

I tore off yards of it. Much of the color of the original design had been transferred to the back of the hideous 1870 paper. With the bonnet box as a guide, I took a faded piece of the original and repainted it in the right colors. I took it to Strahan and took the bonnet box too and left it with them to help their designer. I heard nothing from them and I assumed that they had decided not to reproduce it. They had, in fact, made the copy but, because of a change in management, no one knew that I was supposed to have some rolls of the paper; no one knew to whom the bonnet box belonged.

Many years later I took them another paper to copy. I asked about the Hollister paper and the bonnet box. I described the paper, its color and general look. I said I wondered if the box might still be with the originals of other old papers.

"I'll go and look. Is it oval or round?" a helpful young man asked.

"I think it's round," I said.

"And you're quite sure you didn't take it away."

"Quite sure," I said.

I suppose he must have had some Vermont blood.

He came back looking glum and said, "You were mistaken."

"It's been lost then, but thank you for looking," I said.

"It's oval," he said and pulled it out from behind him.

I almost cried, I was so glad to see it.

The paper was out of print. They had only a sample left but that they gave me. They also reproduced three other papers I found — one from Rich's great-great-grandfather's house in North Montpelier, one from a paper, put on for the wedding of his great-uncle John Van Rensselaer Kent, on the walls of the Robinson house in Calais, and one from the Brick House.

The project I enjoyed most was rescuing the original wallpaper in the hall of the Brick House from under two layers of modern paper. The old pattern had bunches of grapes and scrollwork and panels of marble, over which the grapes hung. It was a hand-blocked paper and the colors with which it was printed — shades of gray and white, accented with brick red — had come off on the back of the paper pasted over it in 1870.

I saved these mirror images. Where there was a gap in the original paper, I would find the right pattern, tear it off with a feather-edged margin and paste it over the empty space. Unless you examined the wall closely it was almost impossible to see where the gaps had been. One of Kenty's Bryn Mawr friends, Elizabeth Monroe, helped me a great deal. She carefully removed a piece of the original paper, enough to show the whole design, from a dark place in the upper hall. We sent it to Strahan's in Chelsea, Massachusetts, makers of some of the finest papers. They reproduced it, giving us enough to do the other two halls of the house and returning the original piece. This Elizabeth put back on the wall so neatly that I could pass it without noticing it had ever been removed.

About 1950 I became interested in stenciled walls. The Brick House had become the Kent Museum and Nora Gallagher had given it her collection of weaving equipment. It was housed in the part of the old store where boots and shoes used to be made a hundred years earlier. Plaster had crumbled and fallen off the walls. It was still lying where it fell.

I swept up plaster and dumped it on the compost heap. This was an improvement, but the room was still an unattractive background for Nora's looms and spinning wheels. I decided to have the walls covered with Sheetrock and to stencil them with old designs. Fortunately by this time I had met Ralph Weeks.

One day when I was enjoying the sunshine on the front porch a young man appeared with a can of roofing paint and asked if I would like the porch roof painted. He had heard in East Calais that it needed it.

I said that I supposed it did and asked when he could paint it. Vermonters usually temporize in such matters. I had once asked another painter when he could come to work.

"Well," he had replied, "maybe — if the weather holds up and the paint I'm putting on down in Gospel Hollow dries good and if we don't have company — my wife's sister's family from Ohio might drop in anytime — and if I don't get this distemper that's around, I might possibly get up to Kents' Corner perhaps Thursday — or maybe Friday — pro-ably."

I had almost never heard a promise to come to work that was not cautiously embellished with the word "pro-ably."

It was rather a shock to have the young man say: "My name's Ralph Weeks. I'll be here tomorrow morning at seven o'clock."

He came promptly and has been coming ever since. He does painting, carpentry and plumbing. He changes electric fuses. He makes the hi-fi work by snapping a tube with his forefinger. He makes picture frames to surround the windows through which you look into miniature rooms. He runs cement mixers to make dams for ponds, picks peas, builds dormers, whittles a piece of fretwork for the top of a grandfather clock, saws out a properly curved scroll for the bottom of a Chippendale mirror. He cleans stovepipes. I have never seen him cook anything, but he was a cook in the army. He gave me his rule for bread.

It begins: "Take fifty pounds of flour . . ."

Naturally I told him about my plan for the walls of the weaving room. By the time I had cut the stencil, he had the room really clean, the floor sanded and the Sheetrock up. Pearl Bullock and I did most of the stenciling in places where we could reach easily but Ralph did the oak leaf and acorn border near the ceiling. I used to stand below his stepladder, wash the back of the stencil with turpentine each time it was used and hand it back to him, keep just the right color and depth of paint ready in an old tin pan so he could touch his brush into it.

I used designs from Janet Waring's book on stenciled walls — patterns in pinkish red and soft green rather like the Tudor rose. I drew the designs on heavy brown paper, cut out the patterns with a razor blade, shellacked both sides of the paper. They are still in excellent condition — in case I feel another attack of stenciling coming on.

However my favorite wall decoration is not stenciled. It is in the Old West Church on the second floor, near the entrance to the balcony. In 1877 Blanche Kent took her six-month-old son to church. She decided to sit, not in the Kent pew, a pine box near the pulpit, but at the back of the balcony so she could take him out easily if he cried.

The friend with her pointed to the section of plastered wall near the balcony door and said: "Blanche, that plaster looks damp. Do you suppose it is?"

"We'll see," said Blanche and pushed her son's bare foot against it.

It was damp.

My favorite wall decoration is the print of Ira Rich Kent's foot.

27

Neighbors

A VERMONT HABIT, slightly bewildering to outsiders, is to call a house by the name not of the present occupant but by that of someone who lived there twenty-five years ago. Among the various roofs Rich had to keep shingled was that of the Delaney place. This story-and-a-half house faced the mill pond and the sunset. Its south side looked down the valley, past the lady elm, to Spruce Mountain. Mrs. Delaney arrived from Ireland when she was about sixty years old in time to be Rich's nurse in 1876. When he went to boarding school at Goddard Academy in Barre, ten years later, she was given a pension by Rich's father and the use of the house for her lifetime. She lived to be more than a hundred years old.

In 1912, when I made my first visit to Kents' Corner, Mrs. Delaney gave me, as a wedding present, something she had treasured since 1815 — a small wooden doll. Her joints still work well. Her face, hands and feet are all delicately carved and painted. If she had a dress it should be something a lady would have worn to a dance on the eve of the battle of Waterloo.

After Mrs. Delaney died, the house stood empty awhile. Later it was rented to a succession of John Graham's hired men. Rich stated mildly that it was not being improved. He told me that if I had any friends I would like for summer neighbors, he would give them the house and the small piece of land, fenced off from the farm, on which it stood. It wasn't, he said, much of a present. All you could say for the house was that its situation was attractive, its foundation and roof in good repair and that whoever lived in it would have good neighbors, the Fitches up the hill. However, if someone liked Vermont . . . liked fixing up a place . . . if I could think of anyone . . .

I had already thought of them — James Aldrich, head of the boys' department at the Park School and his wife Esther. James, known as "Sir" to both boys and girls at the school, was a Vermonter. Esther, a niece of Ida Tarbell, came originally from Titusville, Pennsylvania. She gave one the impression that she had been present when the first oil well in the United States began to gush in Titusville — if she had not drilled the well personally.

When we first met, the best seller of the moment was a pamphlet called *Acres of Diamonds*. It was a sermon really. The author had a formula for health, wealth and happiness: you could achieve all three by buying the pamphlet for ten cents — a bargain certainly. The author practically had his own acre of diamonds and without the trouble of digging them up.

I went to call on Mrs. Aldrich not because I had an inkling that I was going to make one of the best friends I ever had but because my conscience was at work. It told me I ought to call on the wife of the new master. They lived in an apartment on Walnut Street. I rang the bell. Someone called down "Who is it?" in a genial tone that implied that, of course, it was someone delightful.

I said: "It's Mrs. Kent, Sam's and Posy's mother."

"Mrs. Kent? That's wonderful! Come right up, Mrs. Kent, and behold me in my new dress — Acres of Diamonds."

So I went up, laughing, and beheld her, a tall woman in a crisp gingham dress with rather less than an acre of small green diamonds on a white ground. I don't think I ever saw her that she didn't make me laugh. It was her genial acceptance of the peculiarities of the world and of those of its inhabitants rather than the exact thing she said that made all her friends laugh. She was, in fact, inimitable.

That summer Grandma Kent lent the Aldriches for a few weeks Remember Kent's pioneer cottage — as she called it. This gave them a sample of life at Kents' Corner so that they could decide whether they wanted the Delaney place. Esther's aunt, Ida Tarbell, joined them. She was to me a mythical figure, known only through her books on Lincoln, on Napoleon and through her muckraking articles on the oil industry. I never supposed a muckraker would be gentle, charming and tolerant but Aunt Ida, as we all soon called her, was all three. She liked Kents' Corner and soon after she came she told Esther she would help her fix up the Delaney place; that she would give her the money to do it at once instead of leaving it to her.

There was no doubt that it needed fixing. Never having been in it except under Mrs. Delaney's management, I naïvely supposed that it was a matter of paint and new wallpapers. As soon as I stepped through the front door and almost fell over a bright blue kitchen sink with a hand pump, I realized that changes were needed. One of the recent tenants had placed the sink in this central position. It was in the bedroom. The living room too had an unusual arrangement. Along its rear wall was a row of small cubicles, also an improvement since Mrs. Delaney's day. They extended into the kitchen, right up to the cast-iron stove. Each held a hen's nest. One thing I will say for this interior decor — when you cooked a poached egg, you could be pretty sure it would be fresh.

In the kitchen was a large barrel. It contained old boots, broken glass, rags of interesting tints and textures, cabbages, beets and several cockroaches. It was this collection that made me speak, I'm afraid in a slightly critical tone, to Alice Graham, John's wife, about the recent tenants' methods of housekeeping.

"Oh well," she said tolerantly, "they were just young married folks."

It was extraordinary what an attractive place the Aldriches made out of this rural slum. I never saw it when its basic pattern was not peace and order and hospitality. Still, as a souvenir of old times, Esther would greet me at the front door, saying: "Welcome to Roachcroft!"

My children were so pleased with this remark that they had writing paper printed for her with "Roachcroft, Calais, Vermont" on it. She used it too.

They and their friends started speaking of her as the Duchess of Roachcroft. They addressed her simply as "Duchess." "Sir" Aldrich was promoted socially. He became a duke, by marriage, and was called "Duke" by the entire population of Kents' Corner, Maple Corner and parts of North Calais, East Montpelier, Plainfield, and Adamant.

About the time they were fixing the house, I met Dwight Keniston. I had heard that antique dealers got him to repair such treasures as tavern tables with three legs missing; that he made the new ones so well that dealers sometimes had him make a fourth leg and started work all over again with the original one. Mr. Keniston had a lathe, an unerring eye in using it and a sense of texture and color in bringing out the full beauty of wood. He fixed an old chest of mine so well that I decided he ought to be making antiques instead of tinkering with them.

I bought a book of measured drawings of pieces in the Metropolitan Museum. Using it, he made a butterfly table, some banister-back chairs and a Chippendale mirror. For the Duchess he made a seventeenth-century dining table, at which I had some of the best meals I ever ate, old armchairs topped with a carved sunburst and one of the butterfly tables. He also turned on his lathe the pieces for a mirror frame.

I painted the picture for the top of it, copying it from one that had been hanging in my dining room as long as anyone could remember. Painting on glass is nervous work. You have to do it not only wrong side to but inside out. No mistakes can be made; it has to be right the first time. The painting, a bowl of fruit lurking between red curtains, came out pretty well. We hung it just above where the blue sink and the pump used to be — an improvement, I used to think.

Mr. Keniston's granddaughter now runs my favorite beauty shop. She too seems to enjoy working on antiques. It is certainly not her fault that, when I look in the mirror at my newly arranged hair, I notice that I don't look quite so well as one of her grandfather's seventeenth-century armchairs. After all, the material used always affects the completed masterpiece to some extent. Besides I am about forty years older than the chairs.

In 1927 I made a mistake — in fact several. I put a low bookcase in front of one of Posy's windows to hold her toys. In bending over it to open the window, I slipped and fell. I did not go to an orthopedic doctor at first, but I had my back strapped up by a fine old-fashioned surgeon. He would probably have made a good veterinarian. He thought a woman ought to be as strong as a horse. He told me to go right on driving Sam out to Milton Academy every day. I could do anything I felt like doing; it would work out in time — that's what he said.

So I did my spring gardening, washed the china and glass on the highest cupboard shelves, cleaned out the dark closet under the stairs, reorganized both the attic and the cellar. Before long I had a splendid case of sciatica. It was worse if I sat down than if I lay flat or stood up. I was in bed for several months with an excellent orthopedist dropping in occasionally. For two years, even after he allowed me to be out of bed, I almost never sat down.

This peculiarity became so well known that, when I went to the Delaney house, the Duchess used to say: "Come right in! Which will you lie on — a hooked rug or a braided one? Or would you rather just lean on the mantelpiece?"

My journeys to Calais at that time were by night train in a lower berth. Luckily I had written the rough draft of my first book, *Douglas of Porcupine,* while I could still sit down. I revised it standing at my old schoolmaster's desk in the living room of the White House. I had planned to write the book for some time but I had resolved not to try to be a writer until the day my youngest child went to school.

One bright September morning I had taken Posy to the Park School. Then, equipped with a pad of yellow paper and several sharp pencils, I went to the Brookline Public Library and started writing my book. The background of it was Iron Bound, thinly disguised as Great Porcupine Island. The story was to be a combination of *Treasure Island* and *Little Women.* It followed this pattern so faithfully that it is still my favorite of all my books.

That first morning everything went well — my pencil sped quickly over the paper. I was never at a loss for a word. I knew my characters, since they were my own family with an extra boy added to balance things. I knew the house, since it was my grandfather's, every foot of the island with its iron-bound cliffs, every anemone in the rocky sea-washed cave where, in due time, the treasure would be found.

The children from the school next door came out shrieking and howling as I wrote but they did not disturb me. I was in a world much more real than theirs. I heard them again later. My hand kept moving across the paper. It never occurred to me that time was passing until my characters began to eat a meal. Feeling hungry, I glanced at my watch. Its opinion, obviously wrong, was that it was two o'clock. The library clock thought so too.

I was supposed to call for Posy at twelve. Since 1919 I had been picking up children at school. I had never been a minute late.

What would the school think? What would happen to Posy? Forgetting about the Douglas family, I drove rather fast.

The lower school was shut. At the upper school no one had ever heard of Posy. She must, I realized, have been kidnapped. Who could resist her charms? I hurried home, expecting to find a ransom note on the front steps.

I will not say that Goldie greeted me disapprovingly — she was too kind to do that in the presence of my distress — but I did feel a certain lack of enthusiasm about the writing of books in her voice. The school had telephoned, she informed me, and Aunty had gone for Posy in a taxi.

"They're out now," she said. "They're off to the police station and then to the hospital in case Miss Edgerly can identify a woman that's unconscious after an accident."

I telephoned the police and the hospital that I was at home. Both greeted, with a certain reserve, my explanation that I had been in the library writing a book. I never learned what they thought I was really doing. Aunty was more credulous but she did say she thought it would be better if I did my writing at home.

"And are you going to?" asked Margaret Whitney. "Won't you be interrupted by people dropping in and telephone calls?"

"I'm going to write in the guest room on the third floor and I've told Goldie not to disturb me for anything less than a broken leg," I said.

A few days later came the sound of footsteps running fast upstairs, a loud knock on the door and Goldie's voice saying: "Come quick to the phone, Mrs. Kent — your friend Miss Whitney's just broke her leg in three places!"

This was Margaret's formula for inviting an author to come and eat broiled squabs and mushrooms sous cloche and chocolate mousse with tiny sponge cakes the weight of thistledown. I accepted.

When *Douglas of Porcupine* was neatly typed — not by me — I took the script and put it on the desk in Rich's study across the hall from my writing room. I told him that I did not want to embarrass him by submitting it to Houghton Mifflin — he had recently gone to work there — but I would be grateful if he would read it. When he had, I said, I hoped he would do what he thought best — submit it to a magazine, to a literary agent, to another publisher or throw it in the wastebasket. I had absolute trust in his judgment. He didn't need to tell me what he'd done with it. And I wouldn't ask.

He said politely that he was sure he would enjoy reading it. I heard nothing about it for months. I suppose I must have had some confidence in it. When Posy came home from school one day and asked me to tell her all about ancient Tyre and when I realized I didn't know anything about it, I began to study the subject and to plan a story with Tyre as the background.

By the time I had read and taken notes on all the books I could find about Tyre, my orthopedist had told me to stay in bed with a pillow under my knees and none under my head. This is a better position in which to write a book than you might think. I had my paper on a clipboard. I wrote in pencil. I held the board over my head where I could look up at it.

This was such a tiresome process that I never wrote a sentence unless I was sure of exactly what I meant to say down to the last comma. The result was that *Two Children of Tyre* needed less revision than any book I have ever written. It was printed almost exactly as I first wrote it. Posy was a great help. As soon as she came home from school, she would rush upstairs and present herself at my bed, saying: "Read me our story, please — and tell me what will happen tomorrow!"

What more inspiration could a writer ask?

By the time I had finished the book, I was allowed to get up every day. My doctor said I might try going to New York. Rich wanted me to go with him to Atwater Kent's spring party, given for the artists on his radio program. Atwater was the first advertiser who consistently put good music on the air. Up to the time he started his program, the fact that you could hear anything at all — "Home on the Range," soap operas — simply by turning a few knobs was mysterious and exciting enough. On Atwater's program, you heard Metropolitan stars sing, famous violinists and pianists playing. I wish I could hear those programs again with their maximum of music and minimum of advertising.

On our journey, since I still could not sit down without discomfort, I stood leaning on the back of my Pullman chair most of the way to New York. I had to sit down at lunchtime. My order was small.

"Don't you want any dessert?" Rich asked.

When I said I thought not, he put his hand into his inner breast pocket, pulled out a paper and handed it to me saying: "Perhaps you'd like this instead."

It was a letter from a publisher, not Houghton Mifflin, accepting *Douglas of Porcupine*.

My back stopped hurting for the first time in months.

"Oh Rich," I said, "how I love that editor! Did you see the nice things she said? When will they publish it? Do you suppose anyone will buy a copy?"

"Not so fast," Rich said. "Houghton Mifflin is making you a better offer."

Publishers competing for my work! This must be happening to someone else!

I said, "Don't you think I ought to stick to my first friends? Wouldn't it be sort of mean to leave them now?"

However I allowed myself to be persuaded to become a Houghton Mifflin author; I've never regretted it.

When I had signed the contract, right among the Melba toast

crumbs, Rich said, "I hope you are going to be a good author."

"I hope so too," I said. "I hope we'll sell lots of books."

"That," he said, "is not what I meant."

I asked what a good author was.

It seems that a good author is diligent, prompt in delivering manuscripts, careful about correcting proofs, willing to accept editorial suggestions. He should put any pride and temperament he has into his work, not into relations with his publishers.

"Remember," Rich said, "that the editor who reads your book is probably the most intelligent reader you'll ever have. If he thinks it needs changes, it almost certainly does. Don't forget that the publisher's interest is the same as yours. You both want the book to be a success. He'll do his best to make it so. You must work with him."

I made splendid resolutions about being a good author.

I'm still trying.

I was so excited about my book being accepted that Atwater's splendid party was almost an anticlimax. After we had seen the broadcast through a special peephole in the studio wall, we went to a hotel where Atwater had engaged the whole lower floor for the evening. There was an elaborate supper with champagne, eaten while a floor show went on. There was dancing to the latest thing in jazz by men in evening clothes and by seals in business suits. The men had famous names but they could not equal the seals.

We stayed long enough in New York for me to stand up through *The Green Pastures*. We had a box so I could stand in the back of it and not be in anyone's way. Then I rode back to Boston, standing or walking through the train, and went back to bed. The trip had not helped my sciatica. My doctor said he thought we should consider an operation. He called in a surgeon, a high potentate who beamed kindly at the suggestion.

I asked for details. It would mean three or four months in the hospital in a plaster cast, he said. I brought up the sordid matter of expenses. He figured it all out for me, doctors' fees, hospital, nurses, physiotherapists. I am not sure whether the plaster for the casts was included but the sum was considerable. He was the kindest and the best of men, but surgeons like to show their virtuosity in challenging circumstances and they like to help people. He naturally looked pleased when I confided to him that I had slightly more than the amount he'd named in the savings bank.

"But," I went on, "I am going to use it the way I'd planned — for my daughter's coming-out party. I'll just have to get well some other way."

So I did.

Fortunately my back recovered soon after Kenty's coming-out party. I had been improving steadily but it was the dance, with Ruby Newman playing "Night and Day" and "Three Little Words" and "Tales from the Vienna Woods," that completed the cure. I got so I could sit at a desk and write, drive my car, even sit down while I shelled peas. I have also shelled a good many lying flat on my back on a Gloucester hammock. I have cut green beans too in this position. I have even husked corn. I don't recommend husking corn on your back. Corn silk is too adhesive, especially in your hair.

Having spent all my savings on the party and cured my back in the process, I now needed to earn some money. It seems incredible but, just at this time, I was offered cash to lecture to women's groups. Of course, I realize we had gone off the gold standard but even to be paid paper money for my conversation was pretty remarkable, I thought. My publishers encouraged me to accept the invitations. I was terrified — the first few times I couldn't eat anything but milk toast for days beforehand — but somehow I managed to keep the engagements.

One thing you find out, if you speak before women's organizations, is your lack of importance. What to you is a crisis, to your listeners is a trivial matter. You learn this beforehand by listening to the report of the last meeting. I would be trembling, of course, but my teeth did not chatter loud enough so that I did not learn that they were economizing on me. The month before they paid a hundred dollars. (They were giving me twenty-five.) Next month, the chairman assured the members, they were going to have someone really first class. His price was two hundred and fifty. They must all be on hand. Extra guest tickets would be available at two dollars. Their list of expenses was varied. The treasurer read them all including a dollar to the Red Cross.

Once a man came especially to introduce me. First he was glibly introduced by the chairwoman. She gave him a piece of paper. From this he read that our speaker today, well known to all, was the author of *Douglas and the Porcupines, Two Children of Tyresan* (or did he say Tarzan, I wasn't sure) and of editorials in *The Boston Globe*. It was a privilege to have me with them, he said, and he would now present . . .

He turned to me and said loud enough so everyone in the room could hear him, "What's your name?"

Meekly, I told him.

"Louiser Anderson Katz," he repeated and sat down, leaving me to face the amount of applause suitable to an economy speaker.

The club on these occasions, having paid money, is in no mood for frivolity. The faces of the audience bear expressions that seem to say, "All right — try to make me laugh, stupid. You can't do it."

I did though a couple of times.

Audiences containing even a few men are less rigid than the purely feminine kind. Sometimes a man says "Ha! Ha" at nothing special so loudly that the assembled wives and maiden aunts look disapprovingly at him instead of at the speaker. Of course clubs are

not all alike. Now the one I am thinking of at the moment —
yours probably, dear reader — is full of generous, sensitive intelli-
gences. Their faces glow with enthusiasm. The speaker feels witty
and charming. She would gladly come and talk for nothing. In
fact it is quite possible that she does.

When, about 1930, I first started giving my lecture on old pottery and porcelain, color photography was a novelty. There were
only a few men around Boston who were experimenting with Agfa
color plates and just one woman, my friend Sally Russell. The reason I was invited to talk about old Chinese porcelain was that I had
written an editorial called "Mysterious Lowestoft." It explained
how Chinese-export porcelain became confused with Lowestoft.
Dishonest antique dealers in England a century ago passed off Chinese pieces, decorated in Canton with coats of arms, as the extremely rare armorial pieces from the small pottery at Lowestoft.

The name is still used carelessly even now although the person
using it knows perfectly well that he is talking about china made in
the potteries at Kingtehchen, where the right kind of clay still exists.
He knows too that it was carried over mountains on the backs of
coolies and down small streams and great rivers to Canton or Nanking or Foochow where it was decorated.

The same shaped sugar bowl or plate or tall chocolate pot might
be painted with Chinese patterns or — if it were going to England
or America — it might have an ermine-draped shield with a coat of
arms and a gold-starred border of dark blue. If it were to be sold in
France, it might be wreathed with garlands of flowers. The Dutch
taste was more severe; Chinese artists copied black and white engravings of scriptural subjects to meet it, with the result that Moses
in the bulrushes and Pharaoh's daughter both looked slightly Chinese. Turkish coffeepots and cups had remarks on them in Arabic
script. Pieces intended for America often showed clipper ships or
gold eagles. Somehow both ships and eagles had a Chinese air.

I started photographing our family pieces in black and white. Margaret Wight, to whom I showed my first pictures, said that they must be in color. Sally Russell could easily show me how, she said. I thought it was asking a good deal and said so, but Margaret was so firm that I asked Sally if she would mind giving me one or two lessons.

She gasped slightly. "I think it might take more than that," she said, "but come along tomorrow and we'll try."

It took several months of hard work, much of it Sally's, before the pictures were ready. Including choosing backgrounds, arranging china so that each piece was in focus, setting up lights, calculating exposure times, it took about three hours to make a picture. After each Agfa plate was exposed, we developed it in Sally's darkroom. This took about fifteen minutes. There were several processes to go through before we could check the final result. If it did not satisfy Sally, we did it all over again. She had not only the desire for perfection and the knowledge of how to achieve it, but also the photographer's essential tool — patience.

The developing was mostly done in the dark. We could not use a red light, I learned, because the plates were especially sensitive to red. An occasional flash of pale bluish-green light was allowed at certain intervals, but most of the time we were rocking a plate back and forth in a chemical bath to the loud ticking of the time-clock. To get one picture taken, the plate developed, dried, backed with glass, the two pieces of glass taped together, the thumb spot put on the proper corner so that plate would be in the right position in the projector was a good morning's work.

However, by the appointed day, I had enough pictures for my lecture. I managed to get through it without any calamity. Before long I had slides for three more talks; one on old costumes, one on flower arrangement, one a collection of outdoor scenes called "New England is a Garden." Margaret Wight did a great deal of work on the costumes. We had some lay figures, which used to lurk in her house or Sally's or mine. They frightened visitors in all three houses by their sudden stately colonial appearance. To come into a room and find one staring at you — they all seemed to have excess thyroid — was like finding yourself in a story by Hawthorne or Poe. I was delighted when I had helped dress one of the ladies in ancient brocade for the last picture and could begin on the flower arrangements.

Margaret Wight also helped with these. Theresa Cunningham arranged one of my favorites. Members of garden clubs used to call me in when they had an especially handsome bouquet on hand. They made appointments with me as if I were a doctor. I would arrive with my Graflex camera, my heavy suitcase full of equipment — special light, yards of light cord, reflectors, a dark cloth to put over my head — while I brooded on my subject. I was as conscientious a photographer as Matthew Brady. No guilty flower escaped my lens and shutter.

I earned a good deal of money by my lectures but I do not advise writers to take up this pastime. In my opinion writers should stick to writing, compared to photography a restful pursuit, especially if you have a corn barn — and I did.

28

Corn Barn

IN 1932 Rich gave me an unusual present for the twentieth anniversary of our wedding. The corn barn — the Vermont term for what other people call a corn crib — stood across the road from the White House.

"I'll have it cleaned out and moved across the road for you," Rich said. "It can go on the back lawn near those old apple trees and lilacs."

He had just brought me a suggestion from Houghton Mifflin for another book to write. He added, "You know, I feel like one of those old men who go out with a cart and bring home washing for the wives to do. At least I might give you a quiet place to write."

"Of course I'd love it," I said, "but wouldn't it be a lot of work?"

"Oh, just a few days to move it," he said lightheartedly. "Then you'll need a fireplace. I'll get Levi Ainsworth to build you a chimney — that'll take a little while, of course."

It took three weeks just to get the corn barn into its present position. There were no tractors in the neighborhood then. Rollers made of whole tree trunks were put under and in front of the corn barn. Teams of horses pulled it, a few inches at a time, from one roller to the next. As soon as a roller was empty, it was carried to the front. The weathered gray building had looked small among the burdocks across the road. When it was perched on the rollers it loomed up like a cathedral — one that might fall on someone any minute.

The horses would stand panting in the hot sun while the movers changed the rollers. Then there would be shouting, cracking of whips and angry whinnying as the horses tugged at the chains between them and the building. More often than not, the chains broke. We borrowed others from Clyde Fitch, John Graham, Lewis Bancroft, Julius Wheeler, Elgin Mann and other good neighbors. I took all the chains, when the moving was finished, to the local blacksmith to have him mend them.

When I opened the trunk of my car and showed him what was in it, he said, "Hm — guess the depression's over!"

He was the last of our local smiths. Once a customer complained of his charge for replacing a horseshoe. He said he could get the best doctor in Montpelier to come and see him for less than that.

"Hm," said the smith. "Is that right? And can he shoe a horse?"

During the moving it occurred to me that if the corn barn could be lightened by even a few hundred pounds it might be easier for the horses to get it going. The outside boards were nailed on with cracks between them more than an inch wide so that air would circulate through the building and dry the corn. I suggested that, since the boards would have to be taken off anyway and fitted tightly together, they might as well be removed now and be carried on a wagon to the new site when they were needed.

Naturally no one paid any attention to this pindling advice or to my saying that old chests, winnowing fans, hoes, rakes and hundreds of handmade bricks could be taken across the road separately. The movers went on shouting and cracking whips as horses panted and chains whanged apart. They did — because Rich had told them to before he left for the peace and quiet of Boston — shovel out about half a ton of pedigreed ancient corn, straw and accompanying rats' nests. They did not, however, intend to have a woman interfere with their manly sports.

It took a whole day just to drag the corn barn across the narrow graveled road. One night the front gable end, hung with lanterns, just edged out into the east side of the road. The next night the rear gable end, also illuminated, touched the west side. Now it had only to travel through the muddiest part of the field below the carriage house, around it, around the barn, past the ice house, past the woodshed, through the Joe-Pye-weed, through turtlehead and arrowhead, crushing wild orchis and blind gentians, till it came to the spot where it now stands.

Grandma Kent's contribution to my wedding present was the discovery and purchase of a little tumbledown house on the other side of town. Sam and various nephews who were staying with us, helped to take down the interior woodwork — wide boards, handmade moldings, the panel over the parlor mantel — and transport them to Kents' Corner. They also brought old bricks, hand-forged latches and hinges and the many-paneled front door.

Most of the woodwork had been painted a dingy leaden gray. The children and their friends and I spent much of that summer scraping off this paint with curved pieces of broken glass. When I went to an auction, I would take a piece of molding from the old mantelpiece, also glass and steel wool with me, and uncover the dull gold pine as the bidding went on. By the time the corn barn was cleaned, railings made for the stairs, outside boards fitted together to fill up air spaces, other gray boards found for the resulting gaps, the roof shingled and the chimney built, we had the inside paneling ready.

George Coffrin, who had worked as a boy with his father building the round barns on East Hill, did the carpentry. His bills — as usual — were neatly written on pieces of curly maple or pine from the woodshed. I never paid any bills with so much pleasure.

Before we went back to Brookline, I started to do my daily stint
of writing in the corn barn. I worked at Remember Kent's dinner
table, made of a single board sawed from a primeval pine. Dorman
Kent said his grandfather had told him that Remember and his
wife Rachel each used a pewter plate and a silver spoon. Food for
their eight children, seven boys and a girl, was served in a wooden
trencher that ran almost the length of the table. Rachel would put
eight heaps of — say — saltpork with cream gravy, mashed potatoes, sliced beets and carrots in the trencher. The children would
go at the food with their pewter spoons. If Ira did not eat all his
portion, Abdiel would finish it for him.

When dishwashing time comes, I often wish I had such a handy
arrangement. I always hoped that the trencher would turn up under some heap of shingles or under the eaves. I suppose, a hundred
years ago, some pampered pony may have eaten his oats out of it.
Perhaps the rats from the corn barn now make their nests in it in
one of the cow barns. I have never found it or seen one like it.

At an auction in Waterbury, as I sat polishing a piece of molding, a bundle of old napkins was put up for sale. I saw a corner of
what looked like a piece of old glazed chintz. Part of the pattern
was the shade of greenish blue I had used in the corn barn to paint
the new wood of window frames and of the stair railing. Thinking
there might be a yard of it I recklessly bid a dollar. There was
twenty yards, enough for the corn barn's six new windows.

We painted the floor a deeper shade of the same blue and covered the center of it with handwoven rag carpeting. Old chests and
spinning wheels found their way into the corn barn. There soon
was no excuse for not writing there: Rich had given me Ira Kent's
comfortable tavern chair to sit in and Kenty had made me a sign
for the door.

It said: "Danger! Author at work. Keep out. This means
YOU!"

The only trouble with this type of announcement is that there are always some people who say, usually with a superior smile, "I saw your sign but, of course, I knew you didn't mean *me!*"

Who was it I did mean? I used to wonder.

It was a mistake, I soon realized, to have put that handsome brass eagle knocker on the door and to have had that millstone from the first mill in Calais dragged a mile uphill so visitors could stand on it while they knocked.

I worked out a good system for securing peace and quiet. I had an old fiddle-back maple bed set up, among the spinning wheels and wool winders, upstairs in the corn barn. I did my writing while the family were having their breakfast and before visitors had laid their plans for kindly interruptions of a writer's idleness.

The corn barn continued to turn out books. All I did was to sit there and hold the pen. I had plenty of time because Pearl Bullock had fallen into the benevolent habit of walking down the road from her house to mine and doing whatever she thought would be helpful. Her judgment was excellent. I would emerge from writing *Jo Ann, Tomboy* or *He Went with Magellan* or *The Terrace* and find her washing a window, hulling strawberries for shortcake, braiding a miniature rug or baking Mrs. Appleyard's oatmeal lace cookies.

Mrs. Appleyard and Pearl appeared in my life about the same time. Luckily we all three became friends. It was a case of two's company, three's friendship. The only time Pearl spoke crossly to me during the twenty-five years she helped me was once when I asked her if she would mind baking a sponge cake.

"The trouble with you is," she said, "you're too polite. Don't keep asking me if I mind. Just say, 'Pearl, make a sponge cake!' Now what do you want for lunch?"

"Cheese soufflé, if you don't m———. Cheese soufflé," I said so brusquely that it's remarkable the soufflé didn't fall flat.

How lucky it was that it rose and how lucky I was to have a corn barn in which to sit and write while it was rising!

I had decided to follow Rich's suggestion of making a book out of the short pieces I had written for the Boston *Herald*. I had pasted them neatly in a scrapbook. When I read them over, I found the effect both choppy and monotonous. Because I was allowed only a certain amount of space in the *Herald*, I had become quite adept at compressing my small ideas into a small space. This habit — an easy one to unlearn, I notice — made reading over the editorials rather like tripping over bricks on a Beacon Hill sidewalk. You had to keep stopping and pick yourself up. I decided — the idea was extremely distasteful — that work, a great deal of work, would have to be done.

When Rich made his next visit to Kents' Corner, I told him my idea, which was to make a seasonal book out of some of the editorials, to write more pieces for each season, and to group them around one central character.

"A woman," I said, "not like me. Someone genial, a cozy, friendly type — more like Esther Aldrich."

"Not a bad idea. What do you think of calling her?"

"Mrs. Applegate," I said.

"That sounds as if you shut people out — she ought to welcome them in. Call her Mrs. Appleyard," he said.

Since he was my favorite editor, I took his advice and went to work on *Mrs. Appleyard's Year*.

I grew fond of her as I wrote. I have never — for excellent reasons — quite accepted being identified with Mrs. Appleyard. It's one of those awkward cases of a split personality. Mrs. Appleyard has all the pleasant traits. Mine are the uninteresting ones.

I am the one who kicks herself out of bed in the morning and sits writing neatly on ruled paper with a manuscript pen. I am the one who pays her bills so promptly and whose checkbook has been honestly balanced every month since August 1912. I am the one who, when cooking, carefully follows her own printed instructions, measuring every teaspoon of cinnamon, every drop of peppermint extract.

Who — I wonder — is it who conducts wars on carpet beetles? Who moves an old Delft sugar bowl a quarter of an inch so it balances perfectly with the teapot? When an earthquake knocks a precious Bristol bowl off the shelf and breaks it into twenty-eight pieces, it is not Mrs. Appleyard, I hope to tell you, who puts the pieces together. To do that she would have to lay aside her dashing ways and think like a bowl. You must brood over the fragments until you feel the emotion of bowlishness. I doubt if Mrs. Appleyard can submerge her personality in a lot of broken pottery.

I found out that others notice the difference between us when I went across into the next county to luncheon last summer.

"I am going to put you next to Mrs. Edwards," my hostess told me. "She says she's always wanted to meet you."

Mrs. Edwards had been beside me about two minutes when she stated: "You're not a bit like what I thought you were going to be."

"Perhaps I can be more like it if you'll tell me how it was," I said.

"I thought you were going to be little and dumpling and rosy-cheeked and cute," she said wistfully.

There really didn't seem to be much I could do about it.

I was pleasantly surprised when *Mrs. Appleyard's Year* appeared on the best-seller list in *The New York Times*. Just above it was *The G-string Murders* by Gypsy Rose Lee. This happy literary combination climbed slowly up the list, with Mrs. Appleyard always slightly behind. By the time they were halfway up the ladder of fame, the country was involved in the Second World War and Sam was with the Mountain Troops.

For a time he was the only private. He had the boots of forty-five officers to polish. One morning his friend and Harvard classmate, John Pierpont, arrived at the camp so there were two privates. Naturally with so many officers around, there were copies of the *Times* in camp. One day Sam saw that *Mrs. Appleyard's Year* had moved ahead of *The G-string Murders.* He got permission to hitchhike to the nearest telegraph office so he could send me a message of congratulations. He had it written down.

It said: "Good for you. See you have outstripped Gypsy Rose Lee. Love, Sam."

"You cannot," the clerk said primly, "send this obscene message. You may say 'surpassed.' That will be two-fifty."

Sam said, "I should spend two and a half dollars to say 'surpassed!'" hitchhiked back to camp and sent his congratulations by mail.

29

Cake and Confetti

JUST BEFORE I met Pearl and Mrs. Appleyard, I took a trip to Arizona. Like Henry Thoreau, who fell in love with a pond, I fell in love promptly with the desert. I loved mesquite, either growing or burning in a fireplace. I loved a climate where there was cats' ice in the gutters in the morning and hot enough by noon so that you needed the shade of tamaracks. I loved cactus — cholla cactus with its strange electric radiance, cactus like barrels or organ pipes or twisting ribbons, saguaro cactus, lying like long dead alligators or thrusting dark arms against a sky full of stars. I loved the Grand canyon.

I planned to be the first woman from Boston to photograph the canyon in color.

It was almost sunset when we arrived at the canyon. Pink light was changing to purple the blue shadows of its red and ivory towers. I threw my handbag down on a bench. A benevolent couple on the next bench smiled kindly upon me as I hurried to set up my camera and covered my head with a black cloth. The glowing color was changing every minute but I took some pictures anyway. The dear old senior citizens were gone when I had finished my work. So was fifty dollars from my pocketbook. The picture was not bad but a little overpriced, I've always thought.

I was luckier the next morning. I was out at dawn, alone with the canyon, except for some deer, who had no financial interest in my work. When the canyon became visible, as light flowed down into it, I felt as if I were present at the creation of the world. I feel it again as I look at a picture I took just after sunrise that day.

Mabel Kent had given me the trip so I could be with Prentiss for his vacation. We went to a ranch near the Mexican border. Horses were included in our board. We rode out into the desert every day with vultures swooping over us, ready to pick our bones and any others that were left lying among the cactus. I liked crossing the border. Everything on the other side looked romantic.

When we stopped at our own post to report, we would call, "going out, back soon," to whichever officer was sitting tipped back against the wall with his khaki coat unbuttoned and his cap on the back of his head.

Things were different on the Mexican side. Dark figures with serapes draped in just the right folds stood dramatically against pink cement walls. There were always two of these guardians, leaning on their rifles, shooting flashing glances over the desert, looking grimly at us as we said, *"Aqui no más,"* to tell them we would not be long in their country. As they waved us on, the vultures glided above us. There seemed to be more of them sailing on the hot Mexican air currents than there were on our side.

All the front doors of the village would be open. In each one a fat woman sat behind her treasure — an American sewing machine. While she sewed, she called across the street to her neighbors or screamed at her children as they fought in the dust. Her seat was a vantage point from which she missed nothing. Her aged mother, forty-five at least, drove the goats to the river. They dragged a cart just big enough to hold a can of water, the family supply for the day.

When the mother came back, she ground corn with a pestle in a bowl of rough stone. Later she made tamales or enchiladas or cooked frijoles. The men leaned against walls looking handsome. Basically it was rather like a morning in Calais, Vermont, except that there the men leaned against clapboards and the women served muffins made of corn meal carefully packaged with all the life-giving substances removed. Instead of frijoles there would be baked beans from a can without those hot peppers loaded with vitamin C.

We had Mexican food at the ranch and I quickly acquired a taste for it as well as for the desert and for western ballads sung to the guitar. I still wake sometimes in green, well-upholstered Vermont and feel homesick for a breath of that clean dry air, for sculptured rocks, for the smell of a fire of mesquite branches. I feel somewhat as a man did in a Colorado garage when he saw Lew Manly's Vermont license plate.

"You're a long way from home," he announced. "I was back there once myself. You know, I reckon, if you'd scrape all that mess of grass and ferns and trees and stuff off it back there, you'd have some mighty pretty country."

I am not ready to display enough energy to follow his suggestion but I have moments — especially when I notice the forest of weeds among my tomatoes — when I understand how he felt.

When I left the ranch, I went to stay with Ada McCormick. When Ada found out that I had known the Richard Cabots and Dr. Cabot's mother, nothing would do but for me to come and stay. She had asked me if I knew them because she was writing a book about them. She said she wanted to pick my brains so it would be a good idea if I moved into her guest room. My brains did not really have a great deal to offer but that did not prevent my enjoying the house in the desert.

It had a cactus garden, palms and tamaracks. Jasmine with Arizona pyrrhuloxias flying in and out of it grew outside the living room window. These birds look like grayish cardinal grosbeaks lightly touched with pink until they open their wings which are lined with flaming rose color. Every time this happened was a moment of pure joy to me. Near the jasmine was a lawn like a 9 x 10 green velvet rug. Like all the best outdoor carpeting it was waterproof. A network of small fountains sprayed it every day and kept the grass growing. Perhaps there were other green lawns in Arizona but this is the only one I remember. It was a jewel, as unexpected as an emerald set in a piece of cinnamon toast.

The windows of my room opened on mountains ten miles away. In that clean clear air they looked as if I could reach out and touch them. They changed color constantly. They were a herd of pacing elephants one minute, a wall of rock with sea-blue pools shimmering in it the next. The glow before dawn scattered burning coals all over them but they did not burst into flames, only faded suddenly to rose, to brick red, to brown.

I had never managed to change from my eastern time schedule. I woke at four o'clock, seven by my inner clock, when it was still dark and coyotes were howling and barking at a bright white moon.

I made brief visits to Los Angeles and Santa Barbara. Sally Russell was on her way west and we met on the train by appointment. It was on time and I got on exactly at the right moment. It was eight o'clock when I joined Sally and Ben, her husband, in the dining car. Almost as soon as I sat down, the pheasants which Ben had shot in Georgia were brought in, beautifully roasted. There was bread sauce and other nutritious delicacies. Celery had been elegantly braised. Popovers had practically exploded. Brandied marrons glacés were lavished upon the ice cream.

The last time I ate on a train there was no dining car. I bought a ham sandwich. The ham, several fragments of it, was well throttled by tough lettuce and wads of fluffy plaster of Paris bread. I thought wistfully of that meal with Sally. Why hadn't I photographed it? Even projected on a screen it would have been more nourishing than that sandwich.

In Santa Barbara the gardens were full of flowers, which in Vermont would be deeply covered with snow. Larkspurs, roses and daffodils were all in bloom at once. I saw a citrus tree with oranges, limes, lemons and grapefruit growing on it. You could get your morning orange juice, your grapefruit for your dessert at lunchtime, the lemon for your afternoon tea and a lime for your beverages all off the same tree — an economy measure.

We went to a lecture where "Chinese" Wilson spoke. He had brought trees from China to New England. Many of them — flowering crabs and cherries — still grow in the Arnold Arboretum. After the lecture he answered questions. One lady, who wore pearls the size of kumquats, asked him what was the most beautiful place he had ever seen.

He smiled kindly upon her.

"I wish I could say what you would like me to say, California," he said gently, "but I must be honest. No country is completely beautiful that doesn't have four seasons."

It's true, I realized. Larkspurs in Santa Barbara do not grow with the passionate abandon of those in Vermont who know it is now or never. Wisteria in Maryland has a special brilliance of color. Tulips in New Jersey, dogwood in Connecticut, laurel in New Hampshire all show they know that their moment has come. In Massachusetts forsythia cascades over old stone walls making sunshine on gray days. *Linnaea borealis* on Iron Bound tells where its pink bells are by sending out great wafts of fragrance.

In Vermont experts on fall foliage run back twenty years as they appraise it. They remember the year when every maple had a Persian rug of leaves spread out beneath it on snow. They say the swamp maples are a brighter crimson than last year, the elms especially golden, the sugar maples dappled with the clearest vermilion for years.

They say: "About every five years ash leaves look like these — as if they'd been dipped in chocolate sauce."

They show you stone walls with poor man's daphne running along them. It has scarlet berries now. No rich man's garden has anything more thrilling to show than its first lilac-pink blossoms in early spring, I thought, and knew I must start east.

Soon after I got back to Arizona, I heard from Kenty that she was engaged to Lorie Tarshis; that they would like to come home and be married in Brookline at Easter.

I got out a pencil and began to make a list on the back of an envelope. Awning, punch, wedding dress and veil, wedding cake, dress for Posy . . .

I must have the dining room ceiling done over, I thought, and added it to the list. The last time it was done was the year we moved into the house. A non-union plumber, an old family friend, was putting in a bathtub. Union workers were toying with the hot water tank. They all left at the same time. The steam fitters did not mention to the plumber that they had turned on the hot water. I happened to be in the dining room.

I was almost drowned.

The resulting hole in the ceiling — it was large because it took me some time to get down to the cellar to shut off the main — had been replastered but I could always see where it had been. As soon as I got home I had the old marks smoothed off and the ceiling painted. It looked beautiful for three days.

The morning Kenty and Lorie Tarshis were to arrive, an ancient lead pipe decided its life work was over. The plaster gave way and fell on its regular place, right on the silver tea set on my grandfather's Queen Anne lowboy. I was mopping up water and plaster when I heard a car door slam. I looked out the window. Kenty and a young man with light curly hair were running up the front walk. I liked him before he even reached the front steps and I always have.

The hole was filled up again before the wedding but I could always see where it had been. I gave up the idea of concealing the scar and lived amicably with it for another twenty years or so.

We addressed and mailed the invitations soon after Kenty and Lorie came. The whole family got together in the playroom, just as if we were getting out a rush order of lead soldiers, directed them, filled them, stamped them. Wedding presents began to come in and Kenty wrote notes thanking the givers. She kept at it while I made the basis for the punch. She was still writing when it was time to put on the wedding dress. An occasional bride still persists in the old-fashioned custom of acknowledging presents. For the last four I sent, I received one delightful note. I believe this is rather above average.

Rich had ordered the ingredients for the punch. I had told him exactly what I needed. I thought it was rather a strange mixture but I poured everything in anyway on top of that mixture of tea and crushed lemons and oranges that Mrs. Appleyard has often recommended. When Rich came home that evening I gave him a sample. I wanted to be sure it was quite all right. He sipped it, and kindly praised the flavor.

But when he had finished the glass, he remarked thoughtfully, "If you want your guests to spend their time rolling happily down the front lawn, I suggest you keep on just the way you've started. What on earth did you put into it?"

It seems that the proportions of the recipe were overly generous. The rule for the punch is in the back of ". . . with Kitchen Privileges" under the title of "The General's Punch." The book is out of print but you might be able to get a second-hand copy. I bought one lately for ten cents — and well worth it in my opinion.

Not having a personal liking for the mixture I did not drink any punch.

Yet the wedding becomes a little blurred from now on. I remember that Arthur and Rebecca Perry took all the out of town ushers to stay in Dover, that the Davols' guest rooms were full of Kenty's Bryn Mawr classmates, that Rich gave the proper arm to his daughter so he did not have to jump over her train. I remember Goldie's smile as I came into the church on Sam's arm and that not only had the church hardly changed at all, but that Rich wore the cutaway he wore at our wedding. It fitted him perfectly.

Posy looked very grown-up in her first long dress. It was nice to see her without her glasses. She first started wearing them when she was the smallest child in the Winsor School. The principal of the school always remembered the day she saw Posy wearing two pairs of glasses, one on top of the other.

"Why Posy," she said, "did you mean to put on two pairs of glasses?"

"My mother bought me two pairs," said Posy firmly.

The principal had to call me to come to school and explain that it was customary to wear one pair at a time.

I remember that at the wedding Lorie's mother and aunt both looked beautiful and not much older than he did. I remember Kenty and Lorie cutting the wedding cake, beautifully frosted by Katy. Later Margaret Wight and Margaret Whitney wrapped up cubes of it in wax paper and silver foil for guests to take home.

It rained a good deal, I remember, so the awning and the tent were useful. The red carpet was too — every child in the neighborhood raced up and down it with shrieks of delight. Just before Kenty and Lorie left, someone brought Kenty's new accordion and pushed the straps over my shoulders and I found myself playing "Boston Fancy" while graduates of our lawn at Kents' Corner danced and other guests clapped to the rhythm. Suddenly the party was over. The bride and groom dashed down the walk in clouds of confetti and were gone — temporarily.

They were taking a late train so they came back after dinner and talked over the party. What nicer thing could a bride and groom do? We all praised each other. Rich said the punch was just right. Lorie told us the good news that he would be teaching economics at Tufts in the fall. Then it was time to go. They really went back to England this time.

I was not idle in the next few days. I had a book to write — *Paul Revere Square* — and I had to get used to my new bifocals. Try getting confetti out of a Tausendschoen rose bush in bifocals. You can plan your new book at the same time. If you have a good pair of tweezers, you can get enough of the thorns out of your fingers so you can soon hold the pen. You'll hardly have any time — except every minute — to miss your married daughter.

30

Publisher's Holiday

PAUL REVERE SQUARE appeared briefly among the lower names on the best-seller list. My favorite editor asked me to write a sequel to it. I spent a year writing *High Hollow*, which was never published. It was perhaps, a little too innocent for adults and a little too grown-up for children. It was too long and I had to cut it down. Possibly the real book was in what I cut out of it. I was thinking about it when Kenty and Lorie told us they were going to England so he could take the examination for his Ph.D. and asked us to come along too.

I promptly abandoned my papers in the corn barn.

By the time we were halfway across the ocean, Rich had had all the leisure he could stand. He no longer sat placidly watching the waves or dozing over a book. He began doing more and more walking around the decks. When he sat down beside me, he would talk about "his authors." He was afraid they were loafing and not getting their books done.

"Taking trips probably," he said gloomily.

I felt guilty. Here I was, taking a trip instead of sitting in the corn barn cutting another five thousand words, each perfect in its way, out of *High Hollow*. And making it steadily duller. If I could neglect my work right in his company, it did indeed seem probable, with him out of the country, that many writers had relaxed. Luckily at this moment a steward arrived with a radio message for him. As soon as he read it, his face cleared.

"I'll have to go right to Ipswich as soon as we get to London," he said happily, "and talk with Mrs. Havelock Ellis about her husband's papers. There'll be all kinds of problems."

From that moment our trip was a success.

When the *Île de France* steamed into Plymouth Harbor, I wasn't conscious of crying until the tears trickled down my cheeks. I felt as if I were Drake coming home from his voyage around the world or perhaps as if I were some pilgrim who had been to Plymouth, Massachusetts, on the *Mayflower,* who had decided he didn't like it and had come home again. Of course, I told myself as I mopped the tears off, it was just the sun in my eyes.

It was in my eyes a good deal as the train carried us from Plymouth to London. I had only to see a great oak with sheep lying in its shade on closely-nibbled green turf or a village street with thatched-roofed cottages or a church tower covered with ivy to get these attacks of eyestrain. It was partly, I suppose, because I kept hearing my father's voice. He had died in 1931 in his ninety-second year. One afternoon after his walk he had felt tired. He was lying down when I came to see him, as I did every day, but he sat up with his usual welcome: "You come like a boon and a blessing to men."

I had brought some color plates to show him — pictures taken by Sam of Kenty and me the night of her party and some of my flower pictures. He held them firmly against the light of his bedside lamp, seeing them clearly without his glasses, murmuring: "Beautiful — what color! I see every violet! And daffodils — the woods will be starred with them in England soon. They call them asphodels in Greece, you know . . . "

His sense of beauty never left him. While we were arranging for his rooms in a nursing home, flooded with sunshine with trees and grass outside, he had spent a short time in a dark, ugly room. The woodwork was black, the walls brownish, the rugs also brown, the

chairs of the ugly style known as mission. Buildings taller than the
house cut off the November light.

Yet he had something beautiful to show me. He led me at once
to the window.

"You see," he said, "I stand just here at sunset. Between those
two buildings — see? — a splendid ray of sunshine pours right
into this room. I see the sun as it slips down behind that other
building. It was like a hunter's pink coat yesterday. Sometimes I
see a patch of turquoise sky or the edge of a red and gold cloud.
Then it fades but I wait till the afterglow comes. Once when there
were no clouds, I saw the evening star."

I thought of that other room as he looked at the pictures. Where
I had seen only ugliness he had found a flash of beauty. When I
left him that last day I had said as usual, "I'll see you tomorrow,"
but when the telephone rang early the next morning it was to tell
me that he had died in his sleep.

In England he seemed close beside me. He had been right, I saw,
in telling me that there was something special in the greens of English grass. Even Vermont's greenest fields, even the small velvet
square that was Ada McCormick's lawn, had not quite the deep
brilliance of English turf. It was like a drink from a cold spring on
a hot August day.

It was his England I kept seeing — in the looming rocks of
Stonehenge, in the White Horse, edged by green turf on a hill of
chalk, in the view from Robert Andrew's lawn at the Auberies with
the same clouds hanging low in the sky that Gainsborough had
painted. I heard it in church bells, tasted it in a punnet of raspberries at Simpson's in the Strand, felt it in the dank cold sheets of
unaired beds.

I knew now what it meant when his English landlady, Mrs.
Soames, had written to him some years before in Brookline to tell
him she and her husband were expecting him and would be glad to
see him.

"Don't worry, Mr. Andrews," she had written, "about your bed being aired. It will be nice and warm. Soames and I have been sleeping in it for two weeks."

I often wished they had been sleeping a few nights in those I encountered.

At my cousin Gerald's London flat, I saw the Gainsborough painting of Robert Andrews and his wife. None of the photographs I had seen of it had done it justice. I felt as if I could step into the picture, walk past the golden wheat sheaves toward the green field where sunlight touched the fleece of grazing sheep, feel the roughness of the bark of the great old tree and the silken smoothness of my great-great-grandmother's blue dress.

I would not mind her looking prim and a little disapproving as if she were going to say, "Only fancy! Great-great grandchildren in America! — but where is your feather headdress, child? — and your wampum necklace? Now tell me all about living in a wigwam."

She would say "wham-pum" and "wig-wham," of course, so I said shyly: "In America we say 'wom-pum' and 'wig-wom,' Grandmother."

"Very likely," I thought I heard her say coldly, "but I would hardly care to acquire the American accent."

We went to Cambridge where Lorie passed the examination for a Ph.D. in economics, one of the first ever given. He acquired the right to wear a splendid gown and a wonderful floppy velvet hat. We stopped at Boston because Rich wanted to see St. Botolph's church. The St. Botolph Club in our Boston had helped in the restoration of its tower. When we got there, the sexton was just starting to ring the bells. He let Kenty and me ring a few peals of rejoicing over Lorie's degree. My bell was much easier to ring than the one with which I called the family to meals at Kents' Corner.

Our bell had once been on a Russian church. When the Russians discarded it, the Central Vermont Railway bought it and used it for a time on a railroad snowplow. After a few years it was discarded again in favor of a whistle. I bought the bell. Sam and his friend, Paul Kimball, and my nephew, William Frick, got it up to the woodshed roof while I steadied the ladder. The bell weighed about a hundred pounds. There was a moment when it slipped and seemed likely to fall on my head but it didn't. It has a tone as beautiful as that of my St. Botolph bell. For a while it was easy to ring but when the old rope broke, it was replaced with one of nylon, a substance excellent for stockings and all-weather carpets but not, in my opinion, suitable for bell ropes.

Pulling the St. Botolph bell rope made me feel that I might easily be carried to the top of the tower; that I could fly and make music all at once. Rich and Lorie pretended they did not know Kenty and me. They studied the plaque the St. Botolph Club had placed on the wall. To their relief, I'm sure, no opportunity presented itself to ring bells at the cathedrals of Ely, York or Lincoln.

Rich, who had been to Ipswich again about Havelock Ellis' papers, met us in Edinburgh. As we walked along a dark street in a thick fog, I was reminded of something my father once told me that his father had told him. My grandfather, on a visit to Edinburgh, used to walk along a street so dark that a candle burned all day in a certain window he passed. It was always the same in the window: the burning candle, someone writing, his hand moving steadily across the paper. You could not see the writer's face — the shade was always pulled partway down — just the moving hand and the quill pen and the writing on the paper.

"Who do you suppose writes all day here by candlelight?" my grandfather asked his friend, who answered, "Why, it's Walter Scott, writing to pay off his debts. He spent too much on Abbotsford, you know. Another book or two and he'll be squared with the world again. He's an honest man, is Walter Scott."

My father thought Scott might have been writing *St. Roman's Well* which was a favorite of his and of mine. In it Scott wrote of his own times instead of writing about knights in armor bashing each other on the head.

I'll read it again when I get home, I thought.

☆

Back in Vermont everything was peaceful for almost twenty-four hours. Sam and Posy and Anne Reese told us after lunch, the day after we arrived, that they were having a few of our friends in for supper that evening. None of us was to raise a finger. To be sure we didn't, they told Kenty and Lorie to stay in their own house till the bell rang. Rich and I were instructed to write letters in the corn barn and to plan to dress there.

When the bell rang for supper, we found the road and the lawn full of cars; that we were among twenty-eight guests most of whom were staying overnight — in the house or the carriage house or in Kenty's house or in a tent by the brook. For supper two harvest tables had been joined together. One was in the bird room, one in the map room. They met in the wide opening between the two rooms. Suspended over the place where the two tables met was a large arrow marked SALT. It swung around frequently so one group of guests or the other was sitting above it. The tables were covered with white damask and shining with all the best china and glass and silver.

The guests were told to choose hats from the collection in the carriage house. The men were to choose girls' hats and the girls men's. This, Sam explained to us, is because it would not be polite for men to wear men's hats in the house — a subtle point of etiquette not, I believe, covered by Emily Post. So tall beaver hats, Civil War caps, an opera hat that could be crushed flat under the arm, bowlers, the broad-brimmed hat Rich wore in the police strike appeared on girls' heads. Mardi Bemis looked especially dashing in a straw boater with a Lampoon hatband. Boys wore bonnets with rosebuds and feathers and velvet bows.

In this easy version of fancy dress, we sat below or above the salt, according to how the wind blew, eating Pearl's chicken pie and corn fresh from the garden and lima beans with mushrooms. I have seldom enjoyed a meal more. I hadn't cooked any of it. I hadn't marketed for it, or planned it, or even cut the pies. Moreover, my plate rested on a perfectly steady surface. Tastefully dressed in a smocked dress embroidered with rosebuds and with a tall silk hat on my head, I sat happily among the other guests and ate more than I had for a month.

I suppose I knew subconsciously that this meal marked the end of an era for everyone around the table. None of us would be quite untouched by what was going on across the Atlantic. Decisions about our lives were being made by a maniac in Germany. Sam, for instance, thought he was going out to Colorado to be a school-teacher. So he did — but it was also in Colorado that he was trained as a soldier, a member of the Mountain Troops. Kenty and Lorie were happily married but the war was to separate them, temporarily, then permanently. I could not, fortunately I suppose, know these things or that Rich and I would have only a few more years together.

Yet strangely, I felt for a moment as I was putting the hats back into their places in the carriage house, that I had been living in a rainbow; that like all rainbows it would fade — was fading — had faded — was lost in a dark cloud. Then the cloud lifted and I was back in the world I knew.

When the party broke up two days later and Ken Smith was engaged to Meg Home and I was pretty sure Mardi Bemis and Peter Perry were engaged or would be soon, I retreated to the silence of the corn barn and began work on my new book.

31

War—and Peace

RICH WAS HEAD WARDEN for our small section of the town. I was his deputy. One of us was always in reach of the telephone. I had it beside me as I wrote *Mrs. Appleyard's Kitchen.* Just taking a Red Cross course in first aid, learning to be an air raid warden and having the air raid post in our house seemed like natural, simple occupations.

The reason I wrote *Mrs. Appleyard's Kitchen* was that Kenty's friends knew that I had a handwritten cookbook in which I had recorded exactly how we had made those cream puffs or that apple chutney. They used to write, especially after they were married, and ask for the receipts. (I had been taught to say receipt or rule — not recipe.) After a while it occurred to me if I wrote out rules for our various experiments and had them printed, I would have a book that would make a handy wedding present. I was one of my own best customers during the twenty years the book was in print.

I generously gave Mrs. Appleyard credit for my struggles with the kitchen stove though I never heard of her while I was wrestling with split maple, shingles, coal, briquettes and kerosene. Each of these substances has its own virtues and its own drawbacks. You can turn out a good chicken pie or produce a well carbonized casserole with any of them. In fact you can also do both with gas or electricity as I discovered as soon as I used them. When my friends are surprised at my writing cookbooks, I explain that I have two special assets. The first is that I have made all the possible mistakes in cooking so I can warn you gloomily about them. The second is that if — by some happy combination of circumstances — I cook something that turns out well, I write down immediately how I did it so that I can duplicate the result another time.

One of the difficulties of the war years was food rationing, but I was fortunate in undergoing much of it in Elsie's company. Elsie had lived with me as a waitress fifteen years before. In the meantime she had married, had four children and was now a widow. She boarded the children with a friend and earned enough as a cook-housekeeper to take care of them.

I remembered Elsie chiefly as a pretty, good-hearted, careless girl who broke a good many glasses. When I heard from her, I had just discharged Hannah, an excellent cook, clean, neat, of splendid character — as she often told me. It happened that I had gone out one day at lunchtime, but had forgotten something and had come back.

She did not hear me but I heard her. She was being intolerably rude to Aunty. I came in and found Aunty in tears. I gave Hannah a week's wages in lieu of notice, saw her off the place and became a cook temporarily. It was during this period that rationing seemed especially difficult. Rhodes Brothers, where I had done my marketing ever since my marriage, closed its Brookline store. Mr. Hutchins — number 4 — who had always looked after his customers as if they were troublesome but favorite children, had retired.

The new store was one of a chain and quite impersonal or so I supposed at first. Its meat counter, under rationing, seldom contained anything more appetizing than beef liver and pickled tripe. Elderly hamburg was something for which I stood eagerly in line. It was often all gone before my turn came. It took me some time before I realized that the store was not so impersonal as I had supposed. It had special favorites only I was not one of them. Large red-faced men carried off whole hams and roasts of beef, pushing through the patient lines waiting for hamburg to get the bundles. They must have had as many ration coupons as I could have used in a month to get them yet they were never nervously clasping their ration books like me and the rest of the polloi.

They always paid over the counter in generous wads of bills though the other hungry waiters and I had to go through the check out. The manager, tall, strong and genial — to the right people — always waited on them personally. I had already begun to have my own opinion — cynical I'm afraid — about these transactions at the time of the special steak sale. It was a surprise to see all the steaks displayed in the counter. They looked tantalizingly delicious but even a small one would have taken all my ration points for several days so I bought some haddock and went home to treat it kindly.

The daughter of the local veterinary, however, had enough points. She bought a large luscious-looking steak and took it home for her father's dinner. He came in just as she was about to put it under the broiler.

"Where," he asked, "did you get that horse meat?"

She told him where, what she had paid and the number of coupons she had surrendered.

"They are not going to get away with *that!*" her father stated.

They did not.

It was all in the paper. The court fined them several hundred dollars and the judge's remarks, perhaps somewhat inspired by wartime menus, were severe. Another time punishment might not be so light, he said.

I cannot pretend that the other underlings and I did not read this news item without a certain amount of rejoicing. It happened that the day after it was published, I crossed the street just as the manager came out of the store. The light had just changed so that quite a group of his loving patrons crossed at the same time and walked behind him as he went from one door of the store to the other. He looked splendidly tall and strong in his white coat. He was carrying a large joint of succulent meat.

It was a beautiful morning. I was neatly dressed in my new suit of Oxford gray flannel striped with a lighter gray, my black hat with the velvet bow, and my best pink blouse — the one with the ruffles. The emblem of the Mountain Troops, crossed skis in silver and gold, on my lapel, was my only ornament. I wore black suede shoes and gloves. I could hardly have looked more respectable.

It was, I suppose, Mrs. Appleyard who said clearly, just as the patrons drew near the manager: "Horse meat! Horse meat!"

He jumped so that he almost dropped his hunk of beef and scowled suspiciously at all his smiling admirers. Except for the lady in the gray flannel suit, who passed by him with such quiet dignity, I'm afraid he suspected them all.

I went right in and bought half a pound of chicken livers and some mushrooms to celebrate this propitious day — the very day Elsie telephoned and said she would like to come and work for me.

A happy interlude followed. The kitchen, so neat and austere under Hannah, who prayed a good deal and spoke much of sin — other people's naturally — became a warm, genial, rather untidy place. It smelled spicy and appetizing. Elsie was able to subdue wartime materials into excellent meals. We had her children in for gingerbread and milk every now and then or took them to Howard Johnson's for frankfurters and ice cream cones or to Sears Roebuck's for their winter coats. Elsie never spent anything on herself. Every penny she earned was for the children.

I enjoyed their visits but even more I enjoyed Harry's. He came every evening except when there was overtime work at the factory. Harry was a machinist. He did work of great precision on some secret devices that were used by one of the big aviation companies. I have no idea what they were because Harry and I talked of music and writing. Before he became a machinist, Harry was a tenor in the Metropolitan Opera Company. Perhaps when I say that Harry used to love to hear me play the accordion, it may suggest why he never was promoted from the chorus. He was short too and rather plump, but then so was Caruso.

Every night Elsie would say, "Come out for a few minutes when Harry comes, Mrs. Kent. He does love a little music. It rests him after his work."

To help the war effort I would go out. Harry used to join in the music. Sometimes he played his cello, sometimes he sang. "*La donna e mobile*" was our masterpiece, but Harry was not too proud to sing "*Home on the Range*" or "*Over There*" since my operatic repertoire was limited.

After fifteen minutes of music, Harry and I would talk about his story. At first he was myserious about it, as writers often are. They are afraid other authors will steal their ideas. After a time Harry realized that our interests were different. At the time I was working on *He Went with Columbus.* When he discovered by careful questioning that I had no plans for writing a story about a horse or about the Far West, Harry confided his ideas to me. His story was a little like *Black Beauty* with overtones of *The Virginian,* both of which Harry often read, thus illustrating a well-known literary fact: if no one had ever written the first book, a second is rather unlikely.

I would discuss his day's work with Harry before I went back to my desk and *Columbus.* He had often added several sentences to the story. Harry always carried its few sheets in the inner pocket of his coat, drawing them out carefully with an air both bashful and proud. He said I was a big help to him since I had been to Arizona. Harry had never been farther west than Elizabeth, New Jersey, so he regarded me as an expert. I liked the horse in his story. I had ridden no such charming creature on my excursions across the border. It was a beautiful palomino, of course.

Elsie and I both missed Harry's visits when he left for Chicago with the manager of his company. He had only a day's notice. Some of the mysterious devices the company made had been found defective. Harry had been chosen for his special skill to go to the airplane factory and help decide whether the defects had been due to carelessness of manufacture or to sabotage either in Boston or Illinois.

"He'll know if anyone does," Elsie told me proudly. "Only I wish he wasn't going to that dangerous city."

I said that Chicago could be very peaceful. When he came in to say good-bye, I told him about the Coburn collection in the Art Institute. He ought to have gone there on his last afternoon instead of sitting in the park, he told me, when he came back ten days later.

All went well at first. Harry and his boss went over a number of what Harry called "the mechanisms" and found that the defects in them had been acquired after they left the factory. It was sabotage in his opinion. His boss went back to Boston leaving Harry to check the remaining devices. As soon as he had a complete list of the damage done, the airplane people were to call the FBI. Two days after the boss left, Harry had his meeting with the FBI man. It was late on a mild November afternoon when he walked back to his hotel. There was a peaceful green park near it and Harry sat down just before sunset on a bench with thick shrubbery around it.

He had sat there several afternoons before on the way home from work. Each time he had taken his story out of his pocket and had read it over carefully, adding the sentence he had thought of as he was going to sleep the night before. He did so now. The sun had gone down when he finished writing and he put the papers back into his pocket. He was about to get up when the blow came.

He did not feel it as a blow, only as sudden darkness. He had no idea how long it lasted. He must have fainted, he thought, from working too hard, not eating properly. There was no light in the sky now. Fog had drifted in from the lake. Streetlights shone through it dimly. He got up dizzily, managed to follow the path to the street and walked toward the hotel, a block away.

He was less dizzy than before but his head ached violently and he was still unsteady on his feet as he came through the revolving door into the hotel lobby. He remembered that the doorman took him by the elbow and helped him first to the desk where he got his key and then to the elevator.

The next thing he knew it was morning. He was lying on the outside of his bed, still fully dressed, even wearing his overcoat. He went into the bathroom and undressed. The collar of his shirt was stained with dried blood. It had trickled down from a place on his head where the hair was now dry and stiff.

Harry bathed, put on fresh underclothes and a clean shirt, packed his other clothes in his bag. His watch had stopped. He set it by a clock he could see from his window. He had plenty of time to check out of the hotel and catch his train.

The doorman said genially, "How's your head this morning, mister? Make it to your room all right? I told the elevator boy to unlock your door for you. I figured getting the key in the lock might be hard. Oh well, we all have to tie on a few when we're away from home, don't we?"

Harry, who drank nothing stronger than ginger ale, tipped him and asked what time it was when he came in.

"Just about six," the doorman said. "I went off duty right after."

Six o'clock! It was about four when he had sat down on the bench. He wondered if he ought to call the police or the FBI. It would mean missing his train and they'd keep him there. The boss needed him back at the plant, he knew. And he'd had all he wanted of Chicago. He decided to go.

He was on the train, headed safely for Boston. He'd had a good lunch and was back in his seat. He thought of a sentence to add to his story and he made his usual gesture toward the inner pocket of his suit for the papers.

They were gone. Poor Harry!

He worked it out, as he traveled east, that the man who hit him over the head had probably been hired by the saboteurs to follow him every day, had seen him take out the story of the palomino and write his sentence; had reported that Harry took notes each time he left the factory. It seemed important to the saboteurs to find out how much he knew. What, I wondered, did they make out of the story of Tonio, who lived in a cave in the Arizona desert with his palomino. Perhaps they thought it was a code which, rightly translated, would tell about defective mechanisms.

Harry's report on those was safely in the pocket of his overcoat. It was good, he said, that the saboteurs hadn't found it but it was not, like the story of Tonio and his horse, the only copy.

"Write it down again, Harry. Do it while you still remember it," I urged. "You must know it by heart."

He shook his head sadly.

"I guess I just wasn't meant to be a writer," he said. "Or maybe it was the blow on my head. I know the main idea, about the mare bringing up the little boy in the cave, but the words won't come back."

"Perhaps they will later," I said but they had not when Harry went to Connecticut to work at a more highly paid job.

At about the same time an aunt of Elsie's invited her to live with her in Portland, Maine, and to bring the children with her. She and Harry gave me a recording of Cole Porter's songs, favorites of Harry's and mine. We played it the last evening they were there.

Whenever I have played it since, it brings back a world as distant and unreal as Tonio's in the Arizona cave.

During what I used to look back on wistfully as Elsie's visit, Rich and I had been taking our first aid and air warden's courses. Of the first aid course I remember chiefly the expression on my teacher's face as he explained to me how to tie a square knot.

He had an air of quiet desperation as he said: "Yes, that's another granny but I'm going to teach you to tie a square knot if it's the only thing I do in this war."

It is pleasant to report that he succeeded.

He taught me about the pressure points so well — they are handy spots on the body where you can cut off the blood supply to some special area by applying pressure — that I made Rich almost unconscious by pressing a small hollow below his left ear. This was during a demonstration I was asked to give to show I had learned my lesson.

My teacher said: "It is not desirable to cut off the blood supply to the patient's brain permanently, Mrs. Kent."

Our graduation from the air warden's course was different from any other graduation I ever saw. It was a complete demonstration of how Brookline would respond to an air raid alert. From the moment an enemy plane theoretically crossed the Canadian border into Maine, the whole procedure was carried out. We heard the reports from stations along the route, saw the course of the plane and of our planes charted on an enormous map of New England that covered most of the floor of the gymnasium. From our balcony seats we had a good view of girls in uniform placing the indicators, of the major in charge giving instructions and of the stage where representatives of the public services — gas, electricity, telephone,

Red Cross, water, fire protection, police — sat at their telephones.

When the plane crossed a certain line all air raid posts in town were alerted. When the bomb fell in Brookline, the telephones of the public services started ringing. They gave orders for their trucks to go to the damaged area. Up to the moment when the trucks would have left, the procedure was all as it would have been if plane and bomb had been genuine.

When it was all over and the telephones had stopped ringing, the major asked if there were any questions from the graduating class.

There was a long silence. At last a young warden sitting near me got up and said in an anguished tone: "But, sir, why did the bomb have to fall on *Brookline?*"

The major's reply gave me new respect for the army. He explained gently and kindly that he was glad the demonstration had seemed so real.

"These young ladies and I," he said, waving his hand toward his assistants, "have spent the last two days rehearsing with the representatives of the public service here to show you just how the organization which you have joined works. One of the complications was to make sure that the bomb did fall on Brookline. Next week, when we go to the Newton graduation, the bomb will fall on Newton."

A sort of smile of relief went through the balcony. No one had laughed at the young warden's question, not, I think, because we didn't think it was amusing that of all places in the world he thought that Brookline would of course be inviolate. The polite silence in which we had waited for the major's answer was a sign that, for the first time, we all knew that we had a serious task before us.

☆

The other day a young man with whom I was talking was surprised to hear that Boston was blacked out at night during the war.

"Surely," he said, "that was unnecessary. There can't have been any real danger. No plane ever really came, did it?"

"No," I said, "but that may be because of the precautions. Perhaps if all cities had been lighted and no one worrying, it might have seemed worthwhile to Hitler to take the risk of dropping a bomb on New York or M. I. T. or Detroit."

"I shall always think it was ridiculous," said the young man who was born in 1946.

He may well be right. At the time it did not seem that way.

☆

The spies, at least, were real. On the Maine Coast at Hancock Point the fog rolled in one winter night, sometimes in clouds, sometimes changing to an icy drizzle that froze on windshields and made wheels skid easily in slush. A boy about sixteen, son of the local sheriff, had recently got his driving license. He was already a sensible careful driver. He had borrowed his father's car to take a girl to a dance at Ellsworth and he was glad to be back on the point again safely. He drove slowly, bringing the car skillfully out of an occasional skid, hoping that the fog would not thicken.

If it had been thicker, he might not have seen so clearly the two men who came out onto the road from a patch of woods. They must, he thought, have been following the narrow trail that twisted through the woods from a beach not far from the lighthouse. They had just reached the road and were turning toward Ellsworth when his headlights touched their figures.

Usually he would have stopped and offered help to anyone walking on such a night but there was something strange about them; not only their coming out of the woods on that lonely road so late but the way they were dressed. He said nothing to the girl, only drove on, a little more quickly now, left her at her house, drove to his own nearby, woke his father, told him about the men.

"I think they're spies, German spies from a submarine maybe," he said.

The sheriff asked what made him think so. He had so much respect for the boy's opinion that he was already dressing as they talked.

"Raincoats," the boy said, "foreign-looking raincoats. Soft hats with brims. A night like this anyone who knows this place wears a cap and a mackinaw. And high boots — or anyway galoshes. They had on low shoes. One of 'em carried a briefcase."

They were soon in the car, driving through fog and sleet. "We'll just go to Ellsworth and report and let the FBI take it from there. Don't slow down when you see them, just drive steady."

They passed the men again well on the road toward Ellsworth.

"Foreign coats all right," the sheriff said as they left them behind.

I heard the story soon after that night and tell it as I remember it, accurately I hope. Later I was told that the men really had landed from a German submarine, which used the lighthouse as a landmark. Both spoke excellent English. Both were trained physicists. They had planned to pose as German defectors and get jobs that would throw light on America's plans.

Headlights on a foggy night, falling on clothes that looked foreign to the sharp eyes of a sixteen-year-old boy, had helped keep some of our wartime secrets from Hitler.

☆

Aunty became ill in 1943. She may, the doctor said, have had a slight stroke. She was still able to walk quickly up the two flights of stairs to her room, but she suffered from extreme restlessness both by day and by night and she had slight hallucinations. She had always been so accurate and careful in reporting any incident that it took me some time to realize that what she was saying might have no basis in fact at all. She might, on the other hand, be completely herself. It was a question of circulation. The blood supply to her brain was sometimes inadequate, sometimes quite normal.

She had two nurses, one in the daytime and one at night. She still went out for walks around the neighborhood, giving the day nurse plenty of exercise, and she walked around the house, accompanied by the other nurse at intervals during the night.

One day in late September she came back from her walk, looking delighted with what she had seen on Irving Street, near my grandfather's old house, the one with the tower.

"There's the most beautiful tree," she said. "I'm hoping to get seeds or a cutting and plant one for you. It would do well in the front border in between the hawthorn and the flowering crab, I think, and give us flowers in the autumn."

"What is it like?" I asked.

"Twenty feet high, perhaps," she said, "with big heart-shaped leaves and great trumpet-like blue flowers, as blue as the sea at Iron Bound in a southwest breeze, with centers of deep gold."

She sounded so much like herself that for a moment such a tree seemed possible.

"How strange I haven't noticed it!" I said. "You don't think it could be a heavenly blue morning glory climbing on a catalpa, do you?"

She laughed happily. "Oh darling, I'm afraid it's just one of my delusions — only so much pleasanter than most of them," she said. "It was nice to believe it — even for a moment — wasn't it?"

Nicer certainly than a whole train of half-size Hitlers pouring out of the fireplace and shouting "Sieg Heil!" as they passed or than long-dead cousins calling on the telephone to say they would be coming to Sunday dinner or a dog carrying a screaming cat up on the porch.

The night before she died, she was perfectly rational. We had a long conversation about things that had happened in the distant past. Her mind was clearer than mine. In the morning she refused to eat her breakfast. This was so unusual that I asked the doctor to come and see her. Before he came, she asked for a cup of coffee. I was sitting talking to her when the nurse brought it in.

"Give me my handbag, please, Lulie," she said to me. "I must pay for this."

"Oh, the coffee's on the house," I said laughing.

"I pay my way," she said obstinately and handed the nurse a quarter.

It was an example, I thought afterwards, of "the ruling passion strong in death." All through her life she had always done her share — and a little more. Up to her last hour this was so.

The doctor found her very weak.

"It will not be much longer now," he said.

He gave her some pills and gave me a prescription to have filled. I was starting to walk to the village when I heard her voice calling me. I came running upstairs and was there so she saw me and knew me.

Suddenly a great change came over her face.

"Mother," she said, "I'm coming."

The years fell away from her. She looked for a moment as young and happy as a small girl who knows the beautiful thing she sees is for her.

Then the smile faded and her long life of integrity, of courage, of generosity was over.

32

Hospital

NOT LONG AGO I heard a brilliant young mathematician discussing history. He said that what was printed in school books was all wrong: that Columbus did not discover America, that other events were warped in various ways. Realizing that, of course, he knew more than I did, I made no comment until he mentioned fighting the British in World War I. This surprised me a little. I remembered the six Mah-Jongg sets I sold for British relief, and that I bought three of them myself. I thought of the bacon and butter I had gone without so that the British could criticize their flavor so expertly. Yet I could remember no pitched battles between us.

I said hesitantly that I thought the United States and England had been allies against the Kaiser.

The expert thought it over, smiled kindly upon me and said: "Oh yes — sorry! War of 1812 obviously."

What's a hundred years when you take an impersonal view of history?

I just mention the time element so that my grandchildren will not make this particular mistake. Perhaps at the same time they might note that England, France, Russia and the United States were allies in World War II. I remember this because of my beaver coat. I received appeals about the same time for warm clothes for the

British and the Russians. Someone from the British Relief was to be collecting clothes in Brookline the next day. I admired the courage the Russians had shown at Stalingrad and I had read enough Russian novels to know how cold it was there in winter. Still I knew at first hand how it was in England in August.

I rang up the British organization. A very refined English voice said "Aow" and "Quaite" in answer to my announcement that I had a fur coat for them and passed me on to a superior who said the same.

Now my coat was not the last thing in fashion. It was of muskrat with a huge beaver collar. It was voluminous and so long that it revealed only an occasional glimpse of a trim ankle encased in fur and velvet. My car, a pre-war model, had no heater. I used the coat on cold days as a combination coat and laprobe. I knew I would miss it but I was prepared to sacrifice it to someone shivering in a London Subway (tube) on raw July nights.

After waiting five minutes I was able to explain for the third time that I had a fur coat that could be picked up on their rounds the next day.

"Aow!" said the voice. "And is it a naice caoat?"

"It's a nice warm coat," I said. "It's not the latest style but it's not worn at all."

"Aow! Well suppose you bring it in and let us have a look. Eh?"

"Yes and suppose I don't," I said and replaced the receiver gently on the hook.

I was so mad that I gave the coat and another of more recent style to the Russians. Even now when I see a picture of Russian commissars, I study them carefully to see if one of them is wearing one of my coats. The second one was made of silvery-gray fur, very soft and warm, supposed to have come off some mysterious Himalayan rodent. Either coat, topped off with a fur hat, Karakul of course, would, I still think, look well on a commissar.

I did not have a new fur coat till 1957. I here announce that in case of a third World War, I shall be wearing it myself.

In the summer of 1944, as I weeded my vegetable garden and froze its crops, the tide of battle had turned against Hitler. The D-Day landings had taken place on the Normandy beaches. People who had no sons in the service often remarked that it was only a question of time now.

The 87th Regiment of the 10th Mountain Infantry went to Kiska in the Aleutians in 1943. Hearing that Sam and his friend were on their way, the Japanese left. Just about the time Sam was landing on Kiska, I went to the cobbler's to get a pair of shoes resoled. The rubber soles the cobbler recommended were advertised by a poster in the window. The wearer of the shoes on the poster was doing the kind of rock climbing Sam had described doing in Colorado and the climber looked so much like Sam that I could hardly believe he had not posed for the picture. I told the cobbler about the resemblance and when I came back for my shoes, he gave me the poster.

The slopes in Kiska were less steep and rocky than those in Colorado but there was some loss of life in taking the island. The Japanese had left mines on the beaches and various booby traps around their camps. If you straightened a picture of the Japanese emperor in the general's headquarters, you might get your hand blown off.

The real fighting, however, was on the island of Attu. By that time the 87th was on its way back to the Continent. They went to Italy late in 1944 as part of the Tenth Mountain Division with an X on the shoulders of their jackets. Although they were called the Ski Troops, they did very little skiing either on Kiska or in Italy. The necessary substance was usually lacking.

The ski troops had a reputation of being difficult to get into but this was not always so. My nephew, Oliver Andrews, Jr., was sitting in the library at Fort Devens one day. A detachment of new recruits was leaving for Colorado but several had been knocked out by influenza. At the last minute an officer stuck his head in the door.

"Anyone here that can ski?" he asked.

Oliver put up his hand and said he did — a little.

"You're in the ski troops," the officer said and in a short time Oliver was on his way to Colorado.

They arrived late one night, long after the camp was asleep. Oliver climbed into the upper bunk to which he was assigned and went to sleep. When he woke in the morning, he looked down on his bunkmate, noticed something familiar about that bald head and said, "Hi, Sam!"

They went through the war together, usually sharing the same pup tent.

The Italian campaign received little attention in the newspapers. The headlines were all for the fighting in France. Once in a long while I would find a paragraph, tucked into a corner of the paper, about General Mark Clark's troops. They were north of Rome but they could go no farther because the Germans held Monte Belvedere. British, Brazilian and American troops were all held up. The high mountain gave the Germans a position of great advantage. Troops to the east and west of it could not move north because of the artillery fire from Belvedere and no one — the paper said — could possibly attack it from the south.

No one — that is — except the Mountain Troops. Perhaps the Germans too considered an attack impossible. Their sentinels may have been dozing. The arrival of the Americans on that mountaintop was such a surprise that most of the German troops were captured with little fighting. Their artillery was made useless. With Belvedere taken, the whole German line across Italy had to retreat.

The 10th Mountain Troops have two combat ribbons, one for the Asian theater of operations, one for the European. On each ribbon is a small spearhead showing that they were the advance guard in an attack. They were so until they had chased the Germans across the Po and back to the mountains.

The day Germany surrendered, I was at a luncheon at Margaret Whitney's. There were four other guests, but I was the only one who had a son in the service. The newspaper with the big headline GERMANY SURRENDERS came while we were still there. The maid hurried in with it, carrying it spread out so we could all see it.

Everyone spoke to me as if the war were my private one and congratulated me. I had a feeling that it was too soon for me to rejoice. The shadow still hung over me the next day as I went into Jordan's to buy a frying pan. Just how that took me into the porch furniture section, I cannot say. All I know is that I found myself looking down on the scarlet cushions of a couch of redwood from California and hearing my inner voice say: "That will be just the thing for Sam to lie on while he's getting over his wound."

I tried to shake away this idea but it was still so definite that I bought the couch, an armchair, a footstool and two small tables and had them sent to Kents' Corner.

Just as I got home the telephone rang. There was a telegram for Rich and me from the War Department. It regretted to inform us that our son had been seriously wounded. I have since learned that the phrase to be really dreaded is "critically wounded." Luckily Rich was away on business so he did not get the first impact of the news. For some months he had been under Dr. Paul White's care for a heart condition. Dr. White considered it minor but I felt it was not likely to be helped by this news. Rich called me the next evening. By that time I had had a V-Mail letter from Sam. It was dictated to his nurse. It had not occurred to either of them to say what the injury was; I had to make deductions.

He evidently could speak so it was not to his throat or chest. He'd had a good dinner so it was not his digestive tract. He told

me about the view from his window and said he'd been listening to
Aïda on the radio so it was not his eyes or ears. There were a few
words at the bottom of the page in his own Park School manuscript
writing so it was not his right arm. I decided it was either his left
arm or a leg.

I called his wife, Fifine, in Vermont. She had had a letter too—
fortunately before she got the War Department notice. The injury
was to Sam's left arm and shoulder. An air burst, a shell fired from
a German plane, had gone through the edge of his helmet and his
left forearm. His shoulder and his head both had bits of shrapnel
in them. He was in a hospital not far from Florence. He hoped to
be flown home before long.

So, between operations on his arm at Cushing Hospital near Framingham, Sam did lie on the redwood couch, smell the syringas,
see hummingbirds whizzing in and out of the larkspurs. He spent
most of two years in army hospitals. He had fourteen operations on
his arm. Both bones of his forearm were smashed to splinters. His
hand was like a wax hand. It had shrunk in size so it was not much
larger than mine. It was always in a sling, always cold and there
was no motion in the fingers.

Miraculously the surgeons gave him a new hand. They removed
the many splinters of bone from his forearm and the bits of shrapnel from his shoulder and head. Out of a piece of his shin they
made new bones for his forearm. They found the place near his
shoulder where the nerve leading to his hand was still alive. They
gave it a little tube to grow down so it would meet the old nerve
below where it had been smashed. They made an artery out of a
piece of a vein. They grafted skin. They transferred muscular
tissue to his hand. I forget what else Dr. William Littler and his
associates did, but I know that whatever was necessary to make
Sam's hand come alive was done, no matter how much patience
and ingenuity it took.

To some extent this living hand was made possible by Dr. Nancy Bucher, one of Kenty's Bryn Mawr friends who used to visit us at Kents' Corner. She did some of the very early research on penicillin. It was the use of penicillin, the surgeons told me, that saved Sam's hand and arm from osteomyelitis and gangrene. Without penicillin he would certainly have had to lose his arm.

"He's got twenty thousand dollars' worth of penicillin in him and it's certainly worth it," a surgeon told me.

I felt that another person who ought to have credit for this miracle was Franklin Delano Roosevelt. The attitude that everything possible should be done for men injured in their country's service stemmed, I believe, largely from him and persisted after his death. I wonder sometimes if he would have given the final order to drop the atomic bomb. I have never reconciled myself to the idea that the United States of America, the country always counted on for human and humane treatment of people all over the world in time of disaster, is the country that began nuclear warfare. I have heard all the reasons why dropping the bomb is supposed to have been practically a favor to the Japanese people; I know I am showing myself impractical, sentimental and obstinate when I say that I do not agree. In my observation war always makes more problems than it settles. I am thoroughly in sympathy with Senator George Aiken's suggestion that we should announce that we have won the war in Vietnam and go home.

Innocently and ignorantly, I thought, on November 11, 1918, that war was over forever. When the Japanese surrendered in 1945 there was relief everywhere, of course, but no joy and exuberance. Brookline, where I was at the moment, was as quiet as Calais where we went the next day in time for the service of thankfulness in the old West Church. Since I was sure there had never been a good war nor a bad peace, I was thankful already. I felt that we had entered a new world, one I was not likely to understand. For the first time in my life I was showing common sense; the real foolishness had lain in thinking I knew anything.

Rich had promised he would take a vacation that summer but he kept postponing it. He did however spend a few days enjoying his grandchildren. There were two of them — Susan and Andrew Tarshis. They were, of course, extraordinary children. That isn't just my opinion, Rich thought so too. I'm sure the other people who said so couldn't possibly have been insincere about the charm, verve and intelligence they constantly displayed.

I took photographs of them that show some of these traits that summer. Unfortunately on one occasion I failed to snap the shutter of the Graflex at the right moment. If I'd only been a little brisker we might have had a picture showing where Susie threw my father's gold snake ring. I always thought Kenty was like my father. His first school report ("Walter is intelligent but volatile") described her too, so after his death I gave her the ring. Susie also belonged to the intelligent but volatile association — a nature so different from her grandmother's darkly serious disposition. Perhaps that is why Kenty gave Susie the ring to play with.

She held it up, passing it from one hand to the other, admiring the gold as the sunlight flashed on it. I watched the small flashing light in the camera's mirror finder and waited patiently for just the expression of joy I wanted. Unfortunately I waited too long. The expression was charming but the ring was not in the picture. She had already thrown it away just before I snapped the shutter.

Although I thought I knew just where to look, we never found it. We hunted systematically, mowed the grass a few inches at a time around where she was standing, raked it, sifted it. The ring ought to have been there but it wasn't. Gold sinks a certain amount a year, I'm told, so I suppose it's pretty far down by now.

Rich and I drove back and forth between Brookline and Calais that summer of 1945. He was still promising to take that vacation but he never stayed more than a weekend. When the leaves began to turn, I went to Vermont telling him I would stay until he would take some time off and come and get me. While I was waiting for him, I began to do the various chores involved in shutting up the various buildings.

In between these activities I carried out a plan I had had for some years — of painting a chess table for Rich. We had always used my grandfather's chess table, which his children had had made for him with a walnut frame and legs supporting a porcelain top of red and white squares.

Unfortunately there was no space to put the chessmen after they had been captured. Obviously this was more of a problem to Rich than it was to me. I never took enough of his pieces to worry about where I put them. I just used to toss them over on the sofa. Rich used to keep a small table of Remember Kent's beside him, one of those pieces brought by oxteam from Massachusetts.

I decided to greet him on his next visit with a table he would like to play on. There was an old sewing table a little more than two feet square in the house. By the time Rich came I had painted it black and on top had painted a sort of chessboard of black and red squares edged with gold. He was delighted with it and I was much pleased with what he brought me, a copy of my new book *Country Mouse*. Mrs. Appleyard appeared in it and also Posy, thinly disguised. She organized in it, I remember, something called the Anti-Handicraft Society. Kenty and the Duchess were charter members of it. This organization existed in fact as well as fiction but it did not deter me from my work. As though it did not exist I went right on making Sam a special glove to keep his left hand from freezing in cold weather. It was really a mitten rather than a glove. It was thickly and softly padded and made of a number of things including a big piece of chamois leather in which I used to wrap up my silver teakettle. I seem to remember that a hand-knit sock went into its composition. I did not make the sock: I don't know how to knit. I don't know how to shake down thermometers either. When the children were small and ran temperatures, Rich bought me four thermometers. He used to shake them all down for me before he went to work. Helplessness is such an attractive trait in a woman, I always think.

After I finished the glove I made a stuffed elephant for Susie. He was made out of the gray flannel bag that belonged to my coffee urn. His ears were lined with scraps of red velvet that had been waiting to line ears since 1870. I found his shining eyes in the button box. He was mostly stuffed with nylon stockings with runs in them. I found enough absorbent cotton to fill his trunk. Perhaps you never tried stuffing an elephant's trunk. An ivory button hook is a great help.

So the days slipped by until Rich wrote that he would be on the night train Friday morning. As I had done so many times, I drove out of the first sunshine that touched our bright hills, down through ten miles of thick and thicker fog into Montpelier. I sat there shivering in the gray cold. At last I heard the train's melancholy whistle far off down the valley in the darkness and was cheered by it.

33

Late Autumn

RICH WAS DELIGHTED with the chess table and its wide margins. The only time we used it he set plenty of pieces of mine on it. He had to get back to his work. He stayed just three days. They were the most beautiful of the year. On one of them, a real halcyon day with kingfishers darting across the millpond, Pearl fixed a picnic lunch for us and we all three went for a foliage tour to favorite views.

We drove over into Middlesex, back by Shady Rill, up Hunger Brook to look down into the cold foaming swimming hole. It looked strange with scarlet and gold around it instead of the shadowy greens of summer. There had been no heavy frost yet so the lower slopes of the Worcester Mountains were still dappled with orange and scarlet and apricot and pale gold. Open fields were still brilliantly green. Swamps still showed the crimson and deep plum color of soft maples. The river was as blue as the sky. In the distance the mountaintops were deep violet.

There had been a gentle rain the night before. The trunks of sugar maples had been darkened by it. We followed roads where the tree trunks were columns of wrought iron supporting triumphal arches of gold. We passed what we called the tapestry room — half an acre of bright green grass with three walls of maples showing all possible colors.

We drove to the Haydons' in North Calais. There we could look across a familiar valley and, above our own amethyst mountaintops, see the pale blue shadow of the Couching Lion beyond. I never see that valley without remembering Rich's expression of both sadness and happiness as he stood looking out across it.

We left Kents' Corner the next morning and drove home in a leisurely way through the autumn pageants of Vermont and New Hampshire. We ate lunch on the shore of Newfound Lake. The islands and the hills around it seemed to have a special radiance that year. The foliage was so brilliant for the first hundred and fifty miles that it was almost a relief to drive into ugly little brown and green Massachusetts.

Before long we were climbing up the steep curved walk from Hawthorn Road to our gray houses. We owned them both now. Amy Davol had died suddenly one evening after a heart attack. Without her strength and warmth and generosity, Steve's reason for living vanished: he outlived her by only about a year. None of the children wanted the house. Rich bought it, saying we would be able to choose our neighbors if we owned it. We were consistently lucky in them.

I had no cook now. Mackerel came in season, delicious little tinker mackerel like those that used to swim past Iron Bound. I broiled them beautifully. I wreathed them with parsley and water-cress. I sliced cucumbers as thin as ration coupons and marinated them in French dressing with just a hint of garlic. I made sand-wiches and brown bread and cream cheese. I sprinkled potato balls with chopped chives. I glazed carrots.

When we had finished this well-balanced menu, Rich said thoughtfully: "Mackerel is a very nice fish. I wish I liked it."

He didn't like it!

And he had eaten it politely at least once a week in mackerel season since 1912. And he had never said anything.

I knew why: if Aunty and the children and the maids all ate something without protest, he was not going to complicate my life by mentioning his feelings. This was so typical of him that I was hardly surprised.

I said, "Oh Rich! — what else?"

"Nothing," he said. "Just mackerel."

"Well, I've made you a sponge cake for dessert," I said.

"I'll eat mackerel any time if I can have sponge cake afterwards," he told me and was soon tearing it apart with two forks.

Since the closing of the air warden's post, with no necessity to patrol the darkened hill at night, Rich's angina seemed better. Still he had enough of it so that I suggested he should retire from Houghton Mifflin as soon as possible after his sixty-ninth birthday on October 28. He was horrified.

"Retire — I couldn't bear it! The one thing I couldn't stand would be to be idle and useless."

I told him it was not possible he would ever be either. Tufts College — of which he had been a trustee since 1900 — would use all the extra time he had to spend, I said. We'd manage somehow financially and at least he could take an afternoon off occasionally.

"Let me tell them at Houghton Mifflin about your angina and suggest that you might take some vacation that way. You know you never did take the real one you promised me."

He forbade me to mention the angina to anyone but he did take some afternoons off that October. We drove out to Framingham several times to see Sam who was recovering from one of his many operations. One afternoon Rich went with me to Coolidge Corner while I did some errands. He really enjoyed it — going into Pierce's while I gave my weekly order, into a bookstore where I autographed copies of *Country Mouse*, to Howard Johnson's for ice cream cones. A large ice cream cone cost ten cents then. Rich followed his usual practice of eating it with a spoon.

The waiter tried to get him to order a dish but Rich said serenely that he considered the combination of a cone and a spoon ideal. The man went off, shaking his head. He evidently felt that Rich was striking at the roots of American civilization.

We had a great deal of quiet, golden Indian summer weather that fall. Sometimes on the way to Framingham, we left the turnpike and followed twisting roads bordered by the deep maroon and bronze-purple of oaks and the scorched yellow of beeches. We both spoke kindly and a little patronizingly, as Vermonters do, of these color effects and of the occasional bright blue pond we saw. At least in Vermont it would have been a pond. In Massachusetts it was often a lake.

One afternoon at the hospital we found a pianist playing to the men in an almost deserted ward. It was Saturday and many of the patients had weekend passes. We sat there for an hour enjoying the music, which drifted from "Smoke Gets in Your Eyes" to Chopin, Mozart and Beethoven and back again through Brahms and Debussy to "Star Dust." With Sam making a recovery and Rich looking better than he had for months, it was an hour of complete happiness.

On the eighth of November, Rich was taken ill. He went to the Faulkner Hospital that morning. By afternoon he seemed better and even better in the evening when Kenty and Lorie came to see him. After they had gone, I was told to go home and not to worry. If necessary he would have a transfusion in the morning and after that things ought to be all right. I believed it — because I had to, I suppose.

When I called the hospital early in the morning, they said he had had a good night. I was just starting for the hospital when Miss Rodenhiser, Rich's secretary, telephoned me. I had given her a message from him the day before. He had said that he was in the hospital for a checkup and that she was to let him know if anything important came up.

Something had, she said. There was a matter of moving picture and magazine rights for a book. The author's agent, the representative of the magazine and one from the motion picture company disagreed on several points. They all wanted Rich's advice. It all seemed immensely complicated as I wrote it down. There were about ten paragraphs, I think, and they wanted the whole thing cleared up immediately.

I found Rich sitting up in bed looking cheerful. He spoke about Kenty and Lorie, how much he had enjoyed their visit, of how well Lorie had done at Tufts and in the war. I read him Miss Rodenhiser's message. He dictated the answer, paragraph by paragraph, never hesitating for a word. He spoke slowly only because I wrote in longhand. I read the notes over to him. There were no changes to be made. What had seemed to me, with all the different interests involved, incredibly difficult, was now clear and straightforward.

I telephoned Miss Rodenhiser and read the message to her.

"Do you think they will do what he says?" I asked.

"Of course!" she said and — as I heard later — they followed the memorandum exactly.

When I came back into Rich's room he was showing his nurse his new kaleidoscope. I had just made it for him and he had brought it along with him in his bag. They were passing it back and forth and saying, "Oh, look at *this* one!" in the manner of kaleidoscope addicts everywhere.

Rich suggested that I should go out to Framingham.

"Tell Sam about me," he said. "If you call, he might not be able to get to the telephone and a message might disturb him. Perhaps they'll give him a pass this weekend. Don't hurry. I'll be busy all the morning with interesting activities."

I drove straight out the turnpike this time. Sam arranged about his weekend pass. He said later that he could have come back with me if he had only known. I wonder how many times I have said to myself, "If I had only known."

Rich was alone when I came back to the hospital. The change in his appearance frightened me. I tried not to show my anxiety, but I suppose I must have because he said, "The transfusion didn't help — the poor old rusty pipes just wouldn't take it. Now tell me about Sam."

I sat there for a while, talking about the children and the grand-children, how Susie had said, "Grandpa is the best carver. I love to see him sharpening that shining knife!"

Rich smiled happily over that. For a while he seemed to relax and breathe easily but suddenly his breathing changed. The hospital was short staffed because of wartime conditions. It took some time to get a nurse and a doctor.

He still knew me when I came back. As I sat holding his hand, I said, "I saw our bench beside the pond as I drove past."

He said, "That day has been the great blessing of my life," and I said, "Mine too."

They came then to give him another transfusion. They sent me out of the room. As I left him I knew that our life together was over.

34

Kaleidoscope Turns

I HAVE TRIED several times to write about the next few weeks but I find it is not possible for me to do so. Luckily I had hospital work to do.

I had worked during the war several days a week at the Free Hospital for Women which was only a short walk from Hawthorn Road. The task I liked best was putting away clean linen. I did it painstakingly with the folded edges of the sheets toward the front of the shelves. I always — I had learned to do this by reading a book about Napoleon Bonaparte — first removed any sheets left on the shelves, piled the newly washed ones with geometrical neatness on the shelf, dusting it with meticulous care of course, and then laid the sheets I had removed on top of the pile.

Napoleon had stated that this method equalized the wear. Not being fond of conquerors, I do not cherish Napoleon. Still I believe in taking what is good where you find it. So I had long practiced his methods in my own linen cupboard. I felt very competent about using it in the hospital up to the time one of the nurses rebuked me for wasting time.

"Just stick them on the shelves," was her command. "They all get used every day anyway."

I didn't even mention Napoleon. I just did as she said and went into the patients' dining room to set the table for dinner. One of

the many pleasant things about the Free Hospital was the excellent
food and the patients' enjoyment of it. To many of them their operations were the only real vacations they had for years. To have
their meals cooked for them and served to them was a real luxury.
Some of them, of course, had their meals in bed but there was
always a convalescent group able to come into the dining room.

No lunch party was ever more fun for the guests. They had
much in common and talked about it with vim. They told the
bright sayings of their children and grandchildren. They all talked
at once about their operations and all listened — a social technique
demanding much skill. They spoke well of their doctors; each, I
learned, was something extra special. They mentioned the fish
chowder with much the same genial enthusiasm.

I used to change the plates and rinse them at the sink. Often
some large competent convalescent would shove me aside and do
the work a lot faster than I did. I was rather disappointed when it
was discovered that I had once been trained as a librarian. The
library was short of help and I worked there for several months.

My contribution there was needed more than in the linen closet
or at the kitchen sink. The filing system was out of order. Theoretically a patient's records could be found by consulting the card catalog; they could be — if you found the right card. It would tell you
where the folder was that contained the records. That is, it would
unless the doctor had taken it . . . unless he had also taken the
card . . . unless he had mislaid them both . . . unless he had
put both back in the wrong places . . .

The attitude toward doctors, I noticed, was different in the dining room and in the library. He was regarded in the library not as a
combination of Hippocrates and St. Francis but as a spoiled child
who loved to make havoc in the catalog. Enough of my Simmons
training remained so that I had some sympathy with the latter
point of view. The card catalog was no longer alphabetical. Per-

haps it was not strange that Miss Mary E. Browne's card had been put in front of Miss Miriam Brown's, but how did it happen that Mrs. Adah Solomon's turned up in the same drawer?

I sat at a table every day for months and moved cards back into their places in their own drawers. Of course I realized that I was doing a Penelope task except that I did not have to undo my work at the end of the day. Distinguished gentlemen in white coats did that for me. I made some constructive suggestions to the librarian: a) Doctors should not be allowed to remove cards from the files; b) Someone else should put them back. These ideas were not considered any more practical than Napoleon's about linen closets. Still it must have taken several years to make it quite as wild as when I found it.

I finished my cataloging about the time the war ended. I was asked by a friend in the Red Cross to take a course that would train me to become a Gray Lady. They were needed, she said, because so many soldiers were being shipped home. I passed the examination and early in December 1945, I was assigned to Murphy General Hospital in Waltham, eight miles away. We had many days that winter when the driving, slushy at noon, was over glare ice when I came home. If you travel on glare ice long enough, sooner or later you skid. As I went out to the hospital almost every day, I learned not to touch the brake or the clutch, to keep the wheels turned slightly in the direction of the skid and to hope for the best. I was lucky. I never hit anything during this interesting exercise. Compared to my recollection of it, water skiing and surfboarding must be tame occupations. Perhaps an afternoon in a glider might give some of the same sensations. I do not intend to check my ideas about these sports.

I went so often to the hospital that I was soon allowed to buy a gray Red Cross overcoat to wear over my gray uniform with its white collars and cuffs. The coat had a delightfully warm scarlet

lining. Of course I wore a visored cap with it. I looked very professional. I felt I had subdued Mrs. Appleyard.

Such however was not the case.

Everyone was very efficient out at the hospital. I thought that in
my disguise my being a writer would be a secret, but they had already found me out. They acted logically and gave me an enormous book cart to push.

Murphy General — like Cushing and like other army hospitals,
I suppose — was laid out to give the staff as much exercise as possible. It was all on one floor and covered acres of ground. Corridors
extended for what seemed like miles. Leading off them were long
extensions, beginning with private rooms, bathrooms and offices,
opening into big wards with many beds, ending in sun porches.
Convalescent patients played games and received visitors on the
porches. By the time I had pushed the book cart up and down the
corridors and through the wards to which I was assigned, I would
be, literally, almost too tired to move.

Besides its weight, there was another difficulty about the book
cart. People, as Rich used to say, are divided into two classes —
readers and non-readers — and it is not possible to make one into
the other. The inhabitants of Murphy General were largely non-
readers. When I brought the cart to a halt and asked a soldier if he
would like a book, a quiet shake of the head was the usual response.
All I had done, probably, was to interrupt the radio program to
which he was listening.

I decided that if I was going to continue to be a Gray Lady and
not a patient in a wheelchair, I would have to find some way of
ceasing to cart books. The idea how to do it came to me one evening as I was skidding home from work.

"Oh," I thought, as I looked down from Belmont Hill over Boston, flashing colored lights, "kaleidoscopes!"

The next day I asked my superiors if they would be willing for
me to try to get the men interested in making kaleidoscopes. I

showed them a favorite one from the many I had made. There was politeness about its jeweled elegance but little interest in my idea. My employers, who evidently found my enthusiasm tiring, as enthusiasm often is, replied wearily that I might try.

The next morning I was in a shop in the North End of Boston getting plain and frosted glass circles cut. The owner of the shop, when he heard the kaleidoscopes were for soldiers in the hospital, offered to cut strips of mirror glass, from a great pile of odds and ends he had, for nothing. When I was carrying on the project, Horace Brown kept me supplied with tubes of two sizes. Alex Hoyle got me a big box of real stained glass. Naturally I had always kept up my habit of picking up attractive specimens from convenient gutters but I needed more glass now than the landscape easily provided.

I started with materials assembled for four kaleidoscopes. In each of the larger tubes I put a smaller tube, mirror strips, a frosted glass circle and a plain one, strips of sticky paper — the kind you lick — strips of cardboard to make the third side of the minor prism. On this I marked lines showing where the mirrors must rest to make an angle of sixty degrees.

I carried a basket. In it were the tube packages, pieces of wallpaper of different patterns, the right size to cover the finished kaleidoscope, and a box containing the colored glass. The whole thing weighed five pounds; approximately half a ton less than the book cart, I figured.

It was with a good deal of timidity that I began my rounds but I need not have worried. On my first day I found three men who, out of a combination of boredom and good nature, were willing to try kaleidoscopery.

I carried my own kaleidoscope with me. I used to stop beside some patient who was lying there doing nothing, and say, "Would you like to see my kaleidoscope?"

Even if he didn't want to, he usually said yes. After all, I suppose he thought, one look can't hurt me much. Pretty soon an unusual pattern would click together and the soldier would say: "Hey! look at this one!"

Then, as he carefully passed it to me, adding, "Look out, don't jiggle it!" I would know that I had built a better mousetrap and that the mouse was in it.

I would ask, "Wouldn't you like to make one?"

He would say he couldn't possibly but I would produce one of the tube packages, show him the assembled materials and say, "Now if you don't mind my sitting down on this chair, I can show you how — it won't take long."

Sitting down — that had been my goal. It felt wonderful. I could draw a long breath and the slight discomfort in my chest would ease off. Sometimes, as I sat there, the book cart with its new attendant, hearty, muscular, twenty years younger than I — I was fifty-nine — would come thundering past. Once I heard the pusher trying to get a non-reader to have a look at a cute book. *Mrs. Appleyard's Year* its name was. No luck! He made a kaleidoscope the next week though.

After a while when I came on duty, I would find slips of paper saying that Private, Corporal, even Major so-and-so would like to make a kaleidoscope. Sometimes I would find a patient entertaining a visitor with his handiwork. That would be a great moment for me.

My favorite one was when I found a young soldier from the other side of the hospital, talking to the nurse in charge.

"Is this ward full of psychos?" he asked.

"This is a ward for men recovering from infectious hepatitis," she said.

"Well, does that make 'em crazy or something? Listen I was just out on the porch — go see for yourself if you think *I'm* nuts — and there's three majors out there looking at the ceiling through telescopes. They keep saying, 'Hey, look at this one,' and passing the things around! They're loopy — they think they're astronomers."

"Those are kaleidoscopes. This lady will show you how to make one," the nurse told him.

"Not me!" he said and fled from this danger.

One afternoon I approached the bed of a new patient, an enormous, friendly-looking man. I went through my usual routine.

He liked the kaleidoscope but he handed it back.

"Lady, I couldn' make wanna dose things," he said firmly. "Look a dese mitts — you think I make wanna dose things wid *dese?*"

He held out two of the largest thickest hands I had ever seen.

"I'll help you," I said, "it isn't really hard."

Between us we managed to assemble it. Then came the moment to put in the colored glass. Usually this took time. The maker would choose the emerald of a gingerale bottle, the ruby of a tail light (I didn't have to break my own — they gave them to me at the garage) or a crystal bead from a broken string. He would try different combinations. Sometimes I would sit there comfortably half an hour while he made up his mind before we sealed the frosted circle into place.

My friend that day wasted no time. He scooped one of his big hands into the box of glass and dumped what he got hold of into the kaleidoscope. It was the prettiest one ever made at Murphy General Hospital.

When the jewels were safely sealed into their compartment and when he and I had passed his triumph back and forth a dozen times, he said: "An wen I gets back to de Bronx and shows de folks dis ting, I gonna hold out my mitts an say, 'Dese are de dainty hands dat made dis ting!' "

I have no doubt that he did.

Another way I had of evading book cart work was playing chess. A good many of the hepatitis patients were not allowed out of bed. I arranged a sort of chess ladder on which was recorded how many games with me each had won. The men's scores were usually pretty good but, probably because they were not feeling well, I did win sometimes. After a time, patients began to recover and were able to play each other. One of them, whom I never had played, went from bed to bed defeating the occupants. He boasted loud and often about these triumphs, stating that he was at the top of the chess ladder.

"You can't be," one of his opponents said. "You've never played Mrs. Kent."

"That won't take long," the champion alleged. "Where is she?"

I was in the next ward kaleidoscoping when they came to bring me the challenge. When I was ready for chess, I found that not only was I to play the champion, the contest was to have an audience. Beds had been moved so the patients in them could look on and there was a ring of chairs for those who were out of bed. We had standees from time to time too.

It is hardly necessary to work up suspense about the game. Obviously I would not be telling this Jack-the-Giant-Killer story if Mrs. Appleyard hadn't won.

There was a reader of my works present who called me that.

"Come on now, Mrs. Appleyard," he said at one point, "don't let him get you down!" A few minutes later, he added, "Atta girl — that hit him where it hurt."

I had done what one would always like to. I had moved a knight checking his king and also threatening his queen. It did not take long after that. With only a little encouragement I could have been carried off the field of battle on the shoulders of my supporters. I disgusted them by telling my opponent, truthfully, that it was just luck; I almost didn't see the play myself until I'd made it.

"You'll beat me next time," I said.

No doubt he would have, but he returned to civilian life without having had his revenge.

35

Company

I HAVE BECOME enough of a Vermonter for the word "company" to have a special intonation, partly dread, partly happy anticipation. No matter how things are the rest of the time, everything has to be just right for company. Neighbors realize your predicament and rally around to help. It is not unusual for them to send in flowers. They are an expression of sympathy and so is a bunch of straw-berry rhubarb or a jar of elderberry jam. When I tell Ralph there will be company on Saturday, he mows the grass Thursday so it will be not too long — and not too short — when the guests drive in on it. He takes the trash to the dump. He washes the footprints of raccoons off the arched porch, waters the petunias and brings in every ear of corn the raccoons have not eaten.

Company in Brookline, especially in wartime, made less of an upheaval. Most of the guests were soldiers who had, I assumed, been in places more uncomfortable than Hawthorn Road. They came and went like members of the family. Sam belonged to a camera club at Cushing Hospital. One evening the whole club came to supper and to see my color slides. The thing that I remem-ber most clearly about that evening is that one of the guests, who was paralyzed from the waist down, was carried up from the street by four stretcher bearers, including Sam. Each of them had one good arm. So did the fifth, who carried the crutches. Even more clearly I remember that, six months later, the man who had been carried up walked in through the front door without even a cane and that, when I asked Sam for a glass of water, he brought it to me in his left hand.

My most distant visitors came from Australia. I tried to think of something to show them that they couldn't see anywhere else and we went to see the glass flowers in the Peabody Museum. After all, the glass flowers are the only ones in the world. On the way over I began to wonder if three strong young aviators might not rather see a basketball game or a hockey match.

They had asked about baseball and football and were a little disappointed to hear that they were not played in the snow. However, unlike some English visitors I'd had, they did not seem to expect to see me in a feather headdress and strings of wampum. One of the Englishmen, when I had driven him to a hilltop in Peterborough one autumn day, had delighted me by looking down on the flaming maples and asking, "But where are the Indians?"

Another of them, when I offered him one of Mrs. Appleyard's specialities — candied sweet potatoes, glazed with brown sugar, sprinkled with chopped peanuts — had said: "Ah! Pumpkin and parched maize! Thank you — no."

My Australian visitors seemed to like American food. I daresay they would have eaten pemmican with genial friendliness. What pleased me even more was that they liked the glass flowers. I could hardly get them away till they had seen every stamen, every petal. Just to give them a well-rounded picture of American life, I sent them to a hockey game too. I hated to see them leave for Europe.

I was not always a host during this time; I was sometimes a guest. I think it was Max Beerbohm who wrote about hosts and guests, praising the latter at the expense of the former. The host I remember was patronizing and dominant, the guest all sweetness and eagerness to please. Perhaps it is a little easier to be a host or anyway a hostess — than to be a guest. The hostess is on her own ground. She knows who she is. The time is in her hand. She can consult her own allergies. She can go into her corn barn and write a book. She can decree picnics at distant fireplaces though her guest may be a finger-bowl type. She can even serve tripe.

Still guests have their peculiarities too. I remember that one day I had two letters in the mail. One guest would like to spend Monday night and bring her youngest son. Another suggested coming Wednesday. She would bring her daughter. They both came Tuesday and there were seven of them. As I supplied fourteen clean sheets, I remember thinking that a sense of time and of numbers are useful characteristics, perhaps more typical of hosts than of guests.

It takes a certain ruggedness to be a host. On the whole, guests are gentler than hosts but I have known some determined guests; determined to be guests, I mean. At one time Kenty was having some repairs made to Remember Kent's pioneer cottage. The entire front of the house had been removed with a view to changing doors and windows. Kenty and her family had moved into Sam's house so she would not have to sleep in a bedroom without a front wall.

One night around midnight my telephone rang. A young man was calling from Rutland. He and his wife were planning to come over and visit Kenty. They wanted directions about the route they should follow. I suggested that since it was seventy-five miles they might prefer to spend the night in Rutland and cross the Green Mountain Range in the morning. He said he was used to night driving and preferred it.

"No traffic," he said.

I gave the directions. None of them including the turns and twists of our gravel roads dismayed him at all.

"Yes, yes," he said, "pass an old white church, three quarters of a mile up and downhill to Kents' Corner. That's fine. And when I get there, how shall I recognize Kenty's house?"

"I think you'll know it," I said. "It's the only house in Kents' Corner with the entire front wall removed."

"Fine," he said. "We'll be along."

They were too, around three in the morning, I heard them arrive. When I drove past the house about nine, they were sleeping comfortably in the big maple four poster, a very attractive young couple with the guest's most important trait — adjustability, I thought.

These were not the only guests who were firm about visiting Kents' Corner. There was also one occasion when we practically dragged the guests in by the hair. It was about 1920. I still had a Model T Ford. Rich and the children and I were visiting his mother in the White House. Rich had planned to take her to Montpelier that day to lunch and to see some of her cousins. Unfortunately at breakfast Grandma Kent broke one of the carved ivory teeth off her upper plate.

Rich saw no reason for changing their plans. They could go to the dentist's, leave the teeth to be repaired and make their visits just the same.

"Looking like this, I suppose? Like an old crone?" said his mother, removing her teeth.

With this gesture she had succeeded in changing from a brisk, handsome woman to someone I could hardly recognize. We obeyed her orders. I went to Montpelier with Rich. Kenty and Sam stayed with her. We took the ivory and gold teeth with us in a neat bag of white suede. The dentist said it would take only an hour but he could not start immediately. We could have them after lunch.

We strolled over to the Pavilion Hotel to have lunch. Outside it Dorman Kent was leaning on a big Packard from Ohio making gestures to the driver.

"Here's Rich right now," he said.

The car was full of cousins of Rich's and Dorman's. There were two Curtiss girls — Caleb's great-granddaughters, as Dorman explained — and their husbands, whose names I can't even remember, and four children, two boys and two girls.

"I was just giving them directions how to get to Kents' Corner," Dorman said. "They're on the way to Maine so the kids can see the ocean. But you'd better tell them how to get there. They want to see Blanche."

"Not till after you've all had lunch with us," I said firmly.

After some argument all eleven of us, including Dorman, went in to lunch. By a fortunate coincidence Rich had enough money to pay for it.

From then on we fought a delaying action. We tried to hurry the dentist but he had had to stop work and pull out an ulcerated tooth. He hoped now to be ready at two. We took our visitors to the State House and showed them the legislative chambers. Dorman pointed out Sleepy Hollow, the part of the house where so many representatives sleep comfortably during the session unless something important like changing the bounty on porcupines comes up. We visited the Historical Society and Dorman gave his famous imitation of Calvin Coolidge. Coolidge spent a whole morning visiting the capitol of his native state. Dorman was his escort. A friend had bet him he could not get Coolidge to say more than twenty words.

Coolidge spoke twice. He said: "I want to see the Catamount," and, after he had seen the stuffed mountain lion or catamount or puma or panther in its glass box, he said, "I have seen the Catamount!"

Dorman swears Mr. Coolidge almost smiled but this seems unlikely. Anyway Dorman lost his bet.

Our guests began to get restless. The dentist still delayed. I had a bright idea.

"You must stay for supper and the night," I said. "Rich, telephone your mother and say we're going to bring our company with us."

The company protested but I would not take no for an answer. I was determined they were not going back and tell people in Ohio that Cousin Blanche was a toothless crone. Finally one of the Curtisses weakened.

Rich went and telephoned. Since the telephone was at the farmhouse this took twenty minutes.

He reported: "She's delighted. Says she'll make you a chicken pie."

Still the teeth were not ready but at last after we had visited the Wood Art Gallery, Rich went into the building next door and came out with a small white bag in his hand. We said good-bye to Dorman, said, "Follow us," to the guests and started through ten miles of dust to Kents' Corner.

"I don't feel right about letting them take our dust," Rich said.

"We've got to be first," I said grimly and sent the Model T buckety buckety over the road, raising clouds of the best Vermont dust.

I drove in the middle of the road so there was no chance of their passing us. All went well until we came to the Old West Church. There the road widened and they drew up alongside us.

"We know the way now," called Ellen.

"Oh," I said, "but — but aren't you going in to see the old church? Rich will show it to you."

As he got out I said to him in a tone of soft ferocity: "Show them everything. Tell them how they put the boards on the pews and gave *Othello*. Show them your footprint in the plaster. *Give me time!*"

Perhaps our visitors had had all the sight-seeing they could stand. As I turned by the Brick House, I saw them behind me, coming down Wheeler Hill. I stopped at the side entrance, for I saw Grandma in her new dress, standing on the porch with the children. I ran up the bank. I plunged through the hydrangeas. With the bag in my hand, I climbed the porch railing. As the Packard drove into the yard, I handed Grandma the bag. I heard the teeth go in with a comforting sort of soft snap.

Slightly flushed, gracious and handsome, she received the company with well articulated welcome.

They stayed almost a week (sixteen clean sheets). The second day we had the chicken pie. It was made out of the only material available in Kents' Corner, a rooster so tough that Grandma had had to chop it up with an axe just before the guests arrived. That's how they would have found her — without her teeth, brandishing an axe — if I had not won my race.

The rooster was several years old, weighed about ten pounds and, after being simmered on the back of the range for eighteen hours, made a very tasty pie. After the company had gone, Grandma went to pay for it.

She said to its former owner: "Lorene, that was the toughest rooster I ever cut or cooked. How do you account for it?"

"Well," said Lorene, "we had him shut up lately. Guess he fretted some."

At least our guests did not fret. The children loved the Sucker Hole in the brook with its hungry fish eager for any worm, its big green frogs lurking among the forget-me-nots, its creamy waterfall splashing down as the sawmill whirred. They preferred it, I heard later, to the Atlantic, which was, they agreed, just a lot of water.

Obviously I had chosen the right company — natural Vermonters. What greater compliment could I pay?

☆

One spring I was at Charlottesville, where Posy was to give a paper at a meeting of philosophers. I not only wanted to hear the paper (I think it was on the Ontological Aspects of Negation), but I wanted to make plans with her about her wedding. I had not seen her since she had written that she was engaged to Arthur Sprague. I had met him in Bryn Mawr where he was a professor in the English Department. He was a well-known Shakespearean scholar and had a special interest in the stage performance of Shakespeare. He knew all kinds of interesting things and I had enjoyed his way of telling about them. He still always greets me with a story that makes me laugh. He was coming to Charlottesville too but not in time to hear about negation. I suspect that affirmation interested him more at the moment.

Doctor Lee, head of the Philosophy Department at Sophie Newcomb, kindly sat next to me while Posy read her paper. There were questions afterwards, which were more confusing to me than the original remarks. Posy answered them so capably that at one point, Doctor Lee whispered to me: "Your daughter is *covering* herself with glory."

Of course a dimple helps.

Posy and I talked over plans for the wedding. She wanted to be married in Calais in the Old West Church, wear the family wedding dress and veil and have lots of people staying in the house. She did not care what we had to eat except plenty of homemade wedding cake. The only detail she mentioned with real determination was that she'd like a supper party the evening before the wedding, followed by charades. The Duchess and Dr. Chew of the English Department at Bryn Mawr were to be in them.

With these instructions I returned to Brookline.

In no time at all, it seemed, I was in Calais baking fruitcake — mountains of it, miles of it — and arranging to have lobsters flown over from Maine for the supper party and explaining to the Duchess that her dramatic talents would be needed. Everyone in the neighborhood began to think of helpful things to do. The Manlys offered their guest room to the bridegroom and I had no trouble finding beds for about thirty other guests. I had a notebook with a page for each guest. I noted his time of arrival and departure, who would meet him at plane, train or bus, where his car could be parked if he were driving.

Glancing back at the notebook, I get the impression that I had thought of everything. So I had, except that some guests telegraphed changes in their plans; the telegrams arrived after they did. Planes were late. Heavy rain made our parking area into a sort of Sargasso Sea. One delightful family of five came unexpectedly. Each member of it thought the others had let us know. Moves, little more complicated than those in a chess game, supplied them all with beds.

Without Sue Lewis from Virginia, who had come to spend part of the summer with us, nothing would have gone right. Her head was far better than my notebook. Nothing was too much trouble for her. She did whatever most needed to be done, whether it was arranging flowers, mopping up spilled milk, meeting a train or adjusting the bride's veil. I suppose she must have slept but I can't imagine when.

The notebook had certain successes. The lobsters flew in on time. The bridegroom arrived. Margaret Wight and Margaret Whitney arranged the flowers in the church. Both had strong opinions but they established Emilie Harrison as umpire and the combination made the church look its best. The supper was excellent and a great treat to me as I had never so much as laid hands on a lettuce leaf or a lobster claw during its preparation.

The great success of the evening was the charade; or rather as is, I believe, not unusual — the performers certainly thought so. The original team met in my bedroom. Planning the charade took place with the usual laughter over the author's own wit. They kept sending out for more actors. They already had enough for the cast of *Hamlet* when they sent for me.

Out of respect for the philosopher-bride, they had chosen the word *negation*. For the second syllable a gay scene in a café was planned. They wanted plenty of beer and they suggested that I had better play the accordion so there would be lots of noise — always the best reason for playing that instrument.

The climax came with the acting of the whole word. The scene was a dialogue between Dr. Chew and the Duchess and she declined him with forms of the monosyllable "no" in a variety of languages and dialects — *Negation,* in fact, though how she could resist his eloquence and charm, was hard to understand.

By midnight everyone had gone to bed in various houses, or so Sue and I thought. We still had work to do. She had pointed out that there would be guests around at supper the next night — a dozen or so — and that it would be a good idea to have some fried chicken on hand. We could do the real cooking at night, cool it and run it briefly in and out of the oven the next evening. I had made a special trip to Montpelier the day before and had brought back a ham and enough chicken for twenty-four people. I had never learned to fry chicken as Sue did. This was my chance, I thought, because, of course, I was acting as kitchen maid and could spy on the chef.

I did not learn this time either. The smell of the frying chicken collected gourmets from the carriage house, corn barn, Kenty's house, Sam's, my own. I was kept busy just defending the chicken from them. All they got were a few wing tips. Some of them ate cereal with bananas.

"What is the proper term for a midnight brunch?" someone asked and another conscientious eater muttered, "Munch, obviously."

At last, around two o'clock the cooking was finished and the guests went hungrily to bed.

The morning of the wedding, like most mornings that summer,

dawned in a dour cold rain. It steamed off after a while and by quarter of three, as we were driving to the church, the sun came out. Everything was blue and green and white — clouds as white as the bride's veil, white meadowsweet with rainbow drops sparkling on it. Robins sang "Cheer up! It's going to clear up!" The air was sweet with red clover.

Lorie was showing some of the last comers to their seats in the pine box pews with their faded blue edges. Kenty was already in the front box with Susie and Andrew and Janet, a bundle of peace. I could hear the tramp of Andrew's new shoes on the hard pine seat. The noise almost drowned the music of the organ. When Sam took me up the aisle and opened the door of the pew, Andrew escaped and made a dash for the pulpit steps.

He was two years old. Whether at this time he thought of entering the ministry and conducting the service, I am not sure.

I have always had a dread of crying at weddings and I have trained myself not to — almost. My method works perfectly so long as nothing unexpected turns up. I make a mental list of all the things that might make me cry and insulate myself against them. Of course, the list is never complete. I notice something new and strange — a gesture, an expression, the flash of sunlight on a soldier's service ribbon, the smell of gardenias, the bride's old nurse in her best dress — and there I am again in happy misery.

This time I knew that my danger lay in thinking about Rich, ten years old, helping his father paint the pulpit with that misty shade of blue, of his voice reading "Let us all praise famous men," of his finding me the piece of his great-grandmother's weaving with which I had covered the kneeling stool, of his expression of peace and contentment as he sat looking out at the stones that marked his ancestors' graves. I had stiffened myself against wedding music and the Bible from which he read the lessons. My grandmother's wedding lace across the white satin of my dress and the orange blossoms caught in the veil and swish of the train across the white carpet would not upset me, I vowed.

And I was successful! Not however, I'm afraid, because of my preparations but because of my special task — keeping Andrew's feet from sounding like cavalry coming during the service. Such was my perseverance that he never made a sound and I never had to use my best handkerchief. The only two weddings at which I did not find at least one tear to wink away were my own and Posy's.

36

Sailors Have Scurvy

WHEN SAM took a job teaching at Hofstra College at Hempstead, Long Island, I became an interior decorator. I began work on his Vermont house. I plastered holes in ceilings and walls. I painted woodwork. I had a new kitchen sink and electric lights installed. I papered walls. I painted floors.

Pearl helped me with the papering. "Who was on the wall?" is a question often asked about this process. Usually Pearl was on the wall while I measured, matched, cut and pasted strips of paper. Sometimes I worked alone and carried on all the processes. I usually worked a six-hour day with sometimes an extra two hours in the evening. I walked to work. This was because there was at that time no safe place to turn a car around near Sam's house. Because of the steep pitches and sharp twists in the road on both sides of his drive, it was a favorite place for strong, swift young men to crash into cars containing elderly ladies.

Recently, because of a fatal accident involving an eighty-year-old woman, the papers were full of suggestions about strict tests for such drivers. During my driving life, three of my cars have been demolished. Each time the police have decided the other driver was at fault. All three were active young men. One was waving to someone on the sidewalk. One was drunk. One was delivering a load of bootleg beer. No one approximately senile has ever hit me. Excuse my mentioning it.

As I walked home from work, I found myself moving like a workman, slowly, steadily, wearily through sun or mist or showers. For the first time in my life I was having that splendid regular exercise doctors recommend so highly. Since Rich died, I had not been able to write. Perhaps it had been true, as many of my friends suspected, that he wrote my books for me. When I was in Portsmouth, Virginia, the winter before, I had spent some time in the library reading the history of the town. I had an idea of writing one of the *He Went with* series about John Paul Jones and I thought my hero might start from Portsmouth. I took pages of notes but they remained only notes. That summer I had an idea for writing *He Went with Captain Cook* and I piled up notes about Cook. I was especially interested in his idea that scurvy was caused by a lack of fresh fruit and vegetables and in his taking condensed orange juice and lemon juice with him on his voyage.

Taking notes was not precisely sedentary work. I did it lying flat on my back after my work as a painter or paperhanger was over for the day. My legs were badly bruised, I noticed: as a result of my work, I supposed. I was so tired by the end of the day that I stumbled against things a good deal.

As I studied about Cook, I grew especially fond of a native of Tahiti called Tupia. He was a gentle but brave man whose great ambition was to see the strange world from which the English captain had come. Tupia knew there were dangers — storms, fierce whales, sharks, hidden rocks, booming cannon — but he was ready to face them all for the sake of the great adventure. Only — poor Tupia — he had not faced the right danger.

The fresh food they had taken from Tahiti did not last long enough. The voyage along the east coast of Australia took weeks and it was impossible to land.

Cook wrote in his journal: "Our poor Indian, Tupia, shows the dark spots on his legs that are the first sign of scurvy."

Many of the crew developed scurvy too. Most of them recovered when they reached an island where there was fresh fruit but some of them died, among them Tupia. With Cook, I grieved sincerely over Tupia's death.

"I must remember to get some orange juice," I thought but I was too busy with the last of my paperhanging to think of it again.

Just after my work was done, I collapsed and went to the hospital in Montpelier. The doctor decided to do a biopsy. He and his assistant were bright and cheerful as I was wheeled in. They were both scrubbing up, each at a separate sink. Over the sound of the water they chatted about their patients.

"Remember that old Mrs. Canton — lived over Marshfield way — we operated on last summer? How is she?"

"Died around Christmas."

"Too bad. And that nice Mrs. Petersham we had in here — how about her?"

"Died too. Just after March meeting."

After a third example of these vital statistics, I said, "I wish, just as a personal favor, you gentlemen would talk about some of your successes."

All they did was to give me a delicious anaesthetic. I was back in my room when I met the doctor again.

"What did you find?" I asked.

"The biopsy's negative. You've just got scurvy is all that's the matter with you."

"Scurvy!"

"Yes — didn't you notice those spots on your legs. They're the first sign of it."

I murmured, "Tupia!" and he said, "Yes — too bad, especially as it's not necessary. Now I'm going to give you a big injection of

Vitamin C and in a few days, if you'll promise to take plenty of orange juice, I'll let you go home."

This is how I first became interested in nutrition. I was fortunate in having found a doctor who was. Most doctors are not. They quote the party line of the American Medical Association: "No one who gets three well-balanced meals a day needs extra vitamins. Vitamins should come from food, not pills."

The only trouble with this statement is that the person who eats three well-balanced meals a day is about as rare as the Vermont panther. I will not expand this remark at the moment. The three-volume treatment of the subject I am planning will have to wait until I am older and wiser.

I was ready to start writing about Captain Cook when I received from a friend in England a review of *He Went with Captain Cook*. It had been brought out by my English publisher and was described as being part of the series initiated by Louise Andrews Kent. I protested to the publishers, who could not understand why I was annoyed and said that they had done nothing illegal. They were so convinced of the propriety of their behavior that they hired half a dozen muscular young men and in a short time added six books to the series. This work would have taken me twelve years. I like to think that if I had written the books they would not have been quite so stodgy as the examples I saw, but I may be mistaken.

This episode shoved me back into being a non-writer for a while. At last, a New York publisher asked me to do a book on the village greens of New England. They had already engaged Arthur Griffin to do the photography. This kind of book was so different from anything I had done before that I thought perhaps if I could do it — it might get me back to writing again even without Rich's help. Houghton Mifflin kindly encouraged me to go ahead on it. It is the only book of mine that they did not publish — except for the foreign language editions, including English.

There are editions of the *He Went with* books in Dutch, Swedish, Danish, Norwegian, Finnish, Portuguese and Spanish. The rights to print some of them in Germany and Czechoslovakia were also sold, but the war intervened and I doubt if they were ever published. Perhaps they were considered subversive — a thought I enjoy. I suppose *Mrs. Appleyard's Kitchen* is probably a subversive work too.

I worked about a year and a half on *Village Greens of New England* and enjoyed it. I was especially flattered, only last year, when a young man in New York, who was working for his Ph.D., wrote and asked me to send him any material I had on the subject that I had not used in the book. It would help him, he said.

I felt so amiable that morning that instead of writing and telling him what I think of literary termites, I just threw the letter in the fire.

37

Heart of the Matter

IN 1948 I made a trip to Portsmouth as I had done for three winters, driving my blue coupé, stopping several nights on the way. It all seemed easy and natural. It never occurred to me that I would not do it again. I stopped to see Mallory and Millie Smith so I could keep a promise I had made and help them refinish their breakfast table. Mallory hired a sander. We took turns using it and in one day got all the shellac finish off. The next day I rubbed in the first coat of linseed and then went on south.

There was no snow and I soon found myself driving past open fields with clean black pigs, apparently molded out of polished iron, in them. It all looked so familiar that I felt like a Virginian, who had been away a long time, coming home. I had this feeling wherever I went — in the colonial streets of Williamsburg, on the white sand of Virginia Beach, even when Bishop Brown, Sue's uncle, drove us down past the Dismal Swamp and into North Carolina.

I was very much pleased when one of the committee for the church supper asked me to speak, after the supper, on writing books. I was pleased partly because it meant that I was still a writer in my friends' minds and partly because I could obviously do something for them that they wanted done in return for all the hospitality I had received. It was so long since I had done any speaking in public that the feeling of tension while I was writing and learning my speech was even stronger than usual. However, I shook it off, reduced the speech to brief notes on cards and learned what was on the cards. This was how Rich had taught me to make a "spontaneous" speech. I spent about a week at it.

The evening went all right until I was back at Sue's in the big mahogany four-poster. Then the pain began to run up my left arm and run down again into my chest, making it hard to breathe. It was, I decided in my wisdom, indigestion brought on by eating that delicious supper and being so fraudulently natural afterwards. I went into the bathroom and took several kinds of pills — I don't know what they were — that I found in the medicine cabinet. At least they must have been harmless, since the heart attack passed off. I did not, of course, recognize what it was at the time. Later the pattern became familiar. In addition to the pills my treatment consisted of lying propped up on pillows and doing a little work on *Village Greens of New England.*

I spent a whole day in bed resting after this episode. The next day I drove Sue and some other friends to have lunch with me out in the country. I did not drive much over fifty miles. A few days later I started on the last of what I called my "seven springs journey." I planned to see parts of spring in Virginia, Washington, Maryland, Pennsylvania, New Jersey, New York and Massachusetts.

Things did not work out just as I had planned. I had another attack of "indigestion" as I carried my suitcases up three flights to Millie's apartment, but I got over it and drove on to the Cadwaladers' in Joppa, Maryland. I was lucky enough to have a bedroom downstairs there. I could easily walk out into the sunshine, breathe in the musky scent of box, enjoy the sweetness of a great wisteria that had taken over a whole tree as its territory, walk down a path edged with daffodils.

It was not until I came to Yarrow West in Bryn Mawr, where

Arthur and Posy lived on the third floor, that I had my official coronary. The only reason I did not dismiss that one as indigestion too was because I explained to Mabel Kent why I could not come to lunch and she sent her doctor to see me.

He told me to stay in bed and I did happily, watching leaves grow, reading, dozing. When Posy had to go out, Carlotta was left in charge of me. Carlotta was a long narrow black and white cat who had great talent as an entertainer. Just to see her fling herself at a screen, claw her way up it and stroll nonchalantly along the top was a pleasure. Arthur entertained me too. He used to come home from his office in the middle of the morning, play a game of Canfield with himself and make me laugh with the latest story he had picked up.

Some of the time I entertained myself remembering old family stories. A favorite about LeRoy and Blanche Kent drifted through my mind one day. They went to a church supper and whist party in Hardwick, Grandma Kent had told me. Their seats for whist were with another couple, whom she did not know, but Roy introduced them. The woman was prim looking and spoke little. The man, who sat on Blanche's right, talked loudly between hands, telling stories at which he laughed heartily.

"And, Lulie, the first time he did it," Blanche Kent said, "he threw himself back in his chair so far that when he straightened up, his left leg raked mine right from my knee to my ankle. I guess you can believe the look I gave him [I could], but he just went on sorting his hand. And after he'd played it — if he didn't tell *another* story and throw himself back laughing and when he sat up again that leg of his raked mine from my knee right down to my ankle. Well, I glared at him and at Roy Kent who just sat there not noticing how his wife was being insulted.

"And the same thing happened after almost every hand. He'd tell another story and throw himself back laughing and rake my leg with his again. And his wife and Roy never noticed a thing. Well, when the game was over, I got Roy Kent out into the street pretty quick. It was bright moonlight and I looked him straight in the face and I said, 'Roy Kent, what do you *mean* introducing a man like that to me?' and he just stared at me and said, 'Why, Blanche, he's a perfectly nice man. Good customer at the store. Keeps a big deposit in our bank. What are you talking about?' And then I told him. 'Roy' — I said — 'every time that man told one of those stories and threw himself back in his chair, when he sat up, why he raked my leg with his all the way from my knee to my ankle. I was never so insulted in my life!'

"And all Roy did was just to stand there in the moonlight, right on Church Street, and laugh and laugh! He laughed so hard, he clutched his arms right around his middle and bent over them choking, swaying back and forth till I was afraid he'd collapse right there in the snow.

"So I took him by the shoulder and gave him quite a shake and I said, 'LeRoy Kent, your wife has been insulted so some folks in other parts of the country would fight a duel, and all you do is double up and laugh. What do you *mean*, behaving so?' And Roy, he stopped laughing a minute and he gasped out, 'Blanche, that man — that man — has a wooden leg!' and then we both laughed all the way home."

I laughed too, up in my room under the eaves in Yarrow West.

Grandma Kent, I remembered, varied swiftly and often between informal geniality and imperiousness, especially with the hired help. Her mood was like a barometer equipped for shooting porcupine quills. It was the part of wisdom to learn the symptoms of coming storms and be ready for thunder and lightning of an especially painful type.

When Mrs. Lillian Ramsbotham first came to act as Grandma's housekeeper, all was calm and serene.

"She's real democratic, isn't she?" Mrs. Ramsbotham observed to me soon after she came. "Why last night she called to me just after I took my dress off. 'Yoohoo, Lilly!' she said. 'Let's go out in the garden and eat cucumbers,' and we went out, both in our slips and ate cucumbers like bananas, only not skinned. In the moonlight. She says a cucumber eaten like that never hurt anyone yet. She ever tell you that?"

I admitted that she had but that I had been too timid to try. Grandma had not been pleased at my refusal. Some folks — she had said — don't know what's good for them. She had given me one of her dark but bright prickling looks. However I was a privileged character — Rich's wife, Kenty's mother and a writer — she used to brag to the neighbors about that, and she was never angry with me for long.

The honeymoon with Lilly Ramsbotham lasted several weeks. Grandma moved back and forth across the road from one of her houses to the other whenever she felt like it. I often heard her calling, "Yoohoo, Lilly! We'll move to Remember Kent's house. Come on over and mop the floor!" Mrs. Ramsbotham's voice would reply, "OK, Blanche — be right over!" and I would see her tall figure equipped with mop and pail, crossing the road. Lilly's patience with washing windows, sweeping, cooking seemed endless but, alas, it was not. On a certain day she alleged it was too hot to pick raspberries. Lightning struck. I drove her back to East Craftsbury.

Little was said except an occasional murmur of "I never knew — I never knew —"

What she never knew, I was too prudent to ask. I never saw her again. Indeed I probably should not remember her now, for she was only one among many helpers I had driven around the country, if I had not heard Kenty reading aloud to a group consisting of Sam and Posy and some of their friends. The book was called *Willy Wolf and Lilla Lamb*. The plot was simple. Willy Wolf was all sweetness, inviting Lilla Lamb to come over to his house. When she came, he continued to be extremely pleasant but about page 10, with Lilla Lamb looking especially white and curly with a blue ribbon around her neck, he ate her up.

The Kent version varied slightly from the original. It went something like this:

> And Willy Wolf, he say, "Yoohoo, Lilla Lamb, come over to my house and mop the floor!" And Lilla Lamb, she say, "OK, Willy Wolf. I mopped the floor." So then Willy Wolf, he say, "Yoohoo, Lilla Lamb, come over to my *other* house and wash the dishes!" And Lilla Lamb, she say, "OK, Willy Wolf, I washed all the dishes!"

By this time I had stopped reading *Vanity Fair* in favor of the new piece of fiction being read in the next room. Could it be that my dear little children, brought up to have such pretty manners, were of a satirical and irreverent turn of mind?

Yes, it could.

Willy Wolf cajoled Lilla Lamb into sweeping, making chicken pie, washing curtains — even into mowing the lawn. The trouble with listening to this story, while I was lying on my bed, was that the tears that went with my suppressed laughter ran into my ears.

Kenty's voice dropped to a note of doom:

> So one day Willy Wolf, he say, "Yoohoo, Lilla Lamb! Go pick raspberries!" But Lilla Lamb, she say, "No, Willy Wolf — it's too hot and besides there ain't no raspberries." And Willy Wolf say, "What you mean, Lilla Lamb, saying ain't no raspberries?" And Lilla Lamb, she say, "No, Willy Wolf, your grandchildren and their friends ate them all up." And Willy Wolf, he was so mad he was going to eat up Lilla Lamb for supper but this kind lady she came and drove Lilla Lamb to East Craftsbury by way of Hardwick and Lilla Lamb lived happy ever after.

This fortunate ending produced a torrent of Yoohoos, OK's and frivolous laughter. It sounded to me a good deal as if my relatives were rolling on the floor. I got up hastily, washed my face with water cold from the spring, made some lemonade and passed a few sugared sponge cakes to the reading club.

I remembered in 1948, as I lay watching Carlotta hurl herself up the screen and then claw her way up the window curtains, that when I got back from East Craftsbury, Grandma had spoken rather tartly to me on the subject of my children eating all the raspberries. I said I was sorry and two days later she offered to give me her emerald necklace, the Russian one she bought in Constantinople after the Bolshevik Revolution.

I said I wanted her to keep it and wear it with her black velvet dress next time she went to New York. I am not sure whether she did. I did not see it again for some years. She was not feeling well at the time of the 1938 hurricane and the doctor told her to stay in bed. He found a housekeeper and a nurse to take care of her. Rich and I drove up from Brookline to see her late in October. We found her happy and and on excellent terms with her helpers.

She said cheerfully, "Well, I'm eighty-eight years old and if I live through the falling of the leaves, I guess I'll live to March meeting — as the old saying goes."

There were still a few leaves on beeches and poplars and larches were still cinnamon gold as we drove home. Only a day or two after we got back to Brookline, the doctor called to tell us there had been an accident.

The hurricane had damaged the shutters on Grandma's house. A carpenter was repairing those of her bedroom windows one afternoon when one of her neighbors sent her in some homemade ice cream. The nurse had brought her a dish of it. When she got downstairs Grandma had called down to her.

"Bring me another dish, please. I'm going to give this to Mr. Dalbee," she said, naming the carpenter.

She handed the ice cream to him, Mr. Dalbee said, through the window. Just as he started eating it, standing on the ladder, she fell, striking her head on the bedpost.

She was still unconscious, the doctor said.

Rich went up by train that night. I followed, driving my car, the next day. She died soon after I got there, never having regained consciousness. Typically, her last conscious act was one of generosity and friendliness.

We left the house as it was for the winter. Rich took her jewelry out of her bureau. He looked for the emerald necklace but it was not there. I suggested that she might have given it to one of her nieces and we had forgotten about it the next spring when we were clearing out the house. Rich found a box of costume jewelry on the shelf of the guest room closet and he put it aside to give to the hospital rummage sale. I glanced at it as we were packing a carton of things for the hospital. Tangled up with coral beads and imitation pearls and shoulder ornaments shining not very brightly with rhinestones, was the emerald necklace.

Rich gave the Remember Kent house to Kenty, Grandma's new Chrysler to Sam, who had a house, and to Posy, who didn't want a house, the necklace. One of the things that helped me get over my coronary was seeing her wear it.

Sam and Edith came to Bryn Mawr and drove me to Hempstead. I began to feel so much better while I was there that I went to a wrestling match one evening. When my hero, in *He Went with Hannibal,* had occasion to wrestle with the villain of the story, the wrestling I had seen at Hempstead sixteen years before came in handy. I always think a writer's mind is rather like a sheet of sticky flypaper. You set it anywhere, tacked perhaps to an old shingle, and whatever sticks to it proves useful sometime. Then all you need is some paper, pen and ink and a few words.

I heard of a young man the other day who was writing a book only — he said — he was having trouble with the words. He couldn't seem to get the right ones. He thought perhaps he'd better find a good stenographer who would advise him which to use and dictate to her. This method would also have the advantage of taking less time than it would if he sat down and wrote.

Fortunately, I had found enough words to write most of *Village Greens* before I had my really bad coronary, the one I had in Vermont in June. This was the one when I rode to the hospital in a hearse thinly disguised as an ambulance. Margaret Curtis rode with me to be sure I was all right. It happened that there was quite a group of people in Kents' Corner that afternoon and also many swimmers just coming out of Bliss Pond. The expression on their faces as they recognized me is still a happy memory. I was not allowed to speak or move so I could only smile to return their look of incredulity.

When I came back, three weeks later, Lew and Sue Manly drove me home and carried me up the front steps. I weighed less than usual because I had been put on the so-called Rice Diet.

"Who is Dr. Rice?" I had asked.

Having always especially disliked rice, I could hardly believe it when I was told that it meant that all I could eat was unsalted rice and fruit. After some weeks of this, I was promoted to a low sodium diet. I have stayed on it for almost twenty years. To the many people who have cooked for me without salt during that time, I bow my head in gratitude. To anyone who has recently been put on such a diet, I will say here that if you go without salt entirely, not taking substitutes that keep the taste for it and the habit of gratifying the taste alive, you will soon cease to be interested in salt, may even — as I do — dislike it.

Several other things helped me recover. One was my bird tree. This was a big maple in my front yard. Many of its branches were bare and it was a natural stopping place for birds. I was allowed to walk once a day from my bed to the couch on the porch. I would take my binoculars with me and watch any sign of motion in the tree. During my mornings that summer, I saw seventy-eight kinds of birds. They ranged all the way from a ruby-throated hummingbird, sitting quietly except for turning his head just enough to let the sun flash on his throat, to an enormous hawk that looked as if he'd just come from the taxidermist and had been fastened to the top branch. Woodpeckers, nuthatches and sapsuckers inspected the tree constantly for grubs. Warblers, vireos and redstarts fluttered in and out collecting insects. Waxwings sat there eating chokecherries. It was a sort of ornithological cafeteria.

One day perfect silence settled down over the tree and over the whole yard. When I focused my glasses on the shape on the top branch, I saw why. It was a northern shrike, turning his head with its fiercely hooked beak from side to side, ready to pounce on any small bird and tear it to pieces. He sat there half an hour. I was as relieved as the purple finches when he finally flew off.

38

Kitchen—and Other—Privileges

MY DOCTOR and all my friends kept telling me I ought to find a nice little apartment instead of living alone in that big house. Their advice was obviously sensible, the kind of thing that would have made a good cross-stitched motto, but no one found an apartment for me. However in June of 1949 I did hear of one that sounded possible. Posy had come to stay with me — I had been overdoing and had been sent back to bed for a few days — and she encouraged me to look at it when I could go out again. I made an appointment. When I called up to see if I could postpone it for a day or two, I was told that without saying anything to me, they had rented it to someone else.

I was feeling crushed when the telephone rang. A voice I did not know asked for me, and when I admitted to being Posy's mother, said, "Oh good. I've tried every Kent in the book and that's my last dime."

Nancy Farwell from Chicago, she said she was, and could I tell her how to reach Posy?

I said to her that I'd shove the telephone over to Posy and I said to Posy, "She sounds so nice — ask her out."

I was right as usual. She was perfect.

She told me that she was going to be married to Craig Leman

and that she was looking for an apartment where they could live while he went to Harvard Medical School.

I said, "Are you having any luck?"

"No," she said. "The only thing I've found is a subbasement on the back of Beacon Hill. It's damp and when I asked about rats, they said there weren't many, and it's too far from school and the rent's too high."

"How," I said after a brief pause, perhaps a second, for consideration, "would you like to live here? And have Kitchen Privileges?"

Nancy did not hesitate much longer than I had. She said she would like to come but she'd have to ask Craig. She and Posy started looking the house over at once and deciding where she and Craig would live. They came in early autumn and stayed seven years.

That summer Kenty returned from California. She and Lorie had been divorced and she had married Albert Gay, a talented photographer, painter and designer of textiles. Her house in California had burned to the ground one day while she was out, leaving her and the children with nothing but the clothes they had on, which had been chosen because they were going on a picnic.

Kenty said cheerfully that having your house burn was one way of getting a completely new wardrobe — the neighbors had been extremely generous. One thing she felt badly about was the flat silver. She had expected to find it in her house across the road from mine in Kents' Corner. It was not there and she decided that she must have taken it to California. She used stainless steel for most meals, getting the silver out only for special occasions. Had it been stolen from Remember Kent's cottage? Or had it been melted to a pool on a California hillside? She had no idea.

Naturally, in such a predicament, she drove over to Marshfield to see Luvia Lafiria. Ever since she was a small child, Luvia has been helping people find things. She is a clairvoyant with a Vermont accent. She has no crystal globe, no dramatic rigamarole. She works in a sunny, spotless Vermont kitchen. You'd probably find her cutting green beans or peeling potatoes and wearing an attractive apron over a crisp print dress. She keeps right on with her work while you state your problem.

Sometimes she cannot help you and says so at once, but it is more likely that she makes some straightforward remarks that lead you to your lost treasure. For years she did this as a neighborly service, but so many people who were strangers to her came and it took so much time from her housework that she now charges a fee.

When she heard Kenty's doubts about the silver, she spoke clearly and firmly.

"The silver," she said, "was not in the fire. It was never in California. But it's not in Vermont either. Now I see it in another state. I can't tell you which one but it's south of here. It's in a house that's kind of high up above a quiet street. First there's a long walk, quite steep, and then a flight of steps. There's two houses at the top of the steps. I see the silver in the right-hand one. Keep on climbing stairs, several flights. Go about as high as you can go. I see a sloping window. Light from it shines down on something maroon in color. The silver seems to be near it. Be sure you go as high as you can go — I don't know's I've helped you."

"Of course you have," Kenty said. "Next time I go to my mother's house in Massachusetts, I'll find it."

So when she drove me home that autumn, the first thing she did was to go up to the third floor. Then she climbed the short flight of steps that leads to the attic, walked to the steps under the skylight, went up them, saw on the ledge underneath a maroon cushion.

The silver, in its flannel bags from Shreve's, was next to it.

Explain this any way you like; it was certainly an easy way to find it.

I cannot remember the names of all the couples who had

Kitchen Privileges during the next two years. I have an idea that sixteen children were born while their parents lived in my house but I can remember only fourteen. Of course I could find out by looking in my diaries, neatly written every day for the last thirty-six years, but it is a point of honor with me not to consult them. They do not have exactly the charm of those of Samuel Pepys. They are not written in code so you can read them yourself if you are interested. However I feel I should report that they are chiefly concerned with the weather (varied), how I feel (mostly terrible) and what I am writing.

Soon after I began to give Kitchen Privileges, my diary began to note every day "worked on k.p." This book told how Mrs. Appleyard had some young couples living in her house and what happened. It is much the best reference book for this experience. Yet, while basically true, it is completely inaccurate. For instance there actually was a set of twins born to one of my favorite couples but the twins arrived quietly in a hospital and they were girls not boys. It was I myself who was interrupted, while making almond meringues, by the FBI and not a young lady named Harriet, who did not exist outside the book. I wish she did. She was a capable cook and I would order one of those meringues from her today if she were around. Also some brown sugar rolls.

Perhaps the most helpful thing about the book — it was published in 1953 under the title ". . . *with Kitchen Privileges"* — is that it contains a section in the back telling how to make the various dishes the characters ate. I wish authors would do this more often except — now that I think of it — modern novels are written chiefly by writers who don't like their characters so the food would doubtless be exceptionally repulsive. I withdraw the suggestion. No doubt readers can think how to combine cornstarch and monosodium glutamate without any ghoulish literary advice from anyone.

I have sampled hospitals in a number of places. One day I was about to leave the Parkway Hospital in Brookline and go to Vermont. I was just dressing for the journey, carefully edging my way into my slip with as few arm movements as possible, when there was a loud knock at my door.

"Who is it?" I called. "I'm dressing."

"Reverend Jones," said a hearty voice. "I'll wait."

I said I was leaving the hospital soon, but he said he'd see me if only for a minute. It seemed like an hour. I sat on the bed. He sat on the only armchair and did his best to make me a better woman, not, I'm afraid, with striking success. He told me much of the dedicated women of his church, which was not mine, and how they raised money for missions and how hard they worked for small sums.

One trouble, he said, was these big national campaigns that sucked all the money out of people's pockets.

"Now, you take this Heart Fund campaign," he said loudly — for since I was obviously ancient he assumed that I was also deaf. "Millions, they're begging for — millions! Can you imagine people giving millions to that nonsense and ignoring us and our work?"

I said, "Mr. Jones, I am sorry if I seem unsympathetic but I feel sure, if it were not for the Heart Fund campaigns of the last few years, that you and I would not be sitting here having this interesting conversation. And now — thank you for your call — but I must finish dressing."

He left.

All he said was, "Well!"

I felt virtuous for not saying any of the smart things I had thought of such as, "And what would the mission do with the money — make more Christians like you?"

No doubt he had restrained himself too.

☆

In 1950 I had a sound idea. I decided I had been ill long enough and that to celebrate my return to health I would embroider a crewelwork bedspread. The idea for the design was inspired partly by a piece of embroidered linen belonging to Margaret Wight, partly by the Indian Tree-of-Life motif that I had already used on the wall of the living room. I found a so-called homespun sheet, woven by my children's great-grandmother Polly Curtiss Kent. Its first hundred and thirty years had gone fairly well. There were a few stains and small holes in the ivory-colored wool. I mended the holes and then made the design so that a leaf or a butterfly or a flower covered them and the stains.

There are four trees on the spread, each growing out of a mound of earth and turf and flowers. Each tree has things in common with the others and also something entirely its own. One thing occurring in all four designs is what is called "the inhabited leaf." This is a traditional design in crewel embroidery. It came from India to Persia, went westward to Turkey and North Africa, traveled with the Moors to Spain and Portugal, thence to Holland, from Holland to England, and in the seventeenth century came to colonial America. The "inhabitation" of the leaf means only that a spray of buds and flowers grows over it.

Certain of the flowers on the trees — tulips and carnations, for instance — are traditional. Others are there because they are associated with someone. There is a spray of chrysanthemums, grown by my grandmother and named for her — the Edgerly Seedling. They used to be in New England gardens seventy years ago but have long been only a memory. There is a cardinal flower to remind me of James Aldrich who planted one for me because I had told him of the way they grew in the swamp at North Hatley. A blue gentian recalls the day I saw Faith Bemis' field full of them. I embroidered a goldfinch sitting on a thistle for Edith Kent, a sunflower for Posy, a bunch of blackberries for Kenty, an iris for Leila Page, blueberries for Nancy Leman.

The spread served its purpose from the first. Every flower and leaf made me feel better. By July I was told by my doctor that I might walk down to my pond for the first time. This was a great day. I dressed for the expedition with special care. I had bought new underclothes recently, including a foundation garment that covered most of me. It alleged on the box that it would mold my figure to new beauty. I put on all new clothes including a new white linen coat and skirt and a broad-brimmed white hat. Since I was planning to embroider while I sat on the new float Ralph had built, I did not wear white gloves.

Things were busy around the pond. Small children were paddling in the shallow place near where the brook flows in among the forget-me-nots. Larger ones were swimming and ducking each other with noises suitable to these activities. Kenty and some friends were diving off the dam. Dogs panted among the lupines. Back on the hillside a young man I knew was raking hay. He disappeared behind a small grove of trees just as I recognized him. I began my embroidery.

Andrew went out past the float, paddling his inflatable collapsible raft — that's what the label said. He was lying on his stomach and making large splashes. The raft was collapsible all right. It turned over about ten feet beyond the float. Strange sounds such as a young bull might make in a small submarine, mixed with whimpers, sobs, coughs and gurgles, came from under the raft.

I called Kenty but there was too much other noise and she didn't hear.

Oh well, I thought, he's the important one.

I put down my work, eased myself into the water. I moved as fast as I could toward the raft but I went so slowly that I thought he would drown before I reached him. The bellows were already almost all gurgles. The water was up around my armpits when I got there. I turned the raft over, towed Andrew in to the float, managed to get him up on it and shake the water out of him. When he began to bellow again, I tried to get out myself, but I had used all my strength. I stood there in the water unable to move an inch.

I was still standing there when the young hayraker emerged from behind the trees.

"Hi, Mrs. Kent, how are you today!" he called.

"Fine, just fine," I said.

"How's the water?" he said.

"Just fine," I said and he drove on.

It's nice to have a reputation as an eccentric. No one thinks there's anything odd about your standing in the middle of a pond dressed in a white hat and a tailored suit.

Luckily Kenty had noticed me. She swam over and helped me back to the float. I squeezed a good deal of water out of myself and after a steaming pause, walked back to the house. Obviously I was better. All my new clothes except my hat were carefully washed but they never quite regained their first gleaming whiteness. The pond water had given them a slightly off-white tone, somewhat like that of the bedspread.

☆

Sometimes Kenty and I have been able to communicate without words. On one occasion I was driving her from Brookline to Calais. Besides my usual luggage I had a very large carton on the back seat. It contained a high, domed glass case of rare stuffed birds, perched on spreading branches. The carton had once contained a radio.

As soon as Kenty got into the car, she asked what was in the carton. I said she could have three guesses. She guessed first a radio, then something else logical and also incorrect. Then she said she would keep her third guess until later and I must send her a message. I drove on, thinking at intervals, forming the words in my mind as if I were composing and sending a telegram: "A case of birds . . . a case of birds."

After about two hours Kenty said, "I'm ready for my third guess now. I think it is a cage of birds."

"Only one letter wrong," I said. "It's a case of birds."

"Oh!" she said, "that's what I thought, but it sounded so silly that I changed it to cage!"

The case of birds arrived intact and improves the bird room by partly concealing some of the poorest of my wall paintings.

Once I received a message, urgent and apparently from outer space. I had always had a longing for a gold chain like one Katharine had inherited from our English great-grandmother. Visitors to India used to bring these chains home to England in the early nineteenth century. The links were of gold, beaten down so thin that the edges are quite sharp. Each link is almost a quarter of an inch across, and its surface is rough to the touch because of a raised octagonal design. Without a magnifying glass it is almost impossible to appreciate the extraordinary delicacy and regularity of this pattern. There are perhaps three hundred of these links in a four-foot chain. The clasps vary in size and shape. A barrel shape, with curves like minute golden ropes and gold rosettes rising out of a background ornamented with the octagonal design, is typical.

I always hoped I would find one of these chains in a jeweler's shop or an antique shop. I was told that there was a good deal of alloy in the gold so the price ought not to be out of my reach especially as they were no longer fashionable. I found one at last and the owner assured me it was a bargain, but it cost enough to feed our family for some weeks so I regretfully left it where it was.

A few years later I was visiting Katharine near Philadelphia. She took me to lunch in town and we looked into the windows of various antique shops. In one I saw a small black and gold lacquer cabinet, the kind New England sea captains used to bring from China in the nineteenth century. The drawers of the cabinets were intended to hold jewelry, but this one had thumbtacks, paper clips and flower seeds in it. I bought it for a small sum. There were plenty of other things I would have liked in the shop. I tantalized myself with porcelain and silver and old prints but everything was too expensive for me so when my cabinet was wrapped up, I put it under my arm and started out the door.

I was actually on the sidewalk when I felt suddenly that I must go back.

I said to Katharine, "There's a sort of alcove there I didn't look at. Do you mind if I go and see what's there?"

We went in again and I handed her the cabinet to carry while I quickly walked straight back to the alcove. There was a china cupboard with open shelves with pieces of Chinese porcelain on them. On the top shelf, a foot above my head, was a flowered bowl. I looked at nothing else but stood on tiptoe and put my hand into the bowl.

As soon as I touched what was in it, I knew what it was. The roughish texture, the sharp thin edges, the chink of metal against porcelain could all belong only to an Indian chain.

I pulled it out, more than a yard of it, saying, "I'm going to have it — I don't care what it costs!"

Katharine kicked me swiftly on the ankle and said, "Shut up, you idiot!"

Good advice, really.

Luckily the proprietor, who was eating his lunch in a room back of the shop had not heard me. His price was moderate and took exactly the amount in bills I had in my pocketbook, leaving me eighty-seven cents in change.

The barrel clasp of my new chain had small turquoises as the centers of the gold flowers on it. I wound the golden string of rough links three times around my neck, fastened the clasp with a faint firm click and walked out of the shop feeling as rich as some nabob's favorite niece.

If you have an Indian chain sent special delivery — well, who needs emeralds?

39

Meeting

PEOPLE SPEND a good deal of time yearning for the good old days. No doubt there were pleasant things about them — for a few people. It was pleasant to ride, warm among buffalo robes, in a sleigh with silver bells. Most people walked, some of them with shoes with holes in them. It was delightful to wake at night and hear music of a violin, a cello or a flute and to realize that there was company downstairs. The music readily available to the general public came from hurdy-gurdies.

Once when Rich and I were first married he asked me what he could give me that I most wanted. I replied that I was perfectly contented with what we had but if he really insisted on knowing, I suppose I ought to tell him that I yearned for a private orchestra that would play the piano concertos of Bach or Schumann or Strauss waltzes or jazz — just whatever I wanted.

He said he was sorry he couldn't give me an orchestra. Yet within a few years my wish came true. I had an Atwater Kent radio and good music — or bad — at my fingertips. Later Rich bought me an excellent record player and enough records to keep it going all day long.

Most television at present seems to be aimed at retarded adolescents yet it still has the power of telling the truth and sometimes does so. Perhaps the most striking example was the McCarthy hearings in 1952. I bought my first TV set so that I would be sure I would know what McCarthy was up to. No doubt he thought that by appearing on TV he would achieve his purpose, which was not, of course, really to expose communism but to make himself powerful. What he succeeded in doing was to show millions of people that he was a fraud and a tyrant; Americans don't like either.

I was present, by means of TV, at one of the great moments of history. In the Senate hearing room McCarthy was leering and browbeating a witness. Suddenly the scene shifted. The reporter told us that something important was about to happen. He himself did not know what it was but he'd been told that we'd better watch the corridor. So we saw it, first just a confused mass of people — some waiting for a chance to get into the hearing, but chiefly reporters with cameras and flashbulbs.

The bulbs began to flash far down the corridor. Then people stood aside, leaving a path for a tall, strongly built man. I recognized Senator Flanders of Vermont and wondered what the paper was that he was waving above his head. In a moment the reporter said in a tense voice, "McCarthy doesn't know it, but Senator Flanders is bringing him a summons to appear before a committee of the Senate and answer charges of behavior unbecoming to a senator . . . here comes Flanders . . . he's almost at the door . . ."

We saw him come through the crowd. Then the scene shifted back to the hearing room. McCarthy was still bullying the witness. Flanders seemed to blow through that room like a breath of clean Vermont northwest wind. Silence fell on everyone in it as he strode across it holding the paper in his hand.

McCarthy blustered, "What's this? What's this?" and took the paper.

As he read it, you could see the change come over him. He

shrank like a balloon with a pinprick in it. Literally he was never the same man again. Neither was anyone else in the room. They regained some measure of freedom from fear. Yet none of them would ever quite recover politically from the dose of truth-serum publicity administered by TV. Men who thought themselves dignified had shown only pomposity. Arrogance, effrontery, cowardice and just plain bumbling stupidity had been keynotes of the hearings. The only person who had behaved consistently with decency, generosity, courage and common sense was Joseph Welch of Massachusetts.

Craig's mother, Dorothy Leman, was with us a good deal of the time during the hearing. She was a congenial watcher and, when we were not engaged in our duty of keeping an eye on McCarthy's work, she made my piano sound the best it ever had. Dorothy's visit coincided appropriately with piano moving. A piano had been moved out of the Kent Museum by some non-experts who assured me they were fully insured against damage of any kind. Perhaps they were. Perhaps that was why they were so cheerful about smashing the piano through the delicate spindles of the stair railing, breaking off the newel post and gouging holes in the wall.

They have not — fifteen years later — got around to paying for the damage yet. It took Ralph and me several days to repair it. He made new spindles and restored the newel post to graceful solidity. I patched plaster and painted. I also, using a nail scissors, that handy tool for an angry paperhanger, cut the proper pieces out of remnants of wallpaper and pasted them on the wall. I am proud to say that the last time I looked for the places where the gouges were, I had difficulty in finding them.

The week Dorothy came to stay, my new grand piano arrived from Brookline. It was new to me but Steinway had made it before I was born, so it was appropriate to the other Victorian furnishings of the Museum. The works had been entirely rebuilt and there was even new ivory on the keys. It arrived one hot June night. The men who brought it were experts. They decided at once not to carry it up the stairs. They took out the frame of one of the ballroom windows. They assured me that there was room for the case to go through.

So there was — with almost half an inch to spare. It was as beautiful as a Beethoven concerto to see them maneuver it. There were three men outside working the rig that hoisted it. The head man stood near the windows and shouted directions. As the piano rose so that its bulk appeared, dark against the moonlit sky, I could see by the candlelight inside, the sweat begin to trickle down the head man's back as he pulled on his rope.

At last the case, padded with an old patchwork quilt, rested on the windowsill a moment, then moved farther into the room. Two of the other men came up now, each carrying two piano legs. Both men were shining with sweat and beaming happily over their achievement. There were a few more shouts from above, a few more sounds of ropes and pulleys. The case thrust itself through the window leaving a margin no thicker than my little finger.

Santo Domingo mahogany shone in the candlelight as the case emerged from its wrappings.

"Where would you like it?" asked the head man in his soft, vibrant, strong voice, as beautiful to me as a viola played by William Primrose in "Harold in Italy."

I showed him. In no time at all the piano stood on its own legs in the right spot.

It is still there.

They drank water; that was all they wanted — water, quarts of it. They drank it, nodding approvingly while Dorothy played Mozart and Brahms. They left to drive back to Boston in the coolness of the night while she was still playing Beethoven. I have heard many concerts in that room since but none I enjoyed more than that first one.

The coincidence that was to change and enrich my life for the

next twelve years took place on July 4. I had promised to be one of
the judges of the floats in the Plainfield Fourth of July parade but I
wished I could stay at home on my cool porch. If I had stayed at
home I might never have met Helvetia Perkins. However, I
dressed myself in red, white and blue (new hat, dark blue blouse,
the almost-white suit I had worn while standing in the pond) and
started for what proved to be a rendezvous with a new friend.

She was a little late.

"She'll be here soon," Robert Mattuck said. "She lives in East
Montpelier, not far away."

Just then a very large Buick drove up and a driver who looked a
couple of sizes too small for it got out. I did not realize at the time
that she was dressed with unusual formality; she had on a dress.
Her straight blond hair was combed in a bang over her forehead
and twisted in a bun behind. She had very bright blue eyes that
looked intelligent, humorous and full of interest in the world.

I went to pay as formal a call as anyone ever pays in Vermont on
her a few days later. I found her dressed in the regular uniform in
which I always remember her — faded blue jeans, an immaculate
white shirt, a sweater, with one button fastened, worn a little thin at
the elbows. She was digging around a tremendous clump of regal
lilies.

Larkspurs, taller than she, were blue towers against the piled
logs at the end of the woodshed. The house was a story-and-a-half
brick cottage with dormers added to enlarge the four bedrooms.

When she asked me to come in I said, "I ought not interrupt
your gardening." And she said, "Oh, I'm no gardener!"

In the years of our friendship, she often made this remark, which
was manifestly untrue as the asparagus bed, the great bushes of peo-
nies, the sweet Williams in dozens of colors all testified. There
were pink roses in bloom too that day and big tubs of white frilled
petunias on the wide granite step of the front door. Being Vermonters to some extent, we went in by the kitchen door.

The kitchen was big enough for a coal range, a gas stove and an enormous table covered with a cloth of plaid red and blue gingham. The woodwork was of gray weathered boards from an old barn. Below white plaster, there was vermilion oilcloth on the walls. Helvetia had her own theory of interior decorating. It was, I figured, as she showed me around the house, that every room should have a surprising note of incongruity. So in the almost rustic kitchen there were Queen Anne chairs around the table and French porcelain and English crystal in the cupboards.

The walls of the parlor were covered with prints of hunting and racing scenes, spirited by and incongruous with delicate French provincial chairs and Oriental rug and cupboards full of beautifully polished silver. The room across the hall had magnificent brocade curtains of faded reds and pinks, a beautiful highboy of French walnut and plain low sofas flanking the fireplace. Most people paint the walls of a north room a cheerful yellow to give the effect of sunshine. The walls of this room were a dull milk-chocolate color. The cheerful note was struck by the gilt of picture frames, by rainbows in the prisms of candelabra, by gold on the backs of hundreds of books. In summer this room was a shadowy cool retreat. In winter the fire of big logs made it into a place of sheltering warmth.

Kenty has told me that an English friend of hers had said that the queerest thing about Vermonters was that while they were supposed to be stiff and unfriendly, they always began their acquaintance with you by showing you all around their houses. I rather think that this peculiarity belongs chiefly to Vermonters-by-transplantation, most of whom have taken an old house in poor condition and have worked for years to make it habitable. It is a triumph that the house is standing up, that water runs into the bathtubs and out again, that fireplaces — if properly cajoled — do not smoke, that electricity has taken the place of kerosene lamps. Naturally we show the results of our labors to anyone who seems at all sympathetic.

It seemed perfectly natural to me to be taken upstairs to see the bedrooms. All four had double views. They looked northwest over gently sloping fields with grazing cattle to dark woods. To the southeast, the pattern was also pastoral but more varied. There was a deep valley where a brook ran down toward the Winooski River, a farmhouse with barns and a tall silo dwarfing it, a square field fenced in by seven tall elms, green pastures, golden hay fields, long files of pines and spruces and pale blue mountains.

All the bedrooms were attractive and individual but Helvetia's own room was spectacular. It was paneled with silver-gray boards from an old barn. Louis Quinze furniture looked completely at home in it. So did portraits in gold frames and a Persian rug and other rugs hooked or braided in East Montpelier.

I liked the room across the hall too. I felt at home there almost the instant I crossed the threshold. I liked the Indian print bed-spread, hung onto the wall, showing ladies on horseback escorted by knights and squires, old prints of Rome with the Tiber slipping past the Castle of Saint Angelo, Victorian landscapes in frames of bright gold over the doors, shelves of books — French, German, Spanish and, luckily for me, English. Like every room in the house, this room had a good writing table with real ink and pens and blotters. It also had plenty of lamps for nighttime reading. While I did not guess that for more than ten years it would be called my room, it all seemed at once like a place I had always known.

When Helvetia returned my call, I was lying on the couch on the front porch reading Gibbon's *Decline and Fall of the Roman Empire.* I am afraid this occupation gave her a misleading idea that I was intellectual. As I was to find out later, she considered herself stupid — she wasn't — and she had an exaggerated respect for in-telligent and intellectual people. She used the terms almost inter-changeably. One of the various differences of opinion that kept our friendship a living thing was that I consider common sense and intelligence necessary tools if intellect is to accomplish anything. Intellect without intelligence strikes me rather like an automobile without a steering wheel — a menace on the road.

Gibbon announced in his preface that he would veil any improper details of history by putting them in the footnotes in the decent obscurity of a classical tongue. I could not do much with the Greek but by working conscientiously on the Latin I was able to absorb a certain amount of impropriety though not, of course, as much as one could acquire from a modern novel without the trouble of translation. I was delighted to give up this occupation and show Helvetia around Kents' Corner.

Among other things she saw my grandfather's chess table and said: "Oh, you play chess! I wonder if I dare to play with you!"

I said she need not worry. She won most of the hundreds of games we played. She had what I regarded as an unfair method of thinking long and deeply about her moves. When my turn came I would assume that I had anticipated all the possible moves and replies. I would move at once and then see what a mistake I had made. We took to having supper at each other's houses so she could beat me often enough. We found it convenient to call each other by our first names.

Hers had been acquired in an interesting way. Her father had retired from business in Chicago when he was still a fairly young man. Taking his wife and five children, he went to live in Switzerland. When the sixth child, a girl, was born he went to register her birth at the American Consulate. This had to be done during the first twenty-four hours of the child's life or she would not be an American citizen. In filling out the blanks, he realized that he and his wife had not decided on the baby's name. He put down the last name — Orr — in the proper place saying he would come back the next day and fill in the first name.

"It must be done today," they told him.

"Oh well," he said, "since she was born in Switzerland, I'll call her Helvetia."

The Orrs returned to Chicago. Helvetia went to Farmington School and Bryn Mawr College, but she also spent a good deal of time abroad. She spoke French beautifully and German. Since she often went to Mexico to visit her daughter, Nora de Brecada, she also spoke Spanish — badly, she said, but I doubt it. She used to make fun of herself for an occasional midwestern turn of speech and she had some favorite Vermont phrases in her repertoire. No midwesterner could ever pronounce the word "water" she said. They always said "waddr." I told her that not only did she say "water" perfectly but — even more remarkable — she said "Mary," "merry," and "marry" so that each sounded different from the others.

I added that I liked to hear whatever she had to say.

I wish I could hear her voice now.

40

Divining Rod

ONE NEW FRIEND leads to others — when the one is Helvetia. I heard men's voices downstairs one morning, and when I came down for breakfast, John Latouche and Kenward Elmslie were sitting at the table. They had come from New York to Vermont to find a place they could buy. They wanted some quiet place back in the hills where they could work. John was writing a musical called *The Golden Apple,* the *Odyssey* in modern dress. He began at once to outline it for us, singing snatches of tunes, acting out all the parts.

I remembered that the Cheringtons' house was for sale and that Kenty was the real estate agent for it. There were, I told them, wild woods around it. Pileated woodpeckers chiseled holes in trees there. Eagles flew over screaming. There was a brook that could be dammed to make a pond. You could look down the valley to mountains ten miles away and not see a house between. There were old stone walls and painted trillium and maidenhair fern falling over slopes in green waves.

John was a short man with thick black hair and intensely blue eyes. They flashed sapphire over these details. Kenward, who was taller and quieter, looked pleased too. By the time I got through telling them about the house, I felt so fond of them both that I made a supremely generous remark.

When they asked if I would introduce them to my daughter, I said, "Certainly. And what is more, I will introduce you to Ralph Weeks. Because you will need to know a carpenter, a plumber, a painter and an electrician. And he's all of them and a dowser besides."

They saw the house that afternoon and bought it two days later.

One of the first things John did was to learn dowsing from Ralph. John was a talented pupil. He came down to my yard and his forked stick dipped in all the right places. When he went back to his apartment on East 69th Street, he took the stick with him. He decided to demonstrate his skill at once to the superintendent of the building.

"Now, I suppose," John said, "there's a pipe somewhere along here where water runs into the building. I'll walk across the pavement and when the stick dips, that will be where the pipe is. See? Now I suppose you know where it is, so just check — will you?"

The superintendent nodded and John started along the pavement, holding the V of his stick up and avoiding contact with a lady with a Pekingese, two chauffeurs and a laundry man. Pretty soon the stick turned down.

"Hi — that's where it is all right, isn't it?" John called.

The superintendent, a man of few words, shook his head.

John went back, started across again. The stick went down at the same place. Again the superintendent shook his head when John asked if the pipe were there . . . and the third time . . . and the fourth . . . "That's queer," John said. "Why the stick's almost taking the skin off my hands. I'd swear there was water there!"

"Oh," said the superintendent, "there's *water* there. You said you were going to find the main pipe. That's where the old well is that we used before we had city water. Pipe's over here."

"So I decided to stick to writing," John told me.

He came to Calais several times that summer with composers,

actors, pianists, writers and painters of pictures in his train. There
was an Indian princess in a beautiful curry-colored sari who made
curry in my kitchen one evening. There was Ruth Yorck who had
left Hitler's Germany and had valiantly supported herself since by
writing in a strange country and a strange language. There were
two beautiful princesses — sisters — from Austria. The elder had
a splendid idea about having the city convert garbage into fertilizer.
Calais was never like this before!

John and Kenward went to auctions and antique shops with
Helvetia and me. They bought a piano that sounded like a banjo if
you pressed the right button, a picture painted on glass of a city
burning and other domestic necessities.

I took them to see the Drennans. There were three sisters living
together in the big yellow country hotel that had once been their
father's. Bessie Drennan was unmarried. The other two were wid-
ows — Blanche Utley and Frances Darling. Blanche was the town
of Woodbury's representative in the state legislature, the oldest
woman representative in the United States, she told me proudly.
She was also, I thought, one with an exceptionally high amount of
both common sense and integrity. Frances ran an antique shop in
the big ballroom in the south wing. There was pretty nearly everything you ever heard of in it; definitely less of everything every
time John Latouche stopped there.

He fell in love with all three sisters immediately. He liked
Blanche because she was shy and timid, afraid of the dark, of dogs,
burglars and porcupines. Especially porcupines. Getting the
bounty raised on them was her chief legislative interest. Before she
went anywhere she would figure out what she was afraid of and
conquer each fear. Frances, the youngest of the three was naturally
intrepid. She kept her sisters in order, drove Blanche's big car with
dash and determination, kept Bessie constantly at work.

Bessie's work had been baking bread and frying doughnuts and

washing dishes but when she was almost seventy she suddenly began to paint pictures.

"Like Grandma Moses," people who had not really looked at
them used to say.

Actually they were quite different. Grandma Moses' pictures
were literal; Bessie's were fantastic. They all started with something she knew about — perhaps a dance in the old hotel or a wedding party coming out of a country church — but something
strange happened while she was painting. Horses and sleigh flew
over the snow instead of plodding through it. Birds were too big
for the trees they perched on. The wind blew smoke two ways at
once. Tombstones floated above ground. There was a blind man
who appeared in many of the pictures. He wore dark glasses and
carried a cane.

"He listens and hears things other folks don't," Bessie told me.
"Sometimes I think he knows more'n the ones that can see."

He was in a picture she painted called Tree of Life. There were
owls and peacocks sitting on the tree. Father Time walked past a
blazing fire, mowing daisies with his sharp scythe. A nicely dressed
lady with bonnet, a shawl and a parasol stood near the tree. Apparently the parasol was acting like a parachute in reverse and taking
her up to heaven. The blind man and two Mexicans were nearby.
They looked on; he listened as usual. Did he hear the swish of the
scythe and the crackle of the fire? Who can tell?

Kenty had bought the first picture Bessie ever sold and I had an
early one too. Frances felt that I had a special interest in Bessie's
work so she used to get me alone and ask me to tell Bessie to finish
her pictures better. My reply may have varied slightly in form
from time to time but it continued to be basically the same; that I
had no intention of telling Bessie Drennan how to paint. I did
sometimes suggest subjects to her and I was always charmed with
the way they came out looking quite different from the way I had

thought of them. Helvetia and I ordered a picture of egg rolling on the White House lawn and we sent it to President Eisenhower from Bessie. I always wondered what he thought of its eerily unreal quality. He wrote her a very nice letter about it which she had framed and hung in the front hall.

She began to sell pictures as fast as she could paint them.

"Blanche and Frances see that I keep at it," she said. "It used to be 'Bessie, have you washed the dishes yet?' Now it's 'Bessie, dear. Never mind the dishes. I'll take care of things — you go and paint. You've only got two of the Four Seasons pictures done that John Latouche ordered, you know' . . . Maybe Frances will think of a fifth season before I get through."

The pictures went back to 69th Street when John left Calais to see about production of *The Golden Apple*. Norris Houghton, who had a house not far from the Eyrie, as John called the former Cherington place, became interested in John's work. The result was that the Phoenix Theater, where Norris was working, produced the musical that fall.

It was typical of John that some of the best seats in the theater on the opening night were saved for elderly ladies from Calais. Blanche did not dare to go to New York but Frances and Bessie went. They telephoned her twice a day to let her know that none of the perils of the great city had caught up with them. They stayed at the Grosvenor Hotel where Kenty and Helvetia and I also stayed. They saw the show only once but Helvetia and I saw it three times, liking it more each time.

During the happy gathering that followed the first performance John introduced me to the editor of one of the sophisticated magazines of the period. Naturally I knew that I had nothing to say that could possibly interest him so, after praising the show, I tactfully let him escape me. The Drennans had to leave so Helvetia and I went too. Kenty and some of her friends stayed for a while.

After I had gone, John introduced the editor to Kenty saying, "This is Mrs. Appleyard's daughter."

"How I wish I could meet her," the editor said.

"You did," Kenty said. "I saw you talking to her just before she left."

"And I didn't know! I didn't tell her that I keep *Mrs. Appleyard's Year* beside my bed and read it at night when the world gets too awful! Why she's saved my life over and over again!"

It just shows you never can tell.

☆

At her request, I painted a very large picture for Helvetia. It had to be very large because there was a certain wall space in my bedroom at her house that she wanted covered. It was three by four feet. Luckily I had a piece of composition board the right size. I decided on an underwater scene. There was an anchor with a sagging chain above it, sea horses, scallop shells, sea urchins and many kinds of fish darting in and out of seaweed. I was delighted with it. Helvetia seemed pleased with it too. Ralph took time off from building the music room to make a frame for it and to nail it to the sloping gray boards of my room.

It was still there when the house was sold after Helvetia's death in 1965. I called the new owners to ask if I could buy it, but they had taken it to the dump some weeks before. I suppose it looked different to them from the way it did to me. I'm hoping that someone who was amused by it may have picked it up on the dump. I mention this because I would still like to buy it.

Fortunately perhaps, I did not do any more painting that summer but went on with my writing. It was a quiet, peaceful time with enough going on in the music room to keep it from being dull. The music room was finished when John Latouche came back from Colorado. He and Harry Martin came to supper the first night he was back at the Eyrie.

One thing I remember about that evening was especially typical of him. He was telling us about *Baby Doe* and its success in Colorado, making plans for the first night of the New York performance. The Drennans and Helvetia and I must all come, he said. This time he wasn't going to hear any nonsense about Blanche staying home.

"I'm going there tomorrow to supper," he said, "and I'm going to make that clear."

I asked him if he was going to work on a new piece this summer.

"No," he said. "I'm tired. I have a Christmas story to write but I don't feel like it. I tell you, Lulie — how about my giving you the idea? You can write it and I'll help you and we can put both our names on it. You'll have all the money, of course."

He named the sum — it seemed large to me — and I said half would be plenty.

Now this offer was incredibly generous, not just because of the money, but because of the idea. Painters sometimes give away paintings. Musicians will sit down at your piano and play for you. An actor will do a scene from his new play. Writers, however, are traditionally economical. An idea is something to be darkly veiled especially from other authors. Painters and musicians, when they get together, talk about their art. Writers talk about their agents and their publishers. Even what dictionary they use is a secret.

John did not stop with telling me about one story. He presented me with three or four ideas and was still pouring them out when he left at midnight.

I never saw him again.

He died the next night of heart failure. He was not yet forty years old.

He no longer had much connection with his native Virginia. He had left there as a small boy with a scholarship to a New York school. He went to Columbia briefly. In his sophomore year, he wrote both words and music for a show. A Broadway producer saw it, took both John and the show to Broadway. He never went back to college. New York itself was his education. He worked, writing for the stage there until the Second World War when he joined the Seabees. Part of his service was in Africa. He stayed there for some time after the war. He wrote a book about the Congo. I had known him — before I ever saw him — because of the book and because of "Ballad for Americans," which I had heard Paul Robeson recite.

He had told me that he thought of Calais as his real home. He liked the old cemetery. It was possible to find a lot in it for him, and he is buried there.

41

Almost a Vermonter

IN 1959 I sold the house on Hawthorn Road and moved to Calais.
How simple that sounds!

I had been furnishing my attic for thirty-seven years. Of course I
had had help. My children had been of great assistance in packing
it solid and my tenants had let many an artifact fall from their
nerveless hands. I had thought I would solve many problems by
inviting the Morgan Memorial to help me, but I found that times
had changed since I had given them almost a truckload of things
during the Second World War.

A muscular-looking young man and his assistant came up and
looked at the couches, chairs, lamps and boxes containing who-
knows-what that I offered.

They were declined in the following statement: "It's too hot, it's
too high up and I'm too tired."

I had put out various odds and ends of cut glass and silver and
china on the kitchen table intending to give them to the Morgan
Memorial along with the furniture. I left them on the table. Within
a few days an antique dealer came in and gave me sixty-five dollars
for them. I got to know a good many antique dealers during this
time. I began at a low ebb socially with one who wore a T-shirt
and dungarees but mounted upwards to one in a brown suit, to

several in plaid sports jackets, and at least to one in a black coat and gray striped trousers. He looked rather as if he were going to be best man at a wedding; he even had a carnation in his buttonhole.

He had trouble with his eyes so his assistant came with him and described objects to him in a kind of shorthand. He also learned a great deal about a piece by leaning his head against it so that he seemed to be listening to it and smelling it. He also ran his fingers over different surfaces. After touching the brasses of my sideboard and apparently listening to the mahogany, he asked my price. I had no place for it at Kents' Corner and none of the children wanted it so I named the price, fifty times what my father had paid for it seventy years ago when he bought it from a junk shop.

My friend shook his head. He launched into an explanation — it sounded rather like a tape recording — of the reasons why he could give me only half as much.

"You see," he said, "Mrs. Kent, I have to sell it."

"Yes," I said, "but I don't."

"Touché!" he said — yes, he really said it — and turned to his assistant. "Write out a check to Mrs. Kent for her price. I daresay we can dispose of it in Texas."

I daresay he did. I wish I had it back. In fact I wish I had most of the things I sold back, including my old typewriter, a shabby but gentle machine. I bought a new one. It was made in Holland and came in a beautifully upholstered case. The Dutch, I've always heard, are a sturdy race and they must be if they are in the habit of using these typewriters. The action of this one was so stiff that even after several trips to the repair shop, it was so hard to press down the A key that I stopped writing on it; I found it annoying not to be able to write *Appleyard*. However, the typewriter was so well upholstered that I used it for a footstool for a while and then gave it to granddaughter Olivia Gay.

The Salvation Army was more cooperative than the Morgan

Memorial. They fell into the habit of calling every few days and removing treasures from a space in the cellar where I had had them placed. Kenty and Pearl came down from Vermont to sort the things in the attic. I hired some boys from the neighborhood to carry things down to the cellar and put them either into a Kents' Corner pile or into the part of the cellar labeled Salvation Army.

I used to stand at the bottom of the front stairs and, as the boys passed by, tell them which pile to put things into. It seems strange that Luvia Lafiria, our clairvoyant, should have been involved in this procession of moving objects, but she was. The summer before I had taken a friend, who had mislaid some papers, to see her. She gave him some advice that helped him find them later. It occurred to me, as I listened to her quiet, sensible remarks, that I too had an interest in a missing paper.

This was a manuscript that I had been asked to read by one of my neighbors. I read it, found it interesting because I was fond of the writer, but had to tell her, regretfully, that I was afraid it was not in its present form suitable for publication. I was sure — and am still sure — that I returned it but several years later she wrote me that she could not find it and asked if I still had it. I was so distressed that, though I was quite sure I did not have it, I went through every filing cabinet, every desk where I had ever kept any papers. I did not find it but still I wondered what Luvia would say.

"I see it," she said, "in a room, conspicuously neat, almost severe in its furnishings."

Since this did not sound like any room of mine, I was much pleased as I agreed that every room I had ever seen of my friend's was outstandingly neat. She had moved recently, I told Luvia, and I had not seen her new apartment but I felt sure that it would be neatly arranged.

Luvia sewed a little on the apron she was making and then said, "There's a kind of odd box in the bedroom. It's cube shaped, maybe about a sixteen-inch cube. It's upholstered in quite a striking pattern of bright blue and green on a white ground. The lid lifts up — it's kind of thickly padded. There are some papers in it. I guess the one you speak of is among them. I hope I've helped you some."

This was not one of Luvia's successes. I wrote my friend, but she had no such box. Still I felt quite sure I did not have the manuscript so I worried about it no longer — until one night during the attic clearing.

The boys had taken down dozens of loads that day and I must have told them where to put hundreds of different items. I had even been down to the cellar on one of my rare trips and had sorted out some things there for the Salvation Army. One of the things I gave them was a large bean pot that fell on my head as I reached up to get a flatiron off the shelf where the bean pot also was. I suppose I was fortunate; the flatiron would probably have been even more painful than the bean pot.

My head ached a good deal and I slept badly, waking often. I seemed to have a perpetual motion picture of the day's work running through my mind. I climbed up on chairs, caught bean pots on the rebound, said "Salvation Army" or "Kents' Corner" as the boys showed me children's toy boats, boxes of tools, an iron-stone bowl and pitcher and . . . and . . .

And a box upholstered with a bold pattern of bue and green on white. About sixteen inches high with a thickly padded lid . . .

And I had said "Salvation Army" . . .

I threw off the bed clothes, shivered my way into shoes and a wrapper and down the twisting stairs into the cold cellar. The box was there, just as I had seen it; just as Luvia had seen it.

It was empty.

With clairvoyance back in Vermont where it belonged, the rest of the moving went on with only the usual smashing and crashing. Before long, the Brookline house was empty and I was lying on the porch at Kents' Corner listening to the brook and the wind in the grass. When the truck arrived, I suggested to the driver that he should take the gate off the hinges so it would be easier for him to back in. Naturally he spurned this cowardly, feminine suggestion. He preferred to crunch the gate off its hinges with the back of the truck while I writhed in anguish.

There are times when I wish I were not always right.

Nevertheless, in spite of shattered minor frames and girandoles, chipped picture frames and handles deftly removed from cups; in spite of the disappearance of a whole barrel of china and my lawn being churned into a substance resembling giblet gravy, I have never regretted the move. I shall always feel grateful to my children for never having tried to make me leave my Brookline house.

When I was ready, it fell from me like an outgrown snakeskin. This is not so easy as it sounds. Once one of my summer visitors, Tony Thwaites, brought home several snakes. One was a very large one called Evangeline. She lived on my back porch in a homemade cage. I was invited by Tony to the skin changing. The snake has to do a lot of preliminary work — writhing, stretching, coiling, uncoiling. It took some time for the skin to crack but it did at last and Evangeline certainly enjoyed her shining new one.

It had also been a good deal of work to crawl out of Hawthorn Road but I liked feeling I was almost a Vermonter.

I said so to my neighbor, Elaine Fitch, and she said kindly, "We don't think of you as a summer person."

This was one of my proudest moments.

When the White House grew unbearably cold that year, I moved into my apartment at Kenty's, which Ralph had fixed for me. He had built bay windows on both rooms, shelves for books and china, a mantelpiece and an entrance porch. He also laid cork tiles on all the floors and built counters around my kitchen unit.

This is about as big as a bureau and contains three top burners, oven and broiler, a refrigerator so well insulated that it doesn't notice when the oven is lighted. There is also a sink about deep enough to float some pond lilies. The unit works by electricity except when a tree falls on the line.

This does not happen often but Kenty's kitchen is equipped with both gas and electricity in case it does. When the furnace was off, we sat by the big open fire. We also, when the power was on, entertained each other at meals more formally. At Thanksgiving and Christmas we cooperated. The turkey was cooked in Kenty's big oven. She made the mashed potato. I cooked the other vegetables and baked mince and pumpkin pies or made plum pudding.

We had, shortly before I moved, started writing articles about Mrs. Appleyard and her cooking methods for the *Ladies' Home Journal*. Collaborating was especially good fun while we lived in the same house, invented ideas for cooking together and talked over what we were going to say in the background material. *The Summer Kitchen,* written by us together and published in 1957, was what had got us started on doing these articles. Dorothy de Santillana at Houghton Mifflin had shown the book to one of the editors of the *Journal* and had suggested that they should get us to work for them. We had been on to New York to meet Mr. and Mrs. Gould and other members of the staff.

We had lunch in a penthouse with a wonderful view of the city. The menu would be photographed and published in the *Journal* later. This was a trial run, cooked in the *Journal* kitchen and beautifully served. Just a little snack: lobster thermidor, hot rolls, a salad that tasted as good as it looked and an arrangement of fruit some old Dutch master might have painted. I seem to remember a small glass of sherry. Not exactly the sort of thing Mrs. Appleyard usually has for lunch.

We both fell in love with the Goulds, their Chinese pottery and bronzes, the rest of the staff, the kitchens and the food. It was decided to photograph the menu for our first article at Kents' Corner. We put in a special electric cable for the photographer's light. It cost the *Journal* two hundred and fifty dollars to have it installed. Everything else was indigenous including a real Vermont freshly killed turkey.

I had naïvely supposed I would do the cooking but a special cook, who knew about cooking for photographic purposes, came. In the party were also the editor in charge of the project, two photographers, one to take the basic picture, the other to make the necessary color separations and an assistant cook, skilled in cutting radishes in fancy shapes and in washing dishes in which food had been photographed. How I wished she would stay forever!

Ralph, of course, was there too, moving furniture and helping to adjust the electric cable. He even carried in the extra turkey for me. The New Yorkers, knowing they were going to a wilderness, had not really believed me when I said I would get a turkey. Perhaps they pictured me out hunting for it with a gun six feet long and not bringing down my bird. Anyway they brought one from New York. Both birds were browned slightly, not roasted for eating purposes, and highlights were applied with Wesson oil. The Vermont turkey turned out to be the more photogenic of the two, I am glad to say.

The dining room table was moved into the living room and placed under the Tree of Life. There was a blank space that troubled the photographers so I painted an evening grosbeak in it while the turkey was cooking. My grandmother's blue Canton was used on the table so that I think of her every time I see the picture. It took two days to get ready to take it and a few seconds to expose the film.

We hated to see our friends go away but we had various perquisites by which to remember them — the two turkeys in my freezer, the electric cable, a carving set which had once been close to the turkey, a glass-lined silver dish, upon which the pumpkin pie had briefly rested, a small ocean of cranberry sauce.

I always wished they would come again but this was their only visit. However we were to see some of our friends on another happy occasion. The *Journal* gave a reception for us at the Ritz in Boston. Many of the staff came over from New York and the food, cooked by the Ritz chef, was all from receipts that had been published in the *Journal.* If I had some chicken livers and a few Chinese water chestnuts and some bacon I would make you an hors d'oeuvre I learned about that afternoon. It was not exactly on my low salt diet but I ate one and have been regretting ever since that I didn't take two.

Editors from Houghton Mifflin and favorite authors were among the guests. In fact, the affair was quite a contrast to winter in Vermont. I loved both. It was a pleasure to look out my bay windows in the morning and see by the blue tracks in the clean snow who had been calling on us — cats, rabbits, or Norwegian elkhounds chasing bounding deer. My bird feeder was a constant source of interest.

So many people around Kents' Corner and Maple Corner put out sunflower seeds that the local birds are pampered and patronizing. We brag about a visit from a red-breasted nuthatch as proudly as we would if a foreign ambassador dropped in to tea, and a purple finch causes great excitement. A cardinal grosbeak was seen in East Montpelier but — as one of my neighbors remarked bitterly, "They'll keep him so stuffed over there he won't have the strength to fly over this way!"

Less exotic birds — chickadees, sparrows, blue jays — were welcome at my feeder. They kept me company while I worked on books of the *He Went with* series — *Champlain, Drake, Hannibal,* on *The Winter Kitchen,* on articles for *Vermont Life.* I have enjoyed these especially because of the pictures. I like the way

Hanson Carroll shows Mrs. Appleyard's masterpieces being prepared outdoors. It gives me an illusion of leading my life in fresh air and sunshine to see steak being broiled in an open field framed by blue hills, trout in a black frying pan near a tumbling brook, a pewter platter of chicken salad in a garden.

All the food in these pictures is edible and has been cooked for the photographer exactly as described in the text. If there is whipped cream on a strawberry shortcake out in a strawberry patch, it is really whipped cream and not a white substance out of an aerosol bottle. Gloria Carroll, who usually does the cooking for Hanson's pictures, told me that, because whipped cream collapses in the sunshine and because it was hard to get camera and shortcake into the right positions quickly enough, she made that shortcake four times before her husband was satisfied with the picture.

Once she was ill and I took over her job, rather inefficiently. It was a great moment when the platter of salad finally came in from the garden. Hanson Carroll, Frank Liebemann and Mrs. Appleyard fell on it like raccoons on Golden Bantam corn and enjoyed it as much, I rather think.

The winter pictures so far have been done indoors but give these gentlemen time: I wouldn't be surprised to find that Mrs. Appleyard had been seen on a ski slope in Mad River Glen making a cheese soufflé or out on her goldfish pond cooking a Vermont paella on skates. They regard nothing as impossible — why should I?

Actually my winter activities have been somewhat limited. I could not walk outdoors comfortably, I found, unless the mercury was at least ten degrees above zero and there was almost no wind. Such days do not come often. When one did, I would venture as far as the Maple Corner Store. This was quite an excursion, downhill and up again over a slippery road, probably a whole quarter of a mile altogether.

On one of these trips I met an elderly gentleman in a brightly plaided mackinaw outside the store. I was not sure I had seen him before but on the principle that it's more polite to speak to someone you don't know than not to speak to someone you do, I said, "Good morning! Lovely day, isn't it?"

I realized at once that I had said the wrong thing. Vermonters, when you praise a whole day, correct you, saying: "Nice *morning*, seems so."

This one was different. He said sternly, "D' you know me?"

I apologized meekly, explaining that I thought I had met him but I was afraid I'd been mistaken. I added that I was nearsighted.

He still looked stern as he announced that he was Ezra James, in charge of the cemetery. I said what a good job he was doing, as indeed he was.

"Mrs. Kent, be'ant you?" he asked.

"Why yes," I said, "but Mr. James, if I don't know you how does it happen you know me?"

He looked me up and down carefully and answered, "You bin *described* to me."

With that he walked on. As I entered the store and took shelter among the ruffled white petunias and the pink geraniums, I realized that, of course, he had seen the date on my tombstone and that he had a natural interest in my health. It had no doubt relieved his mind considerably to be able to estimate that I would probably last till spring.

I have always wondered what that sinister description was. Perhaps it's just as well not to know.

42

Curator

VACATIONING IN MAINE one summer, Helvetia and I decided to visit the Frank Crams and see Iron Bound once more. We drove to Bar Harbor, left the car there and took a small steamer. We had to make special arrangements to stop at Iron Bound. The man who was urging, in a voice like a foghorn, that passengers should use his boat rather than any other, kindly included us in his list of attractions.

"Come aboard, folks, starting in five minutes, see the Porcupine Islands — Bald, Round, Sheep, Burnt and Long! We're going right through the Halibut Hole, folks, and there's something unusual you won't see every day — *we're going to land two ladies on Iron Bound Island!* All aboard that's coming aboard. Any bird-watchers? Bet I'll show you eagles! And ospreys, and guillemots and shag! Booo-ard . . . all aboard . . . !"

The voyage was as advertised. The birds all performed as if they had been trained for the work. There was, to be sure, only one eagle, but its white head shone splendidly as it posed on a dead tree trunk that grew out of a cleft in the bronze purple cliffs. As we passed its perch, it flapped wings like dark sails and plunged on an osprey that had just caught a fish.

As usual, the gangster of the bird world swooped and snatched the falling fish in its yellow claws, then carried it back to its tree and ate it. The passengers enjoyed this scene but there's no doubt that the big moment of the trip was when the two ladies landed on Iron Bound.

"Le vieux quai" built by my grandfather, still looking as it did when John Singer Sargent painted its picture, was there with its big logtower full of rocks, its float and slip, its long railed walk leading to the shore. The tide was right for us to land, not on the float, but on the wharf itself. The steamer, rocking and swaying on the swirling waves, drew up close beside the wharf.

"Just get aloft the cabin, lady," the mate said, doing so with agility, "and I'll give you a hand across."

I was standing on a small railed walk, not more than eight inches wide, that ran around the cabin. Helvetia, ahead of me, was sensibly dressed in dark blue slacks and a sweater. She got up on the cabin roof and jumped across the interval of boiling green and white water with nautical ease. Perhaps if I had had slacks — but it was too late now, I was skirted as usual.

"However," I reflected as I scrambled awkwardly up to the cabin roof, "at least I have on my best slip."

The spectators apparently appreciated it. They applauded as I grabbed the mate's hand and floundered (surely the right word in these circumstances) from the plunging boat across the green gulf to the wharf. It still seemed to sway and dip for several minutes. Even the island itself was not quite steady but at last it settled down. It smelled like itself — of pointed fir trees and seaweed and of something ethereally sweet — a faint whiff of *Linnaea borealis*.

Yes, this was Iron Bound even though my grandfather's house and all the improvements the Blaneys had made to it, all the beautiful things with which they had furnished it, had burned to the ground. Another house they owned on the island burned too. How it happened is a nightmare of which I will not write.

The Crams had moved into the boathouse near the wharf. We spent the night there, a night when the wind howled and the sea dashed on the rocks below us with a furious sound I had long forgotten. The noise did not prevent our enjoying Iron Bound lobsters. Helvetia said it kept her awake, but after the first few shrieks and howls, I slept as if I were eight years old. We went back to Bar Harbor the next day. Luckily the Crams took us in their boat so I did not have any unknown viewers as I scrambled on board and said my last farewell to Iron Bound. I watched it all the way across the bay, saw its dark porcupine-quill trees pricking into the blue sky; still saw them even for a minute or two while we were driving away.

I still see it now but not quite as it looked that day. My grandfather's house in all its native ugliness rises out of a smoothly mown lawn. My mother has just driven a golf ball into the big patch of wild roses. Oliver and I are getting our legs scratched as we hunt for it, but never mind — dinner will be soon. We have already checked the menu and approved it: lobster soup, roast chicken, new potatoes, peas just out of the garden, raspberry and currant jelly, blueberry pie. We have each earned ten cents picking the blueberries . . . and here's the ball . . . and there's the bell . . .

As Helvetia and I drove back to Vermont, I began to wonder what had happened in Calais without my supervision. Nothing much really, I found, just that the Old West Church had been struck by lightning and would have burned down if Anne Stowell next door had not happened to go out into her garden to pick some lettuce for supper. She had seen the flash of lightning five minutes earlier but — since there was no smoke — had thought nothing of it until she saw the weathervane on the spire fall to the ground. She hastily spread the word. Before the fire engine from Montpelier arrived, young men of the neighborhood had put the fire out.

Several of them were members of the Morse family, descendants of Remember Kent. He had helped build the church in 1823, hewing timbers, sawing boards from primeval pines. Sam, another of Remember's great-great-grandsons, climbed almost to the top of the spire and found the place where fire was smoldering but it was a young architect who was visiting him who carried up the water that finally stopped the fire.

I felt unreasonably that the lightning would not have struck the steeple if I had stayed at home and attended to business. To be sure that no other calamity would occur, I sat down and began to make notes for *He Went with John Paul Jones*. Apparently a writer at work has a certain insulating quality; the rest of the summer was placid.

I started to say "quiet" but, with all the concerts that went on, there was plenty of musical sound and fury. Helvetia and Louise Pierce and I went to concerts at Goddard College and at the Adamant Music School. This is still where you can probably find me on Friday nights in August — in the old schoolhouse, listening to Bach and Beethoven and Schubert and Prokofiev. All with pleasure, for I am an undiscriminating listener who likes whatever she hears. I used to feel rather embarrassed by my simplicity but Edwine Behre and Alice Mary Kimball, who have managed to produce music in Adamant for twenty-five years, have assured me that performers are quite tolerant of spellbound listeners, no matter how ignorant.

Perhaps the name Adamant does not sound especially musical to you. Indeed the town's chief industry is a granite quarry. Adamant got its name in this way: it was originally called Sodom but the inhabitants of that section of Calais, strangely enough, disliked that name. They decided to give their post office a name different from any other in the United States. Their granite, they claimed, was especially hard so they decided on Adamant as suitable. No one has imitated them yet.

One of the concerts I liked best was on my new arched porch. Ralph built it out of part of the woodshed. It was finished just in time for the official opening of the Kent Museum. There was chamber music by members of the Vermont Symphony. This was the only time one of my overnight guests brought a harp with her. I wish this happened oftener.

Allan McNeill composed a special Vermont piece for the quintet, which turned out to be a septet. A hummingbird sat on the top of a tall pale blue larkspur and played the smallest piccolo ever heard. On the telephone a barn swallow balanced and twittered an obbligato. The arched porch turned out to be a natural sound box. The guests — about a hundred of them — had chairs on the lawn. Every note of the music, even the hummingbird's solo, was clearly audible. So were the speeches by the governor, by Dr. Arthur Peach of the Vermont Historical Society, by Hollister Kent. Their remarks were not only clear, they were brief and there was time for music in between them. I believe this happy arrangement is more likely to happen in Vermont than in a few other places I think of.

Vermonters know what they think and say it, often tersely. There are exceptions, of course, but on the whole the lady who spoke to Kenty is typical. The guests, having toured the Museum, were having tea at my house.

"And what," one guest said, helping herself generously to Mrs. Appleyard's oatmeal lace cookies, "is *this* museum?"

Kenty said, "Oh this isn't a museum. It's just my mother's house. She lives here."

The lady looked coldly around the room and back at Kenty.

"It is obviously a museum," she said and sampled the sponge cake.

I've certainly enjoyed being curator of it.

43

Practically Perpetual Motion

MY CHILDREN have often surprised me by their educational prog-
ress. When Posy was three years old, Aunty used to read the *Twin
Books* by Lucy Fitch Perkins to her. They rushed through them so
fast that, without my knowledge, they were soon reading about a
ship called the *Numquam Dormio*. Fortunately, in spite of the
rusting of my Latin, I remembered that the name meant "I never
sleep."

Posy's room, between mine and Kenty's, was really a large alcove
big enough to hold her bed and various toys and books. To please
the Park School, I had been careful not to teach her to read, but the
printed page interested her and I was not sure she did not get ideas
from it. One day, after I had put her in bed for her nap — a strate-
gem often practiced by mothers who would like a little rest themselves — I heard her moving around. I went into her room and
found her back in bed, sitting bolt upright with a *Twin Book* open
on her lap.

I explained that this was the time for sleeping, not for looking at
books. I said, in one of those annoyingly kind tones that even a
thoughtful mother will use at times, that she must have a nice long
sleep.

Posy looked severely at me out of brown eyes the size of the
largest chocolate peppermints. Her voice was severe too.

"Don't you know," she said sternly, "that my motto is *Numquam Dormio?*"

Saying meekly that I didn't, I retreated hastily, shutting the door so I could do my laughing on the other side of it.

Posy at six made her first pun, describing the verve and style with which her father drove a car — "My father," she said, "is a Wreckless Driver."

Several years later Posy surprised me by suddenly learning to play the flute. Diane Harrington, who was staying with us, had a flute and she taught Posy, who was older than she, to play it. At Christmas that year I bought a flute. If you took its three sections apart it fitted neatly into a small leather case. The package did not suggest the shape of a flute but Posy must have had extrasensory perception.

When she took hold of it, she turned a strange shade of pale green and whispered, "I can't believe it — it can't be so."

Yet it was, and George Madsden of the Boston Symphony gave her lessons on it. He was such a good teacher that, the following June, I came home one afternoon and found Posy sitting cross-legged on the front steps, playing to an enthralled audience, one member of which was a rather large snake, coiled up and waving its head.

Another surprise was also musical. Posy was a junior at Bryn Mawr. During her Christmas vacation we went to the symphony. Koussevitzky conducted a performance of Beethoven's Seventh Symphony so exciting that during the last movement I felt I might fall over the balcony. Posy was excited too. She reacted differently.

As the applause began, she announced: "I'm going to change my major from English to Philsosophy."

The result is that in 1967 she is Associate Professor of Philosophy and Greek at the University of South Carolina. When she comes to Calais to visit, I sometimes hear sounds from the flute that remind me of a hermit thrush in the woods across the pond and —

more often — silence that means she is writing a book on Plato's use of fallacy or translating the *Euthydemus*. Fortunately her husband, Arthur Sprague, kindly tolerates such activities.

It did not, of course, surprise me when Kenty began to write books. First she collaborated with me. The First National Bank wanted a book made out of blotters. This could not happen at present. Since the unfortunate invention of ball-point pens, blotters are as rare as Audubon aquatints. In the happy days of the depression the First National used to send its depositors a blotter every month. On the back of it would be a picture of the First Glass Factory or the First Grist Mill or the First Steam Engine. The whole collection was turned over to Kenty and me and the pictures were used in a book we wrote about early Boston. It was called *In Good Old Colony Times* — the title of a song written while ink was still blotted with sand.

Kenty also wrote *Young Sailors of Sidon, Look at America* and *The Village that Learned to Read*. She published a paper called *The Calais Independent*. She and I together wrote articles on cooking for the *Ladies' Home Journal*. This all seems natural. The surprise came when she stopped writing and became a social worker. At present she is training social workers for the state of Vermont.

Sam gave me a pleasant surprise in his freshman year at Harvard.

He said, "Mother, how would you feel if your son did not play football and majored in fine arts?"

All the games in which I had seen Sam, from the time he was seven years old, at the bottom of heaps of husky players whirled past me like a vanishing nightmare as I said, "Oh Sam! It would be the most wonderful thing that ever happened."

It worked well. He now makes plans for places all over the world — Vermont, Brazil, Venezuela, West Australia, New York and, even more remarkable, now and then people follow them. He was the manager of the group that chose the site for Brasilia. He and his wife, Edith, and their two older children, Bruce and Polly, all came back from Brazil speaking Portuguese fluently. Edith says hers was only cooking Portuguese — obviously the kind Mrs. Appleyard would have learned if she had been there.

The children — there are four of them now — all keep surprising and frightening me by the things they know. Their talk about mathematics makes me dizzy. Probably they know where galaxies came from and where they go when they expand. I don't worry about them; I find this planet interesting enough. I am sufficiently surprised when I think of Sam, sleeping in a tent in a western Australian desert with kangaroos bounding around, or Edith in Kitimat, British Columbia, reproaching a dog that was trying to open her garbage pail and finding she was talking to a large grizzly bear.

When they are at home, the Kents live in Fayetteville, New York. I spent a winter there once and have visited them at other times. I had Kitchen Privileges. One of them was to bake a cake for Timothy's birthday. The stove was electric. I pushed something that made the oven think I wanted the sponge cake broiled. The result was, I am glad to report, unique. However, it was staunchly eaten and by the time Nicholas' birthday came, I was able to bake an ordinary one. It takes ten eggs. In New York State, they prefer white eggs. You can buy brown ones at a discount. This puts temptation in the way of visiting Vermonters. Mrs. Appleyard yielded to it frequently. After all, people as extraordinary as grandchildren need special nourishment. Of course, I agree because they are my grandchildren too. We also have a great-granddaughter, Polly Christine, in Alaska. Her mother is Maggie, daughter of Sam's first wife, Fifine Johnson. The last I heard of Polly Christine she was having her bottle and there was a bull moose across the road eating the lilacs.

We have a moose in Calais too, I hear, and there has been a bear eating the apples near Sam's house. A deer and a fawn got most of mine. The raccoons just got the corn. The only catamount I have heard of lately screams and yells and spits like forty cats several miles away. We just have foxes barking all night on the hill above the waterfall. It sounds much wilder here than it did in 1912.

Perhaps that is what has attracted some of Kenty's children back from California. All four were there last year. Susan still dominates computers in a San Francisco bank and Olivia Gay is still there in school, but Andrew and his wife Jean have moved back to Vermont. He graduated from Stanford and is now teaching science in Newport, Vermont. Janet also graduated from Stanford and is now doing social work here. This is another educational surprise. I thought she might be a writer. Surely at least one of my grandchildren ought to add something to the shelf of family writings in my music room — so called because my record player is concealed in one of its cupboards.

This room was built because Kenty gave me the original front door of Remember Kent's plank house. It had been removed during some alterations and was in the woodshed. I was afraid some energetic Vermonter would split up its bluish-green panels for firewood so I told Kenty, when she offered it to me, that I would give it a good home. I could have preserved it by nailing it up on the outside of the woodshed, but I have just enough architectural integrity to feel that a door ought to open into something, so I designed a room for the door to open into.

The Kents never throw anything away. There had been plenty of interesting items under the piles of shingles in the woodshed but I had rescued most of them already. There was a table a hundred and fifty years old with a dual personality. It turns into a chair if you lift the top up. It has been known to decide to be a table again suddenly, a painful experience for the occupant. Fortunately no necks have been broken — yet. All we found in our search this time was most of a Chippendale mirror frame, a seatless ladder-back chair, wooden sapbuckets, a few cracked teacups — just whatever had fallen from someone's nerveless hand.

Ralph Weeks measured the woodshed and found an old barn a mile away with enough weathered gray boards to panel the music room. I drew the plans for four walls, the ceiling and the floor. I used the scale I use in making my miniature rooms — an inch to the foot. In a short time the woodshed began to resemble the plans to an amazing extent. Old beams supported the ceiling. A big bay window added space and lets in afternoon sunshine on one side. Morning sunlight pours in through twelve-over-twelve windows and a fanlight over Remember Kent's front door. Cupboards for the record player and to act as an author's desk run along the third side. Across from them are bookcases with arched tops, a mantel-piece, also from Kenty's woodshed, a Franklin stove and wood boxes that can be filled from outside.

As I sit at my desk now, I can see where the chopping block used to stand. Right past it two steps take you to a door that opens on the arched porch. It was also once part of the woodshed. I remember the trail through it. You passed the rain barrel, a tower of sapbuckets, an ancient stove, a fireless cooker and an interesting collection of mops. It was a cozy arrangement but, on the whole, I prefer it at present with the sapbuckets full of white pansies and frilled white petunias, a sawbuck table made by Ralph out of old boards with Hitchcock chairs around it and the chair-table, waiting to knock unsuspecting sitters on the head. Poppies, lupine, phlox and wild sunflowers blossom around the porch in their season. Phoebes and redstarts and hummingbirds fly past it. Maryland yellow throats in their black masks speed by.

When Kenty was about ten years old, I heard her say to a friend: "When my mother makes plans, they happen."

One thing that did not come out just as I'd planned was the

fanlight. I took my design to Mr. Cruikshank in Montpelier. He would, I thought, know where to have it made. He guessed he could order it but — he said, "I don't see much sense in it when there's an old one up over my garage you can have for nothing."

That's how the morning sunlight gets into the music room.

I think something like this is more likely to happen to you in Vermont than in some other places I know.

The arched tops of the bookcases on either side of the Franklin stove were made by sawing a big chopping bowl in half. The eagles that decorate the mantelpiece were, of course, produced by the lost wax process — Mrs. Appleyard's not Benvenuto Cellini's. By the time I made them I had learned to do it without having the gas stove explode and blow me through the kitchen door.

The music room curtains are not really rare old brocade of faded blue patterned with red and gold; nor are they Fortuny prints imitating the brocade. Pearl Bullock and I stenciled them during a happy fortnight in which no company cooking was done. We could not have company because the dining room table was being used for spreading out the curtains. The stencils were given me by Alex Hoyle, who had made them. The material he made with them hung for a time in the Boston Public Library in spaces later filled with murals by Sargent. On the whole I liked the spaces best when Alex's brocade hung there. He had used faded blue denim, stenciling it with Venetian red and gold. So did Pearl and I.

The music room walls of barn boards weathered to different shades of silvery gray make a surprisingly good background for mirrors and pictures in elaborate gold frames. My favorite picture is a portrait of a lady in crimson velvet with a handsome cashmere shawl. I bought her and her sister, who is wearing bronze velvet, at an auction.

Up to the time the pictures had been brought out, things were moving briskly. Crippled hoes and rakes were being put up in pairs. Someone would shout, "Five cents!" and the pair would be knocked to him. When the two sisters were shown to the crowd, no one was in a mood for art. There was a heavy silence, broken only by the auctioneer's plea for five cents to start.

I said, "Five cents."

No one said anything else.

"Five cents," he said, "to that lady over there — is that five cents for the pair, lady?"

"No," I said in a burst of extravagance. "Apiece."

Even though I had paid twice as much as was necessary, I was happy with my purchases as I framed them. I found the frames under the eaves in the shed chamber. As Grandma Kent used to say, "Everything fits at Kents' Corner."

I would add — I refer to my own work — "or pretty nearly."

Among the family writings on the shelves of the music room are some volumes of the *Kents' Corner Grazette*. This publication was edited first by Kenty, later by Posy. The term "Grazette" was invented because "Gazette" did not sound sufficiently rustic to the editors. Perhaps they wanted to suggest the sound of grass being torn away from the soil by Guernseys, Jerseys and Holsteins. Anyway the *Grazette* had a fine rural flavor. It was written by Vermonters for Vermonters.

I felt grateful to my children for including me by courtesy in this category. Of course they knew perfectly well that I was really a foreigner who just happened to marry into their family but they accepted me just the same.

The *Grazette* came out every now and then. The one precious handwritten copy was circulated at five cents a read. Its readers were also, to some extent, its writers. Rich, Mrs. Aldrich and I were all called on for contributions. Naturally each of us was glad to pay for the privilege of seeing our works published in the best manuscript writing. My editorials for the Boston *Herald* appeared first in the *Grazette*. The Duchess of Roachcroft often figured in the social notes. I rather think she wrote them too.

The *Grazette* records expeditions to mountaintops and waterfalls and secret fireplaces where we heated casseroles brought from home, roasted corn in the husks and grilled hamburgers. One of these fireplaces was in Jeffersonville where a particularly lively waterfall shoots ice water down into a big foaming pool.

The Duchess, Marjorie Townsend and I were cooking dinner there one day while our children carried out their usual program of lowering each other over the falls by well-worn ropes. Another group of visitors, without children, watched as they ate their sandwiches. One of the women walked over to the falls and came back looking as if she had suddenly had a look at a scene in the Spanish Inquisition.

She paused by our fireplace and asked, "How do you stand it? Why do you let them? How do you *stand* it?"

We all considered the matter.

How did we stand it? I wondered.

At last Marjorie explained, "Well, you see we're all school-teachers."

This was the first time I had thought of myself as a school-teacher. Yet when I remembered the number of children I had taught to cook, to make beds, to dance "Dargesson" and "Money Musk," to wash dishes, to weed gardens; when I recalled the hours I had played the accordion for dancing on plateaus in the hills, in C. C. C. shelters, on lawns and cow pastures, I thought that perhaps I did have some of the endurance necessary for that profession.

My grandmother gave me two pieces of advice about bringing up children. One was: "Children take a great deal of letting alone"; the other: "Children go through a great many phases." Another wise woman of the tribe, when asked how she brought up her three splendid intelligent, honorable, successful sons, replied: "Cheerful nagging — and looking the other way."

Mothers of America, cheer up; these things are still true.

44

Walnut Street Again

THE OLDER YOU GET, the shorter grow the summers. Winters are long enough in Vermont. So is that part of spring known as mudtime. Lately I have been spending winter and mudtime on Walnut Street in Brookline. My friend Charlotte Sage lives only a few hundred yards from the house where I was born. She has a room she kindly calls mine. It is full of sunshine and friendliness. From my bay window, as I sit writing, I can see houses I have known for almost eighty years. I know the trees too. I am looking at one that I banged my head against in 1892. It was a large tree with very abrasive bark even then. I was blowing whirlpools in my new chinchilla muff and did not notice the tree till it knocked me down. I have approached it cautiously ever since.

Aunty's gate, on which children used to risk their necks, is nearby. So is my octagonal tower. So are the gray houses on the terrace above Hawthorn Road. I drive past occasionally and notice every bud and blossom on trees and shrubs I planted more than thirty years ago. I have favorites on Walnut Street too — a deep rose and ivory magnolia, dark purple lilacs, pear trees, a great copper beech, cascades of forsythia, the big hemlock above the Wishing Stone in Olive Prouty's wall.

Olive asks me up for a delicious unsalted meal now and then.

Also for a literary wrangle. We disagree about practically everything, thoroughly enjoying our differences. We end up laughing so
hard that I can scarcely manage to swallow the macaroon parfait.

One nice thing about her is that, having been a writer herself,
she worries about my writing.

Haven't you got that book finished *yet?* . . . Aren't you going
to read so-and-so's autobiography and get some ideas? . . . Aren't
you getting awfully tired of it? . . . she asks.

The answer to all these questions is No.

She also worries about my literary integrity.

"Now I should think you'd be ashamed to prostitute your talents
the way you did in that cookbook — writing things to go with color
photographs! I'd never expect you to do that."

"I didn't," I say meekly, everytime we have this conversation.
"They took the pictures to go with what I wrote."

She brushes this aside by repeating that she never thought I'd do
it.

"Do you think Willa Cather would do a thing like that?" she
asks.

I say no but add that I do not exactly consider myself in a class
with Willa Cather. We establish a truce. Usually at some point in
the conversation she tells me that she is much older and wiser
than I am. Wiser, I admit, and I daresay she's a year older. However in my my own case I'm not sure that my wisdom is increasing.
I still do foolish things.

I was over seventy that evening I was trying to get a taxi to carry
me up High Street Hill. It was late in the afternoon. Brookline
Village was full of cars edging along bumper to bumper. I kept
slipping out into the street to hail a taxi but they were all in use
already or someone got ahead of me.

Finally a car stopped. The driver opened the front door.

He said: "I'm Ron Harland. May I take you where you are going?"

I said: "Why Dr. Harland — how nice of you! I've met your wife but I don't remember seeing you before." I got in and shut the door adding, "I'm just going up to the top of the hill. I go in my back gate so I don't have to walk uphill from the street. But isn't it out of your way?"

"I don't think so," he said. "How do you suggest I should go?"

This seemed a little odd but then the Harlands had only recently moved into the neighborhood, adding one more doctor to the population of what is now known as Pill Hill. Only I'd thought his name was John; perhaps Ron was his nickname.

I said, "I usually get into the left-hand lane so I can make the left turn easily at the firehouse."

It took some time to do this. By the time we were ready for the turn, Ron — I always think of him as Ron — and I were old friends. We had similar ideas about the sunset (gorgeous), autumn in Vermont (colorful) and how to solve the traffic problem that had brought us together (raise Boylston Street and send the other traffic under it).

"Only," Ron observed, "if that had been done I'd never have met you."

I said we'd have both been at a Neighborhood Improvement meeting sooner or later. Only I supposed his patients kept him too busy. He admitted he had heavy responsibilities. He was just about the age when they are the heaviest — in his fifties, I judged. His hair was beginning to get gray.

"I don't know what your speciality is," I said.

"I don't either really," said Ron.

We were driving up the hill by this time. He drove with deliberate care, trying not to frighten me, probably.

I said as we came to the stone church, "If you'll just stop at Mrs. Newell's driveway, before we come to Irving Street."

"Tell me where it is," he said.

"Don't you know?" I asked . . . and added, "Stop right here."

He stopped, remarking, "I don't know why I should know. I was never here in my life before."

"But — but aren't you Dr. Harland? Don't you live on the next street?"

"I didn't tell you I was a doctor. I told you I was Ron Harland. I live out near Natick," he said.

"I'm so sorry. I misunderstood. I wouldn't have brought you out of your way, but thank you, ever so much. It was awfully kind."

I opened the door.

He said, 'Think nothing of it and now — don't hurry — I'd like to ask you something. Will you answer?"

"Of course," I said.

"Will you marry me?"

"No. Thank you," I said and got out rather briskly.

He blew me a kiss and drove on.

At first I wondered whether I was old enough to go out without a chaperone. I concluded before I crossed the street that I was not likely to be faced with this special problem again and, surprisingly, I have not.

I am able to keep reading a book a day on Walnut Street because Polly Shakespeare, Charlotte's daughter, keeps me supplied with suitable material. She sorts out the mystery stories, identifying those that take place in good society, among well-bred people. I like my murders refined. I am not going to mention the writers whose books seem to me shallower and more trivial every time I read them. In one or two on my shelves I have inserted slips of paper that say, "Remember not to read this again." I intend in the future to take this sensible advice.

Another pleasant feature of the house is that Charlotte's grandchildren drop in from Pennsylvania, Oregon, Uganda or just a few miles away. It's next best to having my own tell me about the world. Wherever they come from, their appetites are, I notice, excellent. I am lucky in having Kitchen Privileges. My favorite one is that I don't have to cook unless I feel like it.

A member of the Sewing Circle of 1906 — Charlotte is the only member of it who graduated from M.I.T. as an architect — asked me how two strong characters like Charlotte and me managed about cooking. She asked, hopefully, I thought, if there were many clashes.

I replied that we had worked out a good system. We avoided difficulties, I said, by having Charlotte stay downstairs and do the cooking while I sat upstairs and wrote about it.

This is true except when Mrs. Appleyard is really needed. Then she may be found slipping a dash of sherry and a few grains of nutmeg into mushroom sauce, toasting garlic croutons for green beans, rolling out two thousand layer pastry for deep dish apple pie.

I had meant to end this book with a chapter on Old Age. I planned to read Cicero's *De Senectute* to see if I still agreed with him and to add some wisdom of my own. I have decided against this plan. After all, what do I know about the subject? I shan't be eighty-one for several weeks yet.

I am writing this on a soft spring morning when crocuses are opening their cups to offer visiting bees a dash of nectar and ambrosia; when scyllas and grape hyacinths are pools of sky on the ground. Snowdrops are almost over but forsythia is coming. It is the kind of morning that makes me realize that it will soon be time to go back to Kents' Corner.

Only first I must finish this book. Luckily Linny Saxton, from Uganda and Milton Academy, came in just now. She was on her way to the Wishing Stone. She knows how to find it; knows that you must lick your thumb, press it hard on the small garnet-colored stone, shut your eyes and draw a long breath. She made several wishes this spring morning. One of them, she said when she came back, was for me.

"I wished," she told me, "that you could finish your book just the way you'd like to."

I would like to finish it with some wishes, but since most of them are impossible, I will not carry them up to the stone.

I wish Rich could know that his children — as he did — have all found the work they like best to do.

I wish his grandchildren could know him.

I wish the Lemans and the Krakauers and their eleven children would drive into my yard at Kents' Corner. Kitchen Privileges are available.

I wish a long line of Mrs. Appleyard's favorite people of whom — as you very well know — you are one, dear _____ , would come too.

I wish the sun would shine all summer and that there would be plenty of rain to keep the grass green and the ponds full.

I wish there would be leaves shining with every rainbow color except blue for the Foliage Festival; the blue can be in the sky and the ponds and the rivers.

I wish I could decide which of the five books I found notes for in that envelope marked "Ideas for this and that" I had better start writing. As I may not have more than twenty or thirty years more of active writing life, I ought to get at it.

I wish I could tell Mrs. Appleyard and me apart.

OLD WEST CHURCH

THE KENT MUSEUM

IMPRESSIONS OF APPLEYARD CENTER